# Genderwatch: still watching...

# Genderwatch: still watching...

*Edited by Kate Myers and Hazel Taylor*
*with Sue Adler and Diana Leonard*

**Trentham Books**
Stoke on Trent, UK and Sterling, USA

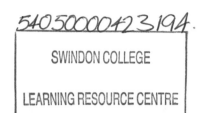
Trentham Books Limited
Westview House 22883 Quicksilver Drive
734 London Road Sterling
Oakhill VA 20166-2012
Stoke on Trent USA
Staffordshire
England ST4 5NP

First published 2007

British Library Cataloguing-in-Publication Data
A catalogue record for this book is available from the British
Library

ISBN: 978 1 85856 401 2

Designed and typeset by Trentham Print Design Ltd,
Chester and printed in Great Britain by Cromwell Press Ltd,
Trowbridge.

## Acknowledgements

*Royalties*

All the contributors of this book have agreed to donate their
royalties to Book Aid International, a charity that provides
books to libraries, hospitals, refugee camps and schools in sub-
Saharan Africa and Palestine. www.bookaid.org

Many thanks are due to many people who gave their time
freely to this publication. In particular, the authors of the
schedules and:

■ the cartoonists who have given permission to reuse cartoons
from the previous edition, Brian Bagnall's widow; Kate
Charlesworth; Sophie Grillet; Cath Jackson; Angela Martin;
Christine Roche; Posy Simmonds

Jacky Fleming has allowed us to use her cartoons for this
edition. www.jackyfleming.co.uk

■ Kate Moorse; Alan Richardson; and Sarah Myers who
assisted with the editing process.

All new illustrations in this edition are by Harriet Seddon

Cover based on a design by Sam Wall

*Photocopying permission*

The schedules in this book may be photocopied free of charge
for use within the school or institution which purchases this
publication. These materials remain the copyright of Kate
Myers and Hazel Taylor with Sue Adler and Diana Leonard and
may not be used or distributed in any way outside the
purchasing institution.

Finally the idea to update the book came from Gender and
Education which also financed the new illustrations in this
edition www.genderandeducation.com

**DISCLAIMER**

*Every effort has been made to acknowledge the source of all
the illustrations used in this book. However it has proved
impossible to trace a few of them, for which we apologise. If we
receive information about any of those we have omitted, we
will of course include them in reprints of this book.*

# Contents

vii   **Contributors**

xi   **Still Watching...**
*Kate Myers*

xiv   **How to use this book**
*Kate Moorse*

## Context for gender equality

1   **'Underachieving Boys' and 'Overachieving Girls' Revisited – Rhetoric and Reality**
*Tim Oates*

8   **Relevant Legislation**
*Graham Clayton*

12   **Every Child Matters**
*Alan Richardson*

## The foundations

16   **School Climate**
*Rosalyn George and John Wudsworth*

19   **Leadership**
*Kate Myers*

24   **Governors**
*Diana Leonard and Frances Migniuolo*

29   **Using the School Budget**
*Hazel Taylor*

32   **Design for Learning**
*Ros Asher*

## Setting the tone

38   **Using Performance Data**
*Hazel Taylor*

42   **School Self-evaluation**
*Alan Richardson*

46   **Continuing Professional Development**
*Hilary Bourdillon*

50   **Performance Management**
*Alan Richardson*

55   **Strategic Management of Information and Communications Technology**
*Avril Loveless and Pippa Totraku*

## Communicating the tone

59   **The Wider School Workforce**
*Hazel Taylor*

62   **Home-School relations**
*Meg McGuire*

65   **Managing Behaviour**
*Lynda Haddock and Leora Cruddas*

69   **Pastoral Care: Care for Pupils as Learners, Persons and Citizens**
*Colleen McLaughlin*

73   **Assemblies**
*Rosie Walden and Diana Leonard*

77   **Breaktimes, Lunchtimes and Playgrounds**
*Hilary Claire and Angela Piddock*

82   **Uniform and Dress Codes**
*Shan Scott*

85   **It's my school: the power of pupil voice**
*Maggie Farrar and Vinsia McQueen*

89   **Lesbian, Gay, Bisexual and Trans Issues in Schools**
*Paul Patrick*

93   **Career Support and Guidance: Choices in the 21st Century**
*Sandra Morgan and Deirdre Hughes*

## Inclusion

98 **Introduction: Gender and Inclusion**
*Hazel Taylor*

100 **Inclusion of Pupils with Special Educational Needs**
*Daryl Agnew and Carole Goodwin*

104 **English as an Additional Language**
*Silvaine Wiles, with Meena Modi and Shahla Taheri-White*

107 **Managing pupil mobility**
*Val McGregor and Karen Benton*

## Pedagogy and the organisation of learning

111 **Introduction: Pedagogy, Pupil Organisation and the Interface Between Gender and Learning**
*Hazel Taylor*

113 **Learning and Teaching**
*Chris Watkins*

118 **Assessment**
*Patricia Murphy*

123 **Literacy**
*Gemma Moss*

126 **Mentoring and Learning**
*Leora Cruddas*

130 **Classroom Interaction**
*Becky Francis*

134 **Study Support and Out of School Hours Learning**
*Tony Kirwan*

138 **Libraries**
*Sue Adler*

141 **Single-Sex Schools**
*Diana Leonard and Debra Murphy*

144 **Single-Sex Classes in Co-Educational Schools**
*Mike Younger and Molly Warrington*

148 **Working with Girls**
*Debra Murphy and Emma Renold*

152 **Working with Boys**
*Trefor Lloyd*

156 **Early Childhood Education**
*Jayne Osgood*

159 **The 14-19 Curriculum**
*Hazel Taylor*

## Subjects

166 **Art and Design**
*Karen Hosack*

169 **Citizenship Education**
*Hilary Claire and Cathie Holden*

175 **Design and Technology**
*Patricia Murphy*

180 **English and Media**
*Jan Shapiro*

183 **Geography**
*Margaret Caistor and Louise Lee*

188 **History**
*Kate Moorse and Hilary Claire*

192 **Information and Communications Technology (ICT)**
*Pippa Totraku and Avril Loveless*

196 **Mathematics and Numeracy**
*Tamara Bibby, Pat Drake, Heather Mendick and Hilary Povey*

200 **Modern Foreign Languages**
*Vee Harris*

## Performing Arts

205 **Introduction**
*Veronica Jobbins*

207 **Dance**
*Veronica Jobbins*

210 **Drama**
*Jan Shapiro*

213 **Music**
*Brigitte Charles and Lucy Green*

216 **Personal, Social and Health Education**
*Janice Slough*

220 **Physical Education and School Sport**
*Anne Flintoff and Sheila Scraton*

224 **Religious Education**
*Joveriah Idrees and Anna Sallnow*

227 **Science**
*Patricia Murphy*

223 **Bibliography**
*Sue Adler*

237 **Index**

# Contributors

**Daryl Agnew** is a Children's Services adviser for the DfES. She has worked as a secondary teacher, as a senior manager in local authorities and as an HMI.

**Sue Adler** works as a librarian in a schools library service, and as a lecturer in education.

**Ros Asher** is an education adviser for Partnerships for Schools, the organisation implementing the Building Schools for the Future programme. She has worked as a teacher, an education adviser and chief officer in local authorities.

**Karen Benton** is a deputy head of a large comprehensive school with a significant number of pupils with high mobility.

**Tamara Bibby** is a lecturer in learning and teaching at the Institute of Education, University of London.

**Hilary Bourdillon** has worked as advisory teacher, humanities inspector and Director of the Open University's flexible PGCE. Currently she is working on the Teachers' TV project.

**Hilary Claire** is a freelance writer, consultant and lecturer in history and citizenship education. She was for many years a primary school teacher, and then a teacher-educator in higher education.

**Margaret Caistor** is a consultant geography adviser. She has been a geography head of department and was an HM Inspector for 20 years with particular interest in geography, equal opportunities and inner-city schools.

**Brigitte Charles** has been a primary class teacher for twenty years in London and Kent. Her specialist area is music education. Her PhD is in gender and music education.

**Graham Clayton** is senior solicitor at the National Union of Teachers.

**Leora Cruddas** is a senior officer in Waltham Forest local authority. She has been involved with learning mentor programmes and investigating ways of meeting girls' needs, with Lynda Haddock.

**Pat Drake** is a senior lecturer in education at the University of Sussex.

**Maggie Farrar** is an operational director at the National College for School Leadership.

**Anne Flintoff** is a reader in Physical Education in the Carnegie Faculty of Sport and Education, Leeds Metropolitan University. She has been involved in school PE – as a teacher, teacher-trainer, and researcher – for over twenty years.

**Becky Francis** is professor of education at Roehampton University. She researches and publishes in the areas of social identities, gender and education, and feminist theory.

**Rosalyn George** is a reader in the Educational Studies Department at Goldsmiths College, University of London. Previously she was an advisory teacher for equal opportunities in the London Borough of Merton.

**Carole Goodwin** is an educational psychologist working for Sheffield Council. She is also a trained person-centred counsellor, group worker and Ofsted inspector.

**Lucy Green** is a professor of music education at the Institute of Education, University of London. Her research is in the sociology of music and music education.

**Lynda Haddock** helps to manage Children and Young People's Services in Newham local authority. She has been involved in anti-racist projects as well as programmes investigating ways of meeting girls' needs in schools.

**Vee Harris** is a senior lecturer in the Department of Educational Studies at Goldsmiths College, University of London, where she co-ordinates the PGCE Modern Languages course.

**Cathie Holden** is an associate professor at the University of Exeter where she teaches on both primary humanities and secondary citizenship PGCE programmes. Prior to this she taught in middle schools for 15 years.

**Karen Hosack** is head of schools at the National Gallery, London. She was formerly head of art and design in a secondary school in Hampshire and has a background in art history.

**Deirdre Hughes** is a university reader in Guidance Studies and head of the Research and Knowledge Transfer Unit, faculty of education, health and sciences, at the University of Derby. She is also director of the Centre for Guidance Studies (CeGS).

**Joveriah Idrees** is head of an RE department in a north London comprehensive school.

**Tony Kirwan** is the joint programme director of Quality in Study Support (QiSS) in the Centre for Education Leadership and School Improvement, Canterbury Christ Church University.

**Veronica Jobbins** is Head of Professional and Community Development at Laban in London and Chair of the National Dance Teachers' Association.

**Louise Lee** is head of geography at the sixth form centre at City and Islington College.

**Diana Leonard** is professor of sociology of gender and education at the Institute of Education, University of London. She has conducted research on gender and special needs in mainstream primary schools, gender and learning, gender and violence in secondary schools and the long-term consequences of single sex and coeducational schooling.

**Trefor Lloyd** is director of Working With Men, an organisation that develops programmes targeting underachieving boys and young men. www.workingwithmen.org.

**Avril Loveless** is a professor of education at the University of Brighton and has been involved in teacher education for many years. Her teaching, research and writing focus on creativity, ICT capability and teacher professional knowledge.

**Val McGregor** is an independent education consultant.

**Colleen McLaughlin** is a senior lecturer at the University of Cambridge Faculty of Education. She teaches, writes, consults and researches on the topics of personal, social and emotional development and well-being.

**Meg Maguire** works at King's College London. Her teaching and research interests lie in the sociology of education.

**Vinsia McQueen** is an assistant head at Park View Academy School in Haringey, London.

**Heather Mendick** is a research fellow at the Institute for Policy Studies in Education at London Metropolitan University.

**Frances Migniuolo** has worked in various education policy settings including local government. She now works as a policy analyst at the Children's Services Network (CSN), a policy advice and information unit supporting local authorities.

**Meena Modi** is the headteacher of Chater Infants School, Watford.

**Sandra Morgan** is a freelance educational researcher/consultant and visiting senior associate at the Centre for Guidance Studies, University of Derby.

**Kate Moorse** has worked as a secondary teacher, a local authority adviser (5-19) and for the Qualifications and Curriculum Authority as a curriculum adviser (3-19). She currently works as a freelance education consultant.

**Gemma Moss** is a reader in education at the Institute of Education, University of London. She writes and researches on gender and literacy and literacy policy.

**Debra Murphy** is director of learning for social sciences at Maria Fidelis Convent school in Camden. She has been involved in running a local authority intervention project aimed at improving the attainment of white working-class pupils.

**Patricia Murphy** is professor of education in the Faculty of Education and Language Studies at the Open University She has researched and published widely on gender in relation to learning and assessment generally and science and technology education specifically.

**Kate Myers** is an emeritus professor from the University of Keele, a senior associate of Leadership for Learning at the Faculty of Education, University of Cambridge and an adviser for London Challenge.

**Jayne Osgood** is a senior research fellow at the Institute for Policy Studies in Education, London Metropolitan University. She writes and researches on gender and the early years workforce and early years policy and professionalism.

**Tim Oates** is group director, assessment research and development, Cambridge Assessment. Previously head of research at QCA, Tim has undertaken evaluation work on all phases of education and training.

**Angela Piddock** is the headteacher of Wilberforce Primary School in Westminster.

**Paul Patrick** has been working for LGBT equality in education since 1974 when he founded the Gay Teachers' Group (now Schools OUT). He is a consultant to the new Commission for Equality and Human Rights. He is also Co-Chair of both Schools OUT and LGBT History Month UK Steering Group.

**Hilary Povey** is a professor in the Mathematics Education Centre at Sheffield Hallam University.

**Emma Renold** is a senior lecturer in childhood studies at Cardiff School of Social Sciences, Cardiff University. Her teaching and research interests pivot around children, childhood and sexuality, young masculinities and femininities and violence and bullying.

**Alan Richardson** is an independent education consultant, and was formerly a secondary school teacher and a local education authority adviser.

**Anna Sallnow** is an RE consultant working in a North London borough.

**Shan Scott** is a deputy director at DfES, responsible for school admissions, organisation and governance.

**Sheila Scraton** is a professor of leisure and feminist studies and pro vice chancellor (research) at Leeds Metropolitan University. She began her teaching career in PE in schools. Since moving into higher education, she has taught and researched in the area of gender, race and equity in PE, sport and leisure.

**Jan Shapiro** leads the Ethnic Minority Achievement Service for Lewisham local authority.

**Janice Slough** is an independent education consultant who has worked with girls and young women as a teacher and youth worker in the area of personal, social and health education.

**Hazel Taylor** is a former secondary headteacher and equal opportunities adviser, and a former adviser to the DfES London Challenge.

**Pippa Totraku** is a senior lecturer in IT in education at the University of Brighton. She was formerly a primary teacher and visiting lecturer. The area of research which is of particular interest to her is trainee teachers' awareness of gender equity in ICT.

**John Wadsworth** is a lecturer in the Department of Educational Studies, Goldsmiths College, London. His interest and expertise is in early years education. He was an advisory teacher for gender and also a deputy headteacher of a nursery school, both in the London Borough of Greenwich.

**Rosie Walden** is headteacher of Drayton Park Primary in Islington, London.

**Molly Warrington** is senior lecturer in geography in the University of Cambridge. Her research interests include contemporary geographies of masculinity and femininity. She was co-director of the DfES-sponsored Raising Boys' Achievement Project (2000-04).

**Chris Watkins** is a reader in education at the Institute of Education, University of London, and an independent project leader with schools and LAs developing their focus on learning. He was one of the organisers of the first conference on gender held in 1982 to address the question Equal Opportunities: what's in it for boys?

**Silvaine Wiles** is English as an Additional Language (EAL) adviser for London Challenge. She was formerly HMI with responsibility for EAL.

**Shahla Taheri-White** is head of Minority Ethnic Curriculum Support Service in Hertfordshire Children Schools and Families. She also runs a complementary school teaching Persian language, literature and culture.

**Mike Younger** is head of the faculty of education within the University of Cambridge. He co-directed the Raising Boys' Achievement Project (2000-04).

*This book is written for all the teachers who want to make a difference
and dedicated to Rosie and her generation*

In memory of Carol Adams (1948-2007)
Inner London Education Authority's
first Inspector for Equal Opportunities

and

Professor Jean Rudduck (1937-2007)
academician with a particular interest in
gender issues and pupil voice

# Still Watching...

*Kate Myers*

The first edition of *Genderwatch!* was published in January 1987. It was the product of the national curriculum body in England's then called the School Curriculum Development Committee (SCDC), *Equal Opportunities in Education Development Project.* The pack of materials was designed particularly for the teacher who said 'I'd like to do something but I'm not sure what to do'. It transpired that there were many such teachers as the initial run of 800 copies sold out within two months.

Several print runs and five years later, the second edition *Genderwatch!: After the Education Reform Act* was published by Cambridge University Press. New topics such as *performance indicators, development plans, appraisal, assessment* and *citizenship* were introduced, indicating how the educational climate had changed in this short period. Times continue to change and so has the focus of some of the schedules in this edition. For example, *local management of schools*, a new issue then as schools were barely getting used to managing their own finances, now becomes *using the school budget*.

There are several new topics which illustrate more recent changes in the educational climate and are also a salutary reminder that even if we successfully address some of the issues related to gender, when new agendas are introduced further issues will arise. Tackling inequalities is an ongoing process. New topics in this edition include *design for learning; early years; English as an additional language; leadership; school climate; mentoring and learning; mobile pupils; home-school relations; uniform; learning and teaching; self-evaluation; lesbian, gay, bisexual and trans issues in schools; study support and out of hours learning; 14-19; pupil groupings;* *pupil voice; the wider workforce; working with girls and working with boys.* Interestingly, although each has been completely rewritten for the current context, the list of curriculum subjects included has not changed.

## So what has changed?

### External factors

Globalisation, new technologies, new patterns of working and changing expectations are all affecting the way we do things and how we behave. The labour market has changed significantly since the first edition of *Genderwatch!*, particularly in respect of the massive decrease in the availability of low-skilled jobs. This has had a significant impact on the pupils (particularly boys) who previously merely served their time at school knowing that jobs awaited them as soon as they were released from their enforced custody. These pupils now have to stay on until the end of the summer term of their final year of compulsory schooling. The sentence is likely to be extended as at the time of writing there is an increasing lobby arguing that the school-leaving age in the UK (currently 16) should be increased to 18.

Cheap migrant labour from the European Union and the developing world has exacerbated the employment issue by providing competition for these scarce jobs. Opportunities in the unskilled sector are contracting, yet both young men and young women reduce their opportunities still further by seeing some jobs as not appropriate for those of their gender.

Simultaneously, the changing times mean that everyone needs new knowledge and skills in order to function both socially and in the employment market. The knowledge society requires a proficient and flexible workforce. This has implications for how both boys and girls construct their view of themselves and their future. It has enormous implications for schools and for the curriculum in helping young people prepare for this very different world.

There have also been major changes in societal attitudes with regard to the way we live. There has been an increase in the number of sole households and of divorces as well as in the number of people living together in heterosexual or same-sex relationships. There has also been a decrease in the numbers of people marrying. This has implications for schools on several levels. For example with regard to home school relations, schools can no longer assume that pupils live with both parents; that the mother is the primary carer; that the carers are in a heterosexual relationship; or that other children in the household are siblings. Just as importantly, schools also have to prepare young people for a world in which they themselves may not end up married with 2.4 children: a world where their gender roles are not quite so clear cut.

The changing patterns of society have brought with them some changes in the way men and women relate to each other and how they see their roles within and external to the relationship. For example, in many parts of the UK the involvement of men in childrearing and domestic tasks is now regarded as the norm rather than the exception. Involvement however does not mean equal sharing. Surveys about housework continue to show that women including those in full-time employment undertake far more housework than men (see for example Yee Kan, 2006). There is increasing concern about the pressures on women, who now expect to be in full-time work but also continue have the major responsibility for childcare and domestic work. The impact on men, particularly those who are unsure of their role in this new situation, also needs to be addressed.

### Within schools

The SCDC's Equal Opportunities Project was conceived because at the time there was increasing concern about girls' education. Although girls' attainment was better than that of boys in many areas of schooling, they were under-represented in significant subject areas and this had a knock-on effect on their A level choices and higher education options, and hence career choice and pay. The Sex

Discrimination Act of 1975 was having some effect but there was no compulsory curriculum at this stage. A significant number of primary and secondary schools were offering distinctly different curriculum experiences, and when pupils were given the opportunity to make choices, many of them chose according to whether they thought subjects were appropriate for boys or for girls.

As Tim Oates points out in *'Underachieving boys' and 'overachieving girls' revisited – rhetoric and reality*, although some of these issues have changed some remain, for example the disparity in the earnings of men and women. With regard to schooling, both boys' and girls' attainment has increased significantly since 1980, although girls have improved at a faster rate than boys. One of the consequences of this is the current concern about boys' achievement. This concern needs to be unpacked. Some boys are not doing as well as they could in our schools but this also applies to some girls. Likewise, some boys are doing very well, as are some girls. A generic concern masks the issues of social class and ethnicity, which are more significant than gender in determining achievement.

### So if gender is not *the* determining factor why write a book called *Genderwatch*?

The reason that gender still needs to be on our agendas is that equality issues interrelate and although gender is not *the* determining factor it is *a* determining factor. There are gender differences within groups, so for example white working class girls tend to do better in school than white working class boys, but they do not do as well as middle class boys. So when we focus on improving attainment, we need to be aware of these differences and try to avoid superficial responses. For example, making schools and schooling more boy friendly, as some commentators are now recommending, is unlikely to help working class girls.

We also have some writers suggesting that hard-wired differences between the sexes mean that their learning needs are completely different. Whatever the significant differences apart from the obvious biological ones between the average boy and the average girl, it is important to remember that the differences within each sex are greater than the differences between them. So, for example, the average 17 year old boy is taller than the average girl of the same age. But the difference between the smallest and the tallest 17 year old boy is greater than the difference between the sexes. So an environment geared only to the alleged needs of one sex would adversely affect a large number of the members of this group. In addition, and perhaps even more importantly, much of our gender identity is socially constructed and schools have an important part to play in enabling young people to widen rather than restrict their horizons.

## Not just about attainment

The introduction in the last edition talked about the importance of value added (a new term for many in those days), suggesting that schools should be aware of how effective they are for all their pupils; schools should have been asking themselves whether they were adding as much value for girls as for boys, for black pupils as for white, for working class pupils as for middle class. Now we know that it is also important to consider how the different equality issues inter-relate. So it is not sufficient to analyse girls' achievement without considering ethnicity and social class factors. For example, how well are white working class girls doing compared with white middle class girls?

The last edition also reminded readers that assessment and exam results are not the only indicators of how well a school is doing for its pupils: 'It is vital to consider the **quality** of the school experience alongside the outcomes.' The majority of readers of this book will, at some time in their lives, have done well academically. We have a responsibility to help all our pupils do the same. However, school should be about much more than this. Schooling has a moral purpose too. What we learn in schools contributes to how we construct ourselves as adults. The experience of the young black woman who is doing well academically but is subjected to daily racial taunts or the gay young man who learns to expect to be bullied are sadly not uncommon. Their schooling experiences will no doubt remain with them throughout adulthood, but they will also be learning experiences for their classmates who will observe an institution tolerating these behaviours. Schools have an important role to play in helping us learn about roles and relationships in connection with gender.

For some time we have been aware that schools do more than transmit subject knowledge to the next generation. In 1968, Jackson used the term 'hidden curriculum' to describe the notion that pupils learn from their school experience as well as what teachers

are trying to teach in the classrooms. Some of these messages are overt, for example how assemblies are organised and conducted. Others may be covert, for example how staff treat each other and how they interact with pupils. More recent research about how our brains work, for example the discovery of the mirror neuron demonstrates how much we learn from observing what is going on around us; hence the importance of school climate and the ethos that pervades the organisation. We are often told that we are what we eat. We are also what we see and what we learn. We make a special effort to learn some things, but others we pick up and absorb through observing the world around us. Schools may not be able to change the world but they can challenge, encourage and widen horizons.

Another reason that attainment – and indeed containment – cannot be the only end tasks of equitable schooling is that, however well girls achieve, they are likely to face sexism when they leave school; hence the continued disparity in earnings in spite of increased attainment and the reality of the glass ceiling. If this is to change, then attitudes have to change too. Schools have a choice either to sanction and maintain the *status quo* or to provide opportunities that encourage young people to question and explore other possibilities.

Good equal opportunities practice is good practice *per se*. It is good for *all* of us. It will not happen though without the concerted effort of those involved in it. There is a continued need to watch. More importantly there is a continued need to do something about what we observe. All of us involved in *Genderwatch: still watching...* hope that this book will help you to do just that.

*Kate Myers*
*January 2007*

## References
Jackson, P. W. (1968) *Life in Classrooms*. New York: Holt, Rinehart and Winston
Myers, K. (1987) *Genderwatch!* London: Schools Curriculum Development Committee
Myers, K. (1993) *Genderwatch!; After the Education Reform Act*. Cambridge: Cambridge University Press
Yee Kan, M. (2006) Measuring Housework Participation: The Gap between 'Stylised' Questionnaire Estimates and Diary-based Estimates. University of Essex GeNet Working Paper No. 20 April

# How to use this book

*Kate Moorse*

*Genderwatch: still watching...* has been designed as a tool to support a school in self-evaluation and curriculum review; as an aid to development planning; and as an aid to staff development and in-service training.

Grouped under seven categories, stand alone sections deal with distinct aspects of the school's life and activity. They are all interdependent and most users will want to work through several components either in conjunction with one another or in a sequence.

The structure of the book seeks to mirror the structure and functions of the typical school. The early sections: *Context for Gender Equality* and *The Foundations* both focus on establishing the conditions that create the climate or set the tone for gender equality within the institution. Whilst they will be of interest to all staff members, they will be of primary interest to those holding a strategic role or management function, and particularly to the senior management team and governing body.

*Setting the Tone* and *Communicating the Tone* are essential reading for all members of the school community, for these deal largely with the way the institution responds to the goal of achieving gender equality. *Setting the Tone* comprises the areas of school activity where gender priorities are able to inform the mechanisms employed to shape and drive the school's social and learning environments. The 'tone' is then conveyed or communicated (*Communicating the Tone*) through the school's daily routines, personal relationships and general ethos of the school, where the experiences gained and messages received by young people will do much to influence the attitudes, values and behaviours that they take forward into teen and adult life.

As well as being directly relevant to the work of individual co-ordinators for the various areas of responsibility, the sections *Inclusion* and *Pedagogy and Organisation of Learning* deal with a wide range of concerns for primary, special and secondary teachers and learning assistants, and should be taken in conjunction with each other and with individual subjects or groups of subjects which comprise the last section, *Subjects*. Within each of the subject schedules there is guidance for the co-ordinator or department manager as well as for the class or subject teacher. Schedules for early years and 14-19 precede these as distinct and discrete topics of interest to specific groups or teams of teachers and other practitioners.

Each schedule comprises a discussion of issues and information about the research findings relating to that area, together with bulleted points for reflection which can be used either by the individual or by a team or group within the school, or indeed as part of a whole school review or in-service training session.

# 'Underachieving Boys' and 'Overachieving Girls' Revisited – Rhetoric and Reality

*Tim Oates*

This schedule challenges some prevailing myths about the relative performance of boys and girls in schooling 5-19. There is a profound need to dispel simplistic representations of gendered achievement in education and training, and in particular, myths around boys' underachievement. Without evidence-driven understanding, we risk misunderstanding the real standing of males and females in society as a whole, and consequently of formulating highly defective public policy. Nowhere is this risk greater than in the realm of *boy friendly learning*.

Media focus on so called underperforming boys pays little attention to important subtleties in the nature of the problem and in the research findings. Marks' influential pamphlet failed to highlight that both boys and girls have improved, but boys have improved less (Marks, 2001). And not all boys at all levels and ages are underperforming.

There are no simple explanations for the gender gap. Many factors have an influence: learning preferences deriving from developmental distinctions between boys and girls, pupil grouping in schools, assessment techniques, the curriculum, teaching styles, teacher expectations, role models, and the way teachers reward and discipline. Ofsted have evidence of gendered behaviour by teachers – including setting, attention-management, subject-choice advice, and decisions about entry to tiered papers ... and more (Ofsted, 2003). Gender-stereotypical peer group pressure amongst boys significantly affects their engagement with learning (Warrington and Younger, 2005).

## Dispelling myths 1: it's a new problem

The gender gap is not a new problem; if raw scores in the 11+ had been used to determine selection, then grammar schools in the 1950s and 1960s would have been full of girls. Likewise, the historical figures for O level achievement in the 1960s and 1970s show a gap in gender achievement, roughly 5% difference in pass rate, 10% in some subjects such as languages (Murphy, 1980).

## Dispelling myths 2: it's all about education

Actually it's all about development, including pre-natal development. Babies are actively processing speech *before* birth; they can recognise a story that they have heard while still in the womb (DeCasper and Spence, 1986). Early experiences affect cognitive development. Maternal-infant bonding is crucial to engagement with the world. Work with infants under a year old shows that the nature of the infant-maternal bond affects learning from birth (Oates and Stevenson, 2005). Other research suggests that gendered behaviour is an insidious element in care and development of the child (Seavey *et al*, 1975; Condry and Condry, 1976).

## Dispelling myths 3: it's only a problem in England

Not so. In PISA 2003, (the OECD Programme for International Student Assessment), boys performed significantly better than girls on the combined mathematics scale in 27 participating countries. However, the magnitude of these gender differences was generally small. No gender differences were observed in the twelve countries including England

and in one country (Iceland) girls performed significantly better than boys. As in PISA 2000, girls performed significantly better than boys on the reading test in all but one country in PISA 2003, but the gender gap was far less marked in mathematics. In PISA 2000, no significant gender differences were observed on the science test but in 2003 boys performed somewhat better than girls in twelve countries. In problem solving, girls outperformed boys in only six countries (OECD, 2006).

The findings of PISA suggest that Finland has generally managed to achieve high quality *and* high equality of reading literacy outcomes but it had the widest gender gap in reading literacy on all three subscales. The gender gap seems to have widened not only in Finland but also in the other OECD countries.

## Dispelling myths 4: all girls are better than all boys

Think about it. Whilst this is the implication of many press stories, this would give rise to a distribution like this:

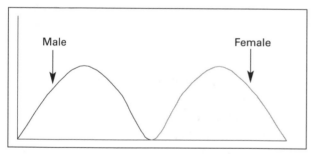

**Table 1: Putative Relationship between girls and boys**

This is clearly absurd. OK, so there is some overlap, perhaps like this?

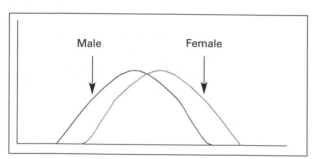

**Table 2: Putative Relationship between girls and boys**

In fact the difference in real data from examinations is actually like this (see Table 3).

The overlap is far more substantial than the difference. In other words, we should remain as concerned about girls in the lower attaining parts of the female population as we are about 'underperforming boys'. Outcomes are not as different as press comment or public perceptions would have us believe.

## Dispelling myths 5: it's all about learning styles and 'lazy boys'

Research suggests that learning styles and approaches to learning are crucial. If we take the data from GCSE mathematics used on page 3 and draw up a new diagram in which the lines show not the attainment of boys and girls but the degree of difference between them, you can see that the difference is at its greatest in the middle area of the distribution. This is vital (see Table 4).

Crucially, boys are more heavily represented at the highest and lowest ends of the distribution. This gives rise to a vital effect, not yet significantly documented. If both boys and girls improve over time, this peculiar distribution, which is present in tests in many different settings and with different purposes, more girls will be included in the top grades, relative to boys. In table 4, if all students (males and females) start scoring 800 where they were previously scoring 700, then many more girls than previously would be in the population scoring 800. In other words, slide the whole distribution up, and you get much greater representation of girls.

This is not the sole explanation for the gender gap, but is a mechanism which is in operation and is part of the picture. As both boys and girls improve, there is a tendency – by virtue of this mechanism – for girls to appear to accelerate ahead of boys.

But there are fundamental issues associated with different approaches to learning. If gender identities are shaped by very early experiences then we shouldn't be surprised by this. Rudduck and Gray have undertaken pupil-based research into differential performance, and remain concerned at the personal and social consequences of many boys' failure to develop engagement with learning and to achieve to a reasonable level whilst they are in compulsory education. Arnot argued that the most significant issue in explaining difference is the way in which boys and girls regard school (Arnot, 1997). Amongst boys, it's 'cool' to be seen not to work or comply. Also boys tend to blame poor performance on externalised factors 'bad teaching', 'wrong test

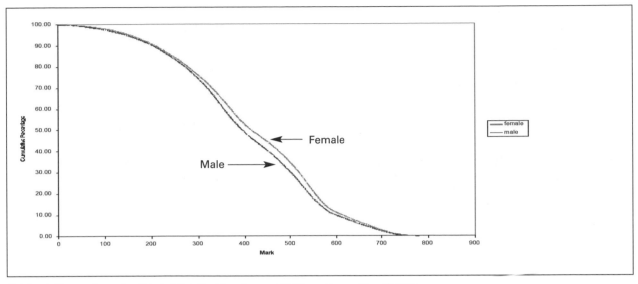

**Table 3: Examples of a Mark Distribution for an OCR mathematics GCSE**

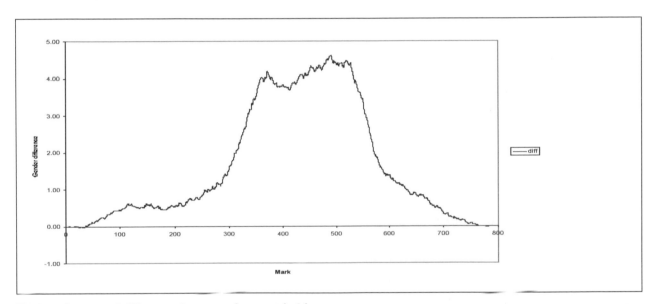

**Table 4: Degree of difference between boys and girls**

questions' while girls tend to blame themselves and their competence, and then work harder. Gender friendship groupings used to cope with transition (Galton *et al*, 1999) reinforce gendered approaches to learning. Rudduck's work on GCSE preparation suggests that boys tend to leave it to the last minute and rely on 'natural talent'; this matters particularly in subjects where you need to build skills and knowledge over time such as languages and English. This adversely affects their performance and affects subject choices post-16. Studies by teachers in schools (e.g. Beacon School, Crowborough, 1993) revealed very different patterns of boys' and girls' homework effort which are heavily embedded in learning identities and cultural models. It is likely to take a lot to shift them.

### Dispelling myths 6: it's all about coursework favouring girls

This is partly true – but it's not a simple issue. Researchers who have disagreed about the educational merits and social justice of new forms of assessment (Marks, 2001; Murphy, 1998) agree that coursework and new curriculum content in the national curriculum and in examinations have had a positive effect on girls' performance. However, the notion that 'it's all down to coursework' is not supported by the evidence. Girls' enhanced performance has not been entirely synchronised with changes in assessment approaches. During the early 1990s, English moved from being 100% coursework, yet as coursework waxed and then waned, the gender gap continued to increase.

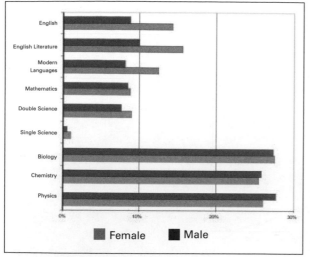

**Table 5: Proportion of students gaining A (within gender)**

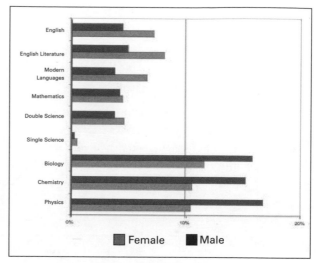

**Table 6: Proportion of students gaining A (relative to cohort)**

Girls do better with coursework, where they can explore a subject discursively. And as boys place emphasis on the 'big bang' of the examination, all the small bits of diligence on the seemingly insignificant pieces of coursework that girls do adds up to a better overall examination grade for the girls. So should we remove coursework because it is not 'gender neutral' or retain it because it helps to reflect better the learning preferences of girls?

### Dispelling myths 7: there are no tests or qualifications in which boys do better than girls

This is a key issue. It is certainly the case that girls' performance has improved significantly. From 1980 to 1995, girls moved from being significantly behind boys in science and mathematics. Over that time, boys' attainment improved significantly, but less

quickly than girls, and therefore the gender gap widened. By 1995, boys' attainment in mathematics and science at key stages 2 and 3 still slightly exceeded that of girls. The detail is vital. What was going on?

The national curriculum had a significant impact. We know that female infants and young children tend to achieve higher levels of language-based proficiency. In the past, they have preferentially favoured language-based learning activities, and avoided areas of activity such as 3D representation in mathematics, something which is cognitively favoured by boys. But the national curriculum cut through these preferences, and compelled girls to study such areas resulting in improved performance. In the 1960s and 1970s some girls' schools had entirely inadequate science facilities. Likewise, prior

| FEMALE | | | | | | MALE | | | | | |
|--------|--|--------|--|--------|--|--------|--|--------|--|--------|--|
| **2001** | | **2003** | | **2005** | | **2001** | | **2003** | | **2005** | |
| GS | 11.62% | GS | 9.66% | GS | 9.62% | GS | 11.88% | GS | 9.98% | GS | 10.12% |
| EngLit | 7.79 | EngLit | 7.36 | EngLit | 7.62 | Math | 10.29 | Math | 7.86 | Math | 7.61 |
| Bio | 6.24 | Psy | 6.24 | Psy | 7.35 | Phy | 6.08 | Phy | 5.58 | History | 5.34 |
| Math | 6.22 | Bio | 5.94 | Bio | 6.05 | Geo | 4.90 | BS | 5.05 | Phy | 5.34 |
| Psy | 5.04 | Math | 4.85 | History | 4.73 | BS | 4.78 | History | 4.79 | Bio | 4.99 |
| History | 4.33 | History | 4.42 | Soc | 4.41 | Chem | 4.61 | Geo | 4.59 | BS | 4.74 |
| Chem | 4.01 | Soc | 4.20 | Chem | 3.94 | Bio | 4.44 | Bio | 4.42 | Chem | 4.73 |
| Soc | 3.85 | Chem | 3.80 | Math | 3.93 | History | 4.28 | Chem | 4.20 | Geo | 4.38 |
| Geo | 3.69 | Geo | 3.39 | Geo | 3.12 | EngLit | 3.61 | EngLit | 3.42 | EngLit | 3.30 |
| BS | 3.44 | BS | 3.07 | Media | 2.98 | PE | 2.88 | ICT | 3.24 | PE | 3.18 |

to the national curriculum, science was poorly represented in teacher training for the primary phase, a circle of negative reinforcement and reproduction.

Mathematics remains an area of national testing in which boys are ahead of girls: in mathematics at key stage 2 level 4 and above (2006 boys = 77%, girls = 75%) and mathematics at key stage 2 level 5 and above (2006 boys = 36%, girls = 31%). But there is a much more significant difference in boys' and girls' attainment embedded in the GCSE and GCE qualifications data, concealed by the way in which the data are normally presented.

Usually, data relating to the numbers attaining a given grade in a qualification are presented as a proportion of the entry. But what if girls are seriously under-represented? Maybe only the high attaining girls enter certain subjects – the figures will then show a higher proportion of girls getting A grades, even though girls overall are poorly represented in the subject. In other words, not many girls do A level physics, but if they do, they get a high grade. What is serious about this is that if girls avoid mathematics and science, it is likely to affect their life chances. If we compare grade attainment with the cohort, and not just those from the cohort who enter for each qualification, we can see that this is the case. The following two tables show the contrast. Look at the way in which table 5 (page 4) is deceptive in terms of girls' lower performance in single science biology, chemistry and physics at GCSE.

And that's another thing – girls are far less likely to do single sciences at GCSE – which in turn affects their progression onto science-based advanced-level study. So while girls are now achieving better academic results than boys at age 16, relatively few are choosing science or science-related subjects for further study. Boys dominate in mathematics, science and technology at A level and far more men than women study these subjects in higher education. This has significant implications for men's and women's career choices and future earnings: 60% of working women are clustered in only 10% of occupations; and men are also under-represented in a number of occupations.

In table 7 note the position of mathematics in the boys' section and in the girls' section. Look also for physics – where is it in the girls' section? It doesn't figure. Then look at the position of psychology in the girls' section. This raises key questions about how girls and boys are advised; how self-perception and peer influences shape subject choice; and what the longer term consequences are for individual progression and for skill supply to the economy.

It is relative attainment between boys and girls which is the vital issue in national testing and GCSE; subject choice is the crucial gender issue in post-16 education and training.

### Dispelling myths 8: women carry through into employment the advantage they gain in education

Not so. While women have made gains and moved towards equal pay and opportunity, the advantage which they hold in education is not carried forward wholesale into society and the economy. The pay gap *is* closing but it still exists. In 2005 women who work full time were paid on average just 87.0% of men's hourly earnings using the median and 82.9% using the mean (Prospect, 2006). Purcell's incisive work suggests that whilst women are increasingly gaining access to previously male-dominated employment, there has been little change in the balance of domestic labour and responsibilities for children. Women are still taking the full weight of domestic responsibilities (Purcell, 2000). The gap in pay and progression between men and childless women has closed. However, for those with children, her work shows that women with high 'control factors' in work – for example, GPs able to specify hours etc – continue to advance in their careers. But for women with low control factors – for example, female bank managers – having children damages their career progression. Taking a career break for child rearing is the dominant factor in inhibiting occupational progression. In addition, where two-parent families decide whose career should be focused upon, even a minor differential in pay can influence that decision – so contributing to the cycle of gendered disadvantage for women.

Occupations remain heavily segregated:

> ...Amongst first degree graduates entering health professions, there were 3.6 times more females than males. This is attributed partly to the popularity of nursing, and to a lesser extent, medicine, as first degree subjects of choice amongst women. At PhD level, those entering health occupations, albeit at a much smaller number than for first degree and Masters graduates, were more likely to be males (3:2 male: female).

Similarly, amongst first degree graduates entering education professions, there were 3.8 times more females than males; for social and welfare professions, 3.7 times; legal professions, two times; scientific research, analysis and development professionals, 1.7 times; and marketing, sales and advertising professionals, 1.6 times. On the other hand, of first degree graduates entering the engineering professions, there were 5.5 times more males than females; for IT professions, 4.6 times, and for other professional, associate professional and technical occupations, 1.4 times... (Prospect, 2006)

Self-perception and labour market positioning seriously disadvantage women too. Female graduates more frequently enter employment for which they consider their degree not to be a requirement:

...Although female first degree graduates were more likely than their male peers to be in health professions or associate professions, they were less likely to report that their degree was a formal requirement and more likely to say that it has not been required for obtaining their employment. Many of the female graduates employed in these occupations were nurses, of which only around half (54%) reported that a degree was a formal requirement. In contrast, relatively few male graduates went into nursing and of those working in the health professions, a higher proportion were employed as doctors, for which a medicine degree, unsurprisingly, was formally required. Of first degree graduates entering work as business and financial professionals and associate professionals, 52.6% were females and 47.4% were males. Males working in these types of jobs, however, were more likely than their female counterparts to believe that their degree was a formal requirement, with 41.3% noting that this was the case compared with 32.5% of females. Female graduates were also more likely to report that their qualification was not required: 21% reported that this was the case compared with 17.5% of males. Female graduates were not only less likely than male graduates to be in IT occupations, they were less likely to be in IT jobs for which a degree qualification was a requirement... (Prospect, 2006)

This suggests a serious, entrenched under-utilisation of skill and learning – the social consequence of personal disadvantage.

## Dispelling myths 9: gender differences are the most crucial in our system

Gender must be placed in the right point on the scale of political and social concerns. Differences in attainment according to gender may be important, but these differences are dwarfed by the differences which are associated with social background. It is not that gender is unimportant – it's just vital to keep it in perspective when forming public policy priorities. Whilst gender is a valuable category for analysis, and causes can be attributed to gendered aspects of educational practice and to gendered attitudes and approaches to learning by pupils themselves, social class and ethnicity are still greater determinants of achievement than gender (Claessen, 2006). Child poverty, irrespective of gender, remains a pressing social policy issue (Robinson, 2001).

## Dispelling myths 10: the gender gap points to a failure at the heart of our education system

Actually our education system could be construed as a success. Both boys and girls have improved significantly over the past two decades. Children go into school with heavily gendered views of occupations; these moderate whilst they are at school due to countering stereotyping, equal opportunity policies etc; and then kick back in again with subject choice (Knipe *et al*, 2002; Jackson and Warin, 2000). School is thus delivering some key social goods and moderating some entrenched disparities.

## Dispelling myths 11: what we need is a 'boy-friendly' pedagogy

This is an oft-quoted position which holds considerable danger. Boaler cuts to the heart of the matter:

....gender patterns are shifting, not because of a climate of boy disadvantage, but because of a climate that is moving closer to equality of opportunity, in which girls are being allowed to achieve. I would therefore like to turn a popular media perspective on its head and propose a history of male overachievement, gained at the expense of the oppression of girls, that is now being replaced by a more equitable system of opportunity in which the group that works hardest and longest is allowed to achieve the greatest rewards... (Boaler undated).

What Boaler goes on to recommend is not a return to methods which advantaged boys, but to methods which advantage both sexes. Her approach is endorsed by the DfES-funded study by Younger, Warrington *et al* (2005), a neglected study which provides a comprehensive, evidence-based set of recommendations for pedagogy. They outlined four classes of intervention strategies:

Pedagogic – e.g. space and time to talk and reflect about reading

Individual – e.g. realistic and challenging target-setting

Organisational – e.g. selective use of single-sex teaching groups

Socio-cultural – e.g. paired reading schemes between year 3 and year 5 pupils

Like Boaler's , their research '...does not support the view that there is a case for boy-friendly pedagogies. Pedagogies which appeal to and engage boys are equally girl-friendly. They characterise quality teaching, and as such are just as suitable and desirable for girls as for boys...'

## Conclusions

By considering the full trajectory of children – from before birth to participation in employment – we can see that the gender gap results from complex processes. My analysis of trajectories through life suggests that the education system is not solely responsible in some way for the gender gap; it is more that social and other stereotypes and pressures impact on education. Where problems are manifest in schools, they require careful remedy.

## References

Boaler, J. (1998) Mathematical equity – underachieving boys or sacrificial girls? *Inclusive Education* I2 (2) p119-135

Boaler, J. (undated) Paying the price for 'sugar and spice' – shifting the analytical lens in equity research. *Mathematical Thinking and Learning* 4 (2&3) p127-144

Claessen, M. (2006) *Gender and Class Differences in GCSE Results*. Cambridge Assessment Internal Report

Condry, S.M. and Condry, J.C. (1976) Sex differences: a study of the eye of the beholder. *Child Development* 47 p812-819

DeCasper, A. J. and Spence, M. J. (1986) Prenatal maternal speech influences: newborns' perception of speech sounds. *Infant Behavior and Development* 9 p133-150

Galton, M., Gray, J., and Rudduck, J. (1999) The Impact of Transition and Transfer on Pupils' Progress and Attainment. *DfES Research Brief* 131

Jackson, C. and Warin, J. (2000) The importance of gender as an aspect of identity at key points of transition. *BERJ* 26 (3)

Knipe, D., Leith, H., Gray, C., McKeown, E. and Carlisle K. (2002) *Betty the Builder, Neil the Nurse: Sex Typing of Occupations in Primary Schools*. Belfast: Equality Commission for Northern Ireland

Marks, J. (2001) *Girls Know Better: Educational Attainment Of Boys And Girls*. London: Institute for Civil Society

Murphy, R. (1980) Sex differences in GCE examination entry statistics and success rates. *Education Studies* 6 p169-178

Oates, J. M. and Stevenson, J. (2005) Temperament and development. In Oates, J. M., Wood, C. P. and Grayson, A, *Psychological Development and Early Childhood*. Oxford/Milton Keynes: Blackwell Publishing/The Open University

Ofsted (2003) *Boys' Achievement*. London: HMSO

Purcell, K. (2000) Changing boundaries in employment and organisations. In Purcell, K. *Changing Boundaries In Employment*. Bristol: Academic Press

OECD 2006 www.pisa.oecd.org/pages/0,2987,en_322523573 1_1_1_1_1_1,00.html

Prospect (2006) www.prospects.ac.uk/cms/showpage/plod cbiFp

Robinson, P. (2001) *Time to Choose Justice*. London: Institute of Public Policy Research

Rodeiro, C. (2005) *Provision of GCE A level subjects*. Cambridge Assessment

Seavey, C., Katz, P. and Rosenberg, Z. (1975) The effect of gender labels on adults' responses to infants. *Sex Roles* 1 (2) p103-109

Stern and Karraker (1989) Sex stereotyping of infants: A review of gender labelling studies. *Sex Roles* 20 p501-522

Warrington, M., Younger, M., and Williams, J., (2000) Student attitudes, image and the gender gap. *BERJ* 26 (3)

Younger, M., Warrington, M., with Gray, J., Rudduck, J., McLellan, Bearne, E., Kershner and Bricheno, P. (2005) *Raising Boys' Achievement*. London:DfES research report RR63

# Relevant Legislation

*Graham Clayton*

## Introduction

This schedule provides a short summary of the main pieces of UK and European Union (EU) legislation dealing with gender discrimination. There are many more gender related measures within the Education Acts and of course extensive legislation making other forms of discrimination unlawful, for example race and disability discrimination. It covers:

- the laws outlawing sex discrimination in employment
- maternity, paternity and parental rights in relation to employment
- other directly relevant statutes affecting employment
- the 2007 Gender Equality Duty
- the impact of EU law.

## Background

The positive duty upon public authorities to promote gender equality under the Equality Act 2006 provides a new legislative focus but the Sex Discrimination Act 1975 and the Equal Pay Act 1970, which the 1975 Act brought into force, remain the mainstay of UK law on gender discrimination. The SDA has been the key gender equality legislation for education since 1975, resulting in many positive changes that have occurred in schooling e.g. girls' access to wider curriculum, but there are still some outstanding issues which it is hoped will be addressed by the Gender Equality Duty (2007).

This is the first major change to sex discrimination legislation for 30 years. Like the race and disability duties, it shifts the onus away from individuals complaining of unfair treatment, and instead puts a positive duty on schools to promote gender equality in all their policies and practices. Schools will have specific duties under the legislation (see below).

### Equal Pay Act 1970 (as amended)

Technically, this Act does not confer a statutory right to equal pay as such. Rather it requires that contracts of employment under which people are employed must legally be considered to contain an 'equality clause'. Though the Act refers to women in comparisons with men it does in fact also confer equal pay rights on men in comparison with women.

Provided there is no genuine material difference between her case and that of the relevant male comparator, a woman is entitled to the same employment benefits as are enjoyed by a male comparator in the same employment if:

a)  the man and the woman are employed to do 'like work'

b)  the man and the woman are employed to do work which has been rated as equivalent in a proper job evaluation study

c)  or, the man and the woman are employed to do work of equal value.

Equal pay law has generated a large volume of case law in both the UK and European judicial systems. There remains a long way to go to achieve genuine pay equality. The law on equal pay allows only for comparisons to be made between a woman and a man in the same employ. Although this allows more than comparisons between people employed by the same employer, there are great uncertainties about securing pay equality across employment sectors, for example amongst employees of different employers paid under the same pay system. The very large majority of teachers in maintained schools are paid under a single statutory pay system, but there are 25,000 or so different decision-making bodies (school governing bodies) exercising discretionary powers in relation to their pay and over 5,000 different employers. This is fertile ground for gender-based pay anomalies within a single pay system, but little opportunity exists for claimants to make claims based on comparisons with other teachers with different employers.

Similarly, the growth of casual short-term and employment agency based employment threatens consistency in equal pay laws. In 2006, the TUC adopted a strong resolution to support equal pay for agency workers.

### Sex Discrimination Act 1975 (as amended)

The 1975 Act makes it unlawful to discriminate on grounds of gender in the provision of a range of rights, benefits and opportunities including, in particular, employment, education and trade union membership.

The Act was designed to outlaw both direct and indirect discrimination. Direct discrimination, that is discrimination for a reason related to gender, has proved relatively straightforward. Examples of direct discrimination include the case of a woman refused an appointment simply because it is thought that 'the school needs a man' and that of a woman denied promotion because she is pregnant or of an age when she might want to have children and go on maternity leave.

Indirect discrimination is more problematic. The intention is to secure the removal of obstacles to rights and benefits which have a disproportionate adverse impact on members of one sex.

In 2001, the situation was improved for claimants in employment cases when the burden of proving a claim was reversed so that it became a burden for respondents in these cases to prove that they have not discriminated. This can be exemplified by a case in which poor recruitment practice seems, for no obvious good reason, to end with a preference for male appointees to senior posts. Though the recruiters may vigorously deny any intention to discriminate, they may well lose to a claimant who demonstrates a serious possibility of discrimination if the recruiters are unable to prove transparent good reason for their decisions.

In 2005, provisions were added to the 1975 Act to make sexual harassment a separate and distinct basis for claims.

## Maternity and related rights

Significant improvements have been made in relation to 'maternity rights' in the employment context in recent years. The Employment Rights Act 1996, as amended by the Employment Relations Act 1999, the Employment Act 2002 and the Work and Families Act 2006 supplemented by supporting regulations, now makes the relevant provision.

Maternity rights fall into four main categories:

■ time off for ante-natal care – that is paid time off during work hours to attend properly authorised ante-natal care appointments

■ maternity leave – a universal right to 52 weeks leave with protection of employee status

■ maternity benefit – rights to Statutory Maternity Pay payable by employers or Maternity Allowance payable by social security – 39 weeks

■ protection against unfair treatment or dismissal – the right not to be dismissed or be made to suffer a detriment in employment for any reason related to pregnancy, maternity or the exercise of maternity rights.

The Health and Safety at Work Act 1974, and the Sex Discrimination Act 1975, as amended, work alongside the maternity rights legislation to give pregnant and post-natal working women additional and parallel rights and protections.

Since April 2003, new fathers have been statutorily entitled to two weeks' paid leave, and employees, both mothers and fathers, who have completed a year's service with their employer have been entitled to 13 weeks unpaid parental leave to care for the child up to the age of five (18 weeks up to age 18 in the case of a disabled child).

Parents of children under six also have the right to request their employers to consider providing them with flexible working patterns. This, however, is limited to a right of request and to have the request considered. If the request has been properly considered on the right criteria, no legal claim can be made against a refusal unless the refusal can be shown to offend the sex discrimination laws.

All these rights are however available only to 'employees', those working under contracts of employment. There is a growing campaign to secure similar rights for other workers who are not engaged in their own lucrative businesses but who, for technical legal reasons, do not qualify as employees. One local authority tried unsuccessfully in 2005/06 to argue that home tutors were not employees. The same argument has been used to deny legal protections to peripatetic music teachers and even casual supply teachers. Casually engaged teachers and other staff are often particularly vulnerable. Employment Tribunals are generally reluctant to exclude such workers from protection but greater clarity is needed in this area of the law.

## Other legislation

Other legislation has been enacted which clearly impacts in areas of employment in which women more commonly work. The Part-time Workers (Prevention of Less Favourable Treatment) Regulations 2000 give part-time workers a range of proportional equality rights and protections. The Fixed Term Employees (Prevention of Less Favourable Treatment) Regulations 2002 have similarly given equal treatment rights and protections to some fixed-term contract holders, including the right to be treated as permanent after four years spent in fixed-term employment with the same employer unless the employer can show justification for continuing the employment as fixed-term. The Employment Equality (Age) Regulations 2006 also provide protections for women whose employment patterns have in the past resulted in their being disadvantaged on grounds of age rather than gender.

## The Commission for Equality and Human Rights and the Gender Equality Duty

The Equality Act 2006 establishes the Commission for Equality as an umbrella organisation to replace the sector based anti-discrimination commissions and has imposed (effective April 2007) a general **positive duty** upon public authorities, that is bodies having 'functions of a public nature' including school authorities, **to promote** gender equality.

■ The **Gender Equality Duty** requires all public authorities and those providing services for public authorities – which include schools and contractors providing services to schools – to produce a three year *Gender Equality Scheme*. In schools, the scheme relates to the workforce, and to the service the school provides: education. With regard to the workforce, the pay duty requires schools to consider setting a

specific objective where they identify gaps between men and women's earnings. The duty also addresses occupational segregation and the concentration of women in lower-paid jobs such as catering, cleaning and caring.

The specific duties require schools to:

☐ set and implement gender equality objectives, published in a scheme and action plan.

In order to set those objectives schools will need to:

☐ gather and use information on how their work affects gender equality

☐ consult relevant stakeholders

☐ undertake gender impact assessments of all policies and practices

☐ report annually and review every three years.

Decisions about action should be prioritised in relation to the severity of the impact of the inequality that has been identified. One of the biggest impacts of the duty for schools will be on the balance of the workforce, particularly in primary and early years settings; on what is being actively done to reduce inequalities in outcomes; and on what is being done to reduce barriers that lead to later inequalities, for example in occupational choices.

GED is about outcomes and can be used to exert pressure. It covers men, women and transsexuals and it is anticipated that it will promote a culture change. However, the Equality Commission faces a daunting task in promoting compliance with the duty, in an environment in which respect for wide cultural diversity is at times in tension with gender equality principles.

It is anticipated that the legal duty will be a focus for promoting good practice rather than a heavily enforced duty, since this is type of legislation is not easily enforced by a stream of governmental orders and directions. Nonetheless, public authorities will need to bring gender equality considerations into all their functions.

## European law

The UK's membership of the European Union means that its internal laws must be consistent with the anti-discrimination laws of the Union itself. Many of the recent developments in domestic law have been enacted to ensure compliance with European Law. Changes to UK law clearly required by EU law can be made relatively easily, without new Acts of Parliament (primary legislation), by the enactment of regulations and orders. Several of the amendments to the early legislation mentioned above have been introduced by this means.

In other respects, again because of the different traditions of UK law, the implementation in the UK of EU directives has, on occasions, proved difficult and controversial. There is a standing requirement that where possible UK laws must be interpreted by courts and tribunals so as to be compliant. The UK Government has, however, on occasions been caught out in non-compliance.

In some circumstances, employees, particularly those in public sector employment, can pursue claims relying on EU law. The overarching European Communities Act 1972 provides the required legal authority. These claims are, however, often complex and expensive to pursue. They are dependent on showing that the EU law under which the claim is made is sufficiently clear and unequivocal to confer an individual right.

The main sources of EU anti-discrimination law are Article 141 of the Treaty of Rome, as amended by the Treaty of Amsterdam and the EU Equal Treatment Directive of 1976, amended 2002. These have the broad purpose of outlawing any gender discrimination 'at all'. There are, however, proposed EU directives with implications for women's employment, which the UK Government has resisted. Most controversial of these is the proposed EU Agency Workers Directive, designed to give equality rights and protections to workers taken into employment through labour supply businesses. In some employment sectors, education being a prime example, the denial of equality rights to workers in this category has statistically identifiable adverse affects on working women.

## Remaining concerns

Some legal mechanisms ought to be found which address inequalities within the labour market as a whole rather than a regime which concentrates on discriminatory acts by individual employers. Greater clarity and far less legalism are needed in the law which permits 'justifiable' discrimination. Discrimination in the casual and 'agency' employment sectors needs urgent attention. Simpler and more effective procedures are needed to tackle gender disadvantage in educational provision.

## Making claims

Access to law remains a major problem. Recent changes have encouraged the resolution of employment disputes without recourse to legal process, but these are controversial and are thought by many to disadvantage employee claimants. The law has become very complex in some areas and difficult for claimants without legal representation. Outside employment, legal recourse is through the traditional court system and is daunting for many claimants.

Employment based claims must now normally start with the presentation of a formal grievance. If the problem is not then resolved, a claim can be made to an Employment Tribunal. Claimants can put relevant questions to the respondent employer. The respondent will reply. There is then likely to follow a series of exchanges about documents, evidence and witnesses. The Tribunal itself will probably convene at least one hearing to manage the claim before it comes to a full hearing.

Appeals from Employment Tribunal decisions can be made to the Employment Appeal Tribunal, but only on a point of law. Beyond that appeals go into the traditional court system.

There is a great deal of advisory material available through the internet including the Tribunal Service site itself at www.tribunals.gov.uk. The Equal Opportunities Commission site at www.eoc.org.uk (from autumn 2007 see www.cehr.org.uk) has a lot of helpful material and there are many other sites worth visiting after searching 'equal opportunities uk'.

However, in the end, there is nothing better than union membership to secure access to advice and representation in pursuing employment related discrimination claims.

### Further reading
Further information and guidance about the Gender Equality Duty (GED) can be found at www.eoc.org.uk or www.cehr.org.uk

GOD THROWS DOWN LOTS OF FRECKLES AND MOST OF THEM FALL ON ME

Helen Crosade

# Every Child Matters

*Alan Richardson*

■ *See also schedules: School Self-evaluation; Pastoral Care: Care for Pupils as Learners, Persons and Citizens; It's My School: the Power of Pupil Voice; Study Support and Out of School Hours Learning; Lesbian, Gay, Bisexual and Trans Issues in Schools; PSHE; Citizenship*

## Introduction

Of all the educational policy development and legislation introduced by the government since 1997, *Every Child Matters* (2003) and the subsequent Children Act 2004 which applies to children and young people living in England, is potentially the most radical and wide-reaching. It has already instigated fundamental structural, organisational and administrative change in local authorities in the ways in which services are provided for children and young people. A model of whole-system change was established with the immediate aim of ensuring more integrated frontline delivery of services, processes, strategies and governance, built around new Children's Trusts and focussing on the needs of children, young people and families.

The legislation was directed towards ensuring the protection and nurturing of the most disadvantaged and vulnerable students which thus shaped the re-organisation of services for children and young people. However, the context in which this was to be achieved was an entitlement to specified outcomes for *all* children and young people. These have become popularly known as the Five Outcomes, which are: be healthy, stay safe; enjoy and achieve; make a positive contribution; and achieve economic well-being. This framework has become the basis of the provision of all services for children and young

people, and the criteria against which the effectiveness of these services is judged.

The concept of targeted services within a universal context is fundamental to an understanding of the rationale of the legislation. Services are not only directed towards disadvantaged and vulnerable children: there is an entitlement for *all* children and young people. Thus *Every Child Matters* and the Children Act are potentially powerful forces for ensuring entitlement and equality of opportunity for all. That having been said, there is very little mention of particular groups of children and young people who may need special consideration. There is a single reference to gender in the Green Paper:

> Outcomes also vary by race and gender. Underachievement and school exclusion are particularly concentrated in certain ethnic groups. Boys have a higher rate of offending and exclusion, while self-harm and eating disorders are more prevalent among girls. (DfES, 2003, p18)

## The Five Outcomes

These represent an entitlement for all children and young people. In many respects, the five outcomes echo the United Nations Declaration of Rights of the Child. They are wide-ranging, and meeting them depends on a community-wide determination and the co-ordinated response of numerous local authority, voluntary and private providers of services. They need to work collaboratively with children's families or the authority itself for children in public care.

Information on individual children collected, stored and shared accurately and effectively is an important element in the monitoring of the five outcomes, and it supports early intervention in cases where they are not being met. While this individual focus is crucial, so is the analysis and interpretation of the data to ensure that there is an awareness of any differences in outcomes for children and young people as a result of gender, ethnic origin, class, sexual orientation or disability.

## Implications for schools
### School culture
If a school is to ensure that it is working towards securing the five outcomes for its pupils, it needs to develop a culture in which each individual is able to thrive and fulfil their potential. It is highly unlikely that authoritarian, directive styles of dealing with and managing pupils will facilitate, for example, feeling cared for, participation in decision making, or feeling safe from bullying, harassment and coercion. If the atmosphere in classrooms and in the school in general is not conducive to pupils developing autonomy and positive attitudes to their education, many aspects of the *Five Outcomes* will be difficult if not impossible to achieve.

### Personalised learning
Personalised learning is a theme which runs through much of the rationale of the government's educational policy since it was first mooted in 2003 and appeared as an element in the New Relationship with Schools (2005). It is seen as being fully consistent with *Every Child Matters*, since its whole rationale is about meeting the individual needs of children and young people. In particular it involves:

- interventions for those falling behind
- extension of provision for gifted and talented students
- development of a tailored curriculum for individual pupils at the risk of exclusion or underachievement
- support and tuition beyond the school day
- individual mentoring and guidance
- extension of support for pupils from minority ethnic backgrounds
- development of effective support for pupils learning English as an additional language.

All of these elements require approaches that recognise the danger of falling into gender stereotypes in addressing them.

### Participation
Involving children and young people in decision making and supporting the community, including

within their schools, is at the heart of the outcome, to make a positive contribution. In many schools, this will need to go well beyond the traditional school council. Schools will not be able to judge their success in meeting some of the five outcomes without developing systematic ways of finding out from pupils about their experiences and feelings. For example, the extent to which pupils feel safe at school – from bullying and harassment, or from discrimination – can only be judged by talking to them or gathering their views in other ways. This will need to be developed in more personal and sensitive areas than has hitherto been the case. It is important that representatives of a full cross-section of the student population is consulted; in the past there has been a tendency for some schools to consult unrepresentative groups – members of the school council, for example – rather than ensuring that there is a dialogue with some students from all the main groups present in the school population, especially those doing less well, like white working class boys and those from newly arrived ethnic groups.

### Extended schools
Clearly, schools are very well placed within the community to provide a wide range of services for children and young people and their families, and many schools have been doing so for some years. The expectation is that, by 2010, all primary and secondary schools will provide access to a core offer of services, in partnership with local providers and agencies. Some of these will be provided away from the school site. The core offer includes access to a menu of activities including sport and study support, childcare from 8am to 6pm, parenting support, swift and easy referral to specialist services such as health and opening up services to the community such as adult learning.

There are important issues which need to be taken into account about the access of girls and young women, especially for those from some minority ethnic backgrounds, to after-school activities. For example, the majority of those students who look after younger family members after school are girls and young women; parents are understandably concerned if their children have to travel home in the dark.

## Partnership working

Improving outcomes for children and young people in sustainable ways involves bringing about fundamental changes in the ways of working with children, young people and families. Services need to be more responsive and better integrated, with access to specialist support available from within universal services.

Local authorities are bringing together partners to plan services strategically across the area, pooling budgets and commissioning schools to deliver services in some instances, to provide services that meet the needs of local communities. It is intended that boundaries between professionals and the services in which they work be removed and that multi-agency teams become the norm. The Common Assessment Framework and the Common Core of Skills and Knowledge for the Children's Workforce are examples of the mechanisms by which the work of those providing services to children and young people will be better integrated. Co-location of services, for example in children's centres and extended schools, has proved to be very effective in promoting this integration, bringing increased understanding of the roles and ways of working of other professionals and increasing the focus on the needs of children. The range of professionals needs to have common understandings about all aspects of equity, and a shared commitment to fostering it. Schools may well need to lead this.

## Information sharing

Traditionally, each service working with children and young people has had its own system and protocol for the gathering, saving and analysing of data. The difficulties in bringing together key information held in different systems have contributed significantly to the failures to identify and help children at risk, which characterised the cases which led to the publication of *Every Child Matters*. Sharing information is a pre-requisite for early intervention to ensure that children and young people get the services they require. If data is to be shared between professionals, not only will effective information systems be needed, but common approaches to confidentiality and access to information will need to be developed. The information gathered and analysed will also provide the basis for identifying inequalities in outcomes or provision for different groups of pupils.

Many of the gender issues raised by each of the five outcomes are covered in detail in other schedules, reflecting the holistic nature of the ECM agenda. The points below focus on its multi-agency emphasis.

### *Issues to consider*
### Be healthy
■ How can confidential advice and information regarding health issues best be made available, using a multi-agency approach, to children and young people, recognising the different needs of girls and boys?

■ How can schools use the skills of external agencies to improve the ways that they promote the mental and emotional health of all children and young people, recognising the different needs of girls and boys?

### Stay safe
■ How can schools ensure that individual pupils do not become isolated or lonely because they are different, for example boys perceived to be gay? What community agencies can support this?

■ How can schools improve their responses to bullying, including homophobia, sexual bullying and harassment, in partnership with other agencies?

■ How can children and young people be placed in situations in which they can safely assess risks and develop strategies to deal with them, for example girls using internet chat rooms, or boys attracted by speed? How can the expertise of external partners help with this?

### Enjoy and achieve
■ How can schools best assess the levels of enjoyment of all children and young people in their school experience and make changes which, as far as possible, maximise it? What evidence from external partners can help them with this?

■ How can schools tackle underachievement amongst vulnerable groups of pupils such as black boys, looked after children, white working class boys? What community links can help with this?

■ How can schools and their partners ensure good attendance, especially amongst some vulnerable groups of girls who, statistics show, are at high risk of teenage pregnancy if allowed to truant on a regular basis?

## Make a positive contribution

■ How do schools develop the kinds of skills that will help pupils in later life such as those of independent learning, thinking skills, collaboration and teamwork? How can external partners help?

■ What activities can be built into the school curriculum to develop enterprise, in ways that are attractive to male and female students, and provide opportunities to apply this to real-life situations?

■ How can boys best be introduced to ideas about nurturing and the responsibilities of parenthood?

■ How can schools encourage pupils not to make gender biased choices in options at 14+ and 16+?

## Achieve economic well-being

■ How can all children and young people be informed about financial issues and become equipped to be economically independent in ways which are both relevant to their needs and which challenge stereotypical ways of thinking about these issues? What enterprise links can support this?

■ How can schools ensure that financial education is embedded in the school curriculum?

■ What steps can be taken to improve the quality of careers advice and education, so that girls and young women appreciate the range of opportunities open to them in a modern economic and work environment, and boys are encouraged to consider non-traditional occupations such as childcare?

*With thanks to Gulshan Kayembe*

## References

Department for Education and Skills (DfES) (2003) *Every Child Matters* (cmd 5860). London: The Stationery Office www.everychildmatters.gov.uk

Department of Health (2004) *The Children Act 2004*. London: The Stationery Office

Department for Education and Skills (DfES) (2005) *Higher Standards, Better Schools for Parents and Pupils*. London: The Stationery Office

PK Research Consultancy and National Children's Bureau (n.d.) *Building a Culture of Participation*. Hove: PKRC and London: NCB

# School Climate

*Rosalyn George and John Wadsworth*

■ *Many of the facets of school climate are addressed elsewhere in* Genderwatch. *See for example schedules: Leadership; Design for Learning; Using the School Budget; It's My School: The Power of Pupil Voice*

## Introduction

The elements that make up the climate of the school are complex, ranging from the quality of interactions between teachers and students to the physical structure of the building and the policies that govern the day-to-day business of the school. Ellis defined school climate as 'an aggregate of indicators both subjective and objective that conveys the overall feeling or impression one gets about a school' (1988:1).

The climate will be affected by the perceptions about the school from parents, carers and members of the wider community as well as students and staff working within it. No one factor can, on its own, determine a school climate or its consequential influence on students' learning and their experience of the school process. It is the interaction between a number of contributory factors that create a 'fabric of support' (Freiberg, 1999) that enables a positive environment for learning and teaching to take place.

The school climate will to an extent be determined by the management or leadership style of the head teacher. Judy Marshall (1994) argues powerfully about female values in leadership and highlights the need for them to complement the traditional male perspectives that have prevailed. We illustrate the complex interplay of elements and factors that contribute to the development of a positive school climate as a weave (Figure 1) echoing Freiberg's 'fabric of support'.

In this schedule we focus on two aspects of school climate that are not addressed elsewhere in this volume – school ethos and policies.

## Ethos

The ethos of a school is created through an interaction between the formal processes governing behaviour, attitudes, relationships and the curriculum alongside the informal messages given out via displays, documentation, newsletters, use of resources and public space.

*NB: There is no hierarchy implied in the order in which we have listed the following.*

### Issues to consider

■ Do displays and notices in public areas reflect the diversity of the school community; promote positive images of women, disability and race?

■ Are languages other than English in evidence?

  ☐ Is information about the school available in languages other than English.

■ Does the documentation produced by the school (prospectus, newsletters etc) demonstrate a commitment to anti-discriminatory practice?

■ Are policies on gender, race, disability and bullying displayed prominently for the benefit of visitors and parents?

■ Is there consistency in the way people are treated?

  ☐ Are women/men/girls/boys treated equitably?

  ☐ Are assemblies and PHSE used to promote the shared values of the school community and an anti-discriminatory approach?

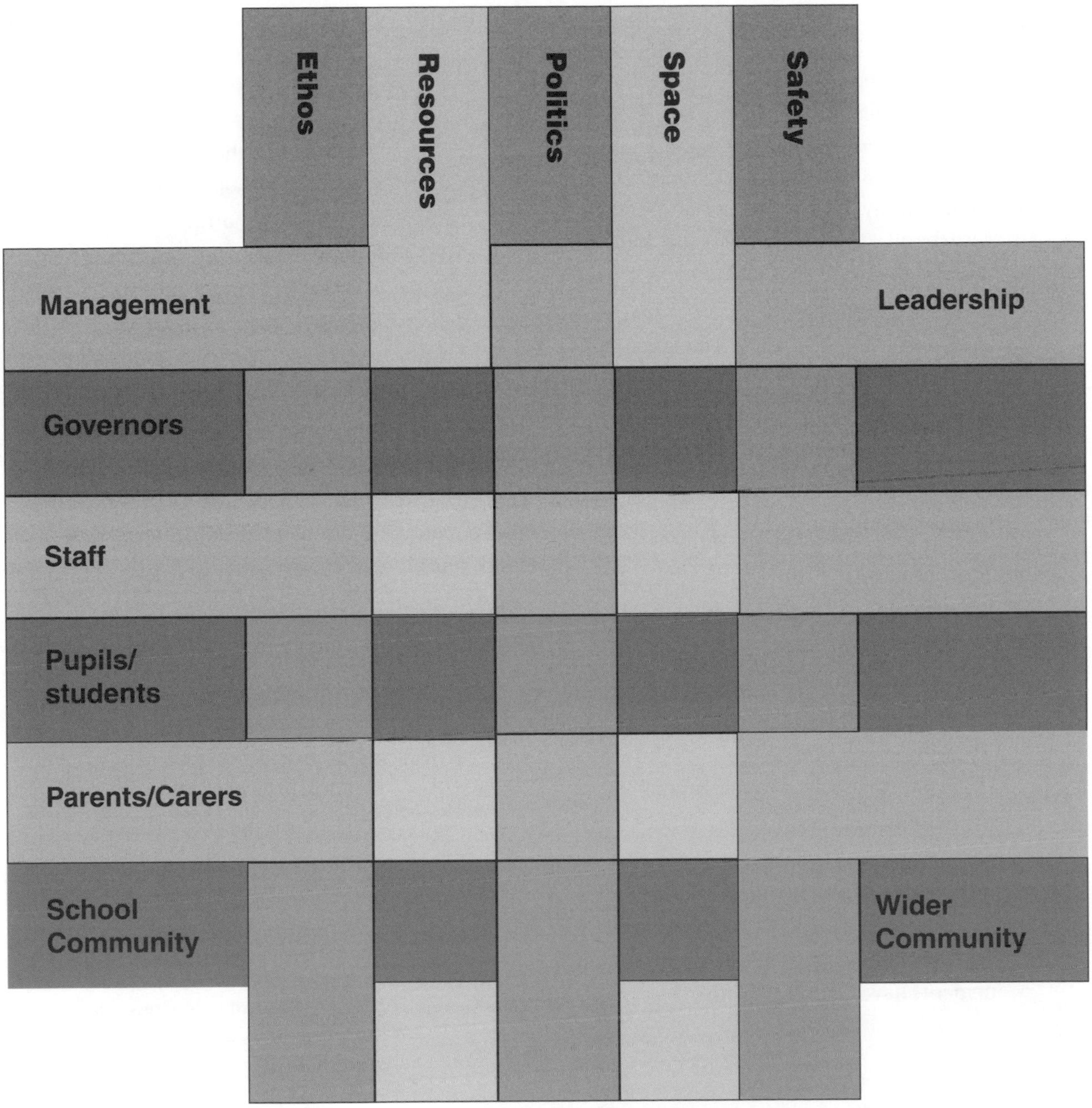

**Figure 1 Weave illustrating elements that contribute to the School Climate**

*This weave illustrates the interrelationships between all the factors that make up the school climate; like the thread in a piece of fabric, each element contributes to the make- up of the whole.*

- Is it clear that the principles of anti-discriminatory practice are non-negotiable?
- Are there facilities for parents/carers and other members of the school community to meet?
- Do staff model good anti-discriminatory practice, in their relationships with each other?
- Are staff respectful of all pupils?
- Is this model of behaviour reflected by the pupils?
- Is there any evidence that stereotypical thinking is challenged?
- Who does the challenging, and is this done in an active or passive way?

- Does the school promote collaborative ways of working between pupils/staff?
- Are there systems in place to induct all new members of the school community into the shared values and ethos of the school?
- What systems are in place to ensure that all new members of the school community are able to play a full and active part in the life of the school?
- Are the different dietary needs of faith groups and other cultures catered for?
- Does the dining hall provide a tranquil, clean and stress-free environment?

## Policies

Policies include those which are statutory, and those which are important to the maintenance of a positive and fair learning environment. It is important that all policies reflect a set of values that are shared and seen to be upheld by all members of the school community. They should be subjected to regular review by all stakeholders to ensure that they continue to meet the changing needs and circumstances of the school.

### *Issues to consider*

- Are there equal opportunities policies in place?
  - ☐ Are they up-to-date?
  - ☐ Are they effective?
- Is there evidence that all members of the school community have had the opportunity to contribute to these policies?
- Is there evidence of a whole-school approach to equal opportunities?
- Is there evidence that issues of equality are dealt with effectively?
- How often are policies reviewed?
  - ☐ Are all parties involved in this process?
- Is there monitoring of equal opportunities policies?
  - ☐ For example, are incidents of sexual harassment recorded and acted on?
  - ☐ How are students and staff made aware that incidents have been dealt with?

- Are there support systems in place for pupils/staff who have been subjected to gender/racist abuse and/or bullying and harassment?
- How are all members of the school community made aware of the equal opportunities policies?
- Are there safe ways of reporting incidents?
- What systems are in place for supporting new members of the school community?
- What systems are in place to ensure that mentors are trained and made aware of and sensitive to issues of equity, diversity?

Where the needs, aspirations and potential of all are valued, nurtured and respected, the school climate is more likely to be one in which issues of gender bias, race equality and disability lie at the heart of all levels and areas of activity.

*A longer version of this schedule is available on http://www.goldsmiths.ac.uk/educational-studies/staff/george.php*

### References

Ellis, T. I. (1988) School Climate, *Research Roundup*, 4 (2)

Freiberg, H. J. (1999) *School Climate: Measuring, Improving and Sustaining Healthy Learning Environments.* London: Falmer

Freiberg, H. J. (1999) *Beyond Behaviourism: Changing the Classroom Management Paradigm*. Needham Heights: Allyn and Bacon

Marshall, J. (1994) Re-visioning organizations by developing female values, in: Boot, R., Lawrence, J. and Morris, J. (ed) (1997) *Managing the Unknown By Creating New Futures*. London and New York: McGraw-Hill

# Leadership

*Kate Myers*

■ *See also schedules: It's my School: The Power of Pupil Voice; Lesbian, Gay, Bisexual and Trans Issues in Schools; Governors; Using the School Budget; Relevant Legislation; Learning and Teaching; Continuing Professional Development; Performance Management*

> Managers are people who do things right, while leaders are people who do the right thing.
> Bennis and Nanus (1985)

> ... leadership has two sides – what a person is (character) and what a person does (competence).
> Stephen Covey (1989)

> Leadership is not something that you learn once and for all. It is an ever-evolving pattern of skills, talents, and ideas that grow and change as you do.
> Sheila Murray Bethelm (1990)

## Leadership at all levels

Leadership can be found at all levels in schools: within the pupil body, the staff body (teaching, paraprofessionals and administrative) and the governing body. It can be seen solely as the province of the head and/or the leadership team or it can be dispersed throughout the school. It can be wielded in a range of ways too – officially, overtly, informally and subtly.

*NB: the term 'staff' is used to refer to all staff employed in the school.*

## Importance of the model of leadership set by leadership team

The model of leadership established by the head and her/his leadership team is of paramount importance. A bullying and hectoring style is likely to be modelled throughout the school and become the way that staff and pupils relate to each other.

There is a range of leadership styles, for example heroic, charismatic, authoritarian, moral, visionary, principle-centred, professional, strategic, transactional, transformational, situational, dispersed, distributed and distributive, shared, invitational, collaborative, instructional, learning centred, teacher centred, and student-centred (all described by MacBeath, 2003). Leaders are likely to mix and match these styles depending on the situation.

Some writers describe these styles as having masculine or feminine attributes. For example, the authoritarian approach is typically seen as masculine whilst the collaborative approach is seen as feminine. It may be true that boys and girls are more likely to develop skills in the areas typically associated with their gender, but it is equally true that both women and men can adopt any of these styles. Bullying and authoritarian female heads exist, as do caring, collaborative male heads. The important issue is that both women and men are free to choose the styles they adopt, regardless of the constraints of their upbringing.

## Issues to consider

■ Given the list of models described above, how would the leadership team describe the predominant style of leadership in the school?

■ How would the staff describe the predominant style of leadership in the school?

■ How do middle managers relate to those they manage and those who line-manage them?

■ How would they describe their own leadership styles and how would those they line manage describe their styles?

- What opportunities are there for staff and pupils to contribute to decision making, and/or make their views known?

- Do these groups consider that the opportunities are effective? Could they be improved?

- Is bullying, sexual or racial harassment tolerated in the school? Are there safe ways that staff and pupils can report bullying, sexual and racial harassment? Is there confidence that these reports will be taken seriously and addressed?

- Is the climate supportive for gay/lesbian and transsexual teachers and pupils, and do they feel comfortable working in the school?

- Are members of the leadership team approachable and willing to discuss these issues? What is the evidence for this?

## Succession planning – particularly of undersubscribed groups

Enduring improvement requires succession planning (Hargreaves and Fink, 2006). This does not mean grooming one person to succeed to the top job, but creating a culture of leadership development throughout the school, for all groups of staff, governors and pupils. There are at least two reasons why schools (and even better, groups of schools working together) should take succession planning seriously. One is the shortage of people applying for promoted posts, particularly at head and deputy headship level. The second is that women and ethnic minority candidates are not represented at this level in proportion to their numbers in the profession.

During the last twenty years there has been an increase in the number of women headteachers, particularly in the secondary sector, where it used to be unusual to find female heads of mixed secondary schools. This is still the case in some parts of the UK, though less so in the urban areas. However, there has also been a decrease in the proportion of men and an increase in the proportion of women in the profession. According to the 2006 figures, 74% of teachers registered with the General Teaching Council (GTC) are female (GTC, 2006). Table 1 below, however, shows that although 64.6% of heads of primary and nursery schools are female, women make up 87.8% of classroom teachers in that phase. Similarly, 67.8% of secondary heads are men, while 43.1% of classroom teachers are male.

A survey of black and minority ethnic teachers (GTC, 2006) implies that ethnic minority staff are not holding posts of responsibility in proportion to their numbers in the profession.

There are some fairly simple strategies that can be adopted to address these issues, and many schools are now putting in place systems to grow their own

**Table 1**

| 2004 figures | % Proportion of male heads | % Proportion of female heads | % Proportion of male DH heads | % Proportion of female DH heads | % classroom teachers M | % classroom teachers F |
|---|---|---|---|---|---|---|
| Special and PRUs | 51.2 | 48.8 | 35.9 | 64.1 | 28.6 | 71.4 |
| Primary and Nursery | 35.4% | 64.6 | 24 | 76 | 12.2 | 87.8 |
| Secondary | 67.8 | 32.2 | 59.5 | 40.5 | 43.1 | 56.9 |

*Source: DfES, 2006*

**Table 2**

| | Majority ethnic % in relation to nos. in profession | Minority ethnic % in relation to nos. in profession |
|---|---|---|
| Heads | 7 | 0.5 |
| Deputy heads | 5 | 1.0 |
| Assistant heads | 4 | 0.5 |

*(N.B. this data is indicative only, as the data was taken from a voluntary sample)*

future leaders. This is not a quick-fix solution: it involves long-term commitment to nurture and encourage future leaders.

These issues also apply to other posts in and related to the school, for example chairs of governing bodies and school bursars.

### Issues to consider

■ Does the leadership team more or less reflect the rest of the school workforce with regard to gender and ethnicity? If not, what long-term strategies are in place to address this issue?

■ What steps could the school take to encourage younger teachers to consider promotion and support them in applying for promoted posts?

■ What career development opportunities are available for the paraprofessionals and administrative staff in the school?

■ How can staff get experience of leadership and demonstrate leadership qualities, for example by chairing working parties, undertaking school-based research, participating in external projects eg local authority, specialist schools and academies trust initiatives?

■ Are members of under-represented groups encouraged to take up these opportunities?

■ Are there opportunities for job shadowing/job placements within the school or between local schools?

■ Is career development seen as an important aspect of performance management?

■ Is continuing professional development (CPD) taken seriously in the school, and is someone with commitment and appropriate knowledge proactive in encouraging and supporting this area of work?

■ Is attention paid to the gender and ethnic make-up of staff other than teachers?

### Is the school family friendly?

Although attitudes are changing, it is still the case that women staff (teaching and support) are more likely to be taking the main responsibility for child rearing and for caring for elderly or ill relations. These responsibilities will affect their life-styles for a proportion of their careers and may make out of hours work difficult or even impossible. This is one explanation why women are likely to apply at an older age than men for deputy and headship posts (MacBeath and Myers, 1999). Schools can make these crucial years easier or more difficult to navigate for their workforce.

Increasingly, men are becoming more involved in child-rearing and family responsibilities. This trend has encouraged some schools to address family friendly policies for all those involved in family life. However, work-life balance is also important for all staff, regardless of their out-of-school ties and responsibilities. The way these issues are addressed can impact on staff morale, retention, recruitment and absenteeism.

### Issues to consider
### For all staff

■ Is there recognition in the school about how work/life balance can impact on staff morale, retention, recruitment and absenteeism?

■ How are the following issues addressed in order to support work/ life balance but also ensuring that there is no negative impact on pupils:

☐ parental leave

☐ paternity leave

☐ scheme of time off for emergencies

☐ job sharing

☐ working at or from home on occasions when pupil contact is not required eg planning time

☐ ability to change from full to part-time hours

☐ access to workplace or other nursery provision

☐ flexi-time

☐ flexible opportunities for CPD?

(adapted from Dex and Smith, 2002)

### For part-time staff, staff on maternity leave and returners to work

■ Do part-time staff feel involved in school life?

■ Are staff on maternity leave helped in keeping up to date with curriculum and other changes?

■ What mechanisms are in place to ensure that the views of part-time staff are sought particularly if meetings take place when they are not at work?

■ Are part-time staff encouraged to participate in CPD? Are they fully involved in performance management and career development schemes?

■ Is there a system to help staff who have had a career break (often women returners) catch up with the changes that have taken place during their absence?

## Recruitment and retention

### Recruitment

The Gender Equality Duty (GED) (2007) puts the onus on organisations to demonstrate fair treatment of women and men in the delivery of policy and services as well as in their employment. As indicated above, men are under-represented in the profession, and women and ethnic minority staff are under-represented in leadership positions. These issues need to be addressed at national as well as local level, but nevertheless there are some strategies that can be adopted at school level. For example, in the 1980s, an Inner London Education Authority (ILEA) survey found that if they were unsuccessful initially, women were more likely to give up applying for promotion than men (Martini *et al*, 1984). Women tend to internalise failure (blaming themselves) whereas men are better at externalising it (rationalising failure). Offering constructive feedback after interviews can help address this issue.

### Issues to consider

■ Are staff encouraged to apply for promotion (internally and externally) and are they supported in this process, for example given help with application forms and interview practice?

■ Is support and advice available when they fail to get jobs for which they apply?

■ Are interview procedures open and fair? Are a range of stakeholders involved in the interviewing procedures? Does the ethnic and gender make-up of panels broadly represent the pupil population?

■ Does the recruitment material demonstrate the school's commitment to equality of opportunity?

■ Are the questions asked of candidates equitable?

■ Do staff who do not want to or are not able to apply for promotion, feel valued?

The EOC suggest that public bodies should ask themselves the following questions

■ Is there a pay gap between men and women doing the same job or jobs of similar value?

■ How could flexible working help staff, and how will it benefit men and women?

■ How do schools recruit staff, and are they likely to get a good gender balance of candidates?

■ Do they have a gender imbalance? If so, how could this be rectified?

■ Does the school have a good return rate of staff from maternity leave? If not, how could this be improved?

Public authorities will also need to look at how their employment policies affect transsexual men and women.

■ Does the equal opportunities policy and harassment policy cover trans people?

■ Do the school's practices and procedures support the dignity and privacy of trans people?

*Adapted from EOC website August 2006*

### Retention and turnover

Staff leave schools for a range of positive (eg promotion) and negative (eg bullying) reasons. Some turnover is healthy and every organisation needs fresh blood to stimulate and invigorate current practice. Too much turnover, on the other hand, can mean lack of continuity for pupils and their families.

### Issues to consider

■ Are staff turnover figures kept and analysed? Is the analysis by gender, ethnicity and age? Are there discernable patterns?

■ Are all leaving staff (teaching and support) encouraged to undergo an exit interview or fill in an exit survey? How is this information analysed and utilised?

■ Are staff encouraged to undergo regular formal appraisal and request informal feedback and/or career development interviews?

■ Do staff feel appreciated? How is this manifested?

■ Are staff offered new challenges when appropriate?

■ How often are staff surveys undertaken? What action is taken following analysis, and how is this publicised amongst staff?

■ Do different groups of staff (for example by gender, ethnicity, seniority) feel affiliated to and involved with the organisation?

■ Does the organisation provide any practical support to encourage staff well-being, for example access to a nursery, dry cleaning collection, car washing provision?

## Curriculum leadership

Equality issues should inform what is taught and how it is taught. Both are dealt with in more detail elsewhere in *Genderwatch: still watching...*

## Issues to consider

■ Where choice is possible, and over a period of time, is the curriculum selected likely to be of interest to both girls and boys?

■ Are bridging strategies (for example taster courses, single-sex groups) used to encourage pupils to participate in areas traditionally not associated with their gender?

■ Do reports include an equality section, for example reports to governors, reports from HODs, team leaders?

■ When classroom observation is being undertaken (peer, performance management or pupil) are equality issues included in the schedule, for example girl/boy participation in the lesson?

■ Are line managers briefed about equality issues and do they in turn brief others?

■ Do all subject areas, particularly those traditionally associated with one gender, offer learning environments that feel safe and attractive for both girls and boys?

## References

Bennis, W. and Nanus, B. (1985) *Leaders: The Strategies for taking Charge.* New York: Harper and Row

Bethelm, S. M. (1990) *Making a Difference: Twelve Qualities That Make You a Leader.* New York: The Berkley Publishing Group

Covey, S. (1989) *The Seven Habits of Highly Effective People.* New York: Simon and Schuster

Dex, S. and Smith, C. (2002) *The Nature and Pattern of Family-friendly Employment in Britain.* Judge Institute of Management, Cambridge University, Joseph Rowntree Foundation by The Policy Press.

Department for Education and Skills (DfES) (2006) *Statistics of Education: School workforce in England (including teachers' pay for England and Wales).* London: DfES www.dfes.gov.uk/rsgateway/DB/VOL/v000633/index.shtml

Equal Opportunities Commission (2006) *What is the Gender Equality Duty?* website www.eoc.org.uk/Default.aspx?page=17686

General Teaching Council (2006) *Annual Digest of Statistics: Teacher Profiles 2005-06.* London: GTC

General Teaching Council (2006) *Survey of Black and Minority Teachers.* London: GTC

Hargreaves, A. and Fink, D. (2006) *Sustainable Leadership.* New York: Jossey Bass Wiley

MacBeath, J. (2003) The Alphabet Soup of Leadership. Inform No. 2 January *Leadership for Learning Network.* Faculty of Education, Cambridge University

MacBeath, J. and Myers, K. (1999) *Effective School Leaders: How to evaluate and improve your leadership potential.* Financial Times: Prentice Hall

Martini, R. *et al* (1984) *Women's Careers in Teaching: Survey of teachers' views.* London: ILEA

### Useful contact

Worklife Support Ltd

2nd Floor, Hamilton House, Mabledon Place, London WC1H 9BE

Tel: 020 7554 5280, Fax: 020 7554 5239

'We are not a sexist Governing body, so we ask all employees the same question. Now, 'What happens if you become pregnant?'

# Governors

## Diana Leonard and Frances Migniuolo

■ *See also schedules: Relevant Legislation; Using the School Budget; Performance Management; Managing Behaviour; Lesbian, Gay, Bisexual and Trans Issues in Schools; Uniform and Dress Codes; Personal, Social and Health Education; Religious Education; Assemblies; The 14- 19 Curriculum*

This schedule focuses on the role of governors in community schools. Governors' roles will increasingly vary according to the type of school.

## Governors' powers

Governors have a strategic role, working with the headteacher and staff, to shape and monitor the way the school is developing and meeting its goals. It is essential that the governing body understands the need to spend time and resources to combat gender stereotyping and discrimination. The 2006 *Equality Act* places responsibilities on school governing bodies, leadership teams and local authorities (LAs) to treat men and women, and boys and girls, equally and fairly in all that they do. The Gender Equality Duty 2007 (GED) requires public bodies, including schools, to assess the impact of their practices on outcomes for men and women, girls and boys, and transgendered people, to develop action plans to promote equality, and to monitor the outcomes. The GED works in a similar, but not identical, way to the duties for race and disability. All governors' responsibilities have a gender dimension and since they carry full responsibility for the school, they are entitled to, and should, check that the school's policies are being implemented, whether equal outcomes are being achieved and if not, why not.

Governors' responsibility for oversight of how a school promotes equality in its provision, its teaching and learning strategies and its ethos is part of Ofsted's remit. Governors' complacency can jeopardise the school's inspection outcome.

The Commission for Equality and Human Rights (CEHR), which replaces the Equal Opportunities Commission, or any individual who believes that a school is failing to meet its general duty under the Equality Act, can ask a court for a judicial review. It is not left to individuals to take their case to court or tribunal, as it was under the Sex Discrimination Act 1975. The former Equal Opportunities Commission and the CEHR, which will run in parallel for a few years, can also take action against schools by issuing a compliance notice which can be enforced in the courts.

## Governors' main responsibilities
### *The appointment of new governors and the chair and vice chair of governors*

This should reflect the gender, ethnic and social class composition of the governing body itself and the way in which governors interact with each other: who speaks and who gets listened to? Who is asked to chair sub-committees?

### *Staffing*
#### *Appointments*

Governors need to ensure that the school has equitable appointment, selection and promotion procedures for all staff and that they review how these are working. Staff appointments are legally their responsibility. The appointment of headteacher and deputy heads cannot be delegated. Governors can take advice from the local authority governor support section or national bodies such as *Governorline* on a person specification and job description. It is important to test candidates on their understanding of the barriers to equal opportunities in schools and to probe them, for examples of how they have tackled these issues and how they would progress them in the post. The governing body should have the following in place for all appointments:

- training in fair procedures for all involved in interview and selection

- clear and accurate job descriptions and person specifications. The person specification should only include those skills, abilities, experience and qualifications relevant to the job and are required for the post

- separation of information about marital status, age or ethnicity (for monitoring purposes) from the part of the application form used for short-listing

- a panel of at least three people for short-listing and interviewing. The panel should agree on the relevant criteria, based on needs of the post and person specification

- an interview where candidates are put at ease and asked broadly similar questions. Marital status and intentions, number of children and childcare arrangements should not be raised.

Governors also lead hearing appeals against dismissals, and appeals under locally agreed disciplinary and grievance procedures. These require equitable procedures, especially as women continue to be under-represented in leadership posts in schools.

Equal opportunities for staff are as important as for pupils. If pupils see women staff only in lower status roles or areas of the curriculum that are traditionally regarded as 'female' this will impact on girls as well as boys. Governors need a breakdown of teaching and support staff by gender in relation to promoted and senior posts in their school. They also need to know the numbers of part-time staff and their opportunities for CPD and PPA (planning, preparation and assessment) time. They could suggest that more posts, especially senior posts, should be advertised on a job-share basis. Serious gender imbalances need attention.

According to the 2004 DfES Statistics of Education School Workforce in England:

- 41% of men working in nursery and primary schools are in senior management posts (heads, deputy heads and assistant heads) compared with 17% of women

- 13% of men working in secondary schools are in senior management positions compared to 6 % of women.

DfES Statistics for England and Wales (2006) indicate that full-time women classroom teachers in maintained schools earned 7% less than their male counterparts. Only one percent of women teachers compared to 4.1% of male teachers reach the leadership scale in their first four years of teaching.

A General Teaching Council (GTC) (2006) survey of 10,000 teachers found that 26% of women teachers said that factors such as childcare or caring for a relative had limited their opportunities for career progression, as against only seven percent of men.

Staff who want to work part-time have far fewer opportunities for promotion than full-timers. Part-time teachers, like full-time staff, should be entitled to time on a *pro rata* basis for PPA.

It is important for governors on the personnel sub-committee to monitor and press for action to promote more family-friendly working, and to ensure that managers in the school encourage part-time and full-time women staff, including support staff, to develop their careers. Governors should not accept the simplistic explanation that women do not apply for senior posts.

### Pay and conditions of service

Governors must have a clear pay policy which they have discussed with staff. While teachers' pay structure is fixed by law, there is scope for annual progression for classroom teachers and some other discretions. This can lead to significant differences in the pay of teachers, with women teachers overall earning less than men. There are also national agreements about teachers' and support staffs' duties and working time, but governors can make variations where the conditions of service are not set by law.

> A case taken by the National Union of Teachers involved an Advanced Skills Teacher who was told that her pay would be reduced because she was pregnant and the school could not afford to pay her higher salary while she was on maternity leave. (*NUT Teacher Magazine* July/August 2006)

*Performance management policy*

Governing bodies of maintained schools are responsible for a performance management policy and for conducting the performance management review of the headteacher. The governing body has a right to ask for progress reports and to help set the training and development plans for teachers. Some schools also run similar performance management schemes for support staff.

It is essential to monitor that the performance management policy is working fairly. For more detail, see the schedule on performance management.

*The position of staff in the event of school re-organisation or mergers*

Agreed processes must give women staff equal opportunities. If there is already a breakdown of posts by gender and ethnic group, showing grade and responsibilities, and a sound equalities policy on appointments and promotions, it is much easier to focus attention on the need for equality of opportunity in a re-organisation: to monitor who is being made redundant, who is being ring-fenced and who assimilated to the senior posts.

**Curriculum policy and monitoring of outcomes**

*The governing body shares responsibility with the headteacher and the local authority for making sure that the national curriculum is taught and assessments carried out.*

Governors can ask to see teaching materials to ensure that these do not reinforce gender stereotypes. They should ensure education is provided in a balanced way and that indoctrination is eliminated. They can also ask for reports to see how different departments are tackling the issue of equal opportunities in classroom teaching, and whether they have the resources and support to promote such teaching.

*Sex Education*

In primary schools, the governors decide whether or not sex education is taught; at secondary level, where sex education is part of the national curriculum, governors can influence how the topic is approached, and how issues such as homosexuality, sex outside the context of a close and loving relationship, and AIDS information are dealt with. They also decide whether these topics are to be covered in areas other than biology or PSHE.

*Subject and diploma choice and careers advice*

Governors should monitor pupils' subject choices, especially the sex stereotyped ones – physical sciences, IT, languages, dance and various crafts – and the vocational paths, particularly the ones which lead to better training, education or employment opportunities. The governing body can ask what the school might do to get more girls doing physics or team sports, and more boys doing dance or subjects with social care aspects.

Widening pupils' horizons and avoiding gender stereotyped choices is equally important in single-sex schools, where there may be pressure to offer subject choices that follow traditional gender preferences. Governors need to seek to influence parents and carers to see the benefits, especially the economic benefits, of girls taking subjects and training previously regarded as more suited to boys/young men and vice versa. They can encourage the school to make this a feature of its prospectus, to put on events for parents and carers which highlight the broader options open, and to use assemblies to present positive non-traditional role models to pupils.

**Whole school equality policies**

*Governors must ensure the school has equality action plans and policies*

These must promote equality and counter discrimination on grounds of race, gender, disability, religion or belief, and sexual orientation. The policies should cover behaviour by and towards staff, pupils, governors, parents/carers and other visitors, including other users of school buildings, and the services provided on school premises. They should cover direct and indirect discrimination. It is also the governors' duty to make sure all staff understand what indirect discrimination is, and why it is important.

In the GTC report quoted earlier, 50% of teachers in the sample stated that they had received no training in aspects of equality.

It is important to ensure that training is a priority and that good trainers are provided. The LA (or in the case of church schools, the diocesan boards) should be able to advise.

*Establishing the school's policy on admissions*

The admissions code (2006) aims to promote greater fairness in schools' admissions criteria. It is important to note the overt and hidden messages in marketing material and to monitor the equity effects of the admissions processes.

### Agreeing a behaviour policy

This covers, amongst other things, how to handle bullying and harassment by staff or pupils and deciding the critieria for temporary or permanent exclusions. A governors' panel hears appeals about a headteacher's decision and decides whether to uphold it. Governors should make sure the processes are as effective for sexual and homophobic harassment /bullying as for any other form of harassment, for example racism.

### Unauthorised absences and exclusions

Governors should review a range of data to see if any groups are disproportionately represented among those who are absent without just cause, and those who receive punishments, suspensions and permanent exclusions.

### The School Improvement Plan (SIP) and the school self-evaluation process

The school's annual school improvement plan must be approved by the governing body. Governors should use their power to ensure it includes actions to promote equalities and allocates resources for this. Self-evaluation has become the central plank of the school inspection system, and governors are responsible for ensuring the process is carried out effectively. Indeed, they should be involved as partners in completing the self-evaluation form.

## Some other governor responsibilitles

### Managing the delegated budget

All aspects of the budget have an equal opportunities dimension. Who is getting what proportion of the resources? The schedule on using the budget in this volume offers advice on this.

### Deciding on the length of the school day and holidays, and on school uniform

School uniform is not trivial! This issue, and specifically girls' rights to wear trousers to school, is the education topic most often taken to the Equal Opportunities Commission for advice and adjudication.

## Getting things done

It is not always easy to raise gender issues, even when backed up by the GED. Many schools and teachers think that they dealt with gender long ago. It can be hard for an individual governor to raise

such issues without people thinking 'there s/he goes again'.

The aim is to initiate discussion – perhaps using a *Genderwatch: still watching* schedule – with a view to getting a working group established; or to get the relevant member of staff to report on an item. The discussion could be on a specific topic, such girls' low take-up of sport. Or it could be a more general one about what the school is doing to conform to equalities legislation. Alternatively, governors can ask for reports on any aspect of the school from the head. Or they can ask for gender issues to be raised in a letter to parents, or in the school profile that governors have to provide annually, asking parents to let governors know of any concerns. Then issues are seen to come from parents rather than the individual governor.

However, if the head or the chair of governors (or worse the head and the chair) prove hostile to gender issues, there are ways to challenge this. Governors should raise the legal aspects. The requirement to have an action plan is new. Ofsted can be mentioned, and the positive advantages for the school of leading with good practice stressed.

## Governor training

Governors need to be up to date on developments so they can identify ways to promote equal opportunities in their school. They can ask to be shown how to read financial spread-sheets and tables of statistics, so as to understand the strengths and shortcomings of both. Then they will not leave others free to interpret them, and they themselves can pick out gender differences which might otherwise get either overlooked or overplayed.

Funding for governors' training is provided to the school via the standards fund and it is included in the school's delegated budget. Governors should ensure this funding is used for their training, in particular to ensure they have access to good equalities training

### Issues to consider

#### How governors can support the school

There is much for governors to do in order to promote gender equality in schools, but here are some key areas for action.

■ take action to promote a positive ethos for gender equality among the whole school community

- use involvement in headteacher and leadership team appointments to ensure that the selection procedures properly test candidates' understanding of and commitment to equality issues

- become aware of any significant differences in performance between girls and boys, between different ethnic groups, and in patterns of take-up of subjects and courses

- support intervention programmes that address these issues

- monitor the breakdown of posts by gender and grade. Look for ways to ensure women and men are represented in promoted posts and leadership roles and that performance management is done fairly

- get a good training programme in place for all staff and governors – including new staff/governors.

## How schools can support governors

Schools can support governors in executing their equality responsibilities by enabling many of the suggestions made above. The headteacher can influence the chair in their meetings. In particular, to help create a climate in the governing body of active engagement in increasing equality, they can make sure that:

*Governors are fully aware of their duties*

- by summarising their equality powers and responsibilities and referring to them in the headteacher's report and under other agenda items

- by asking each committee to report on equality issues, and ensuring that the staff representative on the committee is well informed

- by asking them to share with staff their ideas, and seek feedback on how their actions to promote equality are perceived.

*Governors are included in school training or have their own*

*Governors have adequate information and feel confident in interpreting it*

- by including gender and ethnicity breakdowns in all data about pupils

- by presenting mini case-studies to illustrate gender and ethnicity and social class effects

- by passing on useful documents that come into the school, or web links.

*Governors have specific equality responsibilities*

- by asking for an equality champion to monitor the issue across all the governors' business

- by including governors on relevant school change teams

- by identifying the contribution they can make as role models and inviting them to meet groups of pupils and parents/carers

- by asking them to be part of the school's processes for dealing with persistent racist/sexist behaviour.

## Further reading

Wragg, E.C. and Partington, J.A. (3rd edition 1995) *The School Governors' Handbook*, London and New York: Routledge.

*DfES A Guide to the Law for School Governors*, regularly updated

*The Times Educational Supplement*

*Gender and Education*

Equal Opportunities Commission, www.eoc.org.uk – see guidance for schools on the GED

Governorline, www.governorline.co.uk – free advice service contactable by phone, text or email.

Advisory Centre for Education, www.ace-ed.org.uk – independent charity offering free advice to parents.

National Governors' Association, www.nga.org.uk

# Using the school budget

*Hazel Taylor*

■ *See also schedules: Performance Management; Governors*

## Equity in budgeting

A school's budget enables action for equity in all areas of school life, and decisions about its use are not neutral. Some equity considerations require action on relatively straightforward gross differences in provision between genders, for example on the quality of girls' and boys' toilet facilities. In other cases, the complex interaction of gender, ethnicity, disadvantage and special need may lead to differences in take-up of opportunities, or in outcomes, for a particular group of pupils, such as girls from a community that has recently arrived in the UK, or indigenous white boys in areas of economic disadvantage and low aspiration. Difficult choices that have to be made on funding grounds need to be informed by an understanding of how gender equity considerations have been taken into account in costings.

At times, provision which addresses a gender imbalance may cost more than provision which does not. Gender equity is not necessarily achieved by spending equal amounts of money on both genders. Achieving comparable outcomes may well cost different sums – the challenges lie in balancing needs and costs in an equitable way.

Equally, decisions may have to be made about priorities within a range of proposals that address imbalances. These need to be made in the light of the school's overall priorities that reflect its values as well as its immediate response to the messages of its self-evaluation. Governors have responsibility for final agreement of the overall budget and need to be able to ask questions about gender equity. Middle leaders with spending powers are responsible for choices of courses, resources, and activities and need to be able to justify them in relation to the needs they have identified. Bursars and other administrative staff need to be aware of how these issues affect the areas they have responsibility for, including building and grounds developments.

## School phase and type issues

Primary, secondary and special schools face differing issues around gender and equity, but the challenge is the same: how to use limited resources to have the greatest impact on identified need, with the least downside. Mixed schools face choices about imbalances between genders. Single-sex schools face choices about curriculum provision of a similar quality to that in mixed schools. They may need to resource upgrades to ensure equity in opportunities in areas traditionally well resourced for the other sex. This can often be the case in aspects of technology and ICT for girls, and health and social care, and aspects of art and design for boys. Budgets always influence decisions about continuing less popular courses, but particular care is needed where there is also a gender pattern with regard to pupil take-up, for example for boys with modern foreign languages.

The three-year budget and the relaxation of restrictions on use of the standards fund bring opportunities and responsibilities. Less bidding saves time, more forward planning is possible, money can be allocated to areas of need which are exactly matched to the school's needs, but more than ever it is important that decisions are related back to values about equity for all groups in the school.

Schools with high pupil mobility are still subject to annual uncertainties about their budgets. *Every*

*Child Matters* has made inclusion of each individual with appropriate provision a necessity. There are still some funding streams that are ring-fenced, such as Excellence in Cities, and some where decisions on priorities for funding are made by local networks, such as Children's Area Partnerships. These too need to have regard for gender equity in their allocations. New allocations of money attached to a particular initiative can require rapid expenditure, and it is particularly important to spend on things which address the causes of any inequities, rather than trying to alleviate symptoms.

Some school specialisms attract additional funding streams, and these can unwittingly lead to imbalances in opportunities (eg sports funding for activities that attract predominately one gender). Private finance initiative (PFI) contracts can reduce flexibility in access to facilities after hours, and this too can have unwitting effects unless monitored. Academies may need to avoid biases inherent in the historic gender positions in the industry or business of the sponsors. Under-performing schools may need to avoid using sex-stereotyped courses as a quick way of improving results while in the longer term disadvantaging the pupils who take them, by discouraging a balanced range of subjects.

Because the budget is essentially an enabling tool, not a provision in itself, decisions about its use need to be informed by all the schedules relevant to the school's phase and type. Suggestions follow for the questions to consider when looking at overall budget management, curriculum costings, costs of the workforce and environment, and evaluating and reviewing value for money from an equity perspective.

### *Issues to consider*
### Budget allocation and management

Linking of pupil outcomes with quality of teaching and learning within the performance management framework has become increasingly transparent, based partly on detailed data on individual and group achievement. The meeting of targets for improvement can be dependent on funding for training, equipment, or new courses. It is important that the budget allocation is equally transparent. Funding must be seen to be used in a gender-fair way.

■ Do all members of staff broadly understand the funding streams coming into the school, and how they are allocated?

■ Are staff helped to understand the complex interplay of gender, ethnicity, disadvantage and level of attainment in differences in the experience and outcomes for specific groups of pupils, and that all factors need to be considered rather than making a decision on the basis of one factor alone?

■ Are staff helped to understand how any school formulae for allocating funds are constructed, and how they are weighted to meet the varying costs of different provision (for example, weightings for practical subjects which take account of smaller group size and the costs of equipment, technicians and consumables)?

■ Are the school's values on inclusion and gender equity clear, and used explicitly to inform decisions on funding (for example, are there guidelines for teams of staff – subject, cross-curricular, inclusion – on what to consider when balancing costs against need)?

■ Is there an explicit process of defining priorities, planning and resourcing, which guides teams in their budget use (for example a school timeline and common format, and easy sharing of information)?

■ How are decisions balanced over time, when one group may receive funding to address a need, while others wait (for example, for how many years may lower attaining boys' catch-up in literacy be funded at the expense of girls' catch-up in science)?

■ Is spending on outreach work from specialist schools scrutinised from a gender equity perspective?

### Curriculum provision

With the return to greater flexibility in the curriculum, especially in key stage 4, and with the need to provide for inclusion, how are curriculum choices and costings evaluated for gender equity? Traditional patterns of funding subjects by pupil numbers and resource requirements may not be flexible enough to meet needs associated with differential performance of particular groups of pupils across subjects.

■ When data analysis reveals differential achievement by gender, within and across classes and subjects, how are interventions costed and costs balanced across groups (eg under-achieving higher ability girls in science at key stage 3, and under-achieving middle ability boys in English in year 10)?

■ Are there differences in costs of extended curriculum activities that are largely gender differentiated (e.g. dance clubs and sports coaching)? Does it matter?

■ How are gender issues taken into account in deciding whether to fund set -up costs for new vocational courses requiring specialist facilities (eg beauty therapy or building skills)? Are these decisions taken in the context of future economic benefits for pupils, as well as motivational appeal, pay-offs in results, and potential removal of demanding pupils from the school site?

## Workforce reform

■ How does the school demonstrate that it is an equal opportunity employer through its staffing structure and the way it is implementing workforce reform? Are governors aware of the gender and ethnic profile of the staff? Are there clear, fundable, career paths in the structures for staff in non-teaching positions (for example, for learning mentors and teaching assistants)?

■ Are new non-teaching positions replacing teacher management posts (for example, pupil support posts to carry out former head of year welfare responsibilities) appropriately paid, and advertised to attract both men and women?

■ Is training for career development included in budgets for teaching and non-teaching staff?

■ Are responsibilities for training built into job descriptions for leaders at all levels, and the costs of that recognised?

■ How is recruitment managed to employ a diverse workforce, and how are recruitment costs evaluated in relation to turnover, and to succession planning?

■ Is there balanced recognition that employing more expensive returners or older entrants to posts may bring greater benefits to the school, and avoid discrimination by cost (for example, taking on women returners after child-rearing breaks, career changers of both sexes, and ethnic minority teachers new to the UK as mature entrants)?

## The learning environment

In deciding priorities for the use of the building maintenance and the capital budgets, do governors and the headteacher take into account information about the sorts of environments which most support the learning of different groups of pupils, and provide for a balanced variety of accommodation and facilities? Where the school does not have control of buildings maintenance, for example in PFI funded accommodation, there may be few ways of influencing some spending decisions, or of scrutinising value for money. How do relevant staff seek to influence and inform about gender equity needs in these circumstances?

■ Do school staff liaising with contract site managers actively inform them about equity issues in site provision and management?

■ Are planned improvements to leisure spaces costed – for quiet areas as well as ball game markings?

■ Are both boys' and girls' toilets and changing rooms refurbished and maintained to similar standards?

■ Are the needs of both genders met in provision of prayer rooms?

■ Are the requirements of disability legislation constantly reviewed?

## Monitoring and evaluating the use of the budget

The budget will hopefully have been agreed by governors to meet the needs of all in the school in the fairest possible way, given all the constraints and difficult prioritising decisions that need to be made. The regular monitoring of the budget can reveal departures from planned expenditure caused by many factors. The evaluation of the budget against the intended outcomes will enable discussions about how effective the agreed balance of expenditure was in achieving them. It is important that gender considerations are included in these discussions, and successes and lessons learned noted for future years.

■ Are governors trained in all equity issues and their interplay and how they can affect budgeting?

■ When the budget is monitored, do governors question underspends and overspends from an equity perspective (for example, does an overspend in special needs relate to a particular group of pupils and, if so, why)?

■ Do teams within the school with budgets include an equity-related analysis when evaluating their budget use (for example, how do the costs of after-school support for particular groups relate to any improvement in their performance)?

*With thanks to Janet Cullen*

# Design for Learning

*Ros Asher*

■ *See also schedules: Breaktimes, Lunchtimes and Playgrounds*

> School buildings should inspire learning. They should nurture every pupil and member of staff. They should be a source of pride and practical resource for the community (*Building Schools for the Future*, 2004)

## New opportunities

*What do we know about how buildings, spaces and design affect girls' and boys' learning?*

Through the Building Schools for the Future (BSF) programme every maintained secondary mainstream, special school and PRU, and 50% of all primary schools in England, should be either rebuilt or significantly refurbished by around 2016. It is critical to consider how buildings and spaces can be flexible and adaptable to different ways of engaging girls and boys in learning.

Girls and boys need school buildings that enable them to feel valued, safe and secure. They need spaces that can support learning that is exciting, relevant and motivating, with inspiring design. They need an environment that is welcoming, inclusive and promotes equality as well as an environment that is healthy and models sustainability.

The rapid development of new technologies enables transformation of educational practice. Learning need no longer be confined within limited spaces, but will be extended through digital technology.

The varied needs and aspirations of different genders and cultural groups need to be reflected in the school's policies, strategy for change, and review of impact associated with any building or refurbishment programme. Staff and pupils must be fully involved from the preliminary design stage to implementation and evaluation.

Focusing on gender and Design and Build projects, the following sections set out:

■ some key outcomes for improving learning

■ considerations for school design and gender

■ processes to support a building or refurbishment project

■ examples of questions and practical activities for staff and pupils.

## Improved outcomes for learners

The design proposals should be set within a clear vision of how the environment will reflect the identity, ethos and culture of the school, and how the refurbishment or building programme aims to inspire the school community and enhance learning for girls and for boys. Design of school buildings and grounds should take account of their different needs and aspirations. Whether a small or large build or refurbishment, the project needs to be integral to school improvement planning, with options that have been assessed and analysed against educational objectives.

Desired outcomes for the building project will focus on:

■ **education performance**: improving opportunities to raise achievement for girls and boys through an appropriate, adaptable, stimulating and high quality learning environment and curriculum

■ **pupil satisfaction**: having a positive effect on girls' and on boys' self-esteem, confidence, behaviour and willingness and capacity to learn

■ **community involvement:** having a positive impact on social cohesion and increasing access and participation through extended school activities and services

■ **design for learning:** improving the organisation and management of learning and extended school use, through flexible and adaptable layout and location of resources, taking account of future requirements for expansion and development of ICT; access and inclusion requirements that enable curriculum and informal areas to be fully accessible to pupils with SEN or disabilities; safety and security considerations; sustainability and environmental design and performance.

## School design and gender

The implications for school design regarding the differing needs of boys and girls are complex. Gender needs to be considered together with learning, special and additional education needs; traditions and aspirations regarding culture, faith, race, ethnicity, values and beliefs; and ways of addressing barriers for vulnerable groups or due to deprivation. Although there is much literature about gender in education and an increasing amount about buildings, spaces and design for learning, with the exception of ICT there is little research that brings these two aspects together. Powerful developments where young people have been engaged in contributing views and developing designs for schools include those organised by the Design Council, Schoolworks, the Sorrell Foundation and the *Guardian* newspaper competition for pupils to define 'The School I'd Like'. However, outcomes have not been analysed according to gender.

## Preparing and developing design projects with a focus on gender

Fundamental considerations arise regarding boys' and girls' needs and expectations of their school environment and the contribution this makes to achieving improved learning outcomes.

The DfES's Building Bulletins for primary, secondary and special schools provide a framework and process for schools to use when developing a strategic plan to support design quality and appropriate specifications for major new building projects or minor refurbishments. This includes key design criteria and issues to be addressed to ensure that the design reflects the school's organisation and preferences, now and in the future. Exemplar designs can be found on www.teachernet.gov.uk/exemplars.

Processes in the DfES Bulletins for finding the right design solutions can be modified and applied, with a focus on gender. For instance:

**Defining objectives** – *compare future school needs with the capacity of the current premises to support them*

■ Define needs and impact by gender according to: the current and projected pupil profile of needs, expectations and education performance; and the 2007 act regarding gender discrimination to improve access, inclusion, participation and achievement

**Identifying strategy** – *ways to overcome issues through design solutions*

■ Identify ways of removing barriers to raise the expectations of groups of girls and/or boys, eg by: faith, culture, race (eg quality and provision of separate prayer or social facilities), SEN, disability; mobility and turbulence, (eg asylum seekers)

**Developing and trialling options** – *a feasibility study from design/building professionals identifying various ways of meeting objectives*

■ Consider a range of layouts for learning spaces, social and leisure activities, eg

☐ zoning according to areas or stage of learning;

☐ multi-functional spaces;

☐ design of fabric and colour;

☐ environment and ambience, including heating, lighting, acoustics and air quality;

☐ messages and modelling, including rooms for specific cultural functions and displays;

☐ how curriculum options, pastoral and registration spaces are catered for through space and design, and how this links to pedagogy and timetabling;

☐ design and use of high specification ICT and blended learning;

☐ the impact of space and seating areas and of time for moving around the building on behaviour and learning;

☐ facilities for girls and boys with complex special educational and additional educational needs.

**Table 1: Strategic processes to inform design and build projects, focusing on gender**

| Strategic Processes | Implications for Gender |
|---|---|
| Leadership and management | How is gender considered in strategic planning, auditing, developing, review and evaluation of school design and build projects? |
| Vision and strategy | How are design and build projects incorporated within the school's vision and strategy for increasing the achievement and inclusion of boys and girls?<br><br>How is this translated into a clear change management and CPD programme?<br><br>Does risk assessment include specific options for girls and boys? |
| Involvement of users | How are female and male staff, pupils, parents/carers and community users involved in contributing to all stages of design and build projects?<br><br>Are the pupils involved representative of girls and boys across the school's community? |
| Infrastructure | How do design and build projects enable an innovative and appropriate infrastructure for current and future learning environments, including ICT developments?<br><br>How is this aligned to CPD programmes? |

**Table 2: Transforming learning through design and build projects, focusing on gender**

| Drivers | Implications for Gender |
|---|---|
| Improving learning and achievement | How can school buildings and spaces for learning:<br>– have a positive impact on girls' and boys' self-esteem and willingness to learn?<br>– accommodate a range of styles that meet the needs of different groups of girls and boys, with spaces that provide a range of learning opportunities and recreational activities?<br>– accommodate particular needs due to a major gender imbalance?<br>– enhance organisation and design of curriculum, specialist and learning resource areas?<br>– provide positive modelling and messages to girls and boys?<br>– respond to girls' and boys' views rather than others' assumptions of their needs regarding space, design and infrastructure, (eg type and use of facilities and spaces for learning, resources storage, dining, play, recreation and social interaction)?<br>– support girls' and boys' willingness to attend school and support positive behaviour? |
| Improving inclusion and social cohesion | How is the school environment and ethos supported by the design and layout of the building and spaces, so that it is welcoming and values girls and boys across all community groups?<br>How can the design and spaces have a positive impact on girls and boys from vulnerable groups, or those who may be disaffected with school?<br>How can spaces for learning, faith activities, recreation, social interaction and dining facilities, encourage social cohesion for and between girls and boys, taking account of culture, faith (including religious requirements and ablutions), race, disabilities and level of maturity?<br>How can the area or site be designed so that girls and boys feel safe and secure, in and around the building? |
| Improving health and safety | How can school organisation and its impact on design and layout cater for different stages of pupils' physical and emotional development (eg grounds, equipment, site access, security, health and safety, energy efficiency, environmental performance, colour schemes and furniture)?<br>How can the design and the environment promote and support healthy lifestyles, including use of ICT, the quality of air, light and acoustics, access to drinking water, ergonomically designed furniture, dining areas that promote healthy eating, exercise areas and open spaces, and the impact of materials, colours and display on girls and on boys?<br>How can the toilets, personal care and specialist hygiene facilities give girls and boys respect and dignity, and enable adequate supervision? |
| Extending community provision | To what extent do buildings, spaces, grounds, design and facilities enable extended school activities and services that value and meet the needs and aspirations of girls, boys, women and men from the school and the wider communities?<br>How can the design of the site be welcoming for multi-generational use by girls, boys, women and men from the local community, in ways that reflect and value culture, beliefs and needs? |

**Information gathering** – *options set out against key objectives, including costs and design quality*

- secure the views and engagement of users, at various stages of the process (pupils, staff, governors, parents/carers, visitors and the wider community);

- draw stimuli from visits to other buildings (not only schools) and use of publications and international research

## Shaping and reviewing design projects with a focus on gender

### *Issues to consider*

The following framework could be used or adapted as a tool to review and identify examples and evidence that inform building and design projects, focusing on gender.

- **Table 1** focuses on strategic processes

- **Table 2** focuses on key drivers for transforming learning

- **Table 3** provides activities to engage girls and boys in the process

---

**Table 3: Examples of discussion areas and activities to engage girls and boys**

Most of the activities are not gender specific, but they can be recorded and analysed according to boys (B), girls (G), and year group (Yr)

**Introduction to the activities for pupils**

Think about the design of the school buildings and grounds:

- inside and outside spaces

- how different parts of the building, grounds, classrooms and furniture are laid out

- the use of inside and outside areas, including the canteen, hall, classrooms, library etc

- the effect of the design, materials and colours

- how the building makes you feel

| Activities and Areas for Discussion | Responses |
|---|---|
| 1. Compare this school building/ grounds to another used for learning, (eg leisure centre, former nursery or school, college, library, museum, other school building (split site), your room at home, cyber café, etc) Which do you prefer and why? | |
| 2. How welcoming do you find the school entrance and why? | |
| 3. Which part(s) of the building(s) do you like spending most time in? Why? Are there areas you feel comfortable in? Where are they? What is it about them that makes you feel this way? | |
| 4. Which part(s) of building(s) do you not like spending time in? Why? What changes would you make to improve it/ them? | |
| 5. Think about somewhere in school where you think you learn most. Describe this space and say what it is about it and the way the equipment/ furniture is set out that helps you learn effectively. | |
| 6. Think about somewhere in the school where you find it difficult to take part in learning. Describe the space and say what it is about the design or layout that gets in the way of your learning. | |
| 7. Think about the change of lessons at break, lunchtime and end of the day. Does the way the school is laid out make it easy to travel around at these times? Is there anything we could do to make it better? | |

**Table 3: Examples of discussion areas and activities to engage girls and boys (continued)**

| Activities and Areas for Discussion | Responses |
|---|---|
| 8. Which area(s) do you like using at breaks and lunchtime? Why?<br><br>How could personal and social areas inside and outside the building meet your needs better? | |
| 9. How safe and secure do you feel in and around the building?<br><br>What kind of design changes would help improve this? | |
| 10. Compare 2 designs: (choose examples from the web, eg www.teachernet.gov,uk/exemplars)<br><br>a) Which would you choose to learn in and why? (eg space, layout, colour)<br><br>b) Which would you choose for a leisure space or a personal or social activities and why? (eg materials or landscaping) | |
| 11. Design your ideal school space to inspire and help you to learn better.<br><br>Set out your specification:<br><br>– the space and what it is used for, (eg lesson, research, whole school assembly/performance, tutor activity) | |
| 12. Design your ideal school space to use at breaks, lunchtime and after school.<br><br>Set out your specification and say what the space is used for | |
| 13. What are your requirements for a school building that would make you feel safe, secure and healthy? | |
| 14. How should the school buildings, spaces and equipment be designed to encourage girls and boys to take part, achieve and enjoy all areas of the curriculum, learning and leisure activities?<br><br>If you could change anything, what would it be – why – how? | |

## Food for thought

Children's voices often produce the most radical and practical views of schools for the future. Here are some of their thoughts to end this schedule:

The basic aspects of the buildings we are taught in do not promote learning, but instead, enhance feelings of negativity. I hate waking up every weekday knowing that this day, one that is so valuable to me, will be spent in a giant magnolia prison. I want colours. I want beauty in my surroundings, but most of all I want to be filled with inspiration by a place that I can call my home from home.

*Angela, aged 15* (*Burke and Grosvenor, 2003*)

A school in a giant submarine with waterproof maps of the underwater world. Private helicopters to fly children to France for their French lessons. Voice-activated pencils. Rocket launch pads to take pupils on trips to distant planets to study the solar system. Canteen robots instead of dinner ladies. Clean toilets, swimming pools, a jug of water in every classroom, enough computers and books to go round, fast food school dinners, comfortable uniforms, flexible timetables, chill-out rooms and quieter school bells.

*Dea Birkett*: The Guardian *June 5, 2001*

## References and further resources

Bhavani, R. (2006) Moving on Up? Ethnic Minority Women and Work. Ahead of the Game: the changing aspirations of young ethnic minority women. In Equal Opportunities Commission *Perform Through Inclusion*. www.eoc.org.uk/research

Basic Skills Agency (2007) The Communication Friendly Spaces Toolkit: Improving speaking and listening skills in the early years foundation stage. Code: A2120 www.basic-skills.co.uk

Burke, C. and Grosvenor, I. (2003) *The School I'd Like. Children and young people's reflections on education.* London: Routledge

Commission for Architecture and the Built Environment (CABE) (2004) *Being Involved In School Design: a guide for community, local authorities, funders and design and construction teams.* www.cabe.org.uk

Department for Education and Skills (DfES) (1997 revised 2007) Building Bulletin 77: *Designing for Special Educational Needs and Disabilities in Schools*

Department for Education and Skills (DfES) (1999) Building Bulleting 91: *Access for Disabled Pupils to School Buildings* (mainly superseded by the Building Regulations)

Department for Education and Skills (DfES) (2000) *Classrooms for the Future: 30 Small Scale Projects and Examples from the 'Transforming Schools' Remodelling Project with 12 Local Authorities.* www.teachernet.gov.uk

Department for Education and Skills (DfES) (2001) Building Bulletin 94: *Inclusive School Designs Outlining Inclusion*

Department for Education and Skills (DfES) (2004) Building Bulletin 98: *Briefing Framework for Secondary School Projects*

Department for Education and Skills (DfES) (2004) Building Bulletin 99: *Briefing for Primary Schools.*

Department for Education and Skills (DfES) (2004) *Transforming Schools: an inspirational guide to remodelling secondary schools* www.teachernet.org

Design Council (2002) *Kit for Purpose. Design Council Report on Resources, Furniture, ICT and Storage.* London: Design Council www.designcouncil.org.uk

Design Council (2005) *Learning Environments Campaign Prospectus: From the Inside Out.* London: Design Council www.design-council.org.uk

> The Toolkit brings together a combination of research evidence, examples of practice and a set of resources to help practitioners working in the Early Years Foundation Stage and Key Stage 1 reconsider how speaking and listening skills can be improved by developing communication-friendly spaces

Department for Education and Skills (DfES) (2004) *Schools for the Future: Exemplar designs, concepts and ideas* www.PfS.ORG.UK/pushingboundaries/exemplardesigns.htm

Flutter, J. (2006) This place could help you learn: student participation in creating better school environments. *Education Review* 58 (2)

Green, H., Facer, K., Rudd, T., with Dillon, P. and Humphreys, P. (2005) *Personalised Digital Technologies Beyond the Broadband Blackboard: digital technologies and learner voice.* London www.nestafuturelab.org.uk

Gordon, T. Holland, J. and Lahelma, E. (eds) (2000) *Making Spaces: citizenship and difference in school.* Basingstoke: Macmillan

Higgins, S. *et al* (2005) *The Impact of School Environments.* Newcastle: Centre for Learning and Teaching at Newcastle University

Space and Schools (2004) *Forum* 46 (1) A special edition bringing together views and articles from teachers, architects, academics, educationalists and policy advisers

Waters, M. (2005) Designs for learning; are we thinking radically enough? In QCA/ DfES (ed) *Delivering Transformational Design in School Buildings*

Woolner, P., Hall, E., Wall, K., Higgins, S., Black, A. and McCaughey, C. (2005) *School Building Programmes: Motivations, Consequences and Implications.* London: CfBT

## Useful Organisations

Becta (Advice on potential for ICT in schools) www.becta.org.uk.

Building Schools for the Future www.bsf.gov.org.uk

Commission for Architecture and the Built Environment www.cabe.org.uk

Learning Through Landscapes www.ltl.org.uk

Partnerships for Schools www.p4s.org.uk

Royal Institute of British Architects (see RIBA Guide for School Building Projects) www.riba.org.uk/go/RIBA/home.html

School-works www.schoolworks.co.uk

Sorrell Foundation www.joinedupdesignforschools.com

## International Resources

Online case studies of school, college and university design and resources on design of learning environments www.designshare.cpom

The Schools Design and Planning Laboratory at University of Georgia www.coe.uga.edu/sdpi

Other Useful Websites

www.schoolworks.co.uk

www.whatkidscando.org

www.designmyschool.com

www.besa.org.uk (British Educational Suppliers Association)

...SO IF 52% OF ALL PUPILS ARE GIRLS, AND 15% OF ALL PUPILS ARE BLACK, HOW MANY WIL PASS THE EXAM?

# Using Performance Data

*Hazel Taylor*

■ *See also schedules: School Self-evaluation; The 14-19 Curriculum; 'Underachieving Boys' and 'Overachieving Girls' Revisited – Rhetoric and Reality*

## Data and gender

Interrogating data on performance can provide valuable information about differentials in access and outcome by girls and boys in subjects across the curriculum. Gender differences in performance matter, because outcomes affect future possibilities for study and employment, and sometimes life choices and chances. Gender differences may reflect school and community assumptions or unconscious expectations about differences between girls and boys which are limiting and unfair to both sexes.

Data about performance that reports on progress and results is *quantitative* – it tells us about numbers of pupils achieving at different levels. Self-evaluation uses *qualitative* data alongside quantitative data. Qualitative data summarises views about the quality of experiences and their perceived impact. Quantitative data provides evidence about disparity and whether an issue needs to be addressed. Together, they often provide powerful evidence about exactly what to change. In addition, qualitative data can give insights into *how* to change it to have the greatest impact. All data needs to be considered reflectively and in as large a context as possible – knee-jerk reactions can lead to ill thought out and sometimes detrimental changes. Caution is always needed when dealing with small numbers.

Data that simply shows that boys and girls from different schools can have different outcomes is of little use, as individual schools vary so widely in their intakes and circumstances. This is a major limitation of league tables. What data can also broadly show,

however, is the value added to a pupil's performance by the school she or he attends. This measure demonstrates the effectiveness of the school in enabling pupils to make the progress that can be expected over a key stage, given the level at which a pupil started – their prior attainment.

Data analysis is valuable from whole-school to individual pupil level, and is of use to governors, classroom teachers and support staff, and teaching assistants. Data is only as useful as the quality of its collection and analysis. Depending on how different data is looked at, different conclusions can be reached. For example, a broad look at whole-school figures might suggest that, overall, girls are doing better than boys, while a closer look could reveal that:

■ girls and boys are outperforming each other in different subjects

■ within a subject, outperformance relates to particular sets of boys or girls, perhaps according to their level of prior attainment, or the teachers of the groups

■ differences between boys and girls are less than those between groups defined by other variables, such as ethnic groups

■ girls and boys outperform each other in different aspects of a single subject, for example in coursework or final examination, and that the weighting of those aspects to the whole creates the overall difference

■ an apparent gender difference, for example that boys outperform girls in one class across the curriculum, may be due to another, unrecognised, variable, such as that a majority of the girls in this particular class are looked-after children, or early stage English language learners, and the boys are not.

Data about gender should always be looked at in conjunction with other key variables in pupil characteristics, including prior attainment, ethnicity and socio-economic background. Overall, differences in outcomes between girls and boys are less than those between pupils from different ethnic backgrounds when other variables are taken into account, and boys' performance overall varies considerably when socio-economic background is taken into account.

## National data and cross-school comparisons by gender

Provision of nationally collected data varies across the UK as elsewhere. This schedule considers practice in England. National data is collected as part of the external accountability framework, and focuses on outcomes as demonstrated by tests or examinations at each key stage. Its purpose is to measure pupils' achievements against predetermined national benchmarks. Gender differences are reported on at a national level, and form part of what is fed back to schools about their own performance compared with other schools.

Each school can compare its own performance with all schools nationally; with other schools with a similar socio-economic profile; and other schools with similar levels of prior attainment. At GCSE, results are presented for the school compared with other schools in all subjects, and allow comparisons to be made between subjects within the school.

This level of data is useful in highlighting broad patterns of performance between girls and boys, but must be treated with caution because:

■ other variables that affect performance are not considered, for example ethnicity or, in key stage 1, that pupils join reception classes in different terms

■ at GCSE, it is not easy to compare like with like because individual pupils take different combinations of subjects, and there are greatly different numbers of pupils entered for different subjects. Beyond the core subjects of English, mathematics and science, it is essential to look at total numbers of pupils of each sex entered, and at which level they are entered, as well as at outcomes by gender. School policy in counselling pupils about option choice will affect the profile of prior attainment of pupils in a minority subject, and where this varies from school to school, comparisons are invalid

■ the issue of value added is not widely understood, and parents and others outside a school can seize on headline figures without being aware of the differences in starting points of pupils from school to school. Publicity suggesting that girls, for example, do better in single-sex schools, can be questioned when prior attainment and socio-economic backgrounds are taken into account.

### Issues to consider at whole school/national comparison level

■ Are there immediate differences in performance between boys and girls in a particular subject? Is this pattern repeated with all ethnic groups? Is it the same for girls who are eligible for free school meals (FSMs) and those who are not? What further investigation is needed?

■ Are there differences in numbers of boys and girls entered for particular subjects at GCSE and A level, or for GNVQs? What further investigation is needed?

■ Where the school's data shows greater difference in performance by gender in a subject than that in similar schools, what action is taken?

■ What opportunities do staff have, collectively and individually, to reflect on the implications of data analysis for the school as a whole and for their subjects, key stages etc.?

■ How does the school support parents/carers in understanding the data?

■ What training have governors had in considering gender and other variables that can affect performance?

### Considering school data – what to look at and how to look at it
#### Summative data

Primary, secondary and special schools have electronic access to summative data about individual pupils' performance in each area tested, that enables them to analyse patterns in considerable detail. Many schools use commercial software to create their own databases for this purpose. The DfES provides detailed data in its PAT – Pupil Attainment Tracker – which is available by September each year giving details about the exact performance of each pupil in each subject. From 2008, Raiseonline replaces the PANDA and PAT and enables every sort of comparison or analysis of an individual's performance that one might need.

However, large data bases can be very intimidating, and data managers can enjoy creating a mystique around their use. They are valuable and need to be widely used, for example by teaching assistants in planning and mapping progress. There are gender issues here in ensuring that all staff get thorough training in using the software, and that assumptions about the capacity both to understand and benefit from it are challenged.

### Formative data

Schools will also collect formative data about pupils' progress in each element of each level, in the core subjects in primary schools, and in all subjects in secondary schools. Within each subject, it is important to look at the data not only at an individual level, and ask what it can tell about that child, but also to look at various groupings of pupils to see what gender issues, if any, may emerge, and what other variables they may be linked with. In a primary schools, teachers looking at data on English in key stage 2 may look at girls' and boys' performance in reading and writing overall and ask questions such as:

- Are there differences? What are they?
- Are they linked with ethnicity?
- Are they linked with eligibility for free school meals?
- Do the patterns vary from class teacher to class teacher?
- Do they reflect differences in mastering particular areas of skill?
- How do they compare with previous years?
- How do they relate to known differences in age-related learning spurts?
- Are pupils at a particular level making less than expected progress compared with those at a higher or lower level?

Considering data needs to be a systematic process, and it is very important not to jump to conclusions on the basis of superficial discussion or generalisation from individual anecdote. When the answers to the questions have been collated and considered, the next step is to formulate hypotheses about what might be going on, and then decide what further evidence might be needed.

At this point, qualitative evidence might be sought. For example, in a secondary school science department, teachers looking at progress in Year 8 might note that girls overall are making similar progress to boys, but that white and African Caribbean girls, the majority in the year, are making slower progress, while Asian girls are making faster progress than the majority of boys. They might additionally note that within a level, two or three concepts seem to prove particularly difficult for the underachieving girls. In pursuing an enquiry they might ask the following questions:

- What do the pupils think?
- Where do the girls sit? Are they bunched at the back of the lab?
- What sort of expectations do the teachers have of the different groups of girls?
- What attitudes do the boys and the girls have to each other, and do these differ by ethnicity?
- What exemplars of the problematic concepts are used in the lessons?
- What activities are used?

Before making a judgment, a rich picture needs to be painted, based on evidence most of which is readily available. Discussion among teachers will reveal assumptions. Lesson observations focusing on the gender issues will provide data. Group or individual interviews with a sample of pupils will yield further material. Then, teachers can come to some tentative conclusions about what might be the causes of the gender difference, and start to think about how to use their findings. If staff have the confidence to include pupils in all stages of the enquiry, much more can be gained, as the pupils respond to the responsibility given to them and to the value attached to their views. An enquiry like this should become a regular part of a school's approach to self-evaluation and, with practice, it becomes both quick and highly reflective. Data used in this way directly generates learning and improvement, and enhances equity.

### Issues to consider at school data level

- What importance is attached to collecting data that highlights gender issues?
- What is collected and who collects it?
- Who looks at the data and how widely are they representative of the perspectives on gender in the school, including those of pupils?
- What training do people receive in the collection and understanding of data? Does the training include understanding of the interplay of variables?

### Using performance data to promote gender equity

Performance data is a tool in the promotion of gender equity and, to be used well, a school needs:

- a clear gender equity policy covering the areas where gender makes a difference to pupils' experience in the school, and setting out its values regarding gender equity
- a commitment to enquiry and to using data to illuminate the circumstances in which gender appears to be impacting on outcomes
- a commitment to the informed use of data at all levels in the school
- an investment in high-quality training in enquiry methods and analysing data.

Without these, attention to gender differences can easily result in superficial actions which have no effect, or exacerbate a difference.

Performance data illuminates gender equity issues in two broadly distinct ways. In the first, it highlights patterns of outcomes where both sexes are apparently receiving the same education, and need to be doing the best that they can, for example in the core subjects throughout their education. Here, both sexes apparently have the same opportunity to achieve, and there should be broadly similar outcomes. Data is used to identify the broad and finer differences in outcome and contribute to the further investigation of what the barriers might be that are causing one group of pupils to achieve less than expected compared with another group. For example, data might show that on entry into secondary school, boys and girls with level 5 in English actually gained that level on the basis of strengths and weaknesses in different parts of key stage 2 SATs, and that the pattern is of boys doing less well in writing. The detailed analysis of this data is used to identify the particular boys involved, and to guide the teaching that will enable the boys to catch up with the girls in this area.

The second major use of data for gender equity occurs where there are opportunities for choice within the curriculum, whether within the timetable or the extended day. Data can be used to improve equity of access and equity of outcome, by illuminating patterns of choice, and differences in performance in areas of choice, and then informing action. This is important at all stages where pupils have to make choices, but is particularly crucial at the end of key stage 3 and during key stage 4, where choices and outcomes have a major impact on future employment and economic outcomes. Data needs to be used to show:

- the patterns of choice in subjects and activities
- any differences in level of entry for examinations

- proportions of boys and girls actually entered for a qualification
- differences in outcomes.

Data can then be used to inform further investigation into:

- the barriers that might be affecting initial choices, for example, perceptions about gender appropriateness for certain courses, such as boys and child care, girls and engineering
- what guides decisions about levels of entry, and whether there are assumptions about, for example, girls' neatness being less of an indicator of high level performance than boys' untidy flair
- what guides entry policy and whether it has gendered effects, for example, in not entering pupils in a particular subject because low grades might affect the school's overall performance figures. This could mean that boys, for example, might end up with nothing to show for studying a modern foreign language
- what differences in final outcomes occur in areas of choice, whether these relate to difference in attainment at the beginning of the course, and what may underlie the differences.

## What data can't tell

Data alone cannot reveal the cause of a difference, nor can it tell what action to take. It alerts, it helps get down to the details of a difference, it reveals complexities, but it does not provide answers. The main caveats in using data are:

- do not generalise from a small sample or ignore information about statistical significance
- do not assume that a broad picture from a large sample applies to everyone
- do not forget that the many variables will be interacting and it is difficult to tell which is the most significant one to tackle
- data is only as good as the accuracy of its collection, and the quality of the reflection on it.

That said, using performance data well is one of the most powerful ways of improving gender-equitable outcomes for all pupils.

### References
Bird, S. and Fowler, J. (2004) *School Improvement: Making Data Work*. London: TEN, www.csn.info (on LA data provision, including useful case studies of good practice in helping schools analyse data about disadvantaged groups)
Fischer Family Trust, www.fischertrust.org/perfomancedataprojects
www.dfes.gov.uk/performancetables

never give

# School Self-evaluation

*Alan Richardson*

■ *See also schedules: Leadership; Performance Management; Using Performance Data; Governors; It's My School: The Power of Pupil Voice*

## Introduction

Self-evaluation is a systematic process whereby the wider school community reviews its effectiveness in order to improve its practice. It plays a key part in tackling any form of discrimination, whether in gender or any other area. It can reveal discrimination that is inadvertent, and can show whether measures designed to combat inequalities are working or not – for example in reviewing the effects of single-sex groupings in a mixed school. Through self-evaluation schools can:

■ design enquiries to find out how effective their gender equity policies are

■ use evidence from self-evaluation to shape changes that are fed into the school's development plan

■ enable all staff to gain skills in data collection and analysis that they can apply to any gender-related concern.

Self-evaluation is both an expectation and a requirement on all schools. Since 2005, external inspection of schools in England and Wales has had as its starting point the school's own evaluation of its work. Evidence for the impact assessment required by a school's gender equity scheme under the 2007 Gender Equality Duty comes from self-evaluation.

Self-evaluation is likely to be more successful in schools which have an open, self-critical ethos and a 'no blame' culture. In this climate, individuals are more prepared to be open about areas of their work which have not been successful. There may well be gender differences in the extent to which this kind of

climate is created. For example, some of the leadership styles associated with women leaders may be more conducive to establishing this kind of culture.

## Who is self-evaluation for?

If schools see compliance with external requirements as the main reason for self-evaluation, staff are unlikely to be committed to doing it, and its impact will be limited. Self-evaluation is essentially for the school itself and its stakeholders. Collecting evidence about the effects of one's practices, in order to adjust them to make them more effective, is at the heart of professionalism. It is also at the heart of learning. Where a particular equity issue, for example the discursive writing skills of many boys, is investigated by teams across the school, differences from subject to subject will be thrown up which can lead to fruitful discussion and plans for change. Understandings, practices and outcomes for pupils and staff improve as a result.

## Issues to consider

■ How do equity issues explicitly inform the self-evaluation process and analysis?

■ What audiences does the school identify for its self-evaluation?

■ How is self-evaluation presented so that participants and audiences see the relevance and value of doing it?

■ How are all stakeholders engaged in a discussion of the purpose of self-evaluation?

■ Is robust evaluation built in to all gender-related innovations in practice?

## What is it for?

In practice, in many schools the purpose of self-evaluation has not been clear and the practice has suffered as a consequence. Looking at a particular aspect of the work in schools can serve multiple purposes. The most obvious reasons for schools to evaluate their work are to:

■ improve experience for all children and young people

■ raise standards, improve teaching and learning

■ find out about the effects of practice and guide changes to it

■ respond to the need to be accountable to the school's many stakeholders.

These clearly overlap, and are broad purposes which encompass a wide range of sub-areas to investigate. While inclusion is an important stated goal in most schools, this is not necessarily reflected in the evaluation of its work. When schools really mean that equality is central to their self-evaluation, these issues will inform both the process and the content of enquiry.

### Issues to consider

■ How can a school establish a clear, widely-accepted purpose for its self-evaluation which has equal opportunities at its heart?

■ How can the outcomes of self-evaluation best be presented and communicated so that they are accessible to the full range of the school's stakeholders?

■ Is data examined from the perspective of equality issues, for example impact on or take-up of particular activities by white working class boys?

■ Is self-evaluation directly linked to continuing professional development and the school's strategies to improve teaching and learning, for example using the school's data about differences in performance by boys and girls in a particular subject or class to inform developments in practice?

## What does it focus on?

The extent of a school's inclusivity should be a major thread of its self-evaluation.

The impact of a school's policies and practice on the particular groups within the school, and aspects of equality of opportunity in themselves should be areas of focus. Campbell *et al* (2001) suggest four dimensions of equality which can guide its evaluation:

■ formal equality of access and provision: concerned with explicit barriers to participation based, for example, on gender, ability or disability

■ equality of circumstance: denial of opportunities because of someone's circumstances, poverty, parents, community factors

■ equity of participation, or treatment: informal aspects of school everyday life that allow some people to be treated less well than others

■ equity of outcome: the inequitable distribution of school benefits such as attainment outcomes.

While there is no shortage of quantitative pupil performance data in most schools, qualitative data – perceptions, views and professional opinions – should also be considered as valid evidence. While analysis of quantitative evidence can suggest what might need to be changed, qualitative evidence can give strong indications of how to change it – for example, one teacher's ceasing to use sexist sarcasm could make a great deal of difference to the girls' performance in that class, but no amount of analysis of the performance data from that class would lead to that conclusion.

### Issues to consider

■ To what extent is equal opportunities represented in the areas of focus of the self-evaluation? Does the school's equal opportunities policy specify a review cycle for its contents, and offer guidance on including all perspectives in subject reviews?

■ How well is self-evaluation integrated with the school's review and planning cycles?

■ Is the school looking at differences between different groups of parents and pupils, for example, in how satisfaction levels amongst parents of girls compare with those of parents of boys, and how these vary when analysed by other factors such as ethnicity or socio-economic status?

■ How does the school use, and feed back, the findings of its self-evaluation?

## Who does it?

Initially and crucially, a school's self-evaluation is a management responsibility. A senior member of staff needs to provide strong coordination and maintain an overview to ensure the coherence of the process and a focus on key priorities. Senior managers need to ensure that it is seen as a whole-school exercise and integral to the school's review and planning cycle – not a duplication of processes already in place. However, as the process becomes more sophisticated and wide-ranging, a wider group of staff needs to be involved, bringing in a range of perspectives and experiences. It will not be possible to evaluate how the school is impacting on different groups – by gender, ethnicity, disability – without directly involving these groups. Even if they are represented within senior management teams, the perspective there will be that of a senior manager.

### Staff

All staff can take part in self-evaluation, for example, in evaluating their own work, their team's work and in giving their views of the operation of whole-school policies. Staff who play a leading or coordinating role need to be representative of the different groups on the staff. In primary schools, the majority of members of teams will be women – teaching and support staff – and it is important fully to involve them, not just in the gathering of evidence, but also in deciding on, for example, the framing of the areas of enquiry and questions to be asked. All staff should be entitled to have their voice heard in the evaluation of the school's work.

It is important that there are measures to support staff in carrying out their own self-evaluation where it links with performance management, and ways of validating the views of individuals. Women tend to underestimate the quality of their own performance in comparison with men. Some schools have countered this by introducing a buddy system in which a colleague works with an individual who prompts and makes suggestions as to the examples of practice which could be quoted as evidence of performance. Also, teams can work together in looking at aspects of their performance which relate to both individual and collective performance.

### Pupils

To provide a really comprehensive view of the school, groups beyond the school staff – pupils, parents, governors, and perhaps outside agencies – need to be involved. Of these, pupils are perhaps the most important. The pupils' voice is an indispensable part of self-evaluation. For example, in looking at aspects of the school's response to the *Every Child Matters* agenda, it is inconceivable that schools could judge effectiveness in meeting the Five Outcomes – for example, Stay safe – without talking to pupils. It is no longer sufficient to use only the school council – a practice often used in the past. A full cross-section ensuring representation by age, gender, ethnicity, class and disability will be needed to provide the rounded view of the pupils' experience of the school.

When involved in self-evaluation, children and young people have been found to be perceptive and reliable observers of practice, and they need to be introduced to ways of working and ways of expressing their views if their contribution is to have its maximum effect. As part of this, it is important to establish protocols to reassure individual members of staff or groups of staff that no inappropriate information from discussions with pupils will be disseminated.

Many schools have found that engaging pupils in the monitoring and evaluation of learning has led to productive changes in pupils' behaviours and improved learning. In one school, pupil observers collected data about off-task talk, and found that many girls engaged in girl talk about personal appearance. When this was reported back and discussed, they became better at self-monitoring, and disruption was reduced.

### Parents

It is a real challenge for many schools to engage a full cross-section of parents and carers. The perspectives of parents and carers across classes and ethnic groups will add to the breadth of feedback and are essential if, for instance, pupils' attitudes to considering non-traditional work areas are to be broadened.

### Governors

Governors retain overall responsibility for endorsing and overseeing a school's self-evaluation. Their actual involvement varies widely. Some governing bodies receive regular briefings, and some nominate a governor to take responsibility for keeping up to date with self-evaluation. Governing bodies become increasingly effective through participating in self-evaluation: it raises their awareness of issues of equality of opportunity and develops their sensitivity to these. Governors cannot escape the statutory function that they exercise in monitoring the work of the school and in acting upon the outcomes, for example in agreeing to fund additional catch-up clubs for underachieving groups.

### Critical friends

Some schools have found the contribution of an independent, external view of their work and of their self-evaluation to be helpful in ensuring that key areas are addressed and difficult questions asked. The critical friend can act as an advocate for groups within the school community whose voice might not be adequately heard.

### Issues to consider

■ Does a full range of stakeholders play a part in the school's self-evaluation? How might a wider range be involved, for example, local supplementary schools?

■ Do those leading and managing self-evaluation in the school reflect the school's make-up or redress imbalances in it? Does it matter?

■ How are pupils involved in collecting and evaluating data about their learning, for example in logging oral contributions of boys and girls over several lessons, and discussing the findings?

■ Is training on the gender issues in self-evaluation included in the governors' development programme?

■ Do those contributing to the self-evaluation include those with an external perspective? Is their role clearly defined, eg as bringing a sharper focus to the analysis of gender or ethnic implications of data?

### How is it done?

The art and science of school self-evaluation has developed over time, and there is evidence, both from inspection and anecdotally, that schools are getting better at it. However, there is still a range of practice both within and between schools, and poor practice occurs in, for example, the gathering and subsequent analysis of data. Unintentionally or occasionally intentionally, bias can affect the conclusions reached, so it is also important for a school to establish the principles to which it will adhere and establish the ethical basis for its evaluation. This is an area to which a critical friend can make a major contribution.

Initially schools adopted a relatively limited range of techniques and gained experience and expertise in using these. As the scope and significance of self-evaluation has increased, a much wider and more imaginative range of methods is being promoted and adopted. MacBeath (2005) analyses a wide array of tools for self-evaluation. Among the more innovative are:

■ group card sorts
■ sentence completion
■ drawings and paintings
■ photo evaluation
■ role play
■ critical incident analysis.

A wider range of participants and this wider range of tools have the potential to investigate some sensitive issues contributing to the school's responses to issues of equality, inclusion and fairness. For example, photo evaluation puts pupils in a position where they can set an agenda for their evaluation and can visually explore areas which they may find too difficult to describe or too sensitive to address by more conventional methods. Group card sorts – where a range of views about aspects of the way in which the school functions, set out on cards, are accepted or rejected and ordered – can distance the groups taking part from identifying the responses themselves and can generate real discussion about the issues raised.

### Issues to consider

■ Does the school keep the process of evaluation under review to ensure that it is capable of addressing sensitive issues such as those which arise in looking at aspects of equal opportunities?

■ Does the school provide training in enquiry methods to groups responsible for monitoring, for example the equal opportunities working party?

■ Does the school use a range of methods to gather the views of aspects of its work?

*With thanks to Gulshan Kayembe*

### References

Campbell, C. Gillborn, D. Sammons, P. Wareen, S. and Whitty, G. (2001) Inclusive Schooling. In *NSIN Research Matters*, London: Institute of Education

MacBeath, J. (2005) *Self-evaluation: Models, Tools and Examples of Practice.* Nottingham: National College for School Leadership

Teachernet (2006) www.teachernet.gov.uk/wholeschool

'BYE, DEAR – YOU FORGOT ONE LAST THING...

# Continuing Professional Development

*Hilary Bourdillon*

■ *See also schedules: Performance Management; Using the School Budget; Governors; Leadership; The Wider Workforce*

> Continuing professional development (CPD) is a term used to describe all the activities in which teachers engage during the course of a career which are designed to enhance their work. ....
> Moreover, because teachers, like the students they teach, think and feel, are influenced also by their biographies, social histories and working contexts, peer groups, teaching preferences, identities, phases of development and broader socio-political cultures, the purpose, design and processes of CPD will need to mirror these if it is to result in effective outcomes. (Day and Sachs, 2004)

## CPD policy and performance management

CPD policy in England advocates that all educational professionals should engage in continuing professional development with the purpose of improving teaching and learning, and further raising standards in schools. For teachers, CPD is linked with performance management within the framework of a professional dialogue between manager and manager. This linkage of ongoing development to performance is dangerously simplistic: teachers' personal experiences and values influence their intellectual and emotional engagement with teaching and learning, and how they respond to various opportunities for development. There are also tensions in making opportunities available. Holistic views of entitlement to CPD (GTC, 2004) encourage a broad view of what may meet needs, while access in reality may be limited to activities which address narrow needs relating to specified aspects of the national standards

for teachers (TDA, 2006). Gender and ethnicity profoundly affect perceptions, access to and experience of CPD, and a school CPD policy based on fairness and equity has to move beyond a prescriptive and minimalist approach.

## *Issues to consider*

How can we ensure that educational policy for CPD is informed by gender and equality issues? The answer to this question doesn't always lie in a school's practices, but through talking to and debating with those who represent educational policy.

In the national context:

- school advisers and external consultants who offer professional development may have useful information about gender, equality issues and CPD. Engage them in dialogue about this and ask questions

- regulatory bodies such as Ofsted may not offer advice and statistics on gender and CPD. It is important not to assume that they are always aware of the issues. For example, the Ofsted (2006) review of CPD in England said nothing at all about gender differences in access and participation in CPD activities

- agencies such as the Teacher Development Agency, set up to secure an effective workforce that improves children's life chances, often hold consultations on teacher and para-professional development. This offers the opportunity to feedback important gender and equality issues

- policy makers can be asked about their monitoring of gender and CPD, for example the take up of funded CPD opportunities

In the school context:

■ does the CPD policy have a statement about entitlement and how do you ensure this includes part-time, supply and non teaching staff?

■ is the process of linking CPD and performance management monitored for gender issues?

## Gender issues in the experience of CPD

The General Teaching Council (GTC, 2005) found that there were gender differences in career expectations which may have had an impact on the pattern of CPD. Female teachers in primary, secondary and special schools were significantly more likely to see their career development in the next five years in terms of strengthening classroom practice, taking on management responsibility (excluding headship) and changing from part-time to full-time teaching. Female teachers were significantly more likely to indicate that their CPD needs had been met, although there were variations here between primary and secondary schools. Female teachers were also less likely to have either all, or part of, their CPD funded.

The survey demonstrated that there were differences in the CPD activities as experienced by male and female teachers. More women participated in activities such as school-based collaborative learning with colleagues whereas men were more likely to experience collaborative learning within a network of schools.

In terms of CPD needs, female teachers were more likely to identify needing classroom-focused development opportunities, such as behaviour management, updating skills and knowledge in the classroom, fostering pupils' creativity, thinking skills, motivating under-aspiring pupils and meeting the needs of minority ethnic pupils. They were less likely to identify needs in the area of management and leadership, such as school leadership and training, school self-evaluation, subject leadership and school finance. Schools need to evaluate CPD in a way which captures gender differences in experiences. Guskey's (2000) influential framework for evaluation is adapted below to include a gender dimension.

### Issues to consider

Are gender issues reflected in the evaluation of CPD, for example:

■ *participant satisfaction*: Are individuals' CPD needs met (including part-time and support staff) and monitored for gender issues? What particular support is given to encourage teachers from black and ethnic minority groups to develop their leadership roles (through schemes for example such as *Investing in Diversity* – see references)

■ *learning questionnaire*: Is data kept on the experiences of female and male teachers' and para-professionals' CPD activities? If so how is it used?

■ *organisational support*: Are there opportunities for all staff to discuss with the CPD leader/senior management, their preferred learning experiences?

■ *participants' use of new knowledge*: Are both women and men supported to move beyond their comfort zone in terms of CPD activities and areas?

■ *student outcome*: Are all aspects of pupil learning and issues of gender, race and social class contributing to the evaluation of outcomes?

■ how is CPD linked to career aspirations, and what support is given to enable the exploration of wider ambitions and possibilities?

■ how are members of under-represented groups encouraged to take up CPD opportunities? This question applies particularly to para-professionals, who have a long history of neglect in terms of access to professional development programmes.

## The feminisation of CPD?

As my opening quote indicates, professional learning needs to take into account personal experiences and organisational cultures as well as the content and style of professional learning experiences. Organisational culture in school is not a given, but the result of how all people involved in the school work together. This has a significant impact on teacher motivation and job satisfaction, and ultimately, change in the classroom.

Capacity building, that is, the creation of a culture that fosters professional collaboration and learning for all involved, is a key element in effective professional learning. This represents a shift from what had traditionally been seen as a 'male values and characteristics' culture (Robertson, 1992) typified by competitiveness, certitude, hierarchical power and a reliance on quantifiable and objective information, rather than what is valued and subjective. Here then, we can see an argument emerging for claims for the feminisation of CPD, much like those claiming the feminisation of leadership.

This argument is based on the contention that qualities and work practices generally described as feminine are more in tune with effective CPD. These include: collaboration, team work, colleague support and networking, with less emphasis on status and communication skills. Some of the literature (Goleman, 1998; Thomson, 1998) alerts us to the value of emotional intelligence of the kind traditionally associated with the feminine, such as intuition, empathetic awareness, and social radar. Intuition and other social assets are now seen as dynamic contributors to a successful organisation. In some tension with this is the agenda for the development of career paths, the emphasis on evidence-based practice and accountability, and the advent of performance-related pay.

Emotional intelligence and an emphasis on relationships is a major plank in programmes for the development of school leaders, such as those organised by the National College for School Leaders (NCSL). This may explain the anecdotal evidence emerging, drawn from participants in the NCSL, which suggests they appeal more to women than men. However, whilst men and women may be drawn to different ways of learning and working, it doesn't mean that all women work in this way and that men do not; or that men cannot learn this way. Whilst it is now widely recognised that feminine traits and approaches are valuable for organisations and professional learning, we need to be alert to the dangers of polarising professional learning approaches by gender. The fact that most CPD activities will be organised around feminine traits belies the gender complexities in professional development.

Life experiences, status and access are more powerful than learning styles in determining engagement in effective, inclusive CPD. It is not because of the learning styles deployed that some women do not participate in or benefit from CPD. Their own aspirations and identities are key factors here, (GTC, 2006), as is their status in the school hierarchy. Women and men in senior management roles are more likely to have their CPD needs met than other teachers (both men and women). All teachers are more likely to have their CPD needs met than the para-professionals in schools.

## Issues to consider

This checklist adds an explicit equity dimension to Ofsted's (2006) headings for the features of high quality CPD:

■ *tailoring the provision*: What types of CPD activities do individual members of staff (teachers and para-professionals) find most effective? For example, how do they identify their needs and does this explore and challenge their aspirations?

■ *organising collaborative projects*: How do you ensure the CPD activities maximise staff confidence?

■ *coaching and mentoring*: Is this developed in a way which is sensitive to the gendered nature of mentoring?

■ *arranging effective staff development days*: Is the timing of CPD activities flexible enough to meet the range of lifestyle demands?

■ *developing the role of the CPD leader*: How is the CPD leader supported by the senior management team to explore and understand gender and equality issues in relation to CPD? What status do they have in the school's hierarchy and to whom do they report?

■ *recognising the need for relevant subject training*: Is the need to update all staff's knowledge and skills in their subject areas/ specialism reflected in the CPD plan? Are all staff given the opportunity to participate in using new technologies (online communities) and resources, for example *Teachers TV*?

■ are external consultants aware of gender differences and equality issues in teacher learning and aspirations?

## CPD for the wider workforce

Many of these issues are also relevant to staff who work in schools in a para-professional capacity. Developments such as the National Agreement for Workforce Reform in England have highlighted the significant contribution made by school support staff to raising standards and the efficient running of schools. Alongside the definition of the roles for these staff, schools are also considering what support and CPD they need. The TDA oversees the qualification and training of support staff and has identified the vocational qualifications which can be tailored to meet the needs of staff (TDA, 2006). These qualifications are accredited through the national qualifications framework (NQF).

This group of para-professionals manifests particular equality issues. The majority of classroom assistants are women and often have life experiences which are of relevance to the classroom and to pupils' learning rather than formal qualifications.

> Most assistants brought parenting skills and previous work experiences to their roles. ... Where assistants came from an ethnic minority group they could offer important additional language skills and cultural understandings and a bridging role between school and community... (Hancock *et al*, 2005 p.11)

This same study found that 'a high percentage of assistants were invited (or required) to attend staff meetings and staff training,' yet 'despite an overall availability, nearly half the assistants said they experienced difficulties attending courses. The main reasons given were lack of availability (particularly in rural areas), family commitments, distance and transport' (Hancock *et al*, 2005, p.11). As with teachers, engagement in CPD is strongly influenced by life experiences, status and access.

### Issues to consider

- How does the school accommodate the professional development of support staff? Does the CPD strategy remove barriers by, for example, providing better access to training and development information? It may be many years since many of them undertook any formal professional development or qualifications, and their learning needs and the emotional support required is likely to be very different from that of most teachers

- Is the professional development for support staff monitored in the same way as the professional development of teaching staff?

- How does the CPD offered strengthen quality and meet the individual needs of support staff? For example, does each role have a clear framework of skills and competences? How does professional development impact on day-to-day practice?

### Teacher knowledge, gender and equality issues

All professional development needs to build staff awareness of the issues of race, class and gender, whether it is subject based or on a whole school issue. In particular, schools need to ensure their CPD reflects the priorities of their Gender Equality Scheme under the UK Gender Equality Duty 2007 (GED). Staff development on equality issues needs to go beyond the legislative requirements. It is a challenging and controversial area which goes to the heart of individuals' beliefs and values.

### Issues to consider

- How does the school monitor the coverage of equality issues in the content of the different CPD areas covered? For example, group work, investigations in science, geography fieldwork, attainment in mathematics

- What work has the school or local advisory service done to enable the school to meet the requirements of the GED?

*With many thanks to Carol Jones, Headteacher of Fulham Cross School, for her comments and discussion.*

### References

Day, C. and Sachs, J. (2004) Professionalism, performativity and empowerment: discourses in the politics, policies and purposes of continuing professional development. In Day, C and Sachs, J. (eds) (2004) *International Handbook on the Continuing Professional Development of Teachers.* Maidenhead: Open University Press

Goleman, D. (1998) *Working with Emotional Intelligence.* London: Bloomsbury

GTC (2004) *Teachers' Professional Learning Framework (TPLF)* London: General Teaching Council. See: www.gtce. org.uk/cpd_home/tplfpubs/

GTC (2005) *Survey of Teachers: Segmentation by Gender.* Slough: NFER. See: www.gtce.org.uk/PolicyAndResearch/ research/survey04/2005survey

GTC (2006) *Annual Digest of Statistics. Teacher Profiles 2005-06.* London: General Teaching Council

Guskey, T.R. (2000) *Evaluating Professional Development.* Thousand Oaks, CA: Corwin Press

Hancock, R. Swann, W. Cable, C and Marr, A. (2005) *Classroom Assistants in primary schools.* London: ESRC No R000237803

*Investing in Diversity.* This is a leadership development programme for black and minority ethnic leaders and aspiring leaders. See: www.ioe.ac.uk/lcll

Ofsted ( 2006) *The Logical Chain: Continuing Professional Development in Effective Schools.* London: HMSO. Document ref: HMI2639. See: www.ofsted.gov.uk

Robertson, M. (1992) Teacher development and gender equity. In Hargreaves, A., Fullan, M. (eds) *Understanding Teacher Development.* London: Cassell

School Workforce Development Board (SWDB) 'Building the school team: our plans for support staff training and development 2005-2006.'

Support Staff CPD information. www.tda.gov.uk/support

Teacher Development Agency www.tda.gov.uk/teachers/professionalstandards.aspx

Teachers TV: programmes on CPD and web pages at www.teachers.tv

Thomson, K. (1998) *Emotional Intelligence.* Oxford: Capstone.

# Performance Management

*Alan Richardson*

■ *See also schedules: Governors; Using the School Budget; Continuing Professional Development; The Wider Workforce*

In 2006, the DfES published regulations which made significant changes to the performance management (PM) arrangements for teachers and headteachers in England and Wales. Its aim was to 'build capacity to enable teachers and headteachers to focus on their core role and enhance their professional status'. This built upon the system introduced in 2000, for which the rationale was the professional development for teachers and the raising of pupil attainment. The linkage of pay to performance is now an integral part of PM. In the review meeting at the end of the performance management cycle the reviewer makes recommendations about the teacher's progression through the pay scales. This is a reflection of the government's commitment to ensure that 'career progression and financial rewards will go to those who are making the biggest contributions to improving pupil progress, those who are continually developing their own expertise and those who are helping to develop expertise in others' (DFES, 2006). This makes performance management high stakes and it is increasingly important that all are aware of the relevant gender issues and the issues, many of them the same ones, which have a particular impact on ethnic minority staff.

While the regulations regarding performance management relate specifically to teachers and headteachers, there are as yet no regulations which relate to support staff, whose numbers have dramatically increased in recent years in line with the government's workforce reform measures. Many, but not all, schools have extended performance management arrangements to teaching assistants, learning support assistants and other non-teaching staff. Many of these staff contribute directly to the learning of pupils, and the large majority of them are women. Most of the issues which arise over performance management of teachers apply equally to support staff.

## Lessons from performance management so far

### Fairness of performance management procedures in practice

From the outset, there have been statements about the need for performance management to be based upon fairness and equality of opportunity: the model policy set out by DfES (2001) has these elements at its core. While few would disagree with this as a basis, in many schools there has been a lack of engagement of staff in the adoption of the principles and few attempts to secure their commitment to implementing them. In order to ensure fairness and equality, staff and their representatives need to be vigilant and to engage in processes which can keep the operation of policies under review.

### Monitoring of policies and procedures

From the early stages of the introduction of performance management, the monitoring of policies and procedures has been widely neglected and was reflected in the Ofsted (2002) report. Between 2001 and 2005, systems in all schools were monitored by threshold assessors appointed by the national agency, Cambridge Education Associates, and even in those schools which were deemed to have well developed performance management systems, the weakest element was their review and monitoring. Thus most schools were making judgements, and continue to make judgements, about the success of their systems on the basis of impressions and anecdote rather than any rigorous review process.

### Professional development for performance management

The training provided for both the reviewer and reviewee is crucial in ensuring that the procedures and the principles underpinning them are fully understood, and that they operate them consistently across schools. Procedures can operate unfairly because of individual perceptions and assumptions, and differences of approach due to gender, race or disability can affect the process. Training for performance management can be lost amongst the numerous changes and developments schools are managing. Time for professional development is at a premium and priorities have to be established. If performance management is not fully integrated with mainstream school improvement and development, like issues of equality it can be marginalised.

## What are the issues and what is to be done?

### Emotional intelligence – school culture

The development of an open, fair and principled performance management system depends on the school culture having these same characteristics. Individuals, in general, need a working environment shaped by good management in order to thrive and develop professionally. Most staff will not approach their professional development positively if they are unhappy about the way the school operates. For example, if staff feel unable to admit mistakes or difficulties because they fear negative responses, it is bound to affect their approach to their job and to performance management. If the school encourages team working and collaboration, sharing experience and individual development within the context of team development, it is likely that female staff in particular will feel comfortable with a way of working that is in tune with their own aspirations. Performance systems in a competitive culture or environment are likely to disengage and disenfranchise women teachers.

The culture of the school will also play an important part in determining the approach of reviewers to background factors and the context in which each member of staff works. For example, a culture which values long hours of work will not be hospitable to

women in particular because of their family or child care responsibilities. Increasingly there are issues of work/life balance which need to be taken into account by managers for men and women staff; indeed this is a requirement for being a good employer.

### Self-assessment and target setting

The starting point in the performance management cycle for each teacher is self-assessment against the objectives set for the previous year. This requires reflection on past performance and honest judgement about whether these objectives were met. The discussion and drawing of conclusions from the lesson observation required for every teacher's performance review should follow a similar approach.

There is evidence of significant gender differences in the ways in which men and women rate their own performance. For example, an extensive study across the Civil Service concluded that men in professional groups were more likely to rate their performance at the highest level than women and that their ratings overall were somewhat higher. It found little evidence that the performance review systems are themselves at fault.

Other research shows that women tend to undervalue the skill level of their jobs more than men, although they are more accurate in their assessment of their performance.

Those managing and participating in performance management in schools need to be aware of differences and to build into the associated training the opportunity to explore approaches to setting and meeting targets or objectives.

### Styles of working/leadership – competitive v. collaborative

Research on gender differences in managerial work indicates little difference in competency. However, gender role stereotyping is pervasive. Women are less likely than men to be perceived by both male and female managers as displaying the characteristics of an effective manager.

> The fact that women are consistently rated lower on 'leadership ability' by managers has important implications since leadership positions may be gender-biased if the more 'transformational' leadership style of women is not valued as equal to the more 'transactional' style of men. (Strebler et al, 1997)

51

Since leadership skills are increasingly seen as important prerequisites for more senior posts in schools, this perception could undermine the promotion prospects of women.

Team working rather than working as an individual is said to appeal to women. In some schools, performance management is seen as purely an individual activity. While this does need an individual focus, it need not be approached only as an individual activity. Many schools seek agreement to have at least one of each teacher's targets common to a team or even across the whole school, and develop ways of reviewing progress towards these collectively. And, while teachers' targets are confidential to them, some school teams agree to share their objectives and support each other in working towards them. The key issue to developing effective teamwork in relation to performance management, is the extent to which staff are committed in practice to the school's aims, direction for development and hence the priorities in the development plan, and within this, to the departmental targets and areas for improvement.

## What is to be done?

*Embed systems and ensure that they are consistent with the culture of the school*

After six years' experience of developing performance management systems in schools in England and Wales it should be possible to integrate the systems with the school's general planning and development processes and to ensure that their cycles are fully coordinated. They should also feed into the school's annual self-evaluation. One London school for instance, devotes one professional development day to its self-evaluation: all staff come together to review the achievements of the previous year and plan for the next. The various strands including the operation and outcomes of performance management are drawn together and fed into the draft of the next year's development plan.

Schools should feel sufficiently confident to adapt the procedures and documents provided by DfES as models to match their individual characteristics and contexts, while continuing to meet the requirements of the regulations.

*Value staff*

In many schools, the rhetoric of headteachers and governors valuing their staff has historically been at odds with how the school operated and certainly with the perceptions of staff. But many schools today have done much to demonstrate that they do value their staff, not only by dramatically improving the physical environment in which they work, but also by their recent policies and practices. In these schools, *all* staff are seen as having an entitlement to professional review and professional development as part of a broader set of entitlements. A middle school in Kent has recently instituted a new approach to such matters which it calls *All Staff Matter*, a reminder that it is the staff whose work will ensure that the approach promoted in *Every Child Matters* is put into effect.

Recognising the individual and collective achievement of staff is a powerful way of showing that the head, senior staff or governors value their work. It is said that women particularly thrive on praise and acknowledgment of their achievement.

*Improve communications with staff*

As new performance management regulations come into effect and new policies and procedures are introduced, staff need to be kept up to date and consulted about change not just on the mechanics of the process but also the intentions and the safeguards being built in to ensure fairness and equality. Questions such as 'How well is our performance management system working?' and 'Are the procedures operating fairly?' need to be asked and addressed straightforwardly and openly.

## Continuing professional development

There will always be tension between institutional needs and the allocation of scarce resources to professional development to meet individual needs. Part of the rationale for performance management is to be able to reconcile the two. Several issues arise about professional development, some relating to access to it and others to what is offered.

Allocation of resources for professional development must be managed carefully so that this it is appropriate and fair. A senior manager should be responsible for collating the professional development outcomes of review statements and monitoring how they are allocated. Part-time staff, predominantly women, are often at risk of being overlooked for professional development so not having equality of access to opportunities. They should have the same entitlement to time for performance management meetings and to professional development opportunities. A pro-rata approach based on full-time equivalence is inappropriate: if a new curriculum approach is to be implemented, part-time staff require the same training as full-timers.

The nature of professional development and how the school approaches it will heavily influence attitudes. Although professional development no longer means 'courses' many schools have yet to adopt more effective approaches which can be sustained, because of money and time. Coaching and mentoring is well developed in some schools and is making a major contribution to individual development in a supportive and flexible way. Peer support can greatly assist developing practice. For example, the use of triads – three members of staff who work together for mutual support – has proved productive, particularly as it dissociates aspects of professional development from hierarchical structures or management judgements about performance.

*Action: Continue to provide training in aspects of performance management*

In addition to training new members of staff and particularly new reviewers in procedures and skills, training is needed in managing equality and diversity to address individual prejudices and develop understanding of how stereotyping works. Governors' training also needs to include updating on gender issues.

*Action: Monitor the allocation of resources for professional development*

Without careful tracking of the spending of these scarce resources, it will be impossible to ensure that they are used for the purpose intended or that they are fairly allocated to different groups of staff.

## Monitoring and evaluation

Monitoring and evaluation have historically been the weak link in implementing performance management. Only by a systematic approach will women staff, staff from ethnic minorities and other groups be treated fairly within the systems. Judgements about the operation of the systems as a whole also require a systematic approach.

*Action: Capture data on the distribution of performance appraisal outcomes (performance categories, pay or bonus decisions) – by race, gender, disability*

At present, most schools lack data about the outcomes of performance reviews. The extent to

which targets have been met, outcomes of lesson observation and the sensitive matter of how staff have progressed through pay scales as a result of performance review, all need to be tracked to inform decisions about the improvement of systems.

*Action: Continue to monitor systems, procedures and management capability to ensure further progress*

It is not only the systems and procedures that need to be scrutinised but also the skills and attitudes of managers (reviewers) in carrying them out. Inequalities in practical aspects, such as the time made available for review meetings, and the conditions under which they are carried out, need to be identified, but so too do the ways in which managers approach the process. Responsibility for this monitoring needs to be clearly identified, and allocated to a senior manager. A small group of staff from different levels might support this process effectively.

*Action: Continue to provide training in aspects of performance management*

While new members of staff and particularly new reviewers need training in the procedures and skills needed, all need training in managing equality and diversity to address prejudices and develop understanding of stereotyping and its effects. Awareness can be raised of issues such as how it is possible to judge others' leadership styles.

*Action: Monitor staff experiences and perceptions of performance management – including checking completed forms, surveys of staff experiences and observing sample appraisal interviews.*

This should be an important part of the overall monitoring of performance management. The idea is to road test procedures for a selected sample of staff over a defined length of time, and to adapt processes accordingly, in particular to ensure fairness and equity. Teachers' perceptions of the process and comparing experiences across groups of staff should throw light on how the procedures are operating in practice.

### Audit trails of paperwork

Schools will need to be able to justify outcomes of performance reviews, judgments of reviewers and decisions about progression through pay scales. These must be supported by rigorous recording processes which enable any member of staff to challenge outcomes if they feel they have been treated unfairly.

Procedures and practices that take full account of how gender, ethnicity, disability, sexuality and age can lead to discrimination, coupled with robust opportunities for training to address particular needs – for example for returners after a career break – are in the best interests of everyone. Pupils benefit from more effective staff and a diverse range of role models and schools get value for money.

## References and further reading

Advisory Conciliation and Arbitration Service (2003) *Employee Appraisal*

DfES (2001) *Performance Management in Schools: Model Performance Management Policy*. London: DfES

DfES (2006) *Education (School Teacher Performance Management) (England) Regulations 2006: A guidance document*. London: DfES

Office for Standards in Education (2002) *Performance Management of Teachers*. London: HMSO

Strebler, M, Thompson, M, and Heron, P (1997) *Skills, Competencies and Gender: Issues for Pay and Training*. Brighton: Institute of Employment Studies

Tamkin, J, Rick, J and Bates, P (2000) *Equity Proofing in Performance Review in the Civil Service.* Brighton: Institute for Employment Studies

# Strategic Management of Information and Communications Technology

*Avril Loveless and Pippa Totraku*

■ *See also subject schedule: Information and Communications Technology*

## Learning in the 21st Century

Digital technologies shape many of the ways in which we conduct our daily social, economic and cultural activities. These are reflected in the life of the school, from daily routines to the design of learning environments. Bold claims are made for the potential of ICT to transform learning and teaching through being embedded in the curriculum and in the management of the school. The potential for transformations does not lie in the characteristics of the technologies themselves, but in the interaction between people and purpose in their use. All staff make decisions about the appropriate use of ICT in the whole school, and those with responsibility for strategic leadership, management and development need to consider how to create an environment for administration, learning, teaching and personal development which expresses understanding of the gender issues associated with ICT.

The schedule on the subject framework for ICT focuses on how members of staff and pupils can be aware of the differences in attitudes and access to ICT. This schedule considers how institutions respond to gender and ICT, and encompasses individuals and curriculum.

## Policy and the quality of ICT experience

The Government's E-learning strategy, Harnessing Technology (DfES, 2005), acknowledges the role that digital technologies can play in an education system which meets the needs of our society at the beginning of the 21st century, and presents a strategic approach to the use of ICT in education, skills and children's services. It proposes that, while integrated access to information and services, and strategic professional development for ICT capability, are useful starting points, the quality of the experience of using ICT can be identified through four key themes: personalisation, flexibility, productivity and inclusion. Staff responsible for the strategic management of ICT may find them useful in reviewing whether their school systems fully address the equity issues implicit in their use.

*Personalisation* focuses on how systems might conform and respond to learners, and offer support for individuals that reflects the diversity in their interests, needs and capabilities. ICT can offer personal virtual space in which learners can make choices and connections in their experience of the curriculum and access to expertise. There are implications for gender and ICT as the offer of a wider variety of choices in curriculum and teaching strategies may lead to gendered responses which need careful attention and monitoring. Certain curriculum subjects might be seen as inappropriate, irrelevant or boring by girls or boys. Indeed, this is particularly true of perceptions and take-up of ICT in the school curriculum. Conversely, unless we recognise some of the benefits of personalisation and the implications for personal access, autonomy and choice, pupils will continue to report frustration and disaffection with their school ICT experiences.

*Flexibility* provides opportunities for choice in the time and place of study, and the different groupings of learners in which that happens. Pupils and staff might wish to work within and beyond traditional school timetables and classroom spaces, but the consequences for school, social and family groupings and priorities have to be acknowledged and discussed.

*Productivity* highlights how ICT might improve efficiency and effectiveness in working practices and communications, for pupils as well as for staff, who need to be active in information retrieval, presentation, record keeping and information management across many dimensions of school life. Access and familiarity with the ICT resources needed to promote efficiency and productivity require levels of competence and confidence with the relevant tools. Perceptions and reporting of ICT skills and techniques are gendered – males are often perceived as, and report themselves to be, more confident with a range of ICT resources, and male pupils remark on the lack of competence and confidence in female staff. There are implications therefore, not only for the role models being presented in school, but also for the provision of appropriate, relevant and focused ICT training in authentic contexts.

*Inclusion* draws attention to the potential of ICT to overcome barriers to learning associated with motivation, engagement, expectations, access and special educational needs. Gender issues cut across these elements of experience, influenced by the themes of parental expectations, popular media, socioeconomic status, the male culture of ICT, age, staff and pupil experience of and attitudes to computers, curriculum design and teaching strategies.

## Reviewing whole-school ICT

The British Educational Communications Technology Agency (BECTA) has collaborated with other key agencies to present an online self-review framework for schools (see matrix.ncsl.org.uk/). The matrix for evaluation, planning and review provides a set of strands and statements to help identify general strengths and needs in the use of ICT across the range of school life. The table below and the following sections add a gender perspective to the matrix.

## Creating the conditions

The ethos of the school should be one in which staff and pupils recognise and value diversity, yet acknowledge the different ways in which gender bias pervades society and influences the choices pupils might make in their perceptions and use of ICT. The school should therefore challenge this bias in its styles of leadership and management, in its policies on teaching, learning and behaviour, and in the attitudes and conduct of staff and pupils. Assumptions about girls' and boys' interest and achievements in ICT can be restrictive and limiting, and the whole school community should be alerted to the gender stereotypes, such as that girls like communicating and collaborating with ICT or that boys like technical details and playing games. Leadership and management teams must discuss how these issues relating to gender and ICT are recognised, monitored, included in planning and target setting, and reported to governors.

| | Personalisation | Flexibility | Productivity | Inclusion |
|---|---|---|---|---|
| **Creating the conditions** | | | | |
| **Designing the learning environment** | **Factors which influence gender identity, experience and opportunity with ICT** parental expectations, popular media, socioeconomic status, the male culture of ICT, age, staff and pupil experience of and attitudes to computers, curriculum design and teaching strategies | | | |
| **Working with pupils** | **Stages of concern** ■ Stage 1: noticing the gender imbalance at home, school and in attitudes ■ Stage 2: changing female participation in ICT activities through role models and collaborative groups | | | |
| **Working with adults** | ■ Stage 3: challenging the dominant paradigm of ICT as culturally and historically male | | | |

### Issues to consider

- What models of confidence and competence in ICT use are promoted by all senior staff, and how is ICT training and support provided to promote such confidence and competence?
- What models of gender expectations are presented by partnerships with the school community – from work experience placements to working with trainee teachers?
- Is there an explicit policy which underpins the use of ICT and promotes a range of experiences for girls and boys?

## Designing the environment

Although access to ICT resources will not in itself bridge digital divides between girls and boys, it is important that the different modes of access provide opportunities for flexibility and personalisation. There needs to be a wide range of access to ICT devices, such as desktops in ICT suites for whole group work; laptops for more flexible working patterns in classrooms; tablet PCs and PDAs for mobility and immediacy in capturing and accessing data; and whiteboards for interactivity and projection. The environment should promote open access to all, and staff should be mindful of the ways in which boys can dominate ICT suites and spaces.

### Issues to consider

- Do all pupils have access to multimedia resources, online materials, secure email, social software and tools for collaboration?
- Is flexible access offered through wireless, broadband connectivity and virtual learning environments which challenges the time, place and manner in which pupils engage in learning activities?
- Do the software resources and associated materials used promote positive gender images, particularly within the predominant male culture of ICT and games?
- Do policies for internet access reflect awareness of issues of safety, privacy, and responsibility?
- Who has responsibility for making these decisions and evaluating developments with colleagues and pupils?

## Working with pupils

Pupils are influenced by and also shape the school ethos in gender matters. They can be made aware of the gender dimensions of ICT use, and suggest how to promote equity. Curriculum planning should reflect awareness of gender-specific and gender-neutral issues, from curriculum choices to curriculum resources. Assessment methods and attainment trends can be reviewed and monitored, and teaching strategies can be observed and reviewed.

### Issues to consider

- What are pupils' perceptions of their experiences of ICT in school?
- How do they use ICT as a tool for learning in the curriculum?
- What are their perceptions of ICT as a discrete subject?
- What are some of the differences between school and home use of ICT?
- Are there gender differences in the pupils' responses? How might staff and pupils discuss the possible reasons and ways forward?
- How is usage and participation monitored, and how are pupils made aware of and able to discuss such monitoring?

## Working with adults

The role models presented by all adults working in and associated with the school are important in addressing gender stereotypes and assumptions. These will include all those seen to be using ICT in the life of the school: teachers, teaching assistants, senior management, technicians, librarians, trainee teachers, administrators, governors, parents, carers and visitors working on a variety of projects, from youth workers to theatre companies. Developing positive and challenging role models might require a range of strategies, from presenting a clear rationale for a shared understanding of gender and ICT when recruiting staff, to devising opportunities for critical, informed and active professional development within the school CPD programme. Parents and the wider community can be used to promote positive role models, and contribute to creative networks and partnerships in the use of ICT for activities within and beyond the school gates.

## Issues to consider

■ How do staff share and develop their understanding of the issues with each other?

■ How might gender and ICT be included in other CPD programmes?

■ Is there a need for focused CPD in this area?

■ How do school staff model their own learning with digital technologies?

■ How might parents be informed of the issues and their influence on gender identities with ICT?

■ How might the school ICT resources be made available to the community for activities which promote and challenge issues of gender?

Each school will need to address these questions in conjunction with other areas of review and evaluation, and each school context will be different in the range of practices, understandings and needs.

## References

DfES (2005) *Harnessing Technology: transforming learning and children's services.* London: Department for Education and Skills

Fisher, T., Higgins, C., and Loveless, A. (2006) *Teachers Learning with Digital Technologies: A review of research and projects.* Bristol: Futurelab

Gansmo, H. (2005) *Primary and Secondary Education: The Distinctive Role of Schools in the Inclusion of Girls in ICT.* SIGIS Strategies of Inclusion: Gender and the Information Society

Green, H., Facer, K., Rudd, T., Dillon, P., and Humphreys, P. (2006). *Personalisation and Digital Technologies.* Bristol: Futurelab

Jarvis, J., Mavers, D., Saxon, D., and Woodrow, D. (2005) *ICT Test Bed: Learner Perceptions of the Impact of ICT on Their Education.* London: DfES

Littleton, K., and Hoyles, C. (2002) The gendering of information technology. In A. Rubin (Ed) *Ghosts in the Machine: Women's Voices in Research with Technology.* New York: Peter Lang Publishing Inc

Livingstone, S., Bober, M., and Helsper, E. (2005) *Inequalities and the Digital Divide in Children and Young People's Internet Use.* London: London School of Economics and Political Science

NCSL and BECTA (2006) *Matrix: Evaluate, Plan, Review.* Available online: [matrix.ncsl.org.uk] Accessed 22nd August 2006

# The Wider School Workforce

*Hazel Taylor*

■ *See also schedules: Every Child Matters; Leadership; Continuing Professional Development; Performance Management*

The wider school workforce in the UK has expanded considerably in the 21st century. Additional posts have been created and existing ones reshaped as a result of the workforce remodelling agenda, the development of extended schools, and the implementation of *Every Child Matters*. A school can now have as many or more non-teaching as teaching posts.

This wider workforce consists of directly employed staff, staff employed by contractors providing a service to the school, and staff employed by other agencies working regularly or intermittently in the school. There may well also be volunteers. The management of these various groups has many gender implications.

Broadly, the workforce in addition to teachers includes:

■ a varied range of school posts supporting pupils and the curriculum directly – for instance teaching assistants, learning mentors, technicians, language assistants, therapists and others working with pupils with special educational needs, examination invigilators, cover supervisors and lunchtime supervisors

■ a complex structure of clerical and administrative staff servicing the overall running of the school and carrying out many duties previously done by teachers – such as financial management, examination administration, data entry and analysis, pupil support, network management and technical support, attendance monitoring, cover,

administration for work-related learning, publicity, admissions, reception and reprographics, among others

■ teams of staff, who may be employed by separate contractors, providing premises management, cleaning and catering services

■ visiting staff from other professional groups – these include psychologists, nurses and nutrition advisers among many others who have a direct impact on pupils' lives. They are attached to schools but not employed by them.

In addition, parents, volunteers, governors and others from the community may visit regularly. They all share an interest in the school and wish to contribute to it.

All of these people influence pupils, and bring with them their own beliefs about gender. As they interact with pupils in informal settings, such as the dining hall or the playground, or work with them individually or in small groups, and as they are not traditional authority figures, they can have enormous influence on children's beliefs and behaviour, and can be very powerful role models.

The school has three responsibilities to them: to be an equal opportunities employer; to induct all of them into the values and practices that ensure gender equality in the school – for adults and pupils alike; and to learn from them where they have valuable experience to contribute.

## The wider workforce and gender equity

Everyone working in the school with reasonable frequency needs to be aware of the school's equal opportunities policy and the values which underpin it. This can be done in a variety of informal ways, and also be a part of a formal induction programme.

Managers can ensure that in establishing working practices, they include guidance on such things as avoiding sexist language and having the same expectations of pupils of both sexes. It is important, too, to include all staff in any training on equity issues, and to make sure it is possible for them to attend. Leaflets and posters in staff areas are useful reminders.

## Issues to consider

Where adults are seen as role models, it is useful to discuss what sort of model is being presented, and what its implicit messages are for gendered behaviours. For example, site management staff may offer male role modelling of practical skills – which is helpful as long as it does not imply that only boys and men can do these things.

- How might gender equity awareness be built into the induction of all new staff?
- How is information made available to non-teaching staff? How are they included in formal training opportunities?
- What use does the school make of the life experiences and role modelling offered by its wider staff?

## Being an equal opportunities employer

Historically, school workforces have been highly gender stereotyped, with female clerical and administrative staff, cleaners, catering and pupil support staff, and male premises managers. This pattern is no longer so obvious, and the increase in the range and levels of responsibility of the wider range of posts has led to better promotion opportunities, a more professional workplace, and the necessity for good quality training.

However, there are still gender imbalances, with jobs needing high level ICT skills attracting men and reinforcing pupils' perceptions of ICT as a boy thing, while pupil support posts attract women, and reinforce perceptions of care as a girl thing. Where this is changing, schools have found that job titles affect the gender of applicants, and that applicants of both sexes are encouraged when the skill set that the post needs is made clear. Unskilled posts vary greatly from area to area in whom they attract, depending on the local labour market. Where they attract people from ethnic minorities, it is important that this is not giving a negative message about the value of minority groups.

The gender balance of the various parts of the wider work force needs to be monitored, and steps taken to improve the balance in areas of obvious disparity.

Non-teaching staff are entitled to a performance management structure comparable to that of teachers but without the compulsory performance/pay progression link, based on review and discussion of performance, and an entitlement to training. This is in place in schools with Investors In People accreditation, and the Investors standards provide useful guidance. For many female employees, this can lead to recognition of talent, and to further qualifications and promotion. When incorporating new posts, it is important to ensure parity for jobs of equal value, and to build in a career structure. Working in a school office is no longer a little job for a local mother, but a serious job for anyone.

Skills for new posts, including advanced ICT skills, can be gained with encouragement to train. When recruiting, it is important to recognise the value of prior experience in a diversity of areas, and to ensure that interviewers are trained in equal opportunities procedures. Disciplinary procedures for any form of sex discrimination are likely to be laid down in local agreements, but where schools are not bound by these, model procedures are available from trade unions.

## Issues to consider

- How and where are posts advertised and presented to attract applicants from both sexes and all sections of the community?
- Are there clear structures for review, training and progression for the wider workforce, and parity of pay for jobs of equal value?
- Is the work of support staff valued by teachers, and their skills recognised?
- Are there clear procedures for the investigation of sexual harassment, bullying, or other forms of sex discrimination?

## Working with contractors and other site users

Obviously, the school does not have control of the recruitment, pay and conditions of staff employed by contractors or external agencies, though any contractor working for a public body is covered by the Gender Equality Duty 2007. However, it can influence, and it can require adherence to its policies concerning behaviour on the premises. School staff can raise awareness of gender and other equity issues with contractors, and achieve a great deal through modelling and negotiation.

It is also important for school representatives in partnerships with outside bodies to raise gender issues and seek to influence practice amongst those visiting the school regularly.

The wider workforce is a valuable resource. It offers models of a wide range of employment areas, it provides essential backup for teaching and learning, and it is a source of employment for the local community. The school needs to ensure that:

■ it has the status it deserves

■ it is recognised as skilled and professional, and is appropriately rewarded.

Good equal opportunities employment practice and induction into the school's procedures and practices will enable everyone to benefit.

*With many thanks to Cheryl Day and Helen Edwards of Clapton Girls' Technology College*

# Home-school relations

*Meg McGuire*

■ *See also schedules: Continuing Professional Development; Governors; Pastoral Care: Care for Pupils as Learners, Persons and Citizens*

## Challenges in establishing equitable home-school relations

Good home-school relations enhance children's progression in school, and active partnership is a key element of contemporary educational policy (Hallgarten, 2000). All schools are required to take steps to ensure that parents and schools work together and that parental partnerships are part of the discourse of compulsory education. 'Parents' is used throughout the schedule to denote both parents and carers.

New Labour has developed a two-fold approach that seeks to:

■ make schools and teachers accountable to parents through monitoring and reporting on their work

■ encourage parents to take on more responsibility for their children's learning and behaviour.

The challenges for schools and parents in establishing supportive and useful relationships are linked to differences in social class, culture and ethnicity, and each of these variables has gender dimensions. Barriers to equity of access to the school, and to mutual understanding, have to be identified then removed so that parents can support their child's learning and schools can plan their teaching in the most effective ways. Men and women from all communities will have differing experiences and beliefs about the education system, relating to their own experience of it, their own culture's perceptions of it, and their aspirations for their children. These may also vary depending on each child's gender.

Research demonstrates that middle class parents are generally better placed to supplement their child's education, for example through private tutors and music teachers, or to get specialist diagnoses of learning difficulties and to ask for extra support in school. It also suggests that middle class parents are skilled at manipulating the system to gain advantage for their own children, for example by accessing a school which scores highly in league tables. It is usually mothers who find information and make visits, while fathers are brought in to support decisions.

Reay (1998) showed how middle class mothers kept a careful watch on the schools attended by their children. They were more likely than working class mothers to approach teachers or send letters to complain or ask for information. Working class parents, again mainly mothers, were more likely to be seen by schools as a nuisance or as less good at parenting. Some studies found that they were blamed for some of the consequences of living in circumstances of relative poverty.

Ethnic minority parents often become anxious about schooling long before the children go to school. They are worried about the possibilities of racism and how this might affect their children. Many are aware of reports about black under-achievement and higher levels of exclusion from school. When their children start school, they invariably feel that their views are not taken into account. Some parents report that schools hold lower expectations of their children. (Cork, 2005; Crozier and Reay, 2005). It is worth reporting the views of a black supplementary school teacher in the study undertaken by Reay and Safia-Mirza (2005: 149):

Our parents feel very strongly that they are not listened to. The education system has a very long history of keeping parents out... I think it's part of that history, you know, 'We're the teachers, we know best'. It's partly to do with class but it is also because whenever they see Black parents opening their mouths they see them as creating discord or problems.

### *Issues to consider*

In developing exemplary practice, schools may find the following sets of points helpful.

### Barriers to approaching the school

■ Which parents might not understand why certain practices are being employed, for example learning through play, and may not feel confident enough to question their child's teacher?

■ Which parents might not feel comfortable or even welcome in their child's school? Black parents in Birmingham reported that they were more often involved in conversations with teachers about their children's behaviour than about their schoolwork (Cork, 2005)

■ How can teachers respond positively to parents who seem threatening, and avoid interpreting interest as aggression?

■ Do teachers want to feel that they are in control in their classrooms and that their expertise is being called into question by enthusiastic but uninformed parents?

■ How do you support those parents facing acutely difficult circumstances, whose anxiety and depression might fuel tensions that flare up when they come to school to talk to teachers about their children?

### Language, assumptions and stereotyping

■ Does the school documentation assume that parents are a homogenous group? What account is taken of gender, class or ethnic differences? For instance, the views of fathers and mothers may differ. How does the school show it recognises the diversity of family structures, including single parents and gay and lesbian families?

■ How does the school show it appreciates the complex circumstances that some families, and mothers in particular, face, such as poor housing, reduced income, lack of wider support, enforced mobility and, possibly, related health problems?

■ Are there flexible and dynamic approaches to arranging meetings that recognise complex working patterns?

■ Is the language in newsletters, documents, and invitations inclusive of all the adults who care for the children who attend the school?

### In-school provision

■ What provision is made in the school to include parents? What written information is provided? What is on the school website? What languages are used?

■ Are rooms available for parents where they can wait or meet one another and exchange information about the school and education in general?

■ Are there any regular newsletters or magazines for parents? If parents are involved in producing them, which parents are involved? Which ones are less involved or not involved at all?

■ What support is given to parents or carers (who may be older siblings), grandparents or other relatives, who are new arrivals to help them to understand the UK system?

■ What attempts are made to reach out to non-resident fathers (or – less often – mothers)?

### The composition of in-school parent groups such as the PTA

■ Is there fair representation in terms of gender, ethnicity, and sexual orientation on home-school committees?

■ Is there access for and representation of parents with disabilities or those parents whose children have learning difficulties or physical disabilities?

■ What steps are being taken to ensure greater representation on school committees? Whose job is this?

■ Which parents hold positions of responsibility? Are they familiar with equity issues? If not, how can they be supported in this area?

### Helping the school staff work effectively with parents

■ Have newly qualified teachers been trained to work in a non-discriminatory and non-stereotyped manner with parents?

■ Have all front line staff been supported through training to deal with parents courteously and respectfully? Do they have easy access to information sheets or volunteer translators in the key languages that are used in the catchment area, so that they can be responsive to new parents whose English is poor?

■ How are school staff supported in their partnerships with parents from any minority group?

## Inclusion

■ Do the school's texts, posters, books and other resources recognise the activism of black and white working class parents who have campaigned for a more inclusive education?

■ Are working class families viewed as 'deficient' implicitly or explicitly by any staff? If so, how are these views challenged?

■ Does the school hold high aspirations for all its children and pupils, and is this reflected in their partnerships with parents?

## Towards better partnerships

Partnerships can be actively encouraged by:

■ developing spaces and opportunities where less privileged parents have a voice and some representation

■ employing an outreach worker to enhance home-school relationships and assure better representation

■ providing spaces for parent-only discussions (taking the T out of the PTA)

■ providing more support through booklets, drop in sessions, parent-led surgeries for parents who want to be more involved in their children's learning, focused to take account of needs at different phases

■ providing more information and training in areas such as ICT, literacy, numeracy, supporting homework

■ establishing newsletters produced by or with parents, available on print and online

■ establishing a regular time each week for teachers, heads of year and mentors to talk with parents

■ providing bilingual staff or other volunteers to translate and welcome

■ formally auditing what is currently provided, setting targets that are implemented with care and sensitivity, monitored and reviewed annually and formally reported to the school governors.

There could be a longer term democratic aim for parents to become more directly involved in wider decision-making about education policy and provision, and not just only in a partnership concerning their own children's education. More teachers could gain some direct experience of the backgrounds of their main groups of children, through paid exchange schemes or community involvement. But any strategy adopted, big or small, needs to be carefully monitored to ensure that any improvements in home-school partnerships do not shore up or contribute towards more inequality in schools.

> The most effective ways of gaining the parents' support and cooperation was to listen to their concerns, consult them about and give them a voice on important issues, both pastoral and academic, and perhaps most importantly, show them respect by acting on their concerns and not merely involving them in a tokenistic way. (Blair, 2001:38)

## References

Blair, M. (2001) The Education of Black Children: Why do some schools do better than others, in: Majors, R. (ed) *Educating our Black Children: New Directions and Radical Approaches*. London: RoutledgeFalmer.

Cork, L. (2005) *Supporting Black Pupils and Parents*. London: Routledge

Crozier, G. and Reay, D. (eds) (2005) *Activating Participation: Parents and Teachers Working Towards Partnership*. Stoke on Trent: Trentham Books

David, M. E. (1993) *Parents, Gender and Education Reform*. Cambridge: Polity Press

Hallgarten, J. (2000) *Parents Exist, OK! Issues and Visions for Parent-school Relationships*. London: IPPR

Maguire, M., Wooldridge, T. and Pratt-Adams, S. (2006) *The Urban Primary School*. Maidenhead: Open University Press (see chapter 5)

Reay, D. (1998) *Class Work Mothers' Involvement in their Children's Primary Schooling*. London: UCL Press

Reay, D. and Safia-Mirza, H. (2005) Doing Parental Involvement Differently: black women's participation as educators and mothers in black supplementary schooling, in Crozier, G. and Reay, D. *op. cit*

Vincent, C. (2000) *Including Parents? Education, Citizenship and Parental Agency*. Buckingham: Open University Press

## Useful contacts

The Advisory Centre for Education, 1c Aberdeen Studies, 22 – 24 Highbury Grove, London N5 2DQ (Tel: 020 7704 3370) www. ace-ed.org.uk (has links to other related sites)

Parentline Plus www.parentlineplus.org.uk (Tel: 0808 800 222)

Fathers Direct at www.fathersdirect.com

There are useful suggestions for schools at www.teachernet.gov.uk/wholeschool/familyand community/workingwithparents/

This site details a training pack for secondary schools, *Involving Parents, Raising Achievement* (IPRA) that can be downloaded or obtained from 0845 60222 60 (Ref: PICE/IPRA). The IPRA pack contains some good ideas for primary schools too.

# Managing Behaviour

*Lynda Haddock and Leora Cruddas*

■ *See also schedules: Design for Learning; Pastoral Care: Care for Pupils as Learners, Persons and Citizens; Lesbian, Gay, Bisexual and Trans Issues in Schools; Breaktimes, Lunchtimes and Playgrounds*

## The context

Initiatives to help schools manage behaviour range from targeted behaviour improvement projects and behaviour education support teams, to anti-bullying programmes, and the national behaviour and attendance programme now incorporated into the national strategy for school improvement.

However, there is more to be done in relation to the identification and monitoring of the significant gender differences in the ways schools respond to challenging and problem behaviours. Who is given sanctions for their behaviour, for example, and who is offered support?

## Labelling pupils

Even in well-ordered classrooms and schools, some pupils experience emotional distress and behave in ways that are puzzling and challenging. Having social, emotional and behavioural difficulties (SEBD) is a tricky label. Emotional difficulties are experienced by everyone at some time in their lives. We must be wary of describing pupils who are reacting to a stressful but short-lived event as having 'special educational needs'.

An important part of teachers' responses to challenging or puzzling behaviour is to reflect on our own reactions to a pupil. We will want to consider whether the learning environment is sufficiently supportive and whether our perceptions of the pupil are influenced by stereotypical assumptions about how boys and girls do, and should, behave.

A further difficulty with the SEBD label is that its application can involve class, gender and culture-based judgements about what are and are not appropriate behaviours. We need methods of assessment that make the judgements as explicit, transparent and negotiable as possible, and that are focused on getting the right help to pupils who need it. There is a prominent gender issue here: typically, two-thirds of pupils who are labelled as having social, emotional and behaviour difficulties are boys – so resources are skewed towards supporting boys. Yet, although they receive more of the available resources, boys are also more likely than girls to be excluded.

## Bullying

Bullying causes misery in children's lives; tackling it successfully involves the commitment of the whole school community. Schools that provide a safe environment for pupils establish an ethos of open communication. Many schools use their peer counsellors and playground buddies to help support children and young people. Vulnerable pupils are sometimes supported by a circle of friends. This approach establishes a tight structure of peer support around a child that is mediated and monitored by an adult.

Teachers should be aware of the different forms that bullying can take between boys and girls. Research tells us that girls' friendships are more intense than those of boys but can also be a source of tension and conflict (Besag, 2006). Girls may be more likely to use covert psychological, emotional or social methods of hurting each other than boys, who are more likely to attack each other physically. The consequence of psychological bullying can be devastating and long-lasting.

Schools naturally reflect the society beyond their gates and sexist, racist and homophobic bullying all take place in schools. Any hostile or insulting action that refers to a pupil's gender, skin colour, cultural or religious background, ethnic origin or sexual orientation is bullying. Such behaviour may take the form of physical, verbal or emotional abuse, insulting comments or 'jokes', offensive graffiti or ridiculing of customs or behaviour. It is important that schools adopt a broad definition of bullying that recognises the different forms that it can take, and make clear that racism, sexism and homophobia are not accepted.

This schedule aims to help schools think about and respond to some of the underlying gender issues in both behaviour management and school support systems. It raises gender issues related to bullying and harassment in schools. The schedule also encourages a better understanding of the links between behaviour and learning, and a deeper understanding of behaviour for learning. Are staff aware of differences between the learning behaviours of boys and girls? How can understanding of learning behaviours contribute to improved behaviour and higher achievement in schools?

## What the research says...
### Resources and targeted support
- Research studies show resources to support behaviour are often skewed towards boys, with fewer girls getting the attention and support they need (Cruddas and Haddock, 2003; Osler and Vincent, 2003)

- Girls often suffer painful emotions silently. They rely more heavily on social support than boys. In many cases, they internalise their difficulties and withdraw from adults and peers. In extreme cases, this can result in self-harm and suicide. Girls, like boys, also 'act out' in ways that schools find difficult to manage. The sanctions that girls receive can be heavier than boys for exactly the same behaviour because of our assumptions about gender-appropriate behaviour

- Many social, emotional and behavioural issues stop girls from learning, including health issues, emotional problems and coping with changes and transitions. But assessment procedures in schools are often pre-occupied with 'challenging' behaviour (Cruddas and Haddock, 2003). Girls are very clear that they need to:

- be supported by better pastoral systems
- be listened to
- be heard above the boys
- be treated as equals
- have dedicated spaces in school
- share problems with each other
- have opportunities in school to explore friendship (Cruddas and Haddock, 2003).

### Classroom behaviour
- Teachers' attention is often directed towards the more dominant boys. By giving attention to boys' challenging and disruptive behaviour, teachers can contribute to some groups of boys distancing themselves from schoolwork – and winning peer support by doing so

- Research on raising boys' achievement (Younger et al, 2005) argues that some boys protect their sense of self-worth by behaviours that prevent them, and others in their class, from achieving well. Younger and Warrington et al argue for a range of socio-cultural approaches to integrate these boys more fully into school life

- Because many research projects have focused on how boys dominate teacher time, classroom space and girls, we know relatively little about girls' relations with each other and how this affects their learning. Hey (1997) writing about how girls negotiate classrooms through the infinite changes of their friendship groups, states:

  As a teacher I too have often witnessed these 'infinite changes,' frequently mopped away tears and lost count of the times the minutiae of girls' passions fractured the rhythms and flows of our official classroom routine. (1997, p27)

- Since girls' friendships have the power to support or disrupt learning, we need a more rigorous understanding of friendships and associated behaviours, and how to manage and support them.

- Not all problematic behaviour involves challenge and acting out. Both boys and girls play truant in mind by avoiding getting involved in lessons, but girls are more likely to use this behaviour in an attempt to be invisible in the classroom. Often these girls are rewarded for the presentation of their work but not sufficiently challenged or stretched in their learning

### *Bullying*

■ Girls may be more subtle and covert than boys are in the ways they bully, and effects can last longer and be more painful than a physical attack. Besag (2006) describes the ways in which girls can use exclusion from a favoured group to hurt their class-mates. Teachers are reported to find quarrels between girls time-consuming and difficult to resolve. Sometimes they ignore the girls' hurtful behaviour or dismiss it as unimportant.

■ Research sponsored by the DfES (2002) in mainly white schools found that a quarter of pupils from minority ethnic backgrounds had experienced racist name-calling within the previous seven days. A third of pupils from ethnic minority backgrounds, interviewed for the same study, described experiences of hurtful name-calling and verbal abuse.

### *Issues to consider*

#### Behaviour management systems

■ Are there negotiated and agreed expectations in the school? Have all members of the school community contributed to their development? Have any differences in responses between boys and girls been analysed and taken into account in policy development?

■ Do all pupils know how their successes, both academic and social, will be recognised and rewarded? Is the progress pupils make socially rewarded, as well as their academic success? Is there an awareness that boys and girls might value different rewards?

■ Are all pupils and other adults in the school aware of the consequences of expectations about behaviour not being met? Are these consequences applied consistently and fairly? Are there any differences in their application between boys and girls?

■ Has there been an audit of trouble spots in the school? Are there any areas where girls or boys do not feel safe? Toilets and changing rooms are often cited by young people.

■ In many secondary schools there are more boys than girls. If this is the case, what is done to ensure that girls feel safe and confident?

■ Is data about the school's behaviour management system analysed? For example, what does the data show about the numbers of girls and boys referred through the systems? Who is punished and who is supported? What does the data on permanent and fixed-term exclusion show?

■ Are there any assumptions made about gender in escalation routes and the ways in which sanctions and support are given?

#### Understanding problematic behaviours

■ How is problem behaviour defined? Does the school have a broad definition of behaviours that cause concern, which includes internalised and externalised behaviour problems?

■ Does the accepted understanding of problem behaviours include those resulting from low self-esteem, difficulties with feelings and self-understanding?

■ How is emotional difficulty defined? Is there an understanding that everyone – boys and girls – experience emotional difficulties at times?

■ What messages are sent by the labels that pupils are given?

■ Is there a difference in the way that girls' problem behaviours and boys' problem behaviours are understood and supported?

■ Is there an awareness of the different social and family pressures on girls and boys? For example, some pupils, more often girls than boys, may have heavy domestic responsibilities, including caring for others, that interfere with their ability to complete homework?

■ Is there a clear focus on behaviour for learning?

#### Classroom organisation

■ Are there opportunities for teachers to observe and discuss patterns of classroom interaction in supportive ways?

■ How are groups within the classroom organised? Are girls used to police the boys, for example in seating plans? Are girls' friendship networks recognised and used to support learning?

■ Are quiet pupils – boys and girls – identified, supported and helped to understand the importance of active participation in lessons?

#### Behaviour in the corridors and the playground

■ Is there somewhere safe for girls to go at break and lunch times?

■ Is there a peer mentoring or playground buddy scheme? If so are there any patterns with which groups of pupils get involved? Are the schemes meeting the needs of both boys and girls?

## Support and pastoral systems

■ Are there girls' spaces in school – a quiet place at lunchtime, girls-only PE classes?

■ Are there spaces where boys who do not want to rush around or play football can be peaceful?

■ Are vulnerable pupils identified prior to transition so that support can be put in place? In secondary schools, are pupils allowed to maintain friendship networks from primary school?

■ In mixed secondary schools, would girls benefit from girls-only clubs in Year 7 (or other year of entry)?

■ Are there procedures in place for listening to pupils' views about all aspects of school organisation? Are the differing views of boys and girls considered? Are the views responded to?

## Bullying and harassment

■ Does the school policy on bullying and harassment recognise that patterns of bullying by different groups may be different?

■ Has consideration been given to designating particular leisure areas for single-sex groups or for younger pupils?

■ Are incidents of bullying and harassment rigorously recorded?

■ What does the data show about the numbers of girls and boys reporting incidents of bullying and harassment? Who is bullied or harassed, and who does the bullying or harassment?

■ Do both boys and girls feel safe to report bullying, racial or sexual harassment?

■ Are there gender differences in the way in which incidents of bullying and harassment are dealt with?

■ Are services and support for lesbian and gay students advertised in the school?

■ Have pupils been asked how safe they feel in different areas of the school? Are possible trouble spots well supervised?

■ Are pupils taught practical ways of dealing with bullies?

■ Are peer counsellors, mentors and buddies aware of the different forms that bullying might take? Are all groups in the school given the same opportunities and encouragement to become peer counsellors?

■ Have parents, governors and the wider school community been involved in developing the school's anti-bullying policy?

## Staff training

■ Have all staff been trained with regard to gender awareness and in ways of supporting the emotional and social development of children and young people? Are new staff inducted effectively into the school's systems?

■ Are staff supported in reflecting on the part their own behaviour, understanding and feelings play in determining a child's behaviour?

■ Are staff supported in their work with challenging and stressed pupils? Are there opportunities to discuss the impact of this work with a skilled professional, either individually or as a member of a staff group?

■ Are staff trained in the use of pupil-centred, problem-solving approaches to understanding and helping to resolve difficulties faced by individual pupils?

## References and further resources

Besag, V. (2006) *Understanding Girls' Friendships, Fights and Feuds.* Buckingham: Open University Press

Circle of Friends. Information available on line from www.inclusive-solutions.com/research

Collins, J. (1998) *Playing Truant in Mind: The Social Exclusion of Quiet Pupils.* Paper presented at the British Educational Research Association Annual Conference, The Queen's University of Belfast, August 27th – 30th 1998 Available online at: www.leeds.ac.uk/educol/documents/000000779.doc

Cruddas, L. and Haddock, L. (2003) *Girls' Voices: Supporting Girls' Learning and Emotional Development.* Stoke-on Trent: Trentham Books

Gender and Achievement website: www.standards.dfes.gov.uk/genderandachievement/

Hey, V. (1997) *The Company She Keeps: Ethnography of Girls' Friendships.* Buckingham: Open University Press

The National Children's Bureau has a comprehensive anti-bullying website: www.gethelpwithbullying.org.uk

Osler, A. and Vincent, K. (2003) *Girls and Exclusion: Rethinking the Agenda.* London: RoutledgeFalmer

Stonewall. The campaign to tackle homophobia in schools can be downloaded from www.stonewall.org.uk/education_for_all

Younger, M. and Warrington, M. with Gray, J., Rudduck, J., McLellan, R., Bearne, E., Kershner, R. and Bricheno, P. (2005) *Raising Boys' Achievement: A Study Funded by the Department for Education and Skills,* (DfES Research Report RR63). DfES Publications (also published on the DfES Gender and Achievement website, www.dfes.gov.uk/genderandachievement)

# Pastoral Care: Care for Pupils as Learners, Persons and Citizens
## Colleen McLaughlin

■ *See also schedules: Every Child Matters; Home-School Relations; Managing Behaviour; Breaktimes, Lunchtimes and Playgrounds; It's My School: The Power of Pupil Voice; Mentoring and Learning*

The phrase *pastoral care* is used in the UK to describe the care, support and guidance aspects of the school's work. Pastoral work is focused on the personal, social, emotional and physical aspects of pupils' development. We know that these aspects of education are very important and closely related to the academic achievement of pupils in school (Rutter, 1991). We also know that, in the reactive and proactive work undertaken in schools, there are significant gender differences and that these have consequences, for example whether you get a punishment or help for a particular action or way of behaving. What pupils learn from how we behave as teachers and other adults in the school, and how we respond according to gender affects them deeply. The ways in which we learn our gender roles is a particularly interesting area to examine since it is often problem-focused and can show us how we have learnt to understand what our gender implies for us.

A useful framework for examining gender and pastoral work is to look at the gendered messages in how the systems operate, and what is learned from them; how staff work with individuals and groups; and how the school interacts with the community and family members.

This schedule aims to help in the development and monitoring of pastoral work that challenges unhelpful stereotypes, and which gives children and young people the opportunity to develop fully. It can be used by individuals or by pastoral staff (for example form teachers, tutors, coordinators of learning, teaching assistants and mentors), senior staff or other groups of staff, in all phases, to discuss and monitor the work in the school. This area is often the most unexamined aspect of a school's work.

## Examples of research studies

We know that pastoral work involves much gender differentiation, and that inadvertently staff may discriminate. For example, research studies have shown the following forms of gender difference and discrimination:

■ in how we allocate resources, including time and money, to pupils on the basis of their gender eg to students with emotional difficulties. Girls and boys get treated differently for the same actions and difficulties according to what we see as acceptable in the different sexes (Osler and Vincent, 2003)

■ in how girls and boys respond to emotional difficulties. Girls tend to rely on social support when they are in difficulty and are more at risk when these relationships are under pressure or become unsupportive. They tend to internalise and withdraw as a way of coping (Dennison and Coleman, 2000)

■ in how we respond to bullying incidents; how girls and boys perceive different forms of bullying; and how girls and boys behave and cope when being bullied (Cowie, 2000; McLaughlin, 2004).

*Issues to consider*
## Organisations, systems and the management of care
*Roles and messages*

■ What messages are sent by the allocation of roles and actions? For example, what forms of discipline are applied by whom? Who undertakes the caring roles? Are there gender differences in the hierarchy of the system?

■ What models of care and support are provided by the system? Are there mechanisms for discussing equal opportunities policy and practice with all staff involved – support staff, lunchtime supervisors, learning and teaching assistants?

■ Is there a pastoral/academic split in terms of how gender issues are dealt with? How are gender stereotypes challenged by pastoral staff?

■ How are meetings conducted and by whom? Is it an inclusive and team-based, cooperative approach? How are the model of care and the style of meetings described?

■ What systems exist for receiving feedback from pupils regarding their needs and pastoral work? Who gets to participate and to be listened to most? What do pupils feel about how the different genders are treated in the pastoral aspects of the school's work?

■ What gender language is used to pupils, and what messages are sent about appropriate gender behaviour?

*Monitoring and using data*
It can be useful to see if there are different patterns for girls and boys in the everyday activities of the school and in the areas of pastoral work. Some of the areas that could be examined are:

■ attendance patterns and gender differences. What patterns are there for girls and boys and how do they differ in different year groups? How does the system respond to these gender patterns? Do either girls or boys truant from particular subject areas, and if so how is this dealt with?

■ referrals to outside agencies, and in particular the differences between referrals for boys and girls who have the same difficulties

■ punishment and exclusion data

■ who gets the attention in terms of the resources of the pastoral team

■ the assumptions made about gender in discussions about pupils or the school's reactions to pupil actions

## Working with individuals and groups
The questions in this section relate to proactive or reactive work with individual pupils or groups. Begin by looking at the balance between proactive and reactive work. Pastoral systems can become fire-fighting systems that do not react constructively to the issues often raised by pupils' challenging behaviours. Rather than focusing on making the pastoral system a support for learning and affiliation with the school it can become a system of negative monitoring. For example, friendship difficulties are predictable. Including an element in the curriculum on relationships and friendships to develop this aspect of social education is more constructive than responding to particular incidents.

*Working with groups*

■ Are there gender stereotypes in the labelling of groups of pupils?

■ How are sexual and gender based bullying treated? Are some forms of bullying treated as more serious than others?

■ If there are anti-bullying and peer support systems in operation, what is the gender balance amongst the pupils involved? Research suggests that girls tend to play a disproportionate role as mentors and peer supporters (Cowie, 2000). How is possible to make caring acceptable to boys if this is the case?

■ What gender models are the pupils acting on in their peer groups? Does this merit some intervention and work with groups?

■ What is the gender and ethnic balance amongst groups and individuals given responsibility?

■ What is the gender and ethnic pattern in the rewards system? Are certain behaviours, which may be gender specific, rewarded more than others?

■ Are certain groups punished more than others? Does it reflect stereotypes about age, gender or ethnicity?

■ What messages are sent by the pastoral system about the inclusion of different groups of pupils in the school, and do they contain gender or ethnic discriminatory elements? We know that schools send messages about who is successful and what is rewarded. The more inclusive and the wider the net that can be cast, the more students will connect to the school and to learning.

### Working with individuals

When we are working with individual difficulties and trying to support pupils, issues related to gender arise. We know that there are differences in terms of gender and culture in how young people respond to distress, for example. Girls tend to rely on social relationships and to internalise distress. Boys often don't have enough relationships to sustain them in times of difficulty. We do know that peer relationships are very important, and that in caring for pupils, we need to build their capacity to communicate about their difficulties and to have a wider repertoire of resources, both internal and external, to draw upon. Some questions that are useful to examine here are:

■ what are the responses of staff to pupils' difficulties, and are there gender and cultural stereotypes in their responses? For example, not taking seriously a boy's loss of a significant relationship?

■ what types of support and guidance, for example about subject choice, are offered to particular individuals, and are there gender stereotypes in this offer? For example, who gets offered counselling?

■ is there a range of support offered that is acceptable to pupils of both genders and different cultures?

■ what do young people themselves feel about the support on offer? What systems are there to consult with pupils?

■ are staff aware of the different expressions of distress amongst pupils of all genders, for example self-harming behaviour?

■ how are peer support and peer counselling developed? Who accesses these services if they exist, and are they representative of gender and culture?

■ are there self-referral systems in place and how seriously are they taken?

■ are there professionals operating on gendered responses? What systems exist for monitoring gender differences in the referral and use of external support systems?

■ are there programmes that develop psychological well-being?

■ are teachers and other staff able to recognise pupils who are getting into difficulties and if not, how might this be developed through continuing professional development?

## How the school interacts with the community and family members

The final area to explore is how the school interacts with the community and family members in terms of gender and culture. This is an important area and the challenges that some community and family members have in accessing the school cannot be underestimated. Some fruitful questions might be:

■ what assumptions are made about the types of family that the child is part of?

■ what gender assumptions are made when communicating with parents and community members, for example when a child is in trouble?

■ what assumptions are made about the lives of family members and their availability when making appointments?

■ is the school's policy and practice with regard to equal opportunities shared with parents?

■ how can the school move towards making all in the community feel safe and welcomed in the school and through its communication systems?

Schools can have a significant impact on pupils' personal, social and emotional development and this in turn will affect them as young adults.

> Schooling does matter greatly. Moreover, the benefits can be surprisingly long lasting. ... School experiences of both academic and non-academic kinds can have a protective effect for children under stress and living otherwise unrewarding lives... Schools are about social experiences as well as scholastic learning. (Rutter, 1991:9)

### References and further resources

Best, R. (2000) *Pastoral Care, Personal And Social Education: a review of research*. British Education Research Association. Available at www.bera.ac.uk

Collins, U. M. and McNiff, J. (1999) *Rethinking Pastoral Care*. London: Routledge

Cowie, H. (2000) Bystanding or standing by: gender issues in coping with bullying in English schools. *Aggressive Behaviour* 26 p85-97

David, K. and Charlton, T. (1996) *Pastoral Care Matters in Primary and Middle Schools*. London: Routledge

Dennison, C. and Coleman, J. (2000) *Young People and Gender: A Review of Research*. London: Women's Unit and Cabinet Office

Lloyd, G. (2004) *Problem Girls*. London: Routledge.

McLaughlin, C. (2004) Bystander behaviour in UK school children. *Pastoral Care in Education*. 23 (3) p17-23

Osler, A. and Vincent, K. (2003) *Girls and Exclusion*. London: RoutledgeFalmer.

*Pastoral Care in Education. The International Journal for Pastoral Care and Personal-Social Education.* Oxford: Basil Blackwell

Rutter, M. (1991) Pathways to adult life: the role of schooling. *Pastoral Care in Education.* 9 (3) p3-10

www.education.unisa.edu.au/bullying

The site is intended to help schools, children and parents in practical ways to overcome the serious problem of bullying.

www.online.curriculum.edu.au/mindmatters

An Australian resource and professional development program to support Australian secondary schools in promoting and protecting the social and emotional well-being of members of school communities.

www.napce.org.uk

National Association for Pastoral Care in Education (NAPCE) Establishes links between all those who have an interest in pastoral care and personal-social education (PSE). NAPCE has a membership, which consists of individuals, schools, LEAs and higher education providers who work in support of pastoral care and PSE at all levels.

my mother says I have to go to school to learn how to deal with the world

I wish there was somewhere I could go where I could learn how to deal with school

# Assemblies

*Rosie Walden and Diana Leonard*

■ *See also schedules: Religious Education; Governors*

Assemblies should be something to look forward to. They can provide occasions for affirming the ethos, values and personality of a particular school; encourage a sense of identity and self-worth in girls and boys from all backgrounds; and promote an awareness of our dependence on each other and on the natural world – as in the example in the box.

When the ethos, management, organisation and content is planned and agreed by staff and pupils, assemblies can help develop a sense of community. They can try to explain to children the importance of listening and reflecting on the big questions of life, including those around gender and the equality of the sexes. But if school values are implicit and not discussed, assemblies can equally pass on unintended messages to pupils, including unintentional and traditional messages about gender.

---

Our whole (primary) school comes together three times a week – Monday, Wednesday and Friday – beginning, middle, end of week.

We re-state our ethos every Monday in our Child of the Week assembly; celebrate it on Wednesday with a Golden Assembly; and show it off on Friday as each class showcases its work.

In deciding which child is the class Child of the Week or which child should receive a Golden certificate, we have had to look at how we, as a school, reinforce our ethos. We reward good behaviour, helpfulness, progress, achievement across the curriculum or in the playground. We have to ensure that we do not always praise our girls for being helpful and our boys for making progress in their work and that the opposite happens; girls are rewarded for academic achievement and boys for kindness and helping clear up the classroom.

We have a new theme every half-term. Learning from past errors we always choose a broad theme, like The Caribbean or Traditional Stories. This enables us to read good, interesting stories to children whilst pulling out the message. We request a variety of books from our local Education Library Service which enables us to expand our choices. Sometimes we use literature with a straightforward message, others with a more elliptical focus. We use the local Agreed Syllabus for RE to find various themes, all of which we use to draw out the messages.

Our assemblies are always interactive, with questions to draw out the message. We use *Espresso* in class with our interactive whiteboards to show different religions/stories in action.

Each one ends with A Thought for the Day – a moment of quiet reflection on the theme of the assembly which, we believe, meets Ofsted requirements for reflection and constitutes 'collective worship' for a multicultural school.

## Collective worship requirements

The requirements for a daily act of worship have changed little since the Education Act of 1944, which established the principle that pupils should be given religious education rather than instruction in non-denominational state-funded schools in the UK, and that worship should be non-denominational. Although confirmed in the 1988 Education Act and since, the requirement for a broadly Christian act of worship in non-denominational schools seems anachronistic in the context of what is, in many parts of the country, a multi-faith and generally secular society.

The following points try to clarify the statutory requirements for county schools. In most schools, collective worship remains the responsibility of the head teacher in consultation with the governors. In faith schools, however, collective worship is the responsibility of the governors.

■ A daily act of collective worship must be provided for all pupils in schools and sixth form colleges and occur on the school premises

■ The parental right of withdrawal and the right of teachers to withdraw from collective worship are safeguarded. However, as part of their duties, teachers may be required to attend assemblies

■ The whole school need not be present at the same time for collective worship and pupils can be grouped in different ways

■ Acts of worship may take place at any time during the school day.

Many teachers are keenly aware that the key figures or role models in most major religious traditions tend to be male. Assemblies nevertheless are an opportunity to draw attention to the many women who, despite these gendered assumptions and within the confines of their position, have been the standard bearers and keepers of the faith. The Hebrew Bible or Old Testament includes biblical heroines such as Ruth and Esther; while Fatima and Ayesha were highly respected and religiously significant wives of the Prophet. In the New Testament there are many examples of Jesus behaving in a caring manner.

The lives of women engaged in social reform, motivated by religious and/or political beliefs, could be included in a Thought for the Day slot: heroines from the past, such as Josephine Butler and Rosa Parks, or the present, such as Daw Aung San Su Kyi

and Gracia Machel, reflect the skills and capacities, and moral values of courage and integrity that schools should be promoting in their pupils. International Women's Day and Black History Week are obvious occasions for special assemblies celebrating the lives of remarkable women. Men who act from social concern also provide non-stereotypical role models, from Dr Barnado to Bob Geldof.

Assemblies are also an occasion when pupils can be encouraged to take leading and public roles. Many adults, particularly women, find speaking in a public forum very challenging. Assemblies can give them the opportunity to develop these skills.

### Issues to consider

■ Do assemblies/collective worship acknowledge and celebrate diversity and affirm children's life stance, religious or otherwise?

■ Is the content pupil-centred, i.e. geared to the interests, concerns and experience of all pupils?

■ What is the religious content? What is the theme? What stories are told, and what messages do they convey?

■ When the achievement of famous and influential people (past and present) are discussed in assemblies, is care taken to ensure that the achievements and contributions of women and minority ethnic/religious communities are seen to be valued by the school? Are areas of concern traditionally associated with women seen to be valued by the school? (Keep a log to check on a gender balance)

■ Do the number of adult women and men speakers (outsiders and staff) remind pupils that women, people from different backgrounds and people with disabilities can and do speak authoritatively – and on a variety of issues (for example, black speakers are knowledgeable about issues other than race)?

■ Are both female and male pupils encouraged to organise and participate in assemblies? When pupils do participate, what are they doing (for example, when playing roles, are all the angels white girls and the shepherds dark-skinned boys?)

■ Do the numbers of male/female and black and minority ethnic pupils who are praised in or who contribute to assemblies over a period of time, roughly represent their numbers in the school?

Do team results announced in the assembly value girl and boy pupils' achievements equally?

■ Do the seating arrangements (either due to pupils' or teachers' decisions) result in segregated or mixed groupings? Does this matter? Are the pupils physically comfortable during assemblies/collective worship?

■ What kinds of display are in the hall where the assembly takes place? What messages may they give to pupils and staff?

■ How many pupils opt out of assembly and what happens to them during this time? Are appropriate facilities available for pupils who wish to worship separately?

### Examples of books and pamphlets on assemblies/acts of worship with good gender practice

Every local authority in England and Wales has a SACRE and an Agreed Syllabus for Religious Education which has lists of books and contacts. But staff training in this field seems to be rarely requested or offered, and gender and equity issues have seldom been central concerns, though this may change in the context of controversies over religious dress.

British Humanist Association *Assemblies not Worship* presents the case against required collective worship www.humanism.org.uk/site/cms/contentViewArticle.asp?article=1247

**For official views see**
Department for Education (1994) *Religious Education and Collective Worship*, circular 1/94

**General advice, see**
Banks, Helen (1988) *Bright Ideas; Assemblies*. London: Scholastic

Leicester, Mal (2004) *Stories for Inclusive Schools : Developing Young People's Skills in Assembly and in the Classroom*. London:RoutledgeFalmer

Myers, K. (1992) *Genderwatch! After the Education Reform Act*. Cambridge: Cambridge University Press

Stowe, Alison (2004) *Developing Collective Worship in a Multi-Faith School* National Teacher Research Panel. A case history of a primary school which Ofsted noted was operating outside the requirement that '51% of assemblies should be 'broadly Christian' in nature', and its subsequent response www.standards.dfes.gov.uk/ntrp/publications/stowe2/

### Monitoring assembly arrangements

The observation form on page 76 can be used to track whole-school or year/group assemblies, to analyse their content as a basis for deciding if arrangements need to be changed. It can then subsequently be used to monitor the success of any changes implemented.

**Assemblies ... taken from p33 of Genderwatch 1992**

Name of school      Filled in by      Date completed

| Group | Content (Write a couple of sentences about the content of each assembly) | Adult Speakers F M Ethnicity (Record numbers) | Teams F M (Record the no. of female and male pupils' teams announced at each assembly) | Pupils named % Ethnicity F M | Organisation (Make a brief note of how the assembly was organised, eg. seating atmosphere, how pupils enter and leave etc.) | Comments |
|---|---|---|---|---|---|---|
| Group 1 F: M: | | | | Praise Reward Punish/ reprimand | | |
| Group 2 F: M: | | | | Praise Reward Punish/ reprimand | | |

# Breaktimes, Lunchtimes and Playgrounds

*Hilary Claire and Angela Piddock*

Good work in equal opportunities begun in the classroom can be undermined or undone during breaktimes. When pupils are moving around the school, waiting in corridors, or are in the playground, the situation is very different from the highly resourced and managed class time. The ratio of children to adults increases dramatically, while there may be little to do. The average amount of space per pupil may also be greatly reduced. Conformity to teachers' rules can simply vanish, and far more powerful out-of-school and peer-group conventions prevail.

Becky Francis summarised some recent research about gendered primary playground interactions as showing how:

> boys use football to enforce a masculinity hierarchy through exclusion of girls and less athletic boys from games,.. and such behaviour and constructions of maculinity can be racist as well as sexist: South Asian boys tend to be constructed as effete by other boys, and hence excluded from activities such as football.
> ...Organised skipping games are an activity from which girls sometimes exclude boys (although some boys are keen to disrupt activities over which girls seemed to have ownership).
> (adapted from Francis, 2004, citing Thorne, 1993; Connolly, 1998 and 2003; Skelton, 1999 and 2001)

In secondary schools, girls may not be skipping but pupils playing football – mainly boys – continue to dominate the outdoor space and there are often no areas for pupils to sit comfortably and chat. In some schools, pupils are not allowed inside during breaks, even in bad weather. The condition of toilets and access to them are a major area of concern for many girls and boys. Lunchtimes can be particularly difficult and be grim experiences for both pupils and the supervising adults.

Such equal opportunities issues relating to playgrounds and breaktimes affect and have implications for the whole life of the school. Hence, dealing with them needs a whole-school approach. Pupils, dinner and playground supervising staff, governors and parents, as well as teaching and support staff, all need to be involved in developing a policy for these areas and times in the school day. The school council should also be involved from the start. Any working group established will have a major task and should be prepared to collect information, collate data and keep everyone informed of progress.

## Developing a whole school approach to improving equity at breaktimes: establishing the extent and nature of the problem

### Getting a working group started

Having gathered together a representative working group, the first activity we recommend is partly an exercise to raise consciousness, and partly to identify issues. Brainstorm thoughts and ideas about the following questions and, as appropriate, note the facts and positive and negative features (see page 78).

### Is any group currently disadvantaged?

The group should next consider whether any group of pupils is currently disadvantaged. This will be based on experience and anecdotes, but will help the group to move from the general issues around breaktimes and circulation spaces to specific equal opportunities concerns. Some hard data is needed to back up hunches, for example about certain spaces in the playground being problematic, or there being particular difficulties associated with moving large numbers of children round the school.

### Starting to collect data about the current situation

It may be possible to involve the children/pupils themselves in data collection. If it is not possible to have whole-school involvement, the school council could ask for volunteers who will work with members of staff.

- Draw out the playground on squared paper
- Also note areas round the school that are already thought to be problematic (stairwells, some corridors)
- Divide the space to be surveyed and monitored into manageable sections, and
- Allocate specific sections and times of the day to small groups

The grid at the bottom opposite may be helpful.

Patterns will soon be perceived – territorial rights exercised over various areas of the playground by different groups. These may or may not be gendered, or based on the year group; different activities may take place in different areas or always in the same area. In both primary and secondary schools, boys will probably be found dominating the larger spaces with football games, and girls and boys who are not joining the football are likely to be squashed into much smaller spaces.

What is likely to be new and of particular interest is any data indicating that certain children are being excluded or bullied, and that some who were believed to be at the heart of trouble, actually are not, though they are scapegoated. It may also become clear that in the freedom of the playground, the school's efforts to integrate white and ethnic minority children, long resident and newcomer children, or boys and girls, seem to have little effect. Research has shown that newly arrived refugees/asylum seekers are often bullied or excluded (Rutter, 1998) and that Asian boys not considered macho or good at football may be bullied by other boys.

### Surveying pupils', parents' and carers' attitudes

Before the group moves into considering what should be changed and how, it is important to survey pupils' attitudes and to gather some information about parents' perspectives.

Collect comments via a suggestion box, newsletters, and the school's web page. Use an interview schedule to collect pupils' views. Interview schedules should cover pupils' experience in particular areas of the school at different times, but also give space for them to note any incidents that have been worrying them – for example, witnessing bullying or sexual harassment and not being able to do anything about it.

Individual teachers and tutors should be encouraged to set up discussions with their own groups. One Year 6 class we know revealed that none of them would use the outside toilets – because they weren't kept clean, there wasn't any toilet paper, there were no sanitary bins for those girls who had reached puberty, and there was no real privacy (Claire, 2004). This issue tends to become worse in secondary schools whether the toilets are indoors or outdoors. As well as the hygiene issues they are often perceived as unsupervised places where bullying is rife. The school council members of the group should make a point of gathering information about anything that is worrying their peers about playgrounds and breaktimes.

In order to give the playground/breaktime project a high profile, an assembly about the issue of breaktimes could be organised involving senior staff and pupils.

### Surveying staff attitudes

It is important to build up a picture of adult attitudes and experience as well as those of pupils. Just as pupils will know about incidents that have not necessarily come to the staff's attention, so staff on duty in the playgrounds may want specific issues discussed. For example, in one primary school, the playground supervisors were very keen to teach some playground games and especially to run girls' football sessions, but they wanted some support from the teaching staff to get this going. It is important for teaching and non-teaching staff to work closely together, because the pupil surveys may reveal that some of the problems experienced in the playground emanate from adult attitudes and stereotypes. For example, some black British boys may feel picked on and scapegoated by staff, which may exacerbate rather than manage perceived behaviour problems (Claire, 2001). Supervisors with rather conventional attitudes may discourage boys from sitting and reading, or express surprise or disapproval at girls kicking footballs around.

| Breaktime Audit | Facts | + features | - features |
|---|---|---|---|
| What is breaktime for? | | | |
| Who is it for? | | | |
| Who is currently responsible for managing breaktimes? | | | |
| What is going on in different areas of the playground/ corridors between lessons? | | | |
| What is causing a problem? When do problems arise (ie which break period?) | | | |
| What are the current strategies for maintaining good order? | | | |
| Anything else? | | | |

| Date and day | Space surveyed | Weather | Surveyed by |
|---|---|---|---|
| **Which break?** Morning: | <u>Junior</u> <u>playground</u> *Benches under cover and area round toilets* | | |
| 10.30 – 35 | Sharon, Marcelle and Kim (all Y5) on benches chatting. Mariam, Aysa, Khadija and Baljeet (Y4)sitting on ground under tree playing with some toy (can't see what it is). | | |
| | Group of girls from Yrs 3 and 4 playing a group skipping game nearby Boys from Y4 run up to the skipping game, try and join; girls shoo them off and they run away. They come back. Girls ignore them. | | |
| 10.35 – 40 | Fuss round the girls' toilets. Y6 Boys jumping up at the wall and peering over. Brenda (Y6) comes out of toilet and shouts at them. Mrs W (on duty) comes up and tells boys off. | | |
| 10.40 – 45 | Mahmoud (Y4) with his sister Seinat (Y3) standing near Y4 girls who are still under tree watching them. Girls ignore them. M and S move near to Y5 girls on bench. They look up and also ignore them. Alex and Jeffrey (Y3) come rushing up to M and S with their arms out playing aeroplanes. They go 'woosh, woosh' very close to M and S. S flinches. | | |
| 10.45 – 10.50 | Bell rings for end of playground. Girls saunter off to line up. M and S holding hands. Boys continue to run around. Mrs W rounds everyone up. Some pushing in the lines. Mahmoud attempting to get into Y4 line. No one makes space. | | |

### Pulling the information together and distilling it

The working group will need to make sense of the data that has been collected. A few main issues should be drawn out and the information which backs this up summarised, for example, that some girls are complaining that they want to join in the football, but the boys won't let them; or that some younger children feel scared of the bigger children in the playground.

### Developing a whole school approach to improving equity at breaktimes

### Issues to consider

■ Involve everyone in discussing proposals for change, and finalising them.

■ Feed back the main concerns to the children. Try and get suggestions from the children themselves about possible changes and initiatives. Expect some that are pie-in-the-sky but also some very sensible, grounded ideas

■ If the playground is not currently zoned with quiet areas, for sitting and reading as well as large spaces for running around and football, consider if this is feasible. This will to some extent depend on the size and shape of the space available. However, without zoning there is the ever-present danger of football dominating the space

■ Consider what is on offer in the quiet areas of the playground, and who is using it. If the resources are girl oriented – girls' books and comics – then it will not be surprising if it is seldom used by boys

■ Put the concerns to parents, and see if they come up with any ideas. The parents in one school organised to convert a section of the playground into a nature area when it became apparent how much their children hated their bleak, concrete space. Some suggestions are really quite cheap – like in primary playgrounds painting snakes and ladders on the playground and allowing the children to use a giant, soft dice. In secondary schools, providing comfortable and safe spaces for those that do not want to be energetic can be easily achieved. In all schools, it may be possible to have a small garden – architects are well aware that the quality of the environment directly affects the behaviour of any community

■ Invite a local arts group in to help the pupils design and make a large mural, or a sculpture for their playground

■ It is worth considering staggering breaks and lunchtimes, so that there are fewer pupils in the space at any one time, shorter queues for food and fewer to supervise

■ In primary schools, run sessions for the helpers in which they learn some games to play with children. Playground supervisors working in all phases should be helped with crowd management techniques. Sergeant major behaviour management by some playground supervisors is at the root of some very aggressive reactions by children – often boys – usually against those weaker than themselves

■ In primary schools, as part of a wider project about the design of the playground, and playground games, ask parents and others in the community to come and teach playground games remembered from their own childhoods – for instance, marbles or hula hoops; group singing games like *The big ship sails in the alley-alley-oh*, *In and out the dusty bluebells* or *Oranges and lemons*; but do make sure that gender stereotypes are not reinforced!

■ Consider training some pupils in peer mediation. This is more formal than a buddy system. Peer mediators are then available to help pupils who are miserable or having difficulties in the playground, and their peaceful conflict resolution strategies can trickle down through the school as the accepted way to behave

■ Contact a local Theatre in Education group which specialises in playground co-operative games through your local authority or the internet. This can help break a macho football-orientated culture dominating a playground and dominating girls

■ Introduce skipping across the school, and other keep-fit activities for breaktime. This is not just about combating obesity, but can give a strong message that activities do not need to be the reserve of one sex: dancers, boxers, athletes and footballers all keep fit by skipping and similar activities

■ Introduce into the playground volleyball and basketball, skittles and apparatus for balancing, again with the aim of providing activities which are not associated with either sex

■ Set aside some days of the week for girls only football and other ball skills – and make sure that there is someone to help the girls with their skills. Encourage discussion in the classroom about inclusion, equality and positive discrimination. If there are no girls in the football team, work towards changing this

■ Consider supervising areas where some pupils can remain indoors, for example, the library, or an area of the hall where large blocks, small world and construction toys can be kept. In secondary schools, offer a wide range of lunchtime clubs and keep a register of who attends. Involve pupils in taking responsibility for indoor spaces that are made available at breaktimes.

Lastly, and very importantly, be particularly watchful if data collection has revealed that any groups are being marginalised or bullied, for example newcomers to the country, whose English is not yet fluent, or when hostility between groups in the community is being brought into the school. If this is happening, then a much more searching programme will be needed to address what are possibly racist and intolerant attitudes, going beyond what happens in the playground. There is no space to address this here but we recommend books by Brown (2001), Dadzie (2000) and Siraj Blatchford (1994).

## References

Brown, B. (2001) *Combating Discrimination: Persona Dolls in Action*, Stoke on Trent: Trentham

Claire, H. (2001) *Not Aliens: Primary School Children and the PSHE/Citizenship Curriculum*. Stoke on Trent: Trentham Based on research in inner city primary schools, children talk about their experience and attitudes to race and racism

Claire, H., (ed.) (2004) *Teaching Citizenship in Primary Schools*. Exeter: Learning Matters

Connolly, P. (1998) *Racism, Gender Identities and Young Children*. London: Routledge

Dadzie, S. (2000) *Toolkit for Tackling Racism in Schools*. Stoke on Trent: Trentham.

Francis, B. (2004) Classroom Interaction and Access: whose space is it? In Claire, H. (ed.) *Gender in Education*, 3-19: a fresh approach. London: ATL

Masheder, M. (1985) Let's Cooperate Pack www.kingsleyhall.free uk.com/masheder.htm

Rutter, J. (1998) *Refugees: A Resource Book for Primary Schools*. London: Refugee Council.

Siraj-Blatchford, I. (1994) *Early Years: Laying the Foundations for Racial Equality*. Stoke on Trent: Trentham.

# Uniform and Dress Codes

*Shan Scott*

## Introduction

Most English schools require pupils to wear a uniform of some kind. A school's uniform or dress code can be a uniquely visible sign of its ethos and culture. But as with many signs, uniform may not always convey what those behind it intended, and may, indeed, give out other messages. In this schedule, uniform is used to cover all forms of required school wear. There is no hard and fast dividing line between uniform and dress code: one school may call its requirement that pupils wear a polo shirt and trousers in school colour with logo a dress code, while another will label the same requirements as a uniform.

This schedule does not set out to analyse the pros and cons of uniform or to advise schools on whether they should have a uniform. The aim of this schedule is to help schools that do have, or propose to have, a uniform, to ensure that the uniform is fair for boys and girls and that it does not convey unintended messages about the abilities of boys and girls, or of appropriate behaviours or activities for them It should also help schools to ensure that uniform policy is sensitive to pupils – boys and girls – from different faiths, cultures, races and social backgrounds. It is intended to be relevant for primary and secondary schools, including for sixth forms.

## The legal position

School uniform is not covered by any statutory provisions. In all categories of maintained school (and in city technology colleges (CTCs) and Academies), the decision as to whether to have a uniform, and what it should be, is the responsibility of the governing body. In making those decisions, as with many other decisions, the governing body must

comply with the requirements of the Race Relations and Race Relations Amendment Acts, the Sex Discrimination Act, the Disability Discrimination Act and the Human Rights Act. There is non-statutory guidance issued by DfES and available at www. teachernet.gov.uk/management/atoz/u/uniform/

## Why have a school uniform?

Schools choose to have a uniform, and what uniform to have, for a number of reasons. Uniform can:

- forge a sense of school community and identity
- demonstrate to pupils and to others that school is a place of endeavour, work and study
- ensure that all pupils are wearing clothes suitable for the activities they will be taking part in. This will both help pupils get the greatest benefit from activities, and minimise health and safety risks
- reduce distractions for both sexes through clothing that can emphasise sexuality
- be popular with parents, not least as it removes the need to decide what the children should wear each day. In research carried out for DfES, 89% of parents with a child who went to state school said they would prefer that their child wore school uniform.

For uniform to succeed in these aims, it must be inclusive of all pupils and equitable between all groups of pupils. Schools will accordingly want to keep inclusivity and equity in mind when choosing and reviewing their uniform, as well as when considering matters relating to enforcement of uniform policy.

## What is included in uniform

In this schedule, uniform covers both day-to-day clothing (including shoes) and items specifically worn for activities such as science, design and technology, art and physical education.

The suggestions the schedule makes in relation to uniform are also relevant to school policies and rules on hair, the wearing of make-up, jewellery (including earrings and other piercings) and tattoos. Tattoos are illegal for those under 18 unless they are for medical purposes.

## Reviewing/changing uniform

It is important to keep uniform under review over time, in order to ensure that it remains fit for purpose and that it is helping to promote an inclusive and cohesive school community. A review may be prompted by feelings among the staff, governors or pupils that the uniform is dated or old-fashioned. It may be that a new faith group has come to be represented among the pupil body and they may ask for – or the school itself may anticipate a need for – the uniform to be adjusted to take account of the dress codes of their faith.

Schools will, however, need to balance the benefits of regular reviews against too frequent wholesale changes to uniform with their attendant costs to parents and in terms of time.

## Carrying out a review

As with the introduction of a uniform, the key to success in reviewing uniform is consultation. The groups identified under new and merged schools above should be consulted. In considering who else needs to be consulted, care needs to be taken to include any new groups or communities that have recently come to be served by the school. The governing body will also want to consult the PTA or other parents' organisations as well as pupils – perhaps via the school council.

## How to consult

There is no one right way to consult. Different schools will have different arrangements to take account of the needs of their communities, and will want to use these when consulting on school uniform matters. It may, however, be useful to bear the following points in mind in relation to consultation on uniform:

- use meetings and displays to show parents, community representatives and pupils what the uniform might look like

- make clear in consultation why the proposals are being made and what the school hopes to achieve
- be clear about the cost of different options and set these out in the consultation.

## Issues to consider

The checklist below is designed to help schools assess existing or proposed uniform for its impact on boys and girls. It is equally relevant when considering the introduction of, or changes to, uniform or when assessing whether uniform policy is enforced fairly as between girls and boys. The questions are not exhaustive: they are examples intended to help schools to reflect on their own arrangements and circumstances.

- Is there any need for boys and girls to have very different uniform? DfES guidance is clear for instance that girls should be allowed to wear trousers.

### Formality

- Is the uniform equally formal or informal for boys and girls? For example, do boys have to wear tailored jackets, whereas girls can wear cardigans?
- Do uniforms for both boys and girls make it easy to move freely?
- Does the boys' uniform or the girls' differ more markedly from the clothes young people would choose for themselves or wear outside school?

### Distinctiveness

- Is the uniform equally distinctive overall for boys and girls? For example, if girls have to wear a skirt with a particular pattern (such as a kilt), whereas boys can wear any plain black trousers, do the boys also have to wear a distinctive tie or blazer?

### Maturity

- Does the uniform allow boys and girls to look their age? Are primary aged boys able to wear long trousers but girls required to wear pinafores?
- Does the uniform encourage boys and girls to act in ways appropriate to their age?

### Flexibility

- If the uniform includes choices of what to wear, is it equally flexible for boys and girls; for example, if there is a choice of black or grey trousers, are these choices equally available to girls and boys?

## Cost

- Does the uniform cost the same for a boy and a girl? Does it matter?
- Is the cost comparable taking into account the whole uniform, including sports kit? For example, do girls or boys require more kit or different kit for different activities?
- Is help with costs available equally for boys and girls? Is the girls' and boys' uniform available from a similar number of providers?

## Enforcement and monitoring of uniform

Just as schools have uniform in part to promote a corporate identity, so pupils will seek to customise their uniform to assert their individual identity. In secondary schools in particular, pupils will want to put their own stamp on their uniform. From year to year, there will be vogues for long and short ties, for shirts hanging out, for skirts that are long and skirts that are short. Each school will decide how rigidly it wishes to enforce its uniform policy.

DfES guidelines explain that head teachers can discipline pupils for breach of uniform policy. DfES does not consider exclusion to be an appropriate response to such breaches, except where it is part of a pattern of defiant behaviour generally.

## Issues to consider

- Is uniform enforced to the same degree for boys and girls?
- Are sanctions for failing to comply with uniform policy applied equitably to boys and girls?
- Where spare items (ties and headscarves for example) are kept in school, are equivalent items available for boys and girls?
- Does one gender generally feel that the other has more leeway in terms of uniform flexibility and the scope to customise uniform?
- Where the school has a school council, are they involved in monitoring enforcement of uniform, and do boys and girls both feel involved in this aspect of the school council's work?

## Sixth form issues

In many schools with a sixth form, uniform requirements are often relaxed or removed for sixth formers, to reflect their increasing maturity and progression towards adulthood. It remains important, however, that any requirements or prohibitions are equitable between male and female sixth formers.

## Physical Education

Adolescents – and particularly girls – are very self-conscious about their bodies. In order to promote active involvement in PE it is important that they are comfortable with what they need to wear. In addition, some faith, cultural and ethnic groups will have views about appropriate dress for PE, as for daywear. Again, consultation is vital; options can include tracksuit bottoms rather than gym skirts, and headscarves (for those who wear them) that fasten with poppers that release easily when pulled and avoid risk of injury in games.

## Dress code for staff

While this schedule is about uniform for pupils, the principles of fairness and inclusivity are also relevant to staff. The NUT guidelines *The Muslim Faith and School Uniform* contain a section on staff dress.

## A note on faith issues

Many schools have pupils of many faiths and none, and have devised uniform policies that both meet the religious needs of pupils, and are distinctive to the school and its ethos. The key to success in this area is consultation and engagement with all parts of the local community served by the school.

The case of Regina (Begum v Head teacher and Governors Denbigh High School 2006 UKHL 15) attracted a good deal of media attention. The eventual outcome was a House of Lords judgement that the school had been within its rights not to allow a pupil to attend wearing a jihab rather than the prescribed school uniform of shalwar kameese. A useful summary of the case is available at www.pinsentmasons.com/media/826963890. For schools considering their uniform policy, it is worth noting that the judgement related only to this specific case – it was not a ruling on whether particular forms of Islamic dress should or should not be permitted in schools. The school concerned had developed its policy in close consultation with the local community including Muslim faith leaders.

## Further resources
DfES Guidance on School Uniform
www.teachernet.gov.uk/management/atoz/u/uniform
The Muslim Faith and School Uniform NUT guidelines available at www.teachers.org.uk.

# It's my school: the power of pupil voice

*Maggie Farrar and Vinsia McQueen*

■ *See also schedules: Assessment; Every Child Matters; School Self-evaluation*

*Editorial note*: as this schedule applies to primary, secondary and special schools, the term 'pupil' is used instead of student.

## Introduction

**M**any schools are committed to the development of pupil voice to make sure all children have a full and engaging life in school and, in so doing, achieve to their full potential. Pupil voice can be seen as an essential component of schools which work in democratic, equal and active partnership with both their internal and external communities.

In this schedule, pupil voice refers to all those initiatives that empower and engage young people as active partners in their own learning and in the school as an organisation. It covers initiatives related to the development of pupil leadership, pupil empowerment and pupil voice. For most schools, the journey of involving pupils begins with asking questions about pupil voice.

## Why pupil voice? The purpose

Why should schools get involved in activities that enhance pupil voice? There are at least three distinct purposes. The first is to help pupils become more independent and confident learners through involving them more effectively in their own learning. The second is to give pupils opportunities to develop their leadership qualities. Both of these can have a profound impact on pupils' achievement and personal development.

The third is to acknowledge that the pupils are critical stakeholders in the organisation, and that the act of engaging in dialogue with them can be integral to school improvement. These purposes are not in conflict. However, they all raise equity issues. With regard to the first, it is possible (as discussed later) that different groups will need different support strategies to help them become more independent learners. Likewise, some pupils will be more confident about taking leadership opportunities; others will need specific encouragement and skill-building. Concerning the third purpose, different groups are likely to have different responses to the school, the staff, its facilities and the education offered. Where numbers are large enough, it is important that feedback is disaggregated so that the views of these groups are noted and compared with others. For example, do the boys who qualify for free school meals feel more strongly about after-school study provision than those who do not?

The development of pupil voice can be viewed as a virtuous circle. The pupils themselves benefit, but they also contribute broader organisational improvement to their peers and the wider community. For schools in England, this links neatly with the *Every Child Matters* agenda, where one of the five outcomes is 'make a positive contribution'.

Once the purpose is established, the process follows.

*For the pupil, pupil voice can*:

- enable pupils to feel engaged in school life and consequently affiliated to the school. Pupils who do not feel affiliated to their school are less likely to achieve (Osterman, 2000)

- aid their learning processes and improve achievement (Flutter and Rudduck, 2004)

- help them understand, participate in and support the democratic process.

*For the school, pupil voice can*:

■ help understand what their pupils care about

■ enhance teacher/pupil relationships

■ improve the teaching and learning process.

Schools need to be aware that the reverse of this can happen if particular groups of pupils, for example those on free school meals or ethnic minority pupils, feel disenfranchised from, or disenchanted with, the process and outcome.

Unless undertaken with an understanding of equity issues, the above may only apply to a proportion of the pupils on roll. It could also have the reverse impact for those not involved.

### Issues to consider

Is the purpose of involving pupils to:

■ get feedback from the pupil body?

■ engage pupils in their learning?

■ encourage pupils to take responsibility for their learning?

■ involve pupils in school life?

■ help them become active citizens when they are adults?

Schools that have engaged in pupil voice activity have done so for a range of reasons. The following list gives an overview of the most common drivers, which connect the engagement, involvement and leadership development of pupils with a school's commitment to continuous organisational improvement and the achievement of children and young people.

### Why pupil voice? The consequences

■ It builds the skills, confidence and motivation young people need to engage directly in the wider improvement of the school, and in particular in the improvement of their learning experiences.

■ It enables pupils to become advocates for their own needs and the needs of others.

■ It lies at the heart of building a sense of community and trust in school and builds effective relationships, which are a prerequisite to further improvement.

■ Pupils are a powerful resource in the development of school and community partnerships and therefore in the extension and enrichment of learning opportunities beyond the school day, week and year.

■ One of the most powerful influences on young people (especially in adolescence) is their peer group. Providing pupil leadership development programmes and opportunities for young people to demonstrate leadership and use their voice, allows the culture and dynamics of the peer group to be focused on engagement and involvement.

■ Young people spend only 15% of their waking time in school; 85% of their time is spent in the home and community. Leadership skills are transferable and leadership opportunities are found beyond the school, thus increasing the school's opportunity to invest in the building of social and intellectual capital within the community.

■ Motivation and re-engagement in learning is linked to pupils feeling that they are empowered to have a say, to make a difference, and to be involved.

In addition, for many schools, a promoting, developing and supporting pupil leader is a tangible realisation of their values.

### The process: ensuring equity

*Enhancing learning: different ways of interacting with pupils*

Using surveys to find out more about pupil attitudes to their school and to their learning is becoming a familiar tool in many English schools. These schools are using the results as evidence for their School Evaluation Form (SEF). Other tools that enable a range of voices to be heard include photo evaluation, making videos, drawing, and role-play (MacBeath *et al*, 2003). More adventurous schools are utilising new technologies such as the My Space and Facebook websites, or MSN messenger to engage in dialogue with pupils. Use of these technologies also enables pupils to develop online communities with pupils in other schools and other countries.

When the aim is to consult pupils about their learning, it is useful to be aware of the different strategies available for consultation, and to understand the different ways in which pupils learn and their preferred styles of communication. Some of these approaches and strategies are commonly associated with girls (eg group discussion and collaborative group work) and others with boys (eg individual feedback and competition). If this is the case generally, there will always be some girls and some boys who do not fit into the typical mould.

Consequently, it is useful to be aware of a range of methods and, over a period of time, employ them with both boys and girls, giving both sexes the opportunity to respond in ways they are familiar with and to develop skills with which they are less familiar. When analysing feedback it is vital to disaggregate how different groups are responding. For example does the feedback from black girls differ significantly from that of the white girls? Do disabled pupils have a particular view that is not raised by other pupils?

### Issues to consider

- Is there a discernable pattern with regard to which tools are more popular with girls or boys?
- Can a combination of ways of communicating with pupils meet the range of preferred styles?
- Are there particular members of staff or the wider school community, such as a critical friend with whom pupils – boys and girls – will more readily communicate?

## Developing leadership and contributing to school improvement

### Which pupils?

Whose voice is heard is a question all schools need to ask when working on pupil voice. The selection of which voices are heard can appear to be exclusive: only a few get the chance, often those who are liked by everyone else, high achieving, or trusted, and usually those approved of by the adults in the school. Some pupils see the selection as a secret process and do not know what they need to do to be recognised as having leadership potential (Jones, 2003). Sometimes it is the most marginalised pupils who have the most of value to say, and yet they often feel disenfranchised by the process. Single-sex girls' schools are frequently more popular than single-sex boys' schools. Consequently, in some areas, mixed secondary schools have more male pupils than female. Schools in this situation need to pay particular attention to engaging with and hearing the voice of the female pupils.

Many schools have established pupil councils. When properly managed, these councils enable pupils to participate in a formal democratic process; they can aid understanding of the benefits – and frustrations – of democracy. These include important lessons about which pupils are likely to get elected and whether the successful candidates think it is important to discover and represent the views of pupils who are different from them. This of course

applies to all age ranges from infant through to secondary.

However, even when well run (ie the pupils are democratically elected, they meet regularly, there is ongoing feedback with regard to their deliberations and they have an impact on school life) not all pupils will be involved in the process. Indeed, traditional school councils are set up in such a way that a pupil needs to be very articulate as well as extremely confident to move through the selection process and succeed in being elected.

### Issues to consider

- When elections are held, which pupils get elected? Are different groups more or less represented in proportion to their numbers in the school, for example girls/boys/ethnic minority pupils, different ages and those on free school meals?
- Does the process used for elections affect who gets elected?
- When should pupils be chosen by election and when are there other ways to encourage representation and involvement? How can a wider, but potentially committed and representative group of pupils be encouraged to participate?

The development of leadership potential in schools can only be achieved by giving pupils a stake in the organisation and by empowering them to make a difference to that organisation.

### Pupil voice or pupil involvement?

Many pupil voice initiatives are conferred by power, position and hierarchy: eg prefects, pupil councils. Pupil involvement on a wider scale can offer more inclusive opportunities and involve more pupils: task teams, innovation groups and change teams. This gives a legitimate voice to those who for various reasons, for example gender, ethnicity, attainment, class or peer popularity, may not have been heard previously.

Establishing pupil leadership teams managed by the pupils gives the pupil body a range of opportunities to be involved. Many schools are developing systematic and imaginative approaches of this kind. One school, Park View Academy in London, has based theirs on four teams which are popular with both girls and boys:

### The ambassador

Ambassadors showcase the school by talking to visitors and speaking to a range of audiences at special events. They speak at local and national events and act as tour guides to visiting educationalists and politicians.

### The interview team

The panel of pupils are part of the school's selection process for prospective employees. They formally question candidates regardless of the level of appointment being made. They provide feedback to the head teacher, forming 25% of the consideration of whether to appoint or not.

### The lunchtime assistants

This team are invaluable to the functioning and experience of the school's mid-day meals service for pupils and staff alike. They organise the queues, ensure fairness of service and assist in the sale of pre-packed lunches. They have a voice in how the service is run and how best to make the session as pleasurable as possible.

### The primary liaison team

The liaison team assist in promoting the school as well as being central to the transition process from primary to secondary. They act as tour guides during prospective parents' visits and accompany staff to primary schools to take part in question and answer sessions. The team also act as classroom assistants and mentors to Year 6 and 7 pupils. They are very proud of the fact that they can speak about their school, often retaining facts regarding the development and progress of the school.

Whilst none of the teams initially had formal positional leaders, the leadership role in each has been assumed by girls. It is interesting to observe that whilst these girls may not feel confident enough to put themselves forward in a public marketing exercise, they are willing to take on a leadership role once they are part of an established team.

### Issues to consider

How can:

■ all pupils be encouraged to have a voice in the life of the school?

■ a climate be established that enables those whose voice is least likely to be heard to become more active?

■ a sense of teamwork and shared enterprise best be fostered once pupils are involved?

Underpinning the notion of pupil voice is an understanding that for pupils, learning to excel is not solely about excelling in the classroom but also about developing a set of competencies increasing their capacity and desire to learn, not only within but beyond the school. That capacity is built around resilience, and a greater understanding of self and others. Some pupil will have opportunities to develop these skills outside of the school setting. We need to find ways to ensure that all pupils have opportunities to develop these capacities.

### References and further reading

Belensky, M., Clinchy, G., Goldberger, N., and Tarule, J. (1989) *Women's Ways of Knowing*. New York: Basic Books
www: BSIP.net/pupilvoice

Caine, R. and Caine, G. (1991) *Making Connections: Teaching and the Human Brain*. Virginia: Association for Supervision and Curriculum Development

Fielding, M. and Bragg, S. (2003) *Pupils as Researchers: making a difference*. London: Pearson Publishing

Flutter, J. and Rudduck, J. (2004) *Consulting Pupils: What's in it for Schools*. London: RoutledgeFalmer

Johnson, K. (2004) *Children's Voices: Pupil Leadership in Primary Schools*. Nottingham: NCSL

Jones, H. (2003) *Leading Learners*. London: Demos
www.ncrel.org/sdrs/areas/issues/pupils/earlycld/ea1lk2.htm

MacBeath, J., Demetriou, H., Rudduck, J. and Myers, K. (2003) *Consulting Pupils: A Toolkit for Teachers*. Cambridge: Pearson Publishing

Osterman, K. (2000) Pupil's need for belonging in the school community. *Review of Educational Research*. 70 (3)

Rudduck, J. (2005) Pupil Voice is Here to Stay! QCA. Qca.org.uk/futures/

# Lesbian, Gay, Bisexual and Trans Issues in Schools

*Paul Patrick*

■ *See also schedules: Every Child Matters; Managing Behaviour; Pastoral Care; Home-School Relations*

Feeling comfortable and confident with one's developing sexuality and gender identity presents a challenge to every young person. It causes particular anxiety and confusion during adolescence, but increasingly affects primary age children. Sexualised behaviour is more frequently presented to young children, whether through styles of clothing, suggestive movement on pop videos, or in the ubiquity of sexually explicit language and discussion. For heterosexual young people, this is a hard enough context in which to discover who you are as a human being with a developing sexuality and gender identity and how this relates to your whole conception of yourself. For those who are lesbian, gay, bisexual or trans (LGBT), who think they may be, have LGBT family or friends, or are called LGBT by others, it is much harder, because schools remain the one place in our society where LGBT lives and experiences are routinely censored from both the formal and informal curriculum, and from any discussion outside the playground.

Elsewhere in society, there is an increased visibility of lesbians and gay men. We have achieved greater legal status and recognition of our rights in civil partnerships, and there are many examples of openly lesbian and gay people getting on with their ordinary and extraordinary lives. However these changes are not mirrored in most schools. Young people who are lesbian, gay, bisexual, or who think they might be, who are thought by others to be, or who have lesbian, gay, or bisexual friends or family, almost uniformly have a hard time in school. Trans young people, those who think they might be or those with trans family or friends, suffer even greater ignorance and almost complete invisibility as well as outright hostility.

At the time of writing there has been no research and no guidelines produced for the tackling of transphobia – the irrational fear and subsequent prejudicial response to trans people – and the effect that it has on young people who are trans or think that they might be. However there are several useful websites listed at the end of this schedule.

LGBT pupils face the confusing and contradictory experience of invisibility – on the one hand they don't exist – and yet they are bullied. This bullying also affects the lives of heterosexual young people who do not conform to a gender or other stereotype. Pupils who feel unsafe, or feel that they have to hide a part of themselves, are likely to achieve less well than those who do not; they are far more likely to truant or leave school early.

There is excellent practice in some schools in ensuring that all pupils feel welcome, and no less ordinary than anyone else – where being lesbian, gay, bisexual or trans is simply part of who they are. However these schools remain few and far between. The areas to address are visibility, safety, and the relationship between the school and the community.

## Visibility

Once the spectrum of human sexuality is openly recognised, it is possible to demystify it, talk openly, reduce fears and challenge prejudices. Schools where LGBT people are visible, so that their sexuality or gender identity ceases to be a mystery to be speculated about, provide a much safer environment for everyone. They enrich everyone's experience by enabling rational discussion about difference to replace irrational and uncontrolled prejudice. To create a climate of visibility, a number of things need to happen:

- the senior leadership team need to indicate in their behaviour and language an inclusion which signals the climate to everyone, and work with LGBT staff to address the visibility issues in the school

- there needs to be training for all staff covering the whole spectrum from awareness raising to developing curriculum materials

- the school's policies need explicitly to recognise the existence of LGBT adults and young people, and indicate that they are included and catered for, for example in the equal opportunities, inclusion and bullying policies

- adults and pupils need to feel safe enough to be out, so that they can be part of the visibility, and provide role models. They need to be respected as an essential part of the educational process

- LGBT adults and young people need to be included in the school's consultation procedures, so that their experiences and needs are taken into account in decision making

- there need to be references to the experience of lesbians and gay men across the curriculum

- there needs to be full coverage of the range of sexuality and sexual experience in sex education, and of the range of relationships in PSHE

- displays need to include images of prominent historical and contemporary gay people – their lives and achievements. The school could use LGBT History Month, which takes place in February each year, as a starting point for this – see www.LGBThistorymonth.org.uk

- information about events, phone lines, support and information groups, needs to be prominently available alongside other such information for pupils

- the school needs to survey its environment for unintended messages, for example the use of words with slang double meanings.

### Issues to consider

- Given the list above, where has the school made the most progress, and what needs most attention?

- How does the school invite the contributions of LGBT staff and young people so that they feel genuinely included and valued?

- How does the school induct new members of its community into its values and policies on sexuality and gender identity?

### Safety

Homophobic bullying is a major component of anti-social behaviour in schools today. The use of sexist and homophobic terms still forms a large part of playground banter, with the word 'gay' commonly used to mean anything dysfunctional or naff. Staff who ignore such language are colluding with it. This sends a clear message that anyone can be picked on at any time.

Abuse from pupils and collusion from staff are not confined to secondary schools. Research by Anderson (2005) makes it very clear that homophobia and the policing of children's gender identity is prevalent in primary and even pre-school classrooms and playgrounds.

This hostility is not directed solely at pupils. A 2006 survey of teachers found that a staggering 75% of LGBT staff had suffered hostility and abuse from pupils and other staff members. A 1996 survey of staff in over 300 schools in England and Wales found that 82% were aware of homophobic bullying in their school. 99% of the schools had an anti-bullying policy, but only 6% of these recognised homophobic bullying. A 2003 Stonewall survey of LGBT found that 79% of respondents under 18 had been called names by fellow pupils, and that 40% of the violent attacks reported had taken place at school. Lesbian and gay teenagers experience abuse both in and out of schools, and can be isolated within their families.

Many develop defences against these experiences that are attempts to block out the pain, but have further negative effects. These can include alcohol and drug abuse, self-harm, truancy and eating disorders. 2006 figures from Childline and the Samaritans suggest that one in five lesbian and gay teenagers attempt suicide. These figures are shocking but not widely known. For many young LGBT, school is not a safe place but another place to be wary.

A major step in making schools a safe place is to have a robust policy on homophobic bullying, and for it to be implemented with confidence and conviction. To ensure a policy is effective, schools need to:

- define and include homophobic bullying in the anti-bullying policy

- provide training for all staff on recognising and dealing effectively with homophobic abuse and bullying – much bullying takes place when teachers are not present
- require homophobic bullies to reflect on their prejudices and develop an understanding of the effects of their actions
- include training on homophobia in peer counselling training
- support young LGBT people who wish to come out, by providing information about people to talk to
- remove offensive graffiti rapidly
- involve pupils in developing and agreeing behaviour guidelines
- monitor and review instances of homophobic bullying, including that of staff, and act on the findings to improve safety.

For an anti-homophobic bullying policy to be effective it needs to be supported by positive LGBT images throughout the school curriculum and personnel.

### Issues to consider

- What information does the school have about the experiences of its LGBT pupils? How could more information be gathered in a way that pupils feel safe to respond?
- What are the strengths of the school's anti-bullying policy? Where does it need to be improved?
- How are non-teaching staff engaged in actively implementing the anti-bullying policy? What feedback do they give about location and types of homophobic abuse?
- How are pupils involved in developing practices that keep everyone safe?

## The school and the community

A school's stance on lesbian, gay, bisexual and trans issues sends messages to its community, and influences community beliefs and behaviours. Schools that take a clear and open stance that recognises the rights and responsibilities of all its pupils and staff in relation to visibility and safety, help to make the community a safer place. The school may fear that openness will attract opposition to its policies. However, there is evidence from Health Education Authority surveys that 94% of parents think schools should play a role in teaching pupils about sexuality, and 80% about HIV. A 2003 survey found that 73% of parents were comfortable

with their child or a close relative's child being taught by a gay or lesbian teacher. The school may also fear hostility from fundamentalist religious groups who believe homosexuality to be wrong. To increase support for policies and withstand opposition, the school can:

- provide clear and straightforward information for parents and others about the school's policies – many objections are based on misunderstandings
- ensure it is well informed about an issue, and can respond rationally and with confidence.

Pupils may have gay parents or carers, and the school needs to make sure that it is welcoming of these, and that they feel comfortable in the school. The school needs to be able to support parents whose children are LGBT and to engage with them whether or not they are supportive of their children. The majority are likely to be supportive, but to want more information, and the school can direct them to appropriate sources.

The school can also both benefit from and contribute to local and national networks that provide information and support for LGBT adults and young people. It can:

- publicise local groups and keep information up to date
- support, or set up, groups of teachers and other education workers with a particular interest in LGBT issues
- invite speakers from national organisations to contribute to assemblies and health education events
- share curriculum materials and access national resource collections to develop new materials.

### Issues to consider

- How does the school communicate its stance on LGBT issues to parents and carers?
- What links does it have with national and local support organisations?
- What messages does it give to the wider community about the value of LGBT people?

A school that addresses sexuality as an inclusive part of its efforts to provide equal opportunities and a secure environment for learning, truly demonstrates that freedom to develop individual confidence and security in sexual orientation or gender identity is central to its commitment to equal opportunities and education for all.

## References

Atkinson, E. (2005) Invisible Boundaries: *Addressing Sexualities Equality in Children's Worlds*. University of Sunderland: MA dissertation

Department for Education and Employment (1999) *Pupil Support*. London: DfEE Circular 10/99

Department for Education and Employment (2000) *Sex and Relationship Guidance*. London: DfEE

Department for Education and Skills (2003) *Don't Suffer in Silence*. London: DfES

Department for Education and Skills (2005) *Report of the Practitioner Group on School Behaviour and Discipline*. London: DfES

Health Education Authority and National Foundation for Education Research (1994) *Report of the Working Group on Sex Education in Scottish Schools*. Slough: NFER

Local Government Act (2000) Section 104 that amended the infamous Section 28

Schools OUT (2006) *School – How was it for you?* www.schools-out.org.uk

Stonewall (2003) *Profiles of Prejudice*. www.stonewall. org.uk

Trenchard, L. and Warren, H. (eds) (1984) *Something to Tell You*. London: London Gay Teenage Group

Wallace, H. (2005) *Time to Think*. www.timetothinkresearch. co.uk

## Useful organisations

The Beaumont Society – UK based transgender support group. www.beaumontsociety.org.uk

Gender Identity Research and Education Society – The aim of this website is to inform a wide public of the issues surrounding gender identity and transsexualism. www.gires.org.uk

The Gender Trust – The Gender Trust specifically helps adults who are Transsexual, Gender Dysphoric or Transgender i.e. those who seek to adjust their lives to live as women or men, or to come to terms with their situation despite their genetic background.. www.gendertrust.org.uk

Mermaids – Mermaids is a support group for gender variant children and teenagers www.mermaids.freeuk.com/

Press for Change – This site aims to be a newspaper, library and resource centre rolled into one. Nowhere else in the world will you find such a comprehensive collection of information about the trans rights campaign, and details about the legal, medical, political and social issues surrounding the people it represents. www.pfc.org.uk

Teachers Support Network and *Times Educational Supplement* (2006) Homophobia and Teaching Staff. www.teachersupport.info

Lesbian, Gay, Bisexual and Trans History Month UK. www.LGBThistorymonth.org.uk

"Frankly, Dinsdale, we like the look of you."

INTERVIEW BOARD

brian bagnall

# Career Support and Guidance: Choices in the 21st Century

*Sandra Morgan and Deirdre Hughes*

■ *See also schedule: The 14-19 Curriculum*

## Introduction

### The context

School leaver destination statistics show that many young people are still following traditional, gender-stereotyped career choices (Women and Work Commission, 2006). These are rarely based upon a single decision point, but on a long series of decisions made throughout their lives. Although young people's attitudes to traditional gender roles are changing, many jobs are still viewed in a stereotypical way by both girls and boys.

The segregation of women and men into different types of employment has a damaging effect on the economy. It fails to make the most efficient use of the potential workforce, contributing to skills deficits and limiting increased productivity. Concentration of women in low paid and low status jobs contributes to the gender pay gap. The OECD, Paris (2002), reports that whichever way this gap is measured, women's hourly earnings remain consistently below those of men in all developed countries.

Bimrose (2006) indicates the gender pay gap has 'serious implications for retirement, when, for example, women in the UK receive 47% lower weekly income than men because of time out of employment to raise children'. These figures confirm the strong pay differentials across sectors and represent a strong incentive for females to be encouraged to choose non-traditional training and work.

Bimrose also identified two types of segregation: horizontal, where women work in a restricted range of occupational areas different from those in which men are employed; and vertical, where women are

employed at lower levels in organisations. While women's position in the labour market is different and unequal compared to men, these trends are exacerbated for some ethnic groups. Platt (2006) finds a 13% full-time, hourly pay gap for women aged 16 to 59 from all ethnic minority backgrounds relative to white men. This is three times higher than the hourly pay gap for ethnic minority men. Higher qualifications (NVQ Level 3 and above) make little difference to the pay gaps suffered by women from all ethnic minority groups. The Equal Opportunities Commission (2006a) reported that Caribbean, Pakistani and Bangladeshi origin women are far more likely to be unemployed than white British women with similar qualifications; they do not get the same pay gains from higher education as equivalent males and are less likely to reach senior positions than white British women.

The Equal Opportunities Commission (2006b) found some increase in women entering non-traditional apprenticeships. However, apprenticeship pay rates showed a 26% pay gap between male and female apprentices and, of those earning less than £80 a week, more than seven out of ten were women. This highlights the need to continue to challenge gender stereotypes, widen choices, improve access and remove barriers for all young people in non-traditional areas of work.

In the 21st century there is a widening diversity of career patterns and expectations. Therefore, it is important to establish an informed culture in which young people and their parents/carers can see how their learning and skill development in school relates to their potential future working lives. A more pro-active approach to reducing gender stereotyping is now required. Research from Construction Skills

(2006), found that young women feel let down by the careers advice they receive and are being put off traditionally male dominated industries. They believe there has been a gender bias in the advice given in school despite attempts to address gender stereotypes.

### Careers education in schools

In England, secondary schools have a statutory responsibility to provide a programme of careers education from Years 7 to 11. Increasingly, some primary schools also include careers work as part of their curriculum.

All schools have a responsibility to ensure that all young people receive careers information, advice and guidance that is free from gender and race stereotyping. In England, the National Education Standards in Careers Education in Schools (DfES, 2007), aim to step up cultural change in order to challenge assumptions about jobs and ensure that all young people are aware of non-traditional career opportunities.

*Shaping a Fairer Future* (Women and Work Commission, 2006) highlighted the need for girls to have a better understanding of the world of work, to experience working in jobs traditionally done by men, and to have access to better careers information, advice and guidance. The assumption is that if girls were made more aware of the consequences of their choices for their future pay and career progression, they just might make different choices.

Children develop attitudes from a very early age which include perceptions of gender and race. Consequently, avoiding all gender and race stereotyping applies equally to all phases of education including nursery and pre-school groups. A study of 6 year-olds and 10 year-olds found that 70% of 6-year-old boys wanted to be sports personalities, rising to 85% by the age of 10. 40% of 6 year-old girls wanted to be nurses and 30% teachers. By the age of 10, one-third of girls wanted to be flight attendants, one-third teachers and one-third hairdressers (Donnellan, 2006).

Bhavnani (2006) finds that Pakistani, Bangladeshi and Caribbean origin girls believe that their careers advice had not opened their eyes to a full range of possible jobs and careers. They were, therefore, not able to fulfil their potential and consider as wide a range of jobs as other young people.

By focusing on equality issues, school and college staff can help tackle stereotyping, raise young people's aspirations and widen the choices available to them. In the UK, a team from Warwick and Derby Universities have developed an innovative National Guidance Research Forum (NGRF) website that includes resources, legislative data and research findings on this topic. From this, an allied European Guidance and Counselling Research Forum (EGCRF) has emerged, focusing specifically on equity issues including those related to gender.

### Issues to consider
### Be pro-active

Young people learn from what they see and hear around them and develop attitudes towards their future working lives. A review of research on young people's decision-making readiness (Webster, 2002, unpublished) identified the importance of cognitive reasoning, emotional intelligence and social allegiances. It is crucial to ensure that a variety of approaches is used, involving all staff and external support agencies, particularly, in England, the Careers/Connexions Services in schools and colleges.

Providing a gender-neutral school environment in terms of role models, books, materials and resources is a shared responsibility. Equality issues should be made a priority and considered at every stage of planning, implementation and evaluation. For example schools can:

- develop a culture of allowing all stereotypical assumptions about particular groups to be effectively challenged
- be aware of the hidden curriculum throughout the school, and actively seek to avoid any gender and race stereotyping and bias
- avoid the use of any spoken and written language that has implications for bias
- develop a critical awareness amongst young people from an early age of the issues of gender and race stereotyping, and of bias in career and subject choice, as well as in language, information, the media and daily life
- raise young people's confidence and self-esteem through personalised and culture-grounded interventions; for example, through raising subject teachers' awareness of gender and race issues to enable them to support and encourage pupils in their day-to-day interactions

- utilise information, advice and guidance (IAG) support services and resources to develop innovative approaches to help young people consider non-traditional choices
- draw on the expertise of others to develop and support gender-free policies and programmes.

## Provide relevant up-to-date information and support its interpretation

Young people access information from a wide range of sources, much of which is unmediated such as that available on the internet. It is important, therefore, to help young people to make sense of information in an unbiased, impartial manner. For example:

- use all materials to combat gender stereotyping in a coherent and integrated fashion to maximise impact
- review the current information provided to young people on non-traditional careers
- where appropriate, use single-sex groups to discuss course and careers information, and its value to them
- provide data in a relevant format, on the qualifications and employment experiences and wages of young people, disaggregated by gender
- provide ongoing support for young people to interpret unmediated information gained from a range of sources; for example, using external sources such as the Careers/Connexions Service, and encouraging teachers to help pupils to understand the information they receive
- ensure that jobs are described in terms of skills and groups of characteristics; for example, jobs that include working with technology could include intensive care nursing, and jobs helping others could include traditionally male jobs not normally associates with this characteristic, such as engineer and computer software designer
- provide information about industries as well as occupations, as some young people have strong preferences against working in particular industrial sectors
- use a range of materials such as DVDs and video portraits to show non-traditional choices
- use role models from non-traditional occupations to discuss their experiences and successes.

## Involve parents and carers

Much information and advice about subject, course and career choice come from parents/carers, friends and relations. Role models within a young person's family and social circle are important. Parents/carers not only support their children throughout their education, but also have a strong influence on the child's decision making. Engaging parents and carers more fully in equity issues would help break down gender barriers. For example:

- provide information to parents/carers on the implications of subject and career choices, including the gender division in education, training and employment
- facilitate opportunities for parents/carers to access course and careers information at relevant stages
- provide information on the implications of changing labour markets for their children's future
- encourage parents/carers to attend taster days in school
- provide support to parents/carers to access and interpret gender-related data and information.

The Canadian Career Development Foundation has developed innovative teaching and learning resources for teachers and advisers working with parents/carers including approaches for tackling gender stereotyping.

## Develop an unbiased, challenging careers education curriculum

Research (Ofsted, 2005) shows that young people gain much careers information and advice from informal sources, raising issues about its accuracy and relevance. The careers education curriculum should be relevant to all young people, reflect diversity and cultural identity, and build on positive images and positive action to ensure that equality of opportunities is met. *The National Framework for Careers Education and Guidance in England* (2003) emphasises the importance of self-development, career exploration and career management.

Programmes should aim to:

- align their quality assurance with national quality standards
- provide an early introduction to recognising and challenging gender stereotyping with relevant gender information on the implications of decision making and career choices

- encourage young people to recognise and respond to the influences on their own attitudes and values in relation to learning, work and equality of opportunity
- use positive images and case studies to encourage non-traditional choices
- use younger role models to promote links with local universities, and employers in non-traditional areas of study and work
- establish the relationship between learning and work from Year 7 onwards through greater use of the work-related curriculum, linked into the careers education curriculum.

## Ensure a gender-conscious approach to career advice and guidance

Impartial, good quality careers advice and guidance can widen young people's knowledge of the opportunities available to them. However, some teachers and advisers see themselves as adopting a gender neutral stance with the wishes of the young person taken as the starting point for advice (Europa, 2005). A *gender-conscious approach* would require gender factors to be made explicit as part of a more challenging practice. Non-stereotyped options would be introduced to multiply the options available to boys and girls; for example, in providing single-sex opportunities, supported by role models, to discuss career choices and their implications.

More encouragement of non-traditional choices both of subjects and courses, and in career choices is desperately needed. For example schools can:

- provide gender-conscious advice and guidance about the opportunities available in terms of further and higher education, and careers
- support young people to raise their aspirations
- provide single-sex opportunities to discuss gender issues
- challenge stereotypical views and provide alternative options
- highlight pay differentials between men and women in work and explore the rationale for this from a critical stance.

## Use work-related experiences pro-actively

The boundaries between education and the world of work are changing fast with an increasing emphasis on work-related learning linked to career exploration. Although work experience could allow young people to try out non-traditional activities, it often reinforces gender divisions, as challenging gender stereotyping and widening opportunities are not seen as priorities by schools. Often pupils' choices are limited by perceptions of the local labour market and what they believe is achievable for 'people like me', which may, for ethnic minority pupils, be tempered by awareness of stereotyping and racism in the workplace. Encouraging pupils to find their own work experience placements in a freedom of choice model can perpetuate inequalities as different pupils have different levels of knowledge of work placements and different levels of access to them through social networks.

A more pro-active approach would:

- encourage work experience coordinators to recognise the gender stereotypical nature of work placements and adopt a widening opportunities approach
- offer additional support for young people choosing non-traditional placements
- encourage taster days for primary and secondary pupils
- offer non-traditional taster courses, with examples of non-traditional role models
- encourage early participation in an unbiased range of work experience placements
- develop follow-up activities from work experience sharing non-traditional success stories from work-experience through videos, photographs, presentations and diaries
- provide a range of role models at Industry Days and other work-related opportunities.

## Develop broader subject and course choices

Young people should not be given the impression that there are jobs for men and jobs for women, but encouraged to make subject choices and follow career paths which interest them and correspond with their skills and talents. In the UK, greater numbers of boys take technical and scientific subjects while girls dominate in English, modern languages, biology and history, and avoid physics and information technology. Such subject choices affect future employment possibilities. Only by changing traditional attitudes to male and female areas of the curriculum and making these attractive to both will equality be achieved. Effective, non-restrictive course options and career guidance give young people access to economic ladders and widen opportunities for personal development.

The 14-19 curriculum changes have implications for career choices with earlier decision making in Year 9. The increased emphasis on vocational education could reinforce stereotypical patterns of race and gender, and restrict choices at an earlier age than before.

Choices of education, training and employment options at 16 plus are also vital. At both transition stages, it is important that all young people are:

■ given equal access to consultation on course/subject options

■ offered gender-conscious careers guidance before choices are made

■ made aware of the implications of their choices for their future careers

■ made aware of the full range of options open to them

■ encouraged beyond conventional choices.

## Conclusion

Opportunities for social mobility have never been greater than they are today. Young people have the potential to explore opportunities in a wide range of careers from across a variety of geographical locations. In addition, opportunities increasingly exist to experience a number of different careers within a single lifetime. Given this potential for diversity it is crucial that young people's choices are not restricted by gender specific assumptions.

## References

Bhavnani, R. (2006) *Moving on Up? Ahead of the Game: the changing aspirations of young ethnic minority women.* Manchester: Equal Opportunities Commission

Bimrose, J. (2006) Guidance for Girls and Women. In Athanasou, C. and Van Esbroeck, R. (eds) *International Handbook of Career Guidance.* Berlin: Springer Science and Business Media

Canadian Career Development Foundation Resources for Work with Parents http://www.qesnrecit.qc.ca/goal/JustForParents_000.php

Careers Scotland (2004) *Gender Stereotyping of Career Choice.* Edinburgh: Careers Scotland

ConstructionSkills (2006) *Three Quarters of Young Women Being Put Off Traditionally 'Male-Dominated' Industries by Poor Careers Advice.* London: ConstructionSkills http://www.constructionskills.net/pdf/news/pressreleases/pr-20060404-positiveimage.pdf

Department for Education and Skills (2003) *Careers Education and Guidance in England: A National Framework 11-19.* Nottingham: DfES

Department for Education and Skills (2003) *Using the National Framework for Careers Education and Guidance.* Nottingham: DfES

Department for Education and Skills (2007) *National Standards in Careers Education in Schools.* Nottingham: DfES

Donnellan, C. and Firth, L. (eds) (2006) *Women, Men and Equality.* Volume 112. Cambridge: Independence Educational

Equal Opportunities Commission (2005) *Action for Change: How careers advice professionals can break down gender segregation in vocational education, training and work.* Manchester: Equal Opportunities Commission

Equal Opportunities Commission (2005) *A Strategy to Build a World-class Workforce for Children and Young People.* Manchester: Equal Opportunities Commission

Equal Opportunities Commission (2005) Gender equality in work experience placements for young people. *Working paper Series 27.* Manchester: Equal Opportunities Commission

Equal Opportunities Commission (2005) J*obs for the Girls and the Boys*. Manchester: Equal Opportunities Commission

Equal Opportunities Commission (2006a) *Moving On Up? Bangladeshi, Pakistani and Black Caribbean women and work.* Manchester: Equal Opportunities Commission

Equal Opportunities Commission (2006b) *Free to Choose: Tackling gender barriers to better jobs: One year progress report.* Manchester: Equal Opportunities Commission

Europa (2005) *Overcoming Gender Blindness in Careers Guidance.* Roskilde: Equal Success Stories www.europa.eu.int/comm/employment_social/equal/data/document/etg4-suc-gm-vocguidance.pdf

European Guidance and Counselling Research Forum (EGCRF) www.guidance-europe.org/country/UK/gen/

Haynes, G., Wragg, C. and Mason, K. (2005) *Equality and Pathfinders.* Manchester: Equal Opportunities Commission

National Guidance Research Forum (NGRF) website www.guidance-research.org/EG/equal-opps/gender

OECD (2002) *Women At Work: Who Are They and How Are They Faring?* OECD Employment Outlook 2002 – Surveying the Jobs Horizon. Paris: Organisation for Economic Co-operation and Development, 63-125

Ofsted (2005) *Developing a Coherent 14-19 Phase of Education and Training.* London: Ofsted

Platt, L. (2006) *Moving On Up? Pay Gaps: the position of ethnic minority women and men.* Manchester: Equal Opportunities Commission

Webster, A. (2002) Decision-Making Readiness Audit: summary and recommendations from the construct review. Bristol University in association with the Centre for Guidance Studies and Sheffield University (unpublished)

Women and Work Commission (2006) *Shaping a Fairer Future.* London: Department of Trade and Industry

# INCLUSION

## Introduction: Gender and Inclusion

*Hazel Taylor*

Inclusion, broadly meaning that all children whatever disadvantages they may face, have an entitlement to provision which addresses the barriers to their equality of opportunity and maximises their life chances, must now be taken seriously by all schools. It is no longer possible to offer groups of pupils additional needs provision which occupies and contains them; it must explicitly seek to enable high achievement and full participation in the school community. Policy for inclusion has developed in response to a number of concerns:

- The focus on raising achievement demonstrated by achieving benchmark targets has led to the increased marginalisation of those not clustered around the benchmark, whether the lowest or potentially the highest achievers

- Many pupils facing poverty, and disadvantage due to ethnicity, disability, mobility or gender are still underachieving in spite of the positive impacts of the national curriculum and a plethora of initiatives to improve teaching and learning

- The ineffectiveness and inefficiency of splitting provision for children across unconnected services, mainly health, education and social care

- The social costs of ineffective education for the marginalised.

It is in these areas that the complexity of interrelated strands of disadvantage presents most challenges. This section of *Genderwatch* considers them through the lens of gender. Though it may not be the most pressing disadvantage, it is always a factor and we must remind ourselves that we have learnt that we do not deal with all aspects of inequity through only focusing on one.

There are schedules on pupils with learning difficulties and disabilities (SEN), on English as an additional language, and on mobility and in each there is some discussion of the general context within which gender is a variable. As Agnew points out, the absence of mentions of gender in the special needs documentation reminds us how easily it is overlooked as a central part of how we experience our lives.

### Gifted and Talented

The most recent area of those now commonly seen as elements of inclusion is that concerned with potentially very high achievers from disadvantaged backgrounds. University entrance continues to be disproportionately dominated by the advantaged. It is felt that many young people with potential may not be acquiring the social and cultural capital that middle class children pick up from home, and that schools with balanced intakes and with more affluent catchment areas are more able to provide. A strand in the policy initiatives to address this, alongside pressure to review university admissions procedures, and the changes to the 14-19 curriculum, is the Gifted and Talented programme. This began as a strand of the Excellence in Cities initiative (1997) and has good intentions, but is highly problematic in practice, not least in terms of gender. Gifted pupils are defined as those with a marked ability in one or more academic subject, while the talented are those with the potential to excel in the arts and sport. The identification and separation of the allegedly gifted raises all the elements of the debate about who benefits and who loses from providing opportunities which are not available to all, and to which access is controlled by unreliable and shifting criteria. From a gender perspective there are several serious concerns:

■ selection is prejudiced by deeply sexist beliefs in the greater potential of boys than girls. When methods other than tests are used in identification of gifted pupils, twice as many boys as girls are likely to be identified. Parents identify two boys to every one girl

■ selection that seeks to alleviate panic at boys' alleged underachievement (Oates, in this volume) panders to beliefs that girls are somehow overachieving and penalises them

■ access to enrichment opportunities for some ignores the fact that in spite of school achievement, girls disproportionately avoid subjects that lead to higher status and higher paid work.

Opportunities for enrichment need to be available to all who are attracted by them, and undoubtedly pupils who could benefit but would otherwise exclude themselves should be directed to them. But as with setting, and tiering in examination entry, exclusion can depress achievement and reduce access to the curriculum, and inclusion can increase pressure. Young men and young women respond differently to demands to achieve, and measures intended to support potential high achievers need to be sensitive to this.

# Inclusion of Pupils with Special Educational Needs

*Daryl Agnew and Carole Goodwin*

■ *See also schedules: Every Child Matters; Home-School Relations; The Wider Workforce; English as an Additional Language*

Note: The terminology changes. Pupils with 'learning difficulties and/or disabilities' (LDD) is the term used within the context of the *Every Child Matters* agenda instead of SEN, as this crosses the professional boundaries of education, health and social services and provides a common language for 0-19 year- olds. SEN is used here, as it is still the term commonly used in schools.

## Introduction

Despite significant developments in social and educational inclusion and the move to integrate services for children and young people, the focus on special educational needs (SEN) has often remained distinct from that of equal opportunities concerning race and gender. Until the introduction of the different types of SEN for use in the pupil level annual schools census (PLASC) in 2004, national data for England on SEN did not include data on the ethnicity and gender of pupils with statements. Scottish and Welsh authorities have been required to report how many children have statements (or 'records' in Scotland) by type of need and gender.

However, a significantly higher proportion of boys than girls have SEN statements: more than twice as many at all ages. Speech and language difficulties are known to be reported more commonly among boys; and for the fastest growing types of special educational needs – behavioural, emotional and social difficulties (BESD) and autistic spectrum disorder (ASD) – boys are more than five times as likely to have these types of needs identified, especially among the middle classes. Furthermore, it is widely recognised that there is a strong correlation between exclusions, poverty, single parents and children with SEN, particularly those with behavioural, emotional and social difficulties.

This marked gender difference raises questions about the extent to which there has been discrimination against girls in terms of the SEN and disabilities agenda and, in particular, insufficient recognition of their social and emotional needs, including their experience of abuse. Girls' needs may remain hidden, rather than there being none. Witness the prevalence of eating disorders such as anorexia and bulimia and of self harm among girls and young women. This is particularly a concern in special schools and pupil referral units (PRUs) where girls are in a significant minority.

Lindsay *et al* (2006), focusing on SEN and ethnicity, analysed the 2005 PLASC data for all children in maintained schools in England and surveyed results from 40 local authorities. They found that socio-economic disadvantage and gender had stronger associations than ethnicity with overall prevalence of SEN and of certain categories of SEN. However, Caribbean origin and mixed white and black Caribbean pupils were around one and a half times more likely to be identified as having behavioural, emotional and social difficulties than white pupils.

Other research has suggested that factors such as racist attitudes and the differential treatment of black pupils could be a reason for their over-representation in the BESD category. However, not all black groups have similar patterns of SEN. Bangladeshi pupils were twice as likely to be identified as having hearing impairment than British white, while Pakistani pupils were between two and two and a half times more likely to be identified as having profound and multiple learning difficulties (PMLD), visual impairment, hearing impairment or multi-sensory impairment, than white pupils.

Local authorities report that a significant and growing proportion of children in care have special educational needs. However, national statistics available on children in care (looked after children) do not include a breakdown by gender. Nor in the Green Paper *Care Matters: Transforming the Lives of Children and Young People in Care* (2006) is there a focus on the differing needs of girls and boys in care or any implications for their support and education.

### The legislative and policy framework

Since *Excellence for all Children* (DfEE, 1997), the Government has sought to increase the inclusion of pupils with special educational needs and disabilities into mainstream schools and to improve provision in both mainstream and special schools.

The *Special Educational Needs and Disability Act* (SENDA) (2001) and the *SEN Code of Practice* (2002), set out the framework for provision for children with SEN. *Removing Barriers to Achievement* (2004), the strategy for children with SEN and disabilities, links to the reform of children's services as set out in *Every Child Matters*, with its focus on early intervention, preventative work and integrated services for children. It aims to improve outcomes for children with SEN and their families.

The Disability Discrimination Act 2005 places a new legal duty, the Disability Equality Duty (DED), on schools (that is, on all maintained primary and secondary schools in England and Wales, including pupil referral units, and also city technology colleges and academies in England) actively to promote disability equality for pupils, employees and service users. This, in turn, has further implications for schools.

Where gender meets disability, inequities can arise because of the tendency to exaggerate gender stereotypes on responding to the disability issue, for example by applying gendered views of coping with pain – bravery or helplessness shown by individuals in response to treatment.

### Inclusion and special educational needs

The particular concern about where children with special educational needs should be educated has been addressed in *Inclusion: does it matter where pupils are taught?* (Ofsted, 2006). This looked at the progress made by pupils in three areas of their learning: academic and vocational achievement, personal development, and social development. The report concluded that the most important factor in determining the best outcomes for pupils with special educational needs is 'not the type but the quality of the provision'.

This survey found that high quality, specialist teachers and a commitment by the senior leadership to create opportunities to include all pupils, including in some cases pupils with severe and complex needs, were critical success factors. Pupils in mainstream schools where support from teaching assistants was the main type of provision were less likely to make good academic progress than those who had access to specialist teaching.

### The interface between gender and special educational need

Within the context described above, this schedule is concerned with the ways in which gender can interrelate with the many types of special need. There is a range of issues that staff in schools need to bear in mind as they tackle the difficult task of ensuring that in attempting to provide for one need, they also recognise others. Staff need to be aware of the following gender/special need interrelationships:

■ where there are uneven numbers of each sex in a category of need, both monitoring the picture, and examining the identification process for any gender bias, for example in reaction to particular sorts of acting out behaviour

■ where one gender is in a minority in any specialist group or provision, noting that all the issues about potential gender discrimination will be present

■ where pupils have serious physical disabilities, being sensitive to developing sexuality and its different impact on girls and boys, and to the need for same sex carers on visits to meet personal hygiene needs

■ where there are mental health issues, making sure that all staff are aware of the very different ways boys and girls can make distress visible, and responding to acting in as well as acting out

■ recognising that while all pupils with special educational needs have emotional needs relating to their perception of their need and what it means for their identity, how these are expressed, recognised and acknowledged can be powerfully influenced by gender

being aware of the tendency for a special need to lead to an intensification of stereotyped gendered expectations and responses – for example, girls being seen as even more helpless, or boys as even more inattentive – and being aware of the risks of double or triple stereotyping when thinking about future aspirations and employment.

### Issues to consider
### At the school (and co-ordinator) level

■ Is there a shared understanding amongst staff about what constitutes underachievement and what is SEN? Are staff aware of the gender stereotypes associated with underachievement and the danger of not identifying some pupils for support because of it (eg quiet and well-behaved girls)?

■ How does the school ensure that at both management and practitioner levels there are high expectations for pupils with SEN and that these expectations are not based on gender stereotypes? Are these high expectations communicated clearly to parents and carers?

■ Is there awareness among staff and governors of the minority ethnic group cultures of pupils with SEN, and the different needs of girls and boys with SEN?

■ What systems are in place for staff to listen to pupils' experience? Is care taken to ensure that both girls' and boys' voices are heard?

■ How well do pupils with SEN respond to school? Is there a difference between male and female pupils? Are there any individuals/groups who find engagement in the work of the school difficult? Are any of these pupils over represented in relation to absence, lateness or exclusion? How does the school act upon these findings?

■ Do senior managers report regularly to governors on SEN and inclusion issues? Is there monitoring of both identification of pupils with SEN and of outcomes for them by ethnicity and gender?

■ Do senior managers report regularly to governors on the progress of looked after children within the school in relation to their ethnicity, gender and/or SEN? Is there recognition of the links between looked after children and their special educational needs?

■ Are the rights of young people with learning

difficulties and disabilities as sexual beings recognised within the school? How are issues of sexuality addressed?

■ Do surveys and pupil questionnaires used by the school fully involve pupils with SEN and/or disabilities? Are the outcomes analysed by gender and ethnicity as well as disability? Are the outcomes used to inform improvements in the school's provision?

### In relations with parents and carers

■ At the key points of transition, particularly at 14 and 16 years of age, are parents and carers encouraged to consider non-stereotypical choices for their children?

### At classroom teacher or teaching assistant level

■ Are girls and boys treated with equity in the identification, assessment and provision for their special educational needs? To what extent do teacher expectations, based on gender stereotypes, influence the overall assessment process for girls and boys with SEN? (See Daniels *et al*, 2000 for an exercise looking at a class and noting 'who needs help and who gets what sort of help' by gender and race, including specifically who gets the expensive in and out of school specialist help.)

■ Is the style of teaching varied in relation to girls and boys to take account of a range of learning styles of the pupils within the class?

■ Is teaching planned jointly by specialist and support staff who are aware of gender issues in learning, even though the teaching may be delivered by the classroom support assistant?

■ Do staff ensure that girls and boys have opportunities to work together in mixed and same-sex groups, and in groups that reflect the range of abilities within the class?

■ Is the low profile that some girls may maintain within the classroom viewed negatively? Are girls' strengths, particularly in communication and emotional intelligence, sufficiently nurtured and valued? Is unusual behaviour (for the age group or a change in the individual child) – willingness to please/conform or interest in sex – monitored as possible indicators of abuse?

■ Are girls' emotional needs recognised as educational needs or are they seen as health problems?

■ Do boys receive more teacher attention for inappropriate behaviour? Are their emotional needs recognised less than their behavioural needs? Do boys receive more provision for their identified needs, particularly their literacy needs?

■ How are pupils with SEN and/or disabilities fully involved in decisions about their learning and behaviour? In particular, how effective is their involvement in meetings such as the annual reviews? If necessary, is support provided to ensure their active involvement? Is consideration given to any gender differences in how pupils may respond to these processes and make adjustments accordingly?

■ If using external agencies either to assess the needs of pupils in classes or to provide specialist support, is consideration given to the dynamics of gender and how they may affect the pupil response?

## Further reading

Audit Commission (2002) *Special Educational Needs: A Mainstream Issue*

Benjamin, S. (2002) *The Micropolitics of Inclusive Education: Ethnography*. Buckingham: Open University Press, on the lives and self image of SEN girls in a secondary school.

Campbell, C. (ed) (2002) *Developing Inclusive Schooling: Perspectives, Policies and Practices*. University of London: Institute of Education

Daniels, H., Hey, V., Leonard, D. and Smith, M. (2000) Issues of equity in Special Needs Education as seen from the perspective of gender. In Daniels, H. (ed) *Special Education Re-formed: Beyond rhetoric?* London: Falmer

Department for Education and Skills (2004) *Removing Barriers to Achievement: The Government's Strategy for SEN*. London: DfES

Lindsay, G., Pather, S. and Strand, S. (2006) *Special Educational Needs and Ethnicity: Issues of Over- and Under-Representation*. DfES Research Brief 757 www.dfes.gov.uk/research/programmeofresearch/projectinformation.cfm?projectid=14467

Office for Standards in Education (2006) *Inclusion: Does It Matter Where Pupils Are Taught?* London: HMSO

Osler, A. and Vincent, K. (2003). *Girls and Exclusion: Rethinking the Agenda*. London: RoutledgeFalmer

Osler, A. and Starkey, H. (2005) *Changing Citizenship: Democracy and Inclusion in Education*. Buckingham: Open University Press

Tilstone, C. and Rose, R. (2003) *Strategies to Promote Inclusive Practice*. London: RoutledgeFalmer

*Skill*: the National Bureau for Students with Disabilities has many useful resources, to encourage discussion between SEN specialists and others on the intersections of gender, race and SEN: eg Maudslay, L., Rafique, A. and Uddin, A. (nd) *Aasha: working with young people with a learning difficulty from a South Asian Background*. Skill: National Bureau for students with Disabilities

Similarly the Joseph Rowntree Foundation eg Bignall, T., Butt, J. and Paragani, D. (2002) *'Something to Do': The Development of Peer Groups for Young Black and Minority Ethnic Disabled People*. JRF: The Policy Press

# English as an Additional Language

*Silvaine Wiles with Meena Modi and Shahla Taheri-White*

■ *See also schedules: Managing Pupil Mobility; Home-School Relations; The Wider Workforce*

Data from one local authority show that minority ethnic pupils are the recipients of a significant amount of racial harassment, and that boys are three times more likely than girls to be perpetrators of racist behaviour and twice as likely to be victims.

> 'Some teachers forget you are learning English and speak too fast in a difficult language.'
>
> 'I have the ideas but the words stick in my mouth.'
>
> 'My English is too plain.' (Ofsted, 2003)

## Equality of access

The key issue for teachers in developing bilingual pupils is how to provide them with equality of access to the wide range of educational opportunities offered by the school. Helping students become fluent and effective users of English so that they can achieve their full potential takes time and is the responsibility of all members of staff. The needs of pupils new to English are obvious, but it is also crucial to recognise the need of more advanced bilingual learners for continuing language support across the curriculum. Pupils with English as an additional language (EAL) spend most of their time in the mainstream and, as their knowledge of English develops, their attainment across the curriculum improves exponentially, with many outperforming their monolingual peers by the end of Key Stage 4.

To a large extent, the gender issues relevant to the teaching and learning of EAL mirror those in the wider school community: the importance of paying attention to classroom organisation, teaching style, the selection of resources, equal aspirations for boys and girls and so on. However, the avoidance of stereotypical assumptions (with reference to gender, class and race), whilst important for all pupils, is perhaps of particular significance for certain ethnic groups and for boys and girls within these groups.

*Aiming High: Raising the Achievement of Minority Ethnic Pupils* (DfES, 2003) identified five characteristics of schools which were associated with successful outcomes for minority ethnic pupils: strong leadership; high expectations; effective teaching and learning; an ethos of respect, with a clear approach to racism and bad behaviour; and parental involvement. For EAL pedagogy to be effective and for bilingual pupils to flourish at school, all of these characteristics need to be present.

The following questions might help teachers to review their practice in relation to these key areas.

### Issues to consider
### Strong leadership

■ Do senior managers make clear their commitment to achieving equality of access for pupils with EAL?

■ Is there specific reference to EAL in the school's vision statement, and documentation such as the school development plan, the self evaluation form (SEF), all schemes of work, and the assessment and equality policies?

■ Do senior managers understand the long-term support needs of many pupils with EAL, insist on a whole-school strategy for support, appreciate what constitutes effective EAL practice, and ensure sufficient staffing and training are available?

■ Is bilingualism/multilingualism valued and celebrated? Is this reflected in the recruitment of teaching and non-teaching staff – male and female?

■ Do senior managers inform the governors about EAL issues and related gender issues (especially as they relate to parents and the community) and see the importance of the governing body reflecting the diversity of the school population?

## High expectations

■ How does the school ensure that, at both management and practitioner level, there are high expectations for all groups, and for both boys and girls within these groups?

■ Is there an ethos that allows stereotypical assumptions about specific groups to be challenged?

■ Are attainment data analysed by EAL, ethnic group and gender?

■ Does the analysis get beneath the global data and look at differences (for both ethnicity and gender) in relation to speaking and listening, reading and writing in English, as well as the various strands of the programmes of study in all areas of the curriculum?

■ What does the school do to close any attainment gaps that emerge?

■ Are grouping and setting policies monitored to ensure that bilingual pupils are placed according to ability and age rather than current level of language development? This is particularly important when pupils are new to English but may, for example, be highly competent in their knowledge and understanding of mathematics and science

■ Is the school aware of local or national action research on the needs of specific groups, for example Pakistani boys' achievement, Turkish boys' attainment in writing?

■ Does the school monitor 14+ options by gender and ethnicity, and seek to ensure balanced choices for all groups to keep pathways open?

■ When pupils arrive mid-term, are their prior attainments (in the first language and other areas of the curriculum) fully assessed, the information shared with all staff, the pupils appropriately placed and their progress monitored? Is care taken not to make assumptions based on gender?

■ Does the school recognise the valuable role played by bilingual teachers, teaching assistants and learning mentors, not only in terms of their linguistic and cultural knowledge and expertise, but in providing male and female role models for minority ethnic pupils, thereby helping to raise their aspirations?

■ Has the school interviewed bilingual pupils about their aspirations and, if these are found to be influenced largely by social and cultural expectations, taken steps to expand their horizons?

## Teaching and learning

■ Has the school sought bilingual pupils' (girls and boys) views on what helps them to develop their English, play a full part in the learning of the classroom and the life of the school more generally?

■ Do ethnic minority achievement (EMA)/EAL staff prioritise support, within the mainstream, of advanced bilingual learners as well as of pupils new to English? Are they aware of gender issues?

■ Is there a focus in all lessons on both language and subject content? Is care taken to avoid sexist language and to ensure that subject content is gender neutral?

■ Has the work been planned in conjunction with mainstream staff/subject specialists, even when the teaching takes place in a withdrawal group? Are gender issues considered when organising the composition of withdrawal groups?

■ Have all staff been helped to develop language aware teaching approaches, either through the experience of working in partnership with EAL specialists or by the provision of training and additional resources? Gender-related ones include:

  – a welcoming environment in which bilingual pupils feel confident to contribute (for example, by giving early stage learners the support they need and more time to respond to questions, making clear that racism, sexism and negative reactions to language and accent variation will not be tolerated).

■ Do teachers ensure that boys and girls have opportunities to work both in mixed and single-sex groups, and in groups which reflect the diversity of the school population?

■ Do teachers set clear ground rules for group work and monitor outcomes for bilingual boys and girls?

■ Do teachers review groups on a regular basis to ensure that both boys and girls have good role models?

■ Do the curriculum and resources reflect the communities and cultures from which the students come in more than just a superficial way? Are topics, themes and materials relevant, interesting and motivating?

■ Are any specific gender issues within cultures recognised and addressed?

■ Do staff understand that even though pupils with EAL will achieve verbal fluency relatively quickly, this may mask continuing difficulties with reading and writing in English? Do they monitor and address any differences between girls and boys in this respect?

■ Have links been made with the community/complementary/supplementary schools attended by pupils to share information, pedagogical approaches and ideas about gender equity?

## Ethos of respect, with a clear approach to racism and bad behaviour

■ Are all pupils' cultures and languages valued not just through display but through the curriculum, with positive role models from both sexes?

■ Are the positive benefits of bilingualism recognised and celebrated?

■ Data from one local authority show that minority ethnic pupils are subjected to a significant amount of racial harassment, that boys are three times more likely than girls to be perpetrators of racist behaviour and twice as likely to be victims. Given the damaging impact of racist behaviour on learning, does the school have clear procedures at whole-school and classroom level for tackling this problem?

■ Is it recognised that where black and minority ethnic (BME) pupils are in the minority in a school, they are particularly vulnerable to racist abuse?

## Parental involvement

■ Do senior managers lead from the front in attempts to engage with the whole school community, not leaving contact with parents of ethnic minority pupils solely to EMA staff?

■ Does the school seek to raise parental expectations for both boys and girls – especially where family and community aspirations for the two sexes differ?

■ Does the school make efforts to gain the confidence of all parents through close contact, openness and respect for their values and beliefs?

■ Does the school monitor attendance at parents' evenings and other school events by ethnicity and gender?

■ Does the school have specific strategies to reduce any gender bias in parental involvement across all ethnic groups?

## References and contacts

Ali, M (2001) *Turkish Speaking Communities and Education: No Delight.* FATAL publications

Department for Education and Skills (2002) *Unlocking Potential: Raising Ethnic Minority Attainment at Key Stage 3.* London: DfES 0579

Department for Education and Skills (2003) *Aiming High: Raising the Achievement of Minority Ethnic Pupils.* London: DfES 0183 DfES website: www.standards.dfes.gov.uk/ ethnicminorities

Gibbons, P. (1991) *Learning to Learn in a Second Language.* Primary English Teaching Association

Gillborn, D. and Mirza, H. S. (2000) *Educational Inequality: Mapping Race, Class and Gender.* London: Ofsted HMI 232

Hall, D. (2001) *Assessing the Needs of Bilingual pupils: Living in Two Languages.* London: Fulton

NALDIC (National Association for Language Development in the Curriculum) www.naldic.org.uk

National Literacy Strategy (2002) *Supporting Pupils Learning English as an Additional Language.* London: DfES

National Numeracy Strategy (2002) *Assessment Toolkit to Support Pupils with English as an Additional Language. Revised Edition.* London: DfES 0319

Ofsted (2003) *More Advanced Learners of English as an Additional Language in Secondary Schools and Colleges.* London: Ofsted HMI 1102

Ofsted (2004) *Managing the Ethnic Minority Achievement Grant: Good Practice in Primary Schools.* London: Ofsted HMI 2072

Ofsted (2004) *Managing the Ethnic Minority Achievement Grant: Good Practice in Secondary Schools.* London: Ofsted HMI 2172

Ofsted (2005) *Could They Do Even Better? The Writing of Advanced Bilingual Learners of English at Key Stage 2.* London: Ofsted HMI 2452

# Managing pupil mobility
*Val McGregor and Karen Benton*

■ *See also schedules: English as an Additional Language; Assessment; Uniform*

## The current context

The non-routine movement of pupils, that is pupil mobility, has implications for many key areas of educational policy and practice, yet it is only relatively recently that this issue has begun to have a higher national profile.

Most schools gain and lose some pupils at irregular times. For some schools, this may mean one or two pupils who come and go in a year; in other schools it may be a hundred or more. Dobson *et al* (2000) concluded that schools with mobility rates above 20% are in a minority, but they can comprise between a quarter and a half of schools in some parts of the UK, for example in London. Although many schools in different parts of the country, both coastal and urban, have high mobility rates, the reasons for this are varied and complex. Most significant are: relocation, abuse of human rights in other countries, war, difficulties in school which lead to official or informal exclusion and the movement of armed services personnel.

In mixed schools, a greater number of boys than girls join as mid-term admissions. Reasons for this vary, but feedback from schools indicates that, in a significant number of schools, this is because more boys than girls have had difficulties settling in schools and therefore have been advised to 'move on' or have chosen to do so. In addition, more boys are likely to experience high mobility because of exclusion, and a significantly higher number of boys are likely to arrive as unaccompanied adults. Unfortunately, reliable data is unavailable, given the nature and profile of both of these pupil groups.

Whatever the context, schools with high mobility rates face considerable challenges. A constant flow of pupils in and out of a school can impact greatly on school administrative systems, on liaison time both within the school and with outside agencies, and on the management and delivery of the curriculum. Pupil mobility in and out of schools has implications for some of schools' fundamental outcomes, in particular, pupil attainment, target setting and attendance.

Since January 2000, schools undergoing inspection have been asked to provide data on pupil mobility and, therefore, national data is available in order to make comparisons, particularly with regards to attainment. In its review of data on mobility and attainment, Ofsted (2002) recognised that the relationship between pupil mobility and attainment is a complex one. Its analysis showed that secondary schools with high mobility levels tended to have lower results, and that almost all schools with mobility above 15% had average GCSE scores below the national average.

## The question of gender

Although schools nationally are becoming more adept at collating and using data to track pupil progress and pinpoint issues for concern, analysis of the progress of pupils with high mobility has to date not taken gender issues sufficiently into account. Pupil case studies and feedback from schools have highlighted the fact that significantly more mid-phase admissions are boys rather than girls. Significantly, the attainment gap between girls from the mobile and stable populations began to close more quickly than for boys.

In addition, more boys than girls who change schools mid-term are likely to experience difficulties in integrating; sometimes these difficulties result in behaviour management issues in the worst cases, even exclusions. Clearly this is a worrying trend and deserves further investigation; unless schools analyse attainment, progress, attendance and behaviour data thoroughly in relation to gender, they will not be able to address the issues of potential under-attainment of boys and girls in this significant pupil group.

## The challenge

Unsurprisingly, recent Ofsted and DfES research on pupil mobility recognises that schools which have a clear understanding of their pupils' mobility and put managerial and organisational structures in place to support effective induction and to provide personal and curricular support, are more likely to settle target pupils swiftly, enabling them to access the curriculum and capitalise on learning opportunities.

Pupils who experience high mobility may well have gaps in their learning. However, it must be emphasised that they may have fallen behind due to tremendous pressures and trauma. When they are adequately catered for, they can and do progress well and make positive contributions to the overall attainment profile of the schools they attend. The attainment data of all of the schools involved in the London Challenge and Secondary National Strategy Mobility Project (DfES, 2004) clearly show that their pupils with high mobility have contributed significantly to their improved results at both key stage 3 and key stage 4.

Planning for pupil mobility requires schools to begin again with new pupils. Sometimes there is little idea of how long they will remain in school. The schools which are most successful in establishing effective work are those which perceive themselves as having mobile pupils as an essential element in their identity. They are seeking to become experts in this field: knowing what is entailed and shaping their provision and deploying their resources accordingly. Below, we offer some pointers for how schools can achieve this.

## Issues to consider
### Initial assessment

In order to ensure that the skills, knowledge and experiences of mid-phase pupils are assessed as accurately and efficiently as possible:

■ minimise the amount of formal testing: many pupils who move from school to school are over tested. In addition, written assessments may obscure the true knowledge and understanding of many pupils, especially those learning English as an additional language

■ rapidly discover as much as possible about pupils' prior schooling and learning experiences, preferably through a senior member of staff interviewing the pupil. Try to glean as much information about pupils' hobbies and interests; this may be particularly helpful for discovering, for example, pupils' extra-curricular or sporting interests. Try not to make assumptions based on gender!

■ where appropriate, involve specialist ethnic minority achievement (EMA) and English as an additional language (EAL) staff in the initial assessment process; particularly when assessing language proficiency and literacy in the home language(s). It may also be helpful to involve interpreters employed by the school or local authority; in some cases, it may be possible to use informal translators, for example, fellow pupils or staff. On occasions it may also be helpful to find same-sex interpreters

■ assess pupils' skills, knowledge and understanding within subjects; this should be done by subject teachers, so that information gathered can immediately be used to establish particular strengths and gaps in learning and, most importantly, to inform pupils' learning

■ rapidly collect and analyse relevant baseline data and information about prior learning for use by staff, so that all information gathered can be used to inform teaching and learning across the curriculum

■ analyse all base-line information on new entrants by gender as well as ethnicity, so that the progress of boys and girls can be effectively tracked and monitored.

## Induction

Ensure that all newly arrived pupils are effectively welcomed and inducted into the culture and systems of the school. Implement an effective induction programme by:

■ organising a swift and effective induction process for all new arrivals which rapidly results in the full integration of the pupils into mainstream lessons as soon as possible. Pay attention to the gender composition of the groups in which the new arrivals are placed

■ appointing an induction coordinator/mentor to oversee the induction of the pupils and to liaise with parents/guardians and key members of staff

■ preparing a full induction for parents/guardians and pupils on the processes and key staff of the school, including timetable arrangements, translated into community languages, as appropriate

■ establishing systems for informing all staff about new arrivals and providing them, before the pupils join lessons, with mini-biographies prepared by pupils themselves during induction, outlining any relevant experiences and interests/hobbies

■ ensuring all pupils are fully prepared with necessary uniform and equipment, arranging financial support as necessary. Be sensitive to the gender issues around uniform

■ enabling induction mentors and/or pastoral staff formally to introduce the newly arrived pupils to the relevant teaching staff and teaching subjects

■ ensuring that induction mentors and/or pastoral staff are aware of gender issues and sensitive to the needs of new arrivals

■ establishing appropriate support for pupils who are learning English as an additional language, keeping any withdrawal/specialist support to a minimum

■ partnering new entrants, wherever possible, with an established pupil from a similar background, with the same timetable and, if appropriate, the same home language and gender

■ providing opportunities during breaks or lunchtimes for pupils to share their hobbies/interests with other pupils; there is much evidence that many new arrivals, both boys and girls, find these informal times of the day the most challenging

■ establishing weekly contact with parents/guardians to feedback on pupil progress.

## Teaching and learning

Ensure that the teaching and learning offered to all newly arrived pupils is appropriately challenging and supportive by:

■ swiftly disseminating relevant assessment data to staff in order to identify gaps in learning, including knowledge and skills

■ ensuring subject leaders maintain flexibility and, where possible, spaces in all pupil groupings and sets, so that new arrivals may be placed appropriately; take care to ensure that pupils are not routinely placed in lower sets/groups, particularly those pupils who are learning English as an additional language

■ trying not to place new female arrivals in groups dominated by boys and vice versa

■ developing units of work and lesson plans to include a range of approaches, activities and materials; some new entrants may have experienced very different teaching styles in the past

■ ensuring these approaches are gender-neutral and avoiding sexist language

■ developing electronic or online versions of schemes of work or lessons, so that pupils may access learning which has been missed

■ deploying additional staff, including teaching assistants, in flexible ways to maximise learning including in-class support, catch-up sessions and coursework support

■ tracking, monitoring and analysing pupil progress by gender regularly, using attendance, behaviour and attainment data

■ organising routine exit interviews with pupils who are leaving to ascertain 'how we could have done it better' and analysing the results by gender

■ reviewing school policy and practice annually, involving pupils who have experienced high mobility and representatives from the school council.

A final note: we are not suggesting that any school should or could tackle all of these areas at once. In fact, quite the contrary: we suggest that any school wishing to improve their expertise in this area should firstly consider the checklist above and then ask themselves the following questions:

- where are we now? What do we know about our pupils with high mobility? What data do we have? What if any are the different needs of male and female mobile pupils?

- which of the areas listed above are potential strengths? Which areas need further development?

- which three priorities will we concentrate upon first? How will we monitor the impact of our actions on the pupils and on the rest of the school?

## References and further reading

Demie, F. and Strand, S. (2004) *Pupil Mobility and Educational Achievement in Lambeth Schools*. Lambeth Education

Department for Education and Skills (2003) *Aiming High: Raising the Achievement of Minority Ethnic Pupils*. London: DfES

Department for Education and Skills (2003) *Managing Pupil Mobility: A handbook for induction mentors*. London: DfES

Department for Education and Skills (2004) *Ensuring the Attainment of Mobile Pupils*. London: DfES

Dobson, J. and Henthorne, K. (1999) *Pupil Mobility in Schools: Interim report*. Research Report 168. London: DfEE

Dobson, J., Henthorne, K. and Lynas, Z. (2000) *Pupil Mobility in Schools: Final Report*. London: DfEE

Lambeth London Borough (2004) *Pupil Mobility in Lambeth schools: Implications for Raising Achievement and School Management*

Newham, London Borough (2003) *Managing Mid-Phase Pupil Admissions: A Resource and Guidance Folder for Schools.*

Office for Standards in Education (2002) *Managing Pupil Mobility*. London: Ofsted

# PEDAGOGY AND THE ORGANISATION OF LEARNING

## Introduction: Pedagogy, Pupil Organisation and the Interface Between Gender and Learning

*Hazel Taylor*

This section of *Genderwatch: still watching...* is concerned with central questions about the impact of gender as a differential in the processes and outcomes of learning. The schedules here take different aspects of provision for learning and ask:

- how do gender and learning interact?
- what makes a difference to how they interact?
- are there really differences in the ways boys and girls learn?
- Are apparent differences actually functions of social constructions of gender, and the learning environment?
- is the organisation of pupil groupings a significant factor in increasing or reducing gendered differences in outcomes?
- what helps pupils of both sexes to learn effectively?

The debate is complex but crucial. As authors throughout the book point out, differences in achievement between boys and girls cannot be discussed in absolute terms. Not only do they vary from school to school and subject to subject, but they interact in different ways with the other variables of social and economic status, and of ethnicity, both of which have more powerful effects than gender alone.

There is confusion nationally about what achieving gender equity in educational outcomes means. Does it mean similar broad outcomes that might be achieved in very different ways, for example in England at 16+, 5 A\*-C GCSEs (or equivalent) using any combinations of subjects to do this? Does it mean similar numbers achieving degrees (or equivalent) but in very different subjects and occupational areas? Or does it mean similar outcomes at the level of comparability with regard to numbers for each pathway in the 14-19 curriculum? And does it seek to increase equity by polarising strategies (which play to differences and increase them) such as changing teaching styles to match alleged learning style strengths while ignoring limitations: 'I'm a kinaesthetic learner, so I need lots of active teaching'; 'I'm interested in football so teach me to read in a stadium'? Or does it seek to increase equity by enlarging strategies, which seek to help learners to expand their conceptions of themselves and others, their interests and their skills? But while men and women continue to be differently valued, inequities in society, the workplace and the home will not be greatly reduced by an evening-up of qualifications.

The paradox is that while the UK government wants comparable outcomes, for example by choice of pathway in the 14-19 curriculum, it encourages the use of pedagogical and organisational tools which reinforce traditional gendered differences. This is because it oversimplifies the issues and creates pressures which encourage the apparent quick fix. The emphasis on personalisation could be a way of enabling each learner to become a rounded learner in a position to make genuine choices in life. It could shift the debate from one about falsely polarised difference between groups to one which recognises genuine individual differences. But personalisation could also become a way of limiting individuals to the patterns and aspirations they are already familiar with. This is likely to happen if learners are not expected to extend their repertoire of skills and knowledge rather than to polarise and maintain their current boundaries. All support for learning must be offered with an awareness of the ways in which gendered assumptions and behaviours are readily reproduced in schools. If we really want genuine equality as opposed to the 'different but equal' illusion, we have to be prepared to spend the time to understand when a bit of polarity is useful, and that enlargement is not the same as convergence. It is the paradoxes that this produces that the schedules in this section grapple with.

Watkins is clear that the challenge is to enable all pupils to extend themselves as effective learners, able to learn actively and interactively, and to do so for their own satisfaction rather than to satisfy external demands. To do this, all need to be supported in understanding how they learn, and how to widen their repertoire and develop the resilience to grapple with things they find challenging. This approach recognises that there may be general patterns of gendered difference in approach to learning, but argues that all are individuals who need to balance their skills. Younger and Warrington advocate an inclusive pedagogy, which provides the conditions in which all can learn effectively; they offer research evidence of what this might look like, arguing that single-sex and mixed groups require the same pedagogy. Kirwan notes that out of hours provision offers a wider range of learning opportunities through which gender inequalities can be addressed.

Debra Murphy and Renold, Francis, and Lloyd draw our attention to the central issues which make inclusive pedagogy so difficult to achieve – the gendered constructs that teachers, other adults in schools and the pupils themselves bring to their classroom practices. It is these which, if unquestioned, replicate the old familiar patterns of inequality in value, aspiration and patterns of achievement, woven through with strands of race and class differences. Exposing, challenging and changing gendered constructs and their effect on learning, needs the involvement of adults and pupils of all ages. This can be done in mixed schools and classrooms, but opinions vary on how different sorts of groupings, including single-sex ones, can be used either to replicate or to challenge and change. Patricia Murphy points out how gendered constructs affect the composition of sets and the choice of tiers for exam entry; Leonard and Debra Murphy describe how co-education can lead to exaggerated gendered behaviours; Cruddas suggests that referring pupils to a learning mentor can be a covert form of pupil grouping, as boys with perceived behaviour problems are singled out of the classroom.

Where can single-sex grouping be useful? Leonard and Debra Murphy show that the superior outcomes from girls' schools are due to other pupil variables, not their gender – higher levels of attainment on entry, social and economic status – and warns of the dangers of the same power struggles taking place between hierarchies of girls that would otherwise be played out between boys and girls. But they can avoid limiting learning. Single-sex groups can be a way of avoiding dealing with issues in mixed classes, and they can set up exaggerated competition between sexes in unhelpful ways. But they can provide transitional support to build confidence, they can equalise the use of resources, they can reduce the desire to play up to stereotypes. They do not in themselves offer a way of improving learning outcomes. Lloyd, Renold and Debra Murphy demonstrate that both boys and girls, and particularly those from poorer socioeconomic groups, suffer from the same issues of lack of confidence and self-esteem, expressed in different ways. Unless schools focus on learning and teaching within the climate for equity that earlier schedules have discussed, single-sex groups will replicate inequities. There is no substitute for a solid understanding of how gender (and ethnicity, and social and economic status) affects teacher and pupil behaviours to underpin all efforts to enable pupils to develop as rounded learners. When this is used to inform all aspects of classroom practice, then not only might there be greater equity in outcomes, but also a greater chance that the positive shift in valuing self and others that is needed to underpin greater equality in the workplace and the world outside the school will be achieved.

# Learning and Teaching
## Chris Watkins

■ *See also schedules: Classroom Interaction; Assessment; Working with Boys; Working with Girls*

## Watching learning

There's no way to watch learning but you can watch for some of the things that are known to enhance learning. And this has great importance for what we call teaching.

In England, the Ofsted inspectors will pronounce on the quality of learning in a classroom, but this is simplified to 'response to teaching'. Similarly, in some of our practices in school, we may call a meeting with a student a 'learning review' but it usually turns out to be a performance review.

## Keeping a focus on learning

It is surprisingly difficult to keep a focus on learning. The word may be used, but often the talk slides off into talk about teaching or performance or 'work'. Learning = being taught is the dominant folk theory and the dominant perspective of policy-makers. Evidence does not support this view, but one of its effects is to sustain other patterns in society, including gender and other differences.

## Learning and gender: the big picture

*Do boys and girls go about their learning differently?* Much attention has focused on gender differences in pupils' public examination results. Differences are quickly explained by recourse to supposed differences in the ways in which boys and girls learn. But this is a facile explanation with little supporting evidence. We need to consider the range of things which may combine to influence examination results, and then seek evidence on their relationship with gender. If we unpack just some of the elements which come into play (see boxes below), we can include other areas.

Starting at the left, the big picture is that there is not much evidence for gender differences in approach to learning, but the more that we move to the right of this set of elements, the more the gendering in society is reflected. The more that we view learning in a way which reflects social process, contexts and cultural values, the more there are likely to be gendered differences. The same point applies to other differences which our society creates: performance differences which relate to social class remain large; those which relate to ethnicity are next; differences which relate to gender are third (Demack *et al*, 2000). The more that social relations or social values enter, the more we see a general effect.

## Is it a matter of 'learning styles'?

It is fashionable to talk about learning styles – and to suggest that boys and girls differ. But the evidence shows that the concept of learning style has a shaky foundation, unreliable measurement and little impact on pedagogy. In the context of these shortcomings, one study identified a new gender difference – in how unreliable the measure was! (Brew, 2002).

| approach to learning | preference for tasks and activities | view of self as a learner | dominant patterns of the typical classroom | attitudes to schooling and achievement | performance in public examinations |
|---|---|---|---|---|---|

*learning orientation*            *performance orientation*

- we believe that effort can lead to success
- we believe in our ability to improve and learn, and not be fixed or stuck
- we prefer challenging tasks whose outcome reflects our approach
- we gain satisfaction from personally-defined success at difficult tasks
- we talk to ourselves: when engaged in a task we talk ourselves through it

*A concern to improve performance*

- we believe that ability leads to success
- we are concerned to be seen as able, and to perform well in others' eyes
- we seek satisfaction from doing better than others
- we emphasise competition, public evaluation
- when the task is difficult we display helplessness: 'I can't do X'

*A concern to prove performance*

Rather than try to squeeze us all into someone else's flimsy pet boxes, it is preferable to consider a well-researched dimension along which we all differ as learners – depending on the context too. The dimension is described above.

## Learned helplessness?

Early studies of this dimension suggested that girls might display greater 'learned helplessness' as learners (Dweck *et al*, 1978). More recent evidence is equivocal, including findings of greater helplessness among boys (Valås, 2001). This is more so with older boys and those facing learning difficulties. A learner's orientation varies according to the context, for example the school subject (Rogers *et al*, 1998), or the activity (Pajares *et al*, 2000). Classrooms can promote a learning orientation (Meece, 2003), although there is probably a dominance of the performance orientation, especially in the later years. Most important, the development of a learning orientation contributes to higher levels of performance, whereas a performance orientation can be associated with lower performance (Watkins, 2001).

Learners also differ in their way of viewing learning: for example, some believe learning is quick, others do not. Girls may be less likely to believe in quick learning and fixed ability (Schommer, 1993), which has additional importance because the more students believe in quick learning, the poorer their school performance (Schommer-Aikins, 2005).

Effective learners are not just learning according to a recipe: they are reviewing how things are going and using this to regulate or drive the way things develop.

Some studies report that girls are more effective at being a self-regulated learner (SRL) (Ablard and Lipschultz, 1998; Bouffard *et al*, 1995).

From this evidence it would be creative to devise credible ways in which boys come to value and develop greater skills of self-regulation.

Preferences for particular tasks in a classroom may also show gender differences, but again the degree of difference and the issues of the wider context are brought to our attention:

> Generally girls tended to be more neutral in their responses, and more tolerant of 'seat-bound' activities than boys,' but 'differences between boys and girls were not great. (Stark and Gray, 1999)

Interaction in the classroom has been much examined, although often with an unexamined view that it is pupils' interaction with the teacher which is all-important. But if we move away from the idea that learning equals being taught, our attention might include the culture of peer relations, and their encouragement (or otherwise) of learning and achievement. One recent study of primary schools found:

> Boys agreed that you could get away with being clever if you were also seen as fashionably dressed or 'hard'; this was a key area of gender difference. Both boys and girls reported 'less pressure on the girls who do well'. (Duffield *et al*, 2000).

## Peer culture

This alerts us to how young people come to present themselves with their peers, and how this accords (or not) with the school culture of achievement. Schools which take care to notice informal leaders in the student peer groups, and support them in affiliating to achievement, may do a service for a wider group of learners.

In peer relationships in the classroom gender differences can show up and girls seem to bring more effective skills of discussion.

> Girls' friendship pairings were found to perform at the highest SRT [science reasoning tasks] levels and boys' friendship pairing performed at the lowest levels. (Kutnick and Kington, 2005)

This is in a situation where no support is given to the processes for working together, and the challenge for educators is to help all our students to learn what many girls may be first to operate. Some studies indicate that when learners are given support to learn about learning together, there are no gender differences in the way that successful small groups operate (Hogan, 1999).

## Affiliation to school

Girls generally show higher levels of affiliation to school and a higher sense of school belonging (Voelkl, 1997), perhaps because their social relations help them colonise the school experience. Boys show evidence of significant social anxiety in secondary school and this influences their view of themselves and their engagement with school goals (Reichert and Kuriloff, 2004). Issues of fitting in and fearing failure are ones which school may either amplify or diminish, especially in the way they construct demarcations between winners and losers. Schools and classrooms can, often unwittingly, contribute to boys' social anxiety by emphasising a public dimension to recognition, and the achievement of recognition through public compliance to some norm or image.

There is no reason to assume that all learners are motivated to achieve in public examinations: many socio-economic differences are re-created on just this, and the way some pupils adapt their experiences in secondary school protect them from something which could bring them another experience of failure. Schools can accentuate or reduce this by the extent to which they offer a wide range of future identities, each of which benefit from school achievement in some way.

### Towards better gender equity in learning

There are differing stances on intervention:

Stance 1: Spot a difference, view it as a difficulty, and treat by separation.

For example, some people generalise to say that boys are more motivated by competition, so they then say that the learning environment should be 'matched' to this, and they sometimes create separate boys' groups with such a culture. But research suggests this is counter-productive: 'Working-class boys seem to experience particular difficulties in such settings' (Daniels *et al*, 2001).

Stance 2: Spot a difference, note what's best for everybody and support accordingly.

To continue the above example, once the difference between girls and boys has been spotted we need to inquire into what is best for learning, review the evidence on what works best for most people (for example Panitz, 2000 on collaborative learning) and then support all learners in becoming more effective in it, with an occasional look at the original concern.

Here we are addressing the relation between pupils' socialisation to date and their socialisation in the classroom, knowing that the role of school is to extend beyond what learners bring. So we can pose key questions about any classroom:

■ does the way that learning is promoted in this classroom serve to confirm or even accentuate the gendered socialisation which pupils have experienced, especially in relation to their views about learning and themselves as learners?

■ or does it extend their repertoire as effective learners?

### The learning culture of the classroom

Two principles support the idea of intervention through the classroom learning culture:

■ the classroom is a powerful context which influences people's views of learning, orientation to learning, performances and differences

■ all learners can be helped to learn approaches to their learning which are new to them.

### Issues to consider

The complex learning culture of a classroom can be examined through what is known about effective learning, and the four headings overleaf.

### Active Learning

When learning is hands on and actively focuses on review, explanation and application, engagement increases. In countries and cultures where girls have not been socialised into an active role, classrooms can help, and performance also increases. In the UK, some evidence challenges the idea that there is a gender difference in preference for active learning: 'In contrast to the teachers' beliefs, these findings indicate that all of their children preferred active learning styles ..., and that most subjects were equally enjoyed by boys and girls. Where there was a difference, it was by achievement rather than by gender' (Holden, 2002).

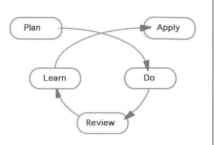

- ■ Does this classroom employ tasks which are engaging to all?
- ■ Is the process of reviewing and making meaning from the experience highlighted?
- ■ Do learners feel there is something consequential to be achieved from applying their learning?

### Collaborative Learning

When learning is collaborative, new shared products are created through the participation of all. In the process of contributing and reconciling, new meaning and understanding is created. Simply placing males and females together under a collaborative learning structure will not ensure that they will positively interact and learn. Attention has to be given to the design of the task, the way of talking which promotes collaboration and learning, and the structure for developing collaboration and interdependence in the classroom.

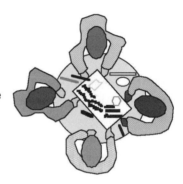

- ■ Does the structure in this classroom promote interdependence?
- ■ Do learners review and develop their talk for collaboration?
- ■ Does the peer culture in this classroom accept and support everyone's achievement?

### Learner-driven

When classrooms engage learners' purposes through choice and planning, and through review, then learners become more engaged, more responsible and more able to direct their learning activity and assess their learning products.

- ■ Does this classroom promote opportunities for learners to choose, to review, and to have their voice heard?
- ■ Does this classroom promote self-regulation on the part of learners?

### Learning about learning

Given that learners' views of learning have such an impact on how they go about learning, it is valuable to create opportunities for surfacing those views and developing them to become richer and more empowered.

- ■ Does this classroom promote a learning orientation, characterised by learners' ability to talk themselves through difficulties, reflect on their strategies, and so on?
- ■ Does this classroom promote the belief that learning is quick, or alternatively that learning sometimes takes time and that it is time well spent?
- ■ Are the stories about learning which circulate in this classroom and school ones which encourage a range of other learners to tell and develop their stories?

## Conclusion

There is some evidence that people for whom the typical masculine or feminine attributes are not central to their identity are also people who have a deep, meaning-directed approach to learning (Severiens and ten Dam, 1997). So our learning focus may provide another reason for questioning traditional polarised gender identities.

■ An effective learning environment is inclusive: it embraces diversity and becomes a resource for learning, rather than inviting people to fit in

■ An effective learning environment is expansive: it helps all people to expand their repertoire, including through learning from each other, rather than keeping them limited by ideas of there being one right way

■ An effective learning environment helps all learners become more versatile and empowered as learners who will meet many situations in life for which a rule could not have been anticipated.

## References

Ablard, K. E. and Lipschultz, R. E. (1998) Self-regulated learning in high-achieving students: Relations to advanced reasoning, achievement goals, and gender. *Journal of Educational Psychology* 90(1) p94-101

Brew, C. R. (2002) Kolb's learning style instrument: sensitive to gender. *Educational and Psychological Measurement* 62 (2) p373-390

Daniels, H., Creese, A., Hey, V., Leonard, D. and Smith, M. (2001) Gender and learning: equity, equality and pedagogy. *Support for Learning* 16 (3) p112-116

Demack, S., Drew, D. and Grimsley, M. (2000) Minding the gap: ethnic, gender and social class differences in attainment at 16, 1988-95. *Race Ethnicity and Education* 3 (2) p117-143

Duffield, J., Allan, J., Turner, E. and Morris, B. (2000) Pupils' voices on achievement: An alternative to the standards agenda. *Cambridge Journal of Education* 30 (2) p263-274

Dweck, C. S., Davidson, W., Nelson, S. and Enna, B. (1978) Sex differences in learned helplessness ii. The contingencies of evaluative feedback in the classroom, and iii. An experimental analysis. *Developmental Psychology* 14 (3) p268-276

Hogan, K. (1999) Thinking aloud together: A test of an intervention to foster students' collaborative scientific reasoning. *Journal of Research in Science Teaching* 36 (10) p1085-1109

Holden, C. (2002) Contributing to the debate: The perspectives of children on gender, achievement and literacy, *Journal of Educational Enquiry* 3, (1) p97-110

Kutnick, P. and Kington, A. (2005) Children's Friendships and Learning in School: Cognitive Enhancement Through Social Interaction? *British Journal of Educational Psychology* 75 p521-538

Meece, J. L. (2003) Applying learner-centered principles to middle school education, *Theory into Practice* 42,(2) p109-116

Pajares, F., Britner, S. L. and Valiante, G. (2000) Relation between achievement goals and self-beliefs of middle school students in writing and science. *Contemporary Educational Psychology* 25 p406-422

Panitz, T. (2000) *67 Benefits of Cooperative Learning*, home.capecod.net/~tpanitz/tedsarticles/coopbenefits.htm

Rogers, C. G., Galloway, D., Armstrong, D. and Leo, E. (1998) Gender differences in motivational style: A comparison of measures and curriculum area. *British Journal Of Educational Psychology* 68 (2) p189-202

Schommer, M. (1993) Epistemological development and academic-performance among secondary students. *Journal Of Educational Psychology* 85 (3) p406-411

Schommer-Aikins, M., Duell, O. K. and Hutter, R. (2005) Epistemological beliefs, mathematical problem-solving beliefs, and academic performance of middle school students. *The Elementary School Journal* 105 (3) p289-304

Severiens, S. E. and ten Dam, G. T. N. (1997) Gender and Gender Identity Differences in Learning Styles. *Educational Psychology* 17 (1-2) p79-93

Stark, R. and Gray, D. (1999) Research report. Gender preferences in learning science. *International Journal of Science Education* 21 (6) p633-643

Valås, H. (2001) Learned helplessness and psychological adjustment: Effects of age, gender and academic achievement. *Scandinavian Journal of Educational Research* 45 (1) p71-90

Voelkl, K. E. (1997) Identification with school. *American Journal of Education* 105 (3) p294-318

Watkins, C. (2001) *Learning About Learning Enhances Performance*. London: Institute of Education School Improvement Network (Research Matters series No 13)

## Further resources

Watkins, C., Carnell, E. and Lodge, C. (2007) *Effective Learning in Classrooms*. London: Paul Chapman/Sage

Watkins, C. (2003) *Learning: a Sense-maker's Guide*. London: Association for Teaching and Learning www.new2teaching.org.uk/tzone/images/Learning_tcm7-26270.pdf

Claire, H. (ed) (2005) *Gender and Learning in the School Years 3-19*. London: Association for Teaching and Learning www.new2teaching.org.uk/tzone/images/Gender_in_education_ATL_tcm7-26272.pdf

Pickering, J. (1997) *Raising Boys' Achievement*. Stafford, Network Educational Press.

# Assessment

*Patricia Murphy*

■ *See also schedules: Learning and Teaching; English as an Additional Language*

Summative assessment (assessment of learning) and formative assessment (assessment for learning, AfL) raise issues about equity. Many research studies have investigated the equity issues of summative assessment. Although the issues are as important for formative assessment, as yet there is little research into this area.

## What do we know about equity and summative assessment?

Across all subjects and all types of assessment, for example national tests, GCSE, and international surveys, boys' and girls' results are found at every grade or level. Consequently any differences between boys and girls cannot be explained by innate differences between them. What does differ for boys and girls is the distribution across grades and levels. There is a tendency for more boys than girls to achieve at the top and bottom of grade or level distributions, and for girls' performance to be bunched in the middle grades or levels. This pattern can vary by subject and, importantly, by school.

When interpreting results, attention is usually paid to which pupils pass or to the overall scores. If equal numbers of girls and boys pass, then it is assumed that achievement is equal and the system is operating fairly. If the outcomes are unequal, it is assumed that the differences in achievement need to be addressed. The same approach is used to monitor the achievement of black and minority ethnic groups.

However, overall scores tell you little about why differences in performance occur. In the same way, similarities in pass rates tell you little about which pupils are achieving the expected level or pass grades, or importantly how they are achieving: which questions they respond to and which parts they fail or succeed on and why. Overall scores cannot illuminate the inter-connections of region, gender, class and race and ethnicity. The categories we use to represent the diversity of individuals are very limited.

## Is assessment of learning objective?

While it is popularly assumed that summative assessment is objective, plenty of evidence shows that it is not. It is often thought that failure to get the right answer indicates a lack of achievement in that area and nothing else. Assessors may intend a single meaning: the one that they feel they have communicated through their words. The pupil, however, has to work it out, drawing on what they know about the subject, the specific question details, and their expectations of the assessment process generally. Differences in interpretation are affected by social and cultural differences and assessment situations are not gender neutral.

Pupils' personal history of experiences of successes and failures combines to create a sense of what they believe they can do. Their self esteem as learners will influence their responses to assessment, as much as what they know about the subject being assessed. Pupils' responses are also affected by:

■ their literacy levels – bilingual pupils may well understand the cognitive demand of a question but not the descriptive context it has been placed in

■ their understanding of the language of assessment – there are class differences in familiarity with formal and specific terms such as explain and describe

- their command of the style of response required by the question – for example, boys are more likely to use a structured, commentary style, while girls prefer to write more reflectively
- their perception of the required behaviour for their gender – for example, boys avoid direct expressions of feeling, preferring to distance themselves from this through use of fantasy
- their feelings about the formal setting of summative assessment and the degree to which they are intimidated by it.

Tests and examinations are always partial selections from a subject. What is selected can advantage some groups because of their particular knowledge. In America, white boys outperformed black pupils and white girls in civics questions, except for those few on black politicians and women's suffrage. Questions embedded in a narrative context are affected by pupils' interpretation of the context. Pupils use the content and context to make sense of the task. There are class, gender and race differences in response to contexts that appear neutral to question setters. For example, more boys than girls failed to answer a question about interpreting a table where the context of the table was about flowers and plants. They reported they did not know about flowers. Boys outperform girls on items requiring a graphic response to the interpretation of graphical data.

### Issues to consider

- Do you make the assumption that summative assessment is objective? What evidence do you use?
- How do you deal with the fact that pupils' beliefs about themselves affect how they react in assessment situations? Girls are more likely to under estimate their abilities and boys more likely to over estimate them.
- Does your school actively teach the language of assessment?
- In revision classes, are pupils given opportunities to discuss what kind of answer particular wording implies?
- If you teach primary children, are there different styles of writing associated with different subjects? Do you help pupils to understand this?
- To help pupils understand assessment and learning criteria, you could, as part of a peer-assessment task, ask them to highlight the evidence they used to judge that a criterion had been met. This could provide the basis for a discussion of style versus criteria.

- Collect together some examples of what you consider to be good and average examples of work that involved a free response. Is style influencing your judgements about achievements and is it associated with certain pupils and not others? You could try this activity with colleagues. Make the examples anonymous, or swap girls' and boys' names to see whether there is a gender – related interaction.
- Do you monitor the content of assessment questions? Select a recent test or examination and ask colleagues to rate which question content they consider to be more familiar to girls than boys and vice versa. They could also discuss whether they felt that cultural knowledge would create problems for other pupils.
- Do you consider content effects with pupils? You could use the same task as above and ask pupils to rate which questions they felt confident to answer, which ones they were less confident about and which they would not attempt. Ask them to discuss their reasons and discuss with them effects that are not to do with their subject knowledge.
- To consider context effects, select examples that use everyday content and/or contexts, which are about social situations involving people, and examples which are very clearly set in school.
- Explore with pupils the questions they prefer and their reasons for this, and what they think the expected response is. Look out for those pupils who pay attention to context and purpose. Which pupils are these, and how does this affect the assessment of their achievements?

### Teachers' expectations and entry levels

Gendered assumptions about pupil characteristics can influence teachers' decisions about which pupils are able or not able to do well in their subjects. Some national tests used in England, and GCSE examinations used more widely in the UK, are tiered. Tiers are differentiated by the grades or levels that can be achieved. Entry to a particular tier can set up floor effects i.e. pupils failing to gain the lowest grade may end up not graded; or ceiling effects ie pupils achieving the highest grade may have achieved higher if allowed access to a higher tier. Schools tend to group pupils in relation to their predicted tier of entry and teach the content for that specific tier, so decisions about tier entry can also restrict the curriculum that pupils have access to.

When mathematics examination papers were divided into three tiers, research showed that teachers tended to allocate more girls to the intermediate tier than boys and the converse with the foundation and higher tiers. These decisions were often influenced by perceptions about girls' lack of confidence as mathematicians, and boys' disruptive behaviour, rather than by prior attainment (Stobart *et al*, 1992). A similar entry pattern was revealed for key stage 3 national tests (Elwood and Murphy, 2002). Boys and girls in single-sex schools had a greater chance of being entered for higher tiers in key stage 3 mathematics and science (Spielhofer *et al*, 2002). Cooper and Dunne (2000) in a study of three schools found that social class and not gender was a major influence on entry to key stage 3 mathematics tiers. The findings about tier entry, although limited, suggest that there are differential effects on predicted and actual achievement related to race, ethnicity, class and gender and that these interact. Furthermore the potential influence of these factors on teachers' expectations and beliefs is pivotal in decision making about test and examination entry.

Schools are expected to meet national standards. This influences which learners they target for additional resources. The GCSE C-D grade boundary is very significant, as schools are judged on the number of passes achieved by pupils. In one study it was found that many schools focused attention and resources on those pupils whose attainment could be improved at the C-D boundary, at the expense of those learners who were considered below that level of achievement. The neglected pupils were disproportionately black, working class and poor (Gillborn and Youdell, 2000). Primary schools focus on the level 3-4 boundary.

### Issues to consider

■ Do you monitor which pupils are entered for which tiers in national tests and GCSE, in relation to race, ethnicity, gender and socio-economic indicators?

■ Do you routinely check predicted achievement against actual achievement at key stage 2 and key stage 3? Which pupils achieve more than expected, and which achieve less than expected?

■ Do you consider ceiling and floor effects in the national tests? For the foundation papers, which pupils are achieving the top levels? Is any group disproportionately represented? In the higher papers, are there pupils not graded?

■ What potential is there for pupils to move between sets in key stages 3 and 4? In which direction is movement generally, for which pupils, and is it for behavioural or for achievement reasons?

### What do we know about equity and formative assessment?

Formative assessment, or assessment for learning, is directed at the individual and his or her learning. Potential sources of inequity arise because it is assumed that AfL techniques are equally accessible to all learners. The techniques also focus on subject knowledge in isolation from social and cultural influences.

### What sort of classroom culture supports AfL?

Assessment for learning entails pupils taking, and being given, more responsibility for their learning. However you cannot assume that this is understood and accepted by all pupils. One teacher introducing AfL in her history classes found a positive impact on girls' achievements but no such impact on boys'. She found that boys are more likely to resent having to take on what they see as the teacher's role, and are less likely to appreciate the value of peer and self-assessment, than girls. There may be several reasons for this.

Research has shown that girls, more than boys, seek really to understand what they are learning, so consequently require more time for reflection. AfL provides girls with the opportunities they value to engage over time with learning criteria and to focus on understanding, which for many girls is more important than grades or marks. Girls more than boys value collaboration and talk about their learning even if the task and the teacher do not encourage this. Boys more than girls show a preference for working independently, and for not seeking help from teachers and peers. For many boys, revealing the need for help is not cool. Effortless achievement is the image to be sought. Boys often rate their achievements more highly than girls and attribute failure to lack of effort; this reflects the nature of the feedback they receive in class. The fear of being exposed in a learning situation with peers affects all pupils, but boys more than girls who, as noted earlier, develop strategies to avoid this. AfL challenges many of the strategies and attitudes that boys develop as part of managing a gender identity; consequently, some boys may feel uncomfortable in peer and self-assessment situations.

### Issues to consider

- Have you considered whether AfL is having a positive effect on the achievement of all pupils?
- Have you asked pupils how they feel about AfL, and what they see as the benefits and the limitations for themselves as learners? You could ask pupils to jot these down anonymously, then use these responses as part of group and class discussion, to see how many and which pupils share these particular views.
- Have you considered that some pupils may have difficulty in developing strategies for collaboration? Your grouping of pupils will be important here. Do some groups work more effectively than others?

### Talking about learning

Many of the techniques of assessment for learning rely on discussion and written products. No hands up; wait time; and peer-assessment are all techniques aimed at providing opportunities for all learners to contribute to discussions and at creating a classroom culture in which the focus is on learning about how to learn. There is evidence that boys can dominate in teacher-pupil interactions and often teachers allow this in order to maintain discipline.

Younger pupils may need to develop the tools for talking about learning as part of AfL. Even then, not all pupils feel equally able to take part in discussions and some have learned to be silent. This may be the case for pupils perceived to have learning difficulties and for bilingual pupils. Some pupils, as noted earlier, may be less familiar with the language used to talk about learning. Peers can be very helpful in supporting other pupils if, instead of being put in the role of judge as in peer-assessment, they are put in the role of advocate.

### Issues to consider

- Do you allow a range of tasks and forms of response so that pupils can reveal what they know in different ways, and have different forms of outcomes to talk about in relation to their learning?
- Do you engage pupils to work together in groups discussing each other's contributions and learning, and their evidence for this?
- Do you give group members the responsibility to report back on another pupil's contribution and learning, and to represent it in the most effective way they can?

This negotiation will help pupils to develop peer-assessment strategies, recognise the complexity of making judgements, and help them to model together ways of looking at evidence of learning and the language to express it.

### Bringing what pupils know and who they are into assessment for learning

The intention is that AfL provides teachers and pupils with information about:

- what has been learned
- how well it has been learned (feed-backward)
- information about the next steps for learning (feed-forward).

It is therefore a means to document pupils' past, present and future learning, i.e. their learning pathway, as well as a means for them to learn about how to learn.

AfL strategies require teachers to focus only on the learning criteria, and pupils' progress in relation to them is judged purely in terms of their knowledge. However, barriers to access, as discussed earlier, can arise because learners do not see the relevance and therefore the point of the learning that they are asked to undertake. This requires a quite different response from the teacher from the one when the learner experiences a conceptual difficulty.

Teachers also need to understand how differences between pupils and what they bring into classrooms, might mediate and constrain their learning. Often the products of learning give insights into the effects of such differences. For example, when given a free choice about genres to use in writing novel openings for GCSE, there were marked differences in those chosen by boys and girls (Murphy and Ivinson, 2005).

### Issues to consider

- Do you ask pupils to share and discuss, not just the criteria, but their views about the point of learning about them?
- Do you monitor the products of pupils' learning in relation to what they consider important, and how this might influence their ability to meet learning criteria?
- Do you use these products as a way of discussing with pupils what learning was allowed and what disallowed by their choices?
- Do you provide opportunities for pupils to talk through their decisions, and what they felt able

booster class acts as a vehicle that will give them more of what they seem to need from the literacy curriculum. Any underlying conditions which produce this state of affairs do not surface as part of the agenda. Managing the problem in this way in effect strips out much discussion of gender politics in the classroom.

Analysing performance data certainly has its uses. It can clarify whether there is a problem that requires attention or not. But there is a difference between identifying a pattern and understanding why it is there. In the 1950s and 60s, the knowledge that boys generally performed worse than girls in the parts of the 11-plus examination designed to test reading and writing led to boys' scores being routinely adjusted upwards. This affirmative action was justified by the widespread assumption that boys were late developers whose linguistic abilities lagged behind girls' right up until puberty (Millard, 1997). The explanation for the data and the way in which that explanation mapped onto a particular context (an education system primarily committed to the production of a highly educated elite), not the data themselves, determined the action taken. This is a salutary point to bear in mind. Data on their own do not tell us how to read them.

### Issues to consider

■ If there are gender differences in the literacy performance data in your school, then what produces such differences? What explanations do you have for why such differences are there?

■ Can you turn your explanations into questions? For instance, if boys score less well in writing because their work is shorter than girls' and they use relatively fewer complex sentences, how do you explain this?

■ What else do you need to know to check whether your explanation is right? Does your explanation invoke stereotyped thinking about boys or girls? Can you find any alternative explanations for the same data? How would you choose between them?

The reasons why many girls consistently outperform boys in literacy have been explored in different ways. Some have focused on the apparent disjuncture between boys' perceived interests and the content of the literacy curriculum (Barrs and Pidgeon, 1993). They have asked if there is too much narrative fiction in the early years curriculum, or whether there is too little use made of technology. Feminists have used

this kind of analysis to argue for a literacy curriculum which can actively challenge, engage and extend both boys' and girls' existing interests, rather than simply reflect them (Millard, 1997; Rowan *et al*, 2002). Others have reconsidered literacy pedagogy, the distinctions it creates amongst literacy learners in the classroom, and how girls and boys react to this environment (Solsken, 1993). This analysis has been used to identify conditions and strategies that can help build and sustain a more inclusive curriculum, capable of enabling both girls and boys to develop the necessary range of skills associated with literacy, and foster their use of reading and writing more broadly (Barrs and Pidgeon, 1998, 2002; Bearne, 2002; Moss, 2002).

## Auditing how children access the literacy curriculum in context

One of the most striking characteristics of the reading curriculum is the central role it plays in highlighting differences between children in primary school classrooms. Children are often seated in class according to their ability in reading. These ability groupings may well determine how children access other parts of the curriculum, the kinds of resources they gain access to and the tasks they are expected to undertake. In many respects, children's status in class and their standing with their peers are built through their relative success or failure at learning to read. In primary schools, a sharp distinction is drawn between those pupils who can read at a level that enables them to function independently in the classroom and those who cannot. Parents wait anxiously to hear if and when their child has crossed that line. Teachers worry about those who seem to be making little progress. Moss (2000) argues that gender differences in literacy attainment are in large part created through this social stratification of the reading curriculum, and the ways in which girls and boys react to their position within it.

### Issues to consider

■ How do differences in literacy attainment manifest themselves in your classroom?

■ Do ability groupings based on reading proficiency show an even spread of boys and girls, or are more boys than girls concentrated in the lowest groups, and more girls than boys in the highest?

■ Are there any differences in the ways in which boys and girls react to their designation as poor readers? As able readers?

■ How does the designation of reading ability shape children's experience of the literacy curriculum?

The literacy curriculum attempts to do several jobs. It tries to ensure that pupils acquire the necessary understanding of the writing system to enable them to function as both readers and writers. It increasingly asks children to reflect on the meanings of the books and other texts they read; to extend their control over the texts that they write; to develop more critical understanding of the functions and purposes that texts of different kinds have within our society; and to read and write more widely for their own purposes. In part, this means taking on board a system and a set of rules that already exists, but then using that system to make something new.

### Issues to consider

■ What opportunities do children have in your classroom to acquire basic understandings of the way in which the writing system works? What status is this kind of work given in the curriculum as a whole? Are boys more likely than girls to shirk these kinds of tasks? How can those who fall behind in basic skills be both challenged and supported in order to make progress?

■ What opportunities do children have to develop their own sense of purpose in reading and writing in your classroom? How much ownership can they exercise over their reading and writing? How much access do girls or boys of all abilities have to opportunities which will stretch and significantly expand their existing competence?

■ What range of books and other texts is promoted in your classroom? Are systems and resources in place actively to support wide reading? What opportunities are there for children across the ability range to choose what they will read? What opportunities do children have to share their reading choices with others, for example through reading diaries; pupil reading circles; paired reading? What opportunities do readers have to recommend texts to each other? How can text recommendations encourage both boys and girls to try unfamiliar texts?

■ How is extended writing supported in class? What opportunities do writers have to plan or talk with others before they write, or work collaboratively on a text? How much choice can writers exercise over how they tackle the task?

Do both girls and boys across the ability range have equal opportunities to use ICT to compose? Does feedback clarify how a text could be improved? Are both girls' and boys' writing held up as models of good practice in class?

■ Does your classroom reflect or challenge stereotyped assumptions about text preferences, for instance, that all boys prefer to read non-fiction, or write action-packed stories; or that all girls avoid reading fantasy fiction and take few risks in their writing?

The questions above are designed to encourage you to audit the opportunities and the resources for reading and writing which the literacy curriculum provides and then identify any gender differences in their distribution and use. Ability groupings are often intersected by gender. Recognising and exploring this intersection in your own classroom is a useful prelude to change.

### Resources

Barrs, M. and Pidgeon, S. (eds) (1993) *Reading the Difference.* London: CLPE

Barrs, M. and Pidgeon, S. (eds) (1998) *Boys and Reading.* London: CLPE

Barrs, M. and Pidgeon, S. (eds) (2002) *Boys and Writing.* London: CLPE

Bearne, E. Multimodal Narratives, in Barrs, M. and Pidgeon, S. (eds) (2002) *Boys and Writing.* London: CLPE

Millard, E. (1997) *Differently Literate.* London: Falmer Press

Moss, G. (2000) Raising Boys Attainment in Reading: Some Principles for Intervention. *Reading* 34 (3)

Moss, G. (2002) Explicit Pedagogy. In Barrs, M. and Pidgeon, S. (eds) (2002) *Boys and Writing.* London: CLPE

Ofsted (2003a) *Yes He Can: Schools Where Boys Write Well.* London: Ofsted

Ofsted (2003b) *English: Improving boys' writing at Key Stages 2 and 3.* Ofsted subject conference report series 2002/03. E-publication

QCA (1998) *Can Do Better: Raising Boys Achievement in English.* London: QCA

Rowan, L. *et al* (2002) *Boys, Literacies and Schooling.* Buckingham: Open University Press

Solsken, J. (1993) *Literacy, Gender and Work in Families and in School.* Norwood, NJ: Ablex

# Mentoring and learning

*Leora Cruddas*

■ *See also schedules: Assessment; Continuing Professional Development; The Wider Workforce*

Mentoring as a strategy for engaging disengaged children and young people has moved to centre-stage in schools in England and elsewhere, particularly North America.

There are many different types of mentors and mentoring. This schedule focuses on learning mentors, who are distinct from other types of mentors in that they work primarily in schools and educational institutions. Their purpose is to reduce any barriers to learning and increase participation in education for all.

They are not teaching assistants, who work under the direction of teachers to provide direct support for teaching and learning. Neither are they special needs assistants, who work under the direction of the Special Educational Needs Co-ordinator (SENCO) to provide support for pupils with special educational needs. Learning mentors are senior support workers with considerable independence, who aim to reduce barriers to learning and participation which lead to underachievement.

With the publication of national occupational standards in England (ENTO, PAULO and TOPSS, 2003a), learning mentors are now a recognised occupational group.

*Learning mentors*
■ identify learning and development strengths and needs with the individual by assessing development in different domains and across different contexts
■ plan with pupils how learning and development needs will be addressed and work with others to ensure that this is achieved

■ support and guide pupils to achieve identified outcomes, using a range of practices including developmental, preventative and therapeutic programmes, group work and family work
■ support pupils' successful transfer and transition in learning and development contexts.

While learning mentoring is widely perceived to have brought about positive outcomes for children and young people (Ofsted, 2003; Morris *et al*, 2004), little attention has been paid to the significant gender issues affecting learning mentors as an occupational group, or to gender issues for children and young people with whom learning mentors work.

*Some gender issues for learning mentors as an occupational group*

■ 81% of learning mentors are women[1]
■ while learning mentors come from a wide range of occupational backgrounds, many have progressed from teaching assistant jobs – which is often low-paid and part-time work, usually carried out by women
■ there is no national pay-scale for learning mentors and no nationally recognised terms and conditions of employment, which results in wide-spread disparity and inequality
■ learning mentors as an occupational group are not regulated and are not required to register with a professional body in order to practice, although the publication of national occupational standards provides the platform for accredited qualifications.

*Some gender issues relating to the cohort of children and young people*

■ more boys than girls are referred to learning mentors – approximately 62% boys compared to 38% girls[2]

■ because most learning mentors are women, there is a danger that the stereotype that only women can fulfil caring roles and do the emotional work is reinforced to children and young people

■ where learning mentors run peer mentoring programmes, it is often the case that more girls than boys are recruited as peer mentors, thereby reinforcing the stereotype described above.

### Issues to consider

#### Recruitment, training and support of learning mentors

The publication of national occupational standards has meant that national vocational qualifications, foundation degree and honours degree provision has expanded across England. Learning mentors now have an occupational home in the Children's Workforce Development Council. However, much more needs to be done, particularly in the fields of regulation, supervision and support. While performance management of teaching staff is now statutory, there is still no entitlement for learning mentors to performance management.

#### Issues for schools

■ Are learning mentor job descriptions based on the recognised national occupational standards for learning, development and support services?

■ Does the school ensure that learning mentors have access to accredited training opportunities?

■ Does the pay scale reflect the level of skill, the ability to formulate solutions and responses to complex problems and situations, and the responsibilities of the job as a senior support worker? How does this compare with other jobs in the school, particularly jobs held by men?

■ Do learning mentors have access to supervision, line management support and performance management?

■ Do both women and men engage with and act as positive role models in the area of emotional work?

#### Issues for policy makers

■ What needs to be done at national level to address the significant gender imbalance in the learning mentor occupational group and in other helping professions?

■ What is being done nationally to address issues of pay, to ensure that there is commensurability between men and women carrying out jobs at similar skill levels – particularly jobs in the helping professions?

### Referrals, assessment and action planning

We have seen that more boys than girls are referred to learning mentors. Referrals are usually made by teachers and other adults. Colley (2003a and b) cautions that many mentoring programmes can fall into the trap of seeking to rectify young people's perceived skill deficits, encourage them to conform, and develop their employability. This is especially the case when assessment practices are carried out by someone other than the mentor and perceived to be an expert diagnosis rather than a process that is carried out with a child or young person.

■ Are referrals monitored to ensure that the needs of both girls and boys are addressed?

■ Is there the opportunity for self-referral and the procedures to support this? Are self-referrals monitored by gender?

### The centrality of relationship

The relationship with the pupil is central to the work of learning mentors. In terms of relationship building, it is important to consider issues of gender and diversity. For example, do young people need the same sex and ethnicity mentors? Or is it more useful to consider:

■ how is work with individual children and young people tailored in a gender-sensitive and diversity-sensitive way?

■ how does the school support all staff in challenging gender and diversity-related blind spots, including gender and cultural stereotyping?

### Monitoring and evaluating outcomes

One of the factors that may contribute towards the skewing of referrals towards boys is the focus on reducing exclusions, so-called anti-social behaviour and crime. If learning mentor programmes are monitored and evaluated against externally imposed hard targets, there is the danger that learning mentoring will fall into the coercive traps that Colley identifies. The focus of learning mentoring and the measures of its success must include qualitative outcomes such as improved self-esteem, confidence, all of which reduce engagement in learning and participation.

The range of outcomes should also be monitored across learning mentor cohorts to ensure that gender stereotyping is avoided; for example, outcomes for boys are often constructed around improving behaviour and for girls as improving confidence and self-esteem.

■ How are the outcomes of the learning mentoring relationship determined? How are stereotypes avoided?

■ Are qualitative outcomes evaluated and included as legitimate measures of success? How do these reflect gender differences?

■ Are a full range of outcomes reflected for boys and girls?

## Values and beliefs

Colley cautions that mentoring can seek to alter young people's values, attitudes, beliefs and behaviours in the attempt to facilitate re-engagement (Colley, 2003b: 529). This is contrary to the value base of learning mentoring which supports practice that is ethical and respectful:

> Practitioners must recognise that the welfare of the children and young people with whom they work is paramount. They must recognise the individuality of each child/young person and promote their learning, development and welfare. This must be reflected in all work with children and young people and their families/carers...
> Practitioners must adopt a client-centred approach based on enhanced inclusion and access, honesty, trust and respect. They will promote equality, respect diversity and challenge stereotypes, helping to improve the life chances of their clients and the overall effectives of the service provision.
> (ENTO, PAULO, TOPPS, 2003a)

Egan (2002) calls respect the foundation value on which all helping relationships are built. For him, respect is not just an attitude; it is a set of behaviours that guide the practitioner's helping relationship. The following questions are designed to stimulate critical reflection on values and beliefs:

■ are the values of learning mentoring developed with children and young people and clearly articulated?

■ is practice inclusive and respectful in that children and young people's values and behaviours are interpreted in the most positive way?

■ is access to learning mentoring monitored in terms of gender and ethnicity?

■ does learning mentoring challenge stereotypes, including gender stereotypes among children, young people and families, and in institutional practices?

■ does the learning mentor practice, promote and enact equality and diversity?

## Peer mentoring and peer support

Many learning mentors set up and run peer mentoring and other peer support programmes. Baker (2003) distinguishes between peer mentoring as an activity undertaken mostly in secondary schools, in which older pupils support young pupils in the traditional role of mentor and guide, and peer buddying which focuses mainly on applying skills of helping in everyday interaction with peers, most commonly used in primary schools. Peer mentoring and buddying can be located in the broader field of peer support as strategies for working with children and young people, which develops positive attitudes towards themselves and others. Baker provides a useful overview of the main peer support programmes currently used in schools: peer mentoring, peer tutoring, peer education, peer researchers, peer buddies, peer mediation, peer counselling and peer listening. By implementing peer mentoring and other types of peer support programmes, learning mentors can increase participation through brokering supportive relationships between peers. However, there are important gender considerations:

■ is recruitment to peer mentoring and peer support programmes monitored in terms of gender?

■ are boys actively encouraged and supported to undertake peer mentoring and support roles in the school?

■ does peer mentor training address issues of gender and diversity? Are gender- and diversity-related blind spots in peer mentors and peer supporters challenged?

■ are there opportunities for peer mentors and peer supporters to reflect on their value formations and behaviours in their work with other children and young people?

■ are referrals to and participation in peer mentoring and peer support programmes monitored to ensure an equal balance of girls and boys?

■ is peer mentoring practice inclusive and respectful of other children and young people's values and behaviours?

Some final areas for reflection and consideration are adapted from Rogers and Freiberg (1994):

■ how do we change the patterns of interactions in schools with regard to gender, class and ethnicity in order to improve the achievement and enjoyment of every child and young person?

■ what support efforts – including learning mentoring – are needed to create meaningful learning communities?

■ how do we transform schools to respond to the needs of every young person?

## References

Baker, J. (2003) *Primary Peer Buddying Programme: Training materials.* Sheffield: Education Directorate

Colley, H. (2003a) *Mentoring for Social Inclusion: A Critical Approach to Nurturing Mentoring Relationships.* London: RoutledgeFalmer

Colley, H. (2003b) 'Engagement mentoring for 'disaffected' youth: a new model of mentoring for social inclusion'. *British Educational Research Journal* 29 (4)p521-542.

Cruddas, L. (2005) *Learning Mentors in Schools: Policy and Practice.* Stoke on Trent: Trentham.

Egan, G. (2002) *The Skilled Helper: A Problem-management and Opportunity-development Approach to Helping.* California: Brooks/Cole

ENTO, PAULO, TOPSS (2003a) *National Occupational Standards for Learning, Development and Support Services for children, young people and those who care for them.* www.dfes.gov.uk/childrenandfamilies/docs/qualification_structure.pdf

ENTO, PAULO, TOPSS (2003b) *Value Base: National Occupational Standards for Learning, Development and Support Services for children, young people and those who care for them.* www.dfes.gov.uk/childrenandfamilies/docs/ value_base.pdf

Morris, M., Rutt, S. and Eggers, A. (2004) *Pupil Outcomes: The impact of EIC.* www.nfer.ac.uk/research/documents/EIC/Pupilout.doc

Ofsted (2003) *Excellence in Cities and Education Action Zones: Management and Impact.* London: Ofsted

Rogers, C. and Freiberg, J. (1994) *The Freedom to Learn.* New Jersey: Prentice Hall

## Further resources

The national website for learning mentors http://www.standards.dfes.gov.uk/learningmentors/

The Children's Workforce Development Council, which has sector skills responsibilities for learning mentors and occupationally similar roles www.cwdcouncil.org.uk

The learning mentor functional map www.standards.dfes.gov.uk/learningmentors/downloads/lmfunctionalmap.doc

Supporting the New Agenda for Children's Services and Schools: the role of Learning Mentors and Co-ordinators www.standards.dfes.gov.uk/learningmentors/downloads/lmssupportingnewagenda.pdf

Value base supporting the national occupational standards www.standards.dfes.gov.uk/learningmentors/downloads/nosldssvaluebase.pdf

## Notes

**1** Data from national survey of learning mentors in Excellence in Cities/Excellence Clusters 2005/06

**2** Aggregate data from a survey of learning mentor cohorts in ten local authorities.

# Classroom Interaction

*Becky Francis*

■ *See also schedules: Learning and Teaching;
Breaktimes, Lunchtimes and Playgrounds;
Citizenship Education; Single-Sex Classes in Co-
Educational Schools; Single-Sex Schools; Working
with Girls; Working with Boys*

Anyone familiar with co-educational classrooms will be aware that classroom interaction is affected by gender. Girls and boys tend to sit separately, unless organised differently by the teacher, and tend to form friendships among their own gender group – even if there are some exceptions, such as genuine friendships formed among a minority of girls and boys, and some heterosexual romantic relationships between pupils. As groups, girls and boys also tend to behave in quite different ways and from pre-school ages onwards, children engage in what Davies (1989) terms 'gender category maintenance work' to produce these differences. It is these tendencies that form the basis for our discussion here, but before proceeding it is vital to pause and consider the complexities at stake.

There tends to be an assumption that biological sex differences programme boys and girls to behave in different ways. So differences in classroom behaviour among groups of girls and boys are usually taken to be natural expressions of sex differences. But evidence of biological differences which might lead to behavioural differences is extremely slight. A large body of child-developmental and sociological evidence shows how children – and adults – actively construct their gender identities. In this view, expressions of gender-stereotypical behaviour are due to individuals seeking to demonstrate their gender allegiance. The desire to be socially acceptable means that behaving in a manner considered appropriate for one's gender becomes crucial from early childhood. Recent research has also stressed the fluidity of gendered behaviour – how children do not always behave in consistently stereotypical ways; and how gendered behaviour may be done differently depending on a child's social class, ethnicity and so on.

To see girls and boys as uniform groups, and to assume simply that boys behave differently from girls, would be to misrepresent gender difference. Nevertheless, it is certainly the case that in general terms children of the same gender tend to gravitate towards one another, and the way in which they express their gender results in different behavioural trends. These also shift and change through schooling, but are always constructed in terms of the relationship of one gender with the other.

## Physical interaction

Boys' physical domination of the classroom and playground space has been well-documented. In the classroom, boys tend quite simply to take up more space than girls. They tend to move about the class more, and to engage in a great deal of physical contact, often aggressive, albeit play fighting.

Skelton (2001) points out that maintenance of aggressive and competitive masculinity involves constant confrontation and challenges between boys. As well as being intimidating, these sorts of practices disrupt the classroom, impeding the learning of boys and girls alike.

This physicality is not restricted solely to male-to-male interaction. Sexual harassment of girls, and sometimes of women teachers, by boys, has been reported by many who work in schools.

## Verbal interaction

Classroom observations since the 1970s and 80s have shown that boys gain far more of the teachers' attention than girls in the same classes. Hence, feminists have argued for many years that girls are marginalised and underestimated both by boys and by teachers. Even today, as a generalisation, boys continue to dominate the classroom verbally.

But more recent research has highlighted the complexity in this area. Occasionally girls may out-voice boys in classrooms, and teachers may also respond to pupils' behaviour and discipline them differently depending on their social class and ethnicity as well as gender. Some studies have indicated that part of the reason that more teacher attention is directed to boys is because they are disciplined more frequently than girls. So although girls' exchanges with the teacher are less frequent than those of boys, girls' exchanges are more constructive and related to the learning task.

Because boys tend to resist the teacher in more ostentatious ways than girls, it is hard to judge whether the disproportionate disciplinary attention that boys receive from teachers is appropriate, or unfair. When girls do behave badly, they are penalised more heavily than boys (Connolly, 1998; Reay, 2001) – again with such tendencies also being influenced by factors such as race and social class. Certainly being loud, disruptive and abusive is an expression of a high-status form of masculinity in school. Such behaviour interferes with the learning of both the boys concerned and that of their classmates.

In primary classrooms the sensible, selfless behaviour adopted by many girls as an aspect of their femininity often involves giving up power to more demanding boys. Girls and less powerful boys are often silenced through ridicule or by sexist/misogynist and/or homophobic abuse. Such abuse has been shown to be a frequent feature in classroom exchanges, further degrading the feminine in the classroom.

## Implications

Such ridicule and marginalisation of girls and non-laddish boys does much to silence girls, and to teach them their place in the classroom. Fundamentally, gendered classroom behaviour supports a hidden curriculum that teaches girls that they are of less value than boys. Boys' domination of space, attention, and verbal interaction quickly becomes seen as normal – and simply extends the norm in other aspects of societal interaction.

In turn, boys experience a competitive masculinity hierarchy in which those who fail to conform may be routinely ridiculed and punished. Such practices often include racism and homophobia, and are based a view of femininity as devalued. Rather than seeing gendered classroom interaction as inevitable, it is important that teachers and educators do what they can to address and challenge these behavioural trends. But how might this be achieved?

### *Issues to consider*
### Classroom strategies: reflection and peer observation

Whatever our intentions and beliefs, teachers are sometimes driven by a pragmatic need to get the job done, and this can involve complicity with gendered patterns in classroom behaviour. Change requires reflecting closely on our own classroom behaviour, asking such questions as:

■ is more time and attention spent on certain groups of pupils? If so, why?

■ do we apply the same expectations to all pupils, and respond to their behaviours in a consistent way in spite of factors such as gender, race and social class?

■ which pupils do teachers like/dislike, and why? Do they go along with gendered expectations, for example expecting boys to behave in laddish ways, or girls to be 'ladylike'?

■ do teachers give more time and mental energy to boys, due to a pragmatic need to hold their attention in order to complete tasks?

■ do they adopt particular approaches with boys, and/or girls – for example, roustabout/gentle?

Of course, teachers often do not realise that they are, for example, spending disproportionate amounts of attention on boys – indeed, research has shown how teachers making a conscious effort to give more attention to girls may still spend substantially more time with boys (Spender, 1982). Teachers can observe themselves, or preferably ask a colleague to observe them, focusing on gender in classroom interaction.

Points to record might include:

■ how much time is spent communicating with boys and girls? (Recording which girls and boys will enable closer reflection that recognises factors such as ethnicity and social class.) The observer might record the amount of time devoted to different pupils or which pupils are addressed.

■ the sorts of attention given to pupils in the class. Which pupils tend to require more discipline? Is praise given proportionately to different groups in the class?

■ what sort of language is the teacher using? Does it differ depending on the gender (or other social features) of the child?

■ what sort of language are the children using? Is it sexist, misogynist or homophobic?

■ what are the social status/power dynamics among pupils in the class? Are some pupils silenced by others? How does gender inform these patterns?

## Points of good practice

■ Be attuned to differences among pupils, but be careful not to apply stereotypes, either in expectations or as an aspect of teaching practices

■ Avoid practices that draw on or heighten gender differences

■ Have clearly articulated rules and punishments for breaches (helping to demonstrate that punishments are meted out fairly)

■ Be aware of classroom power dynamics, and take firm action taken if particular pupils are being silenced

■ Have zero tolerance of misogynist and homophobic verbal abuse, in addition to other forms of abuse.

Good teaching practices of this sort will facilitate change but any real and embedded change must involve pupils too. Pupils must also be encouraged to reflect on gendered trends in classroom interaction, and how their own behaviour contributes to this.

The key method to encourage such reflection among pupils is teacher-led classroom discussion and activities to explore the issue. These can fit in well as an aspect of citizenship education, and are usually greatly enjoyed by pupils. Many relish the chance to explore such issues (see Francis, 2000).

### Activities

The following activities contain similar ideas, but adopt different resources and strategies depending on the age-group. Teachers will of course adapt them according to the needs of their own class. They are intended to run across more than one session. Social identity issues need to be an ongoing theme revisited in different ways.

---

## Thinking about gendered behaviour – Primary age-group

**Aims**: To recognise the influence of gender on behaviour in and out of school

**Materials**: Traditional fairy story (eg *Sleeping Beauty*) and non-traditional fairy story (eg *The Paper Bag Princess*).

**Activities:**

■ Read the traditional story and ask about the roles of the protagonists (eg male prince, active and brave; female princess, passive, reliant). Instigate discussion on whether these roles are consistent in other stories (including contemporary renditions, eg Disney)

■ Instigate discussion as to how we expect males/females to behave, and whether this is fair. Be prepared with non-stereotypical examples to counter stereotypical assumptions

■ Introduce the idea that some of these gender stereotypes affect/constrain our own behaviour (give examples such as girls not boys liking and wearing pink, and boys not girls liking and playing football) – discuss, encouraging children to give their own examples

■ Read the non-traditional fairy story. Discuss what was different about the behaviour of the male and female characters in this story. Encourage children to articulate what they feel about the characters, and to discuss why they feel as they do

■ Ask children to write their own magical adventure story (possibly ask them to incorporate elements that are different from stereotypical tales). Discuss the final products in terms of stereotypical/not stereotypical themes.

<table>
<tr><td>

**Thinking about gendered behaviour – Secondary age-group**

**Aims**: To recognise the influence of gender on behaviour in and out of school

**Materials**: Media materials that present the genders in a stereotypical light – eg celebrity magazines, articles from tabloid newspapers, action movie film footage, etc.

Information on gendered classroom behaviour (eg this schedule)

**Activities**:

■ Initiate discussion of society's views of masculine and feminine attributes and behaviours, asking class to list stereotypical gendered attributes

■ Split class into small groups, and provide each group with a media story/magazine/film extract. Ask them to list the sorts of messages each piece is giving about men, women, and their respective expected behaviour/appearance. Ask each group to feedback to whole class

■ Instigate whole-class discussion as to whether these stereotypes are reasonable, and what their consequences are for men/boys' women/girls' lives

■ Back in small groups, ask groups to discuss whether any gender stereotypical behaviour is evident in school life (it is important to ensure this is not allowed to be personalised) and, if so, feedback to whole class

■ Explain research findings about gendered classroom interaction, and initiate whole class debate to encourage reflection.

</td></tr>
</table>

## Useful Reading and Resources

Much of the work listed below provides invaluable insights and information, but readers may find Salisbury, J. and Jackson, D. (1996) *Challenging Macho Values*. London: Falmer, particularly helpful, as it contains many outlines of workshops and strategies for use in the classroom. For suggested strategies and guidance in questioning gender stereotypes with primary school pupils, see also:

Wing, A. (1997) How can children be taught to read differently? *Bill's New Frock* and the hidden curriculum. *Gender and Education* 9 (4) p491-504

Yeoman, E. (1999) 'How does it get into my imagination? Elementary school children's inter-textual knowledge and gendered storylines. *Gender and Education* 11 (4) p427-440

Websites focusing on using Anne Fine's *Bill's New Frock* as a teaching resource to encourage reflection on gender in the classroom include:

www.the-looking-glass.net/rabbit/2.1/academy.html

www.collaborativelearning.org/catalogue.html

## References

Connolly, P. (1998) *Racism, Gender Identities and Young Children*. London: Routledge

Davies, B. (1989) *Frogs and Snails and Feminist Tales*. Sydney: Allen and Unwin

Francis, B. (2000) *Boys, Girls and Achievement: Addressing the Classroom Issues*. London: RoutledgeFalmer

Reay, D. (2001) 'Spice Girls', 'Nice Girls', 'Girlies' and 'Tomboys': gender discourses, girls' cultures and femininities in the primary classroom. *Gender and Education* 13 (2) p153-165

Skelton, C. (2001) *Schooling the Boys*. Buckingham: Open University Press

Spender, D. (1982) *Invisible Women: the Schooling Scandal*. London: Writers and Readers

# Study Support and Out of School Hours Learning

*Tony Kirwan*

■ *See also schedules: Every Child Matters; Working with Girls; Working With Boys; Libraries*

## What is it?

Study Support is learning activity outside normal lessons which young people take part in voluntarily. Study Support is accordingly an inclusive term embracing many activities – with many different names and guises. Its purpose is to improve young people's motivation, build their self esteem and help them to become more effective learners. Above all it aims to raise achievement. (Study Support: a national framework for extending learning opportunities, DfES 2006)

This broad definition encompasses:

■ homework clubs, and open access sessions in a library and learning resource centre

■ revision and booster sessions, course work catch-up sessions and provision for gifted and talented pupils taking place outside normal school time

■ all the normal sports activities offered by schools

■ creative, artistic and performance activities such as orchestra, choir, solo instrumental tuition, dance classes

■ hobby clubs such as chess, model engineering

■ mentoring and peer education activities

■ opportunities for community service in and outside the school.

Study support activities may take place on the school site or elsewhere such as public libraries, museums and galleries and sports clubs. Activities can take place before school, at break and lunch times, after school and in the evenings, weekends and holidays.

Where extra-curricular activities or enrichment programmes attracted an interested minority, study support aims to increase pupil involvement, while maintaining the enjoyment and voluntary participation of both pupils and staff. Study support activities are one of the most readily available ways for schools to tackle gender inequalities in access to learning opportunities and developmental experiences.

## Issues to consider

■ Does anyone in the school have overall responsibility for the study support programme?

■ Do you use study support activities to address issues in the school improvement plan, including gender related issues?

■ Do you know which pupils go to what activities and, more importantly, who does not go and is this information available by gender?

## What is the connection with other whole-school concerns?

In England study support activities are part of the core offer of extended services which all schools are expected to be making by 2010. Almost all of the wide and varied menu of activities will be study support. It is not the same as childcare provision which has to be consistently and reliably available to meet the needs of working parents. But children who attend childcare should also have access to study support activities. Additionally the Gifted and Talented and Healthy Schools programmes and the PE, School Sport and Club Links programme will be delivering many of their activities through study support.

## What is the evidence that study support makes a difference?

There have been two major studies into the effectiveness of study support, both of which produced significant positive findings. A major longitudinal study tracked 10,000 individual secondary pupils over three years. It compared the attainments at GCSE and the changes in attitudes and school attendance of pupils, matched for gender ethnicity and prior attainment, comparing those who participated in study support activity with those who did not (MacBeath *et al*, 2001).

On average, pupils who participated in study support improved on their predicted GCSE results by three and a half grades, when all results were considered, or by one more A\*-C grade, when only the best five results were considered. Attitudes to school and attendance at school were better for those who participated in study support than for those who did not. The improvement over predicted results was found in all groups of pupils, but there were gender, class and ethnic differences.

Major national research by NFER into the *Playing for Success* scheme have shown similar positive attitudes and impacts on attainment at the primary level (Sharp *et al*, 2003).

## Making it work in schools

One of the key findings of the longitudinal study of secondary pupils was that, although the schools served broadly similar disadvantaged populations of pupils, the participation rates in the same type of activities varied very widely from under 10% to over 90%. The likelihood of participation in study support is not a fixed characteristic of pupils, but depends on how study support is planned, organised, marketed and delivered by the school.

Schools need to plan for and manage study support just as they would manage any other whole-school strategy for raising standards, paying attention to the gender implications at each stage:

■ member of the senior leadership team has responsibility for the overall strategy

■ there is a coordinator or manager responsible for making sure activities happen, and for promoting and evaluating them. It should be noted that this does not necessarily have to be a member of the teaching staff

■ study support activities will feature in school development plans and in school self-evaluation

■ there will be regular reports to governors

■ lots of collaborative work with other schools and with outside organisations will focus on study support.

### *Issues to consider*
### Clarifying purposes and finding out what is needed

The first step in setting up effective provision is to review the school's priorities for improving outcomes, and decide where to focus. The next is to survey pupils' desires and needs, and to have regular formal and informal dialogue with them about what provision they would respond to.

■ What differences in attainment are there between boys and girls? What are the clubs, revision sessions, booster classes or mentoring programmes that address under-attainment?

■ Are there types of behaviour and attendance problems specific to boys or to girls? What sports, artistic or hobby clubs are really open to the groups you are concerned with?

■ If you are already surveying pupils for what study support activities they would like – do you analyse the responses by gender (and by ethnicity, or SEN status)?

### Creating the right ethos

The atmosphere for study support activities needs to be conducive to participation. Pupils need to feel relaxed about trying out something unfamiliar, or talking about feelings. The key question to ask is 'What do I want people to feel when they come in? And when they leave?'

■ Do you relax the school rules about uniform, eating and drinking while working? How do you address members of staff for study support activities? Are there gender differences in the pupils' responses?

■ Do you discuss ground rules for new activities with pupils? Girls are more likely to be willing to discuss the ground rules for a new club or activity. Boys are more likely to want to get on with things straight away and to become bored by too much talking

■ Do you think about when and where activities are held? A football club for Year 7 and 8 girls may be highly popular, but not if it is held in a place where older boys can hang around and make comments!

What assumptions lie behind what you think of as activities open to the whole school? Are boys going to join a dance and drama group that is already full of girls? Will a girl sign up for an introductory session at a climbing wall if ten boys' names are already on the list?

## Involving pupils and letting people know what is going on

Pupils attend study support activities voluntarily. Effective marketing to the different audiences is therefore essential. At primary level, most, but not all, marketing will be directed at parents. If this is always done by letters home with the child, will that exclude children from the more disorganised families?

■ How do you market the overall study support programme?

■ Do you use different approaches to reach different groups?

■ Why do you think those who never or rarely participate choose not to do so? Have you asked them? Do you know if they have caring responsibilities?

■ What do you know about rivalries between groups of pupils? How might this affect who participates?

■ What are the opportunities for pupils to plan, manage, deliver and evaluate particular activities? What assumptions are made about pupil leadership in your school and how does gender bear on these assumptions?

## Creating and running the programme of activities

The overall list of activities in the handbook may be impressively long. Does the programme match the needs analysis? How do you know if those who signed up, turned up?

■ Have you analysed by gender what is actually available for each year group? For example, one Women into Science and Engineering project for Year 10 and 11 and a computer club for girls for Year 7 and 8 does not really constitute opportunities for girls to develop interests in technology. Similarly, the chance for junior boys to audition for a part in the chorus of the annual school musical doesn't offer real opportunities to develop performance skills

■ For girls and their parents particularly, the timing (and offsite location) will affect their participation. How is this taken into account?

■ Have you discussed safety issues or community perceptions of what is safe and what is not? Ethnicity will also be a major influence on perceptions of safety

■ Can the programme respond rapidly to new demands, such as a group for young lesbians and gay pupils?

■ What assumptions do you make about what pupils are likely to be interested in? How have you tested these assumptions? The research evidence is that activities such as sports are more popular with boys, and creative and performance activities with girls. However, the evidence is only about the balance of interests.

## Staff selection training and development

If both boys and girls are to have equal access to the full range of learning opportunities provided by study support a structured recruitment strategy is essential.

■ How do you recruit appropriate staff for a particular activity?

■ What efforts do you make to find role model staff for activities which particularly challenge gender or ethnic stereotypes?

■ Do sessional staff have access to the school's policies and training on equal opportunities issues?

## Measuring the difference it makes

This issue brings us back full cycle to purposes and needs. If you have analysed need (formally and informally) by gender and if you also monitor who is participating in which activities and who is not participating, then you are in a position to discover evidence about the difference that study support is making. Normal school attainment data is usually broken down by gender. Getting qualitative evidence from pupils through structured interviews asking questions such as

■ what did you like about . . . ?

■ what have learned from . . . ?

■ what difference has being part of ... made to you?

is straightforward if it is done little and often. Such focus groups are easier to run if they are made up of either all boys or all girls.

The evidence from the major longitudinal study (MacBeath *et al*, 2001) showed that girls from some ethnic minority groups (principally South Asian) benefited very much more from participating in study support than the whole sample – seven grades better in their GCSE results. White boys improved least – on average two and half grades. However both boys and girls eligible for free school meals improved slightly more than the whole sample average.

- What might your evidence about participation be telling you about your programme, your publicity and your staffing?
- What more might you need to find out?
- What further action can you take, based on your evidence?

## And finally
- It works
- But you have to plan for it and monitor what is going on
- Boys and girls have slightly different needs and respond slightly differently
- Involve pupils in planning, delivery and evaluation to the greatest possible extent. They and their families will have skills and talents undreamt of – until you ask them
- It does not have to be more work for teachers – but when teachers are involved it is often an arena in which they can experiment with teaching and learning
- Keep it fun!

## Further information
Quality in Study Support
www.canterbury.ac,uk/education/quality-in-study-support
DfES Study Support
www.standards.dfes.gov.uk/studysupport
Every Child Matters
www.everychildmatters.gov.uk
Extended Schools- Teachernet
www.teachernet.gov.uk/extendedschools/
University of the First Age
www.ufa.org.uk
The National Youth Agency
www.nya.org.uk
ContinYou
www.continyou.org.uk
Youth Sport Trust
www.youthsporttrust.org.uk

## Research reports and guidance documents
ContinYou (2005) *Taking Part: Making Out-of-hours Learning Happen for Children in Care*

Department for Education and Skills (2006) *Planning and Funding Extended Schools: A Guide for Schools, Local Authorities and their Partner Organisations.* London: DfES

Department for Education and Skills (2006) *Study Support: A National Framework for Extending Learning Opportunities.* London: DfES

Elliott, J., Harked, E. and Oglethorpe, P. (2004) *Lessons from Study Support for Compulsory Learning.* London: University of Sunderland / DfES

Hunter B. (2004) *Putting Young People at the Centre of the Extended School.* Sheffield: The National Youth Agency

Macbeath, J., Kirwan, T. and Myers, K. (2001) *The Impact of Study Support: A Report of a Longitudinal Study into the Impact of Participation in Out-of-school-hours Learning on the Academic Attainment, Attitudes and School Attendance of Secondary School Students.* London: DfES

Sharp, C., Blackmore, B., Kendall L., Greene K., Keys W. *et al* (2003) *Playing for Success: An Evaluation of the Fourth Year.* London: NFER DfES

Wilson, D., Gammie, H. and Moore, J. (2004) *The Study Support Code of Practice.* London: DfES

DON'T BE SILLY—
OF COURSE THERE
WEREN'T ANY
CAVE WOMEN

# Libraries

*Sue Adler*

■ *See also schedules: ICT; Breaktimes, Lunchtimes and Playgrounds; English and Media; Literacy*

Sometimes called the Library or the Resource Centre, and sometimes the Library Resource Centre, the term library is used in this schedule. These learning spaces, often with books and computers together, reflect an institution's ethos and values. So libraries in primary, special and secondary schools can confirm and reinforce prejudice, or actively confront and challenge all forms of inequality and social injustice. At their best they are proactive and vibrant, providing access to information and recreational reading, and promoting independent and life-long learning, with the library accessible to the whole school, and the library staff themselves a resource for all.

The points below relate predominately to gender equality issues in libraries and many apply to classroom book corners too.

## Using the library

When we consider the questions below it becomes clear how varied library usage can be, and that the differences have implications for girls' and boys' learning. As with everything else, gender is one factor, and other identities should not be ignored.

A good way to start considering gender issues in the library is to monitor the way girls and boys use it. Doing such monitoring is time consuming – so try to persuade a colleague to run a statistics project to help get the information, or alternatively carry out spot checks.

## Issues to consider
### Children's use of the library

*Who* elects to use the library most – girls or boys?

*What* are they using it for?

■ Access to books for homework / classroom support?

■ Access to books for recreation and fun?

■ Computer and internet access?

■ Anything else?

*When* are they using it?

Opening hours are an equality issue. Do you see that certain groups who may not have access to computers or a place to study at home use the library out of lesson time? Have you considered that girls who may have childcare responsibilities at home cannot use the library before and after school, but may choose to use it at break time and lunchtime?

■ After school?

■ Before school

■ Morning break, lunchtime?

■ During the school day?

*How* do girls and boys choose to use the library?

### Books

Boys and reading is the subject of much discussion, debate and concern. Do the findings on boys and girls in your school confirm that boys' reading is at a lower level than girls' in both quality and quantity? Issue statistics are easy to get from any computerised library system.

Analyse girls' and boys' borrowing by subject: eg

- fiction
- thrillers/crime
- horror
- romance
- adventure
- graphic novels
- science fiction
- historical fiction
- non-fiction

Computers, magazines, newspapers etc – who uses them? What for?

Observe the behaviour of pupils in the library:

- do girls/boys tend to work together or individually?
- share information and discuss?
- how do girls and boys relate to each other in the library?

## Teachers' and departments' use of the library

In secondary schools, which departments use the library? (Consider the quality of use, as well as the quantity.)

- What are they using the space for?
- Are there any gender issues to address? (Are boys encouraged and assisted to use books as well as computers to obtain information?)
- Are there any differences between the behaviour of women and men teachers in the library, and in their relation to the students and library staff?

## How the library system works
### Classification

Almost all British schools and public libraries use the Dewey Decimal classification system – it's tried and tested and very much better than any homemade scheme. However, there are related gender issues to consider.

- Where are books on women classified – with the subject or with a number for women (usually 305.8)? In other words, is the person's sex the determinant if that person is female, or are her activities the important factor?

For example, does Bessie Coleman sit alongside the Wright Brothers in 'pilots' or has she been sent to a section on women? Is Chinwe Roy with other artists in the 759s or in 305.8? Are Mary Seacole and Florence Nightingale in 'medicine'?

- Where are books on sexual politics? Where are the works of, for example, lesbian poets – with poetry or with sexuality?

### Subject index

- Is there an entry for 'Women' – and if so, is there one for 'Men'? What are the implications of having the first but not the second?
- In secondary schools, are there entries for Feminism? Women's Studies? Men's Studies? Masculinity?
- Does the Subject Index reflect a conscious decision to avoid offensive language in all areas? And does it promote, by example, acceptable and non-offensive language?

## Library staff

Analyse the staff – including volunteers and student/pupil helpers – by gender.

- Are they mostly female? Are children aware that both men and women can be, and are, librarians?
- Does the negative stereotype of the librarian persist (a dowdy middle-aged white woman more concerned with silence than learning)?
- Are the library staff aware of, and committed to, promoting equality in children's learning in the library?

## Library policy

- Does the library have a stated policy of equality?
- Is the library policy within the whole school policy?
- Is there a stock policy that addresses criteria on equality, including criteria for selection of new material, discarding old stock, and suppliers?

## The physical appearance and accessibility of the library

- Is the library accessible to all?
- Is it safe for everyone?
- Does the library look welcoming and inviting to all?
- Are there comfortable places to sit and is it a pleasant environment in which to spend time?
- Do posters, displays and signs reflect a positive stance on equality?
- Does the library, in its role as provider of information, contain posters and leaflets from the local community, and from help lines and advice centres on issues of sexual health, rape,

sexual abuse and sexuality? Some information may be for all schools, others are suitable for secondary schools only.

## Stock

■ Is the stock of the library assessed with gender equality in mind? How is this monitored?

As with much monitoring, involving pupils has the dual advantage of speeding up a time-consuming process and also, much more importantly, raising awareness of the issues for all those involved.

Pupils/students can:

■ count the characters in single titles, listing female and male

■ count, similarly, with a collection of titles, for example, looking at all the books on castles in the library

■ discuss the findings from the above two exercises, extending the debate to include the roles of male and female characters, stereotypes, and then make suggestions for improvements.

Does the library select purchases of stock from small, alternative suppliers and publishers, supporting them when possible?

The 1980s saw a flowering of checklists for libraries, mostly designed to assess individual titles. Few made the point that it was the collection overall that needed to be assessed. However, their value in raising awareness of sexism and other oppressions remains significant.

## Resources

Chartered Institute of Library and Information Professionals (CILIP) (2004) *Sexual Orientation and Libraries: Professional Guidance*, Policy and Research. www.cilip.org.uk/professionalguidance/equalopportunities/briefings/sexuality.htm

Department of Culture, Media and Sport (2001) *Libraries, Museums, Galleries and Archives for All*. www.culture.gov.uk/PDF/libraries_archives_for_all.pdf

Department of Culture, Media and Sport (2003) *Framework For The Future: Libraries, Learning and Information in the Next Decade* www.culture.gov.uk/global/publications/archive_2003/framework_future.htm

Letterbox Library. This is not a library but is a children's bookclub that 'celebrates equality and diversity in the best children's books.' Catalogue and mail-order. www.letterboxlibrary.com

The Network: tackling social exclusion in libraries, museums, archives and galleries. john@nadder.org.uk www.seapn.org.uk

Project SEE (Sex Equity in Education) (1998) *10 Quick Ways to Analyse Children's Books for Racism and Sexism*. Sacramento CA: California State Department of Education

Suffolk County Council (2006) *Equalities Impact Assessment: The Schools Library Service. Suffolk: Schools Library Service*. www.suffolkcc.gov.uk/policy/diversity

YOU MEAN GENDER, CLASS, RACE AND THAT KIND OF THING? IT'S GOT NOTHING TO DO WITH US!

# Single-Sex Schools
## *Diana Leonard and Debra Murphy*

■ *See also schedules: Single-Sex Classes in Co-educational Schools; Continuing Professional Development; Governors; Learning and Teaching; Working with Girls; Working with Boys*

The number of single-sex schools in Britain has been steadily declining. Very few single-sex primary schools or colleges remain in the public sector, and virtually no single-sex state secondary schools in Scotland and Wales. In England, however, there are still significant numbers in London and the South, and in Northern Ireland most secondary schools have religious affiliations and remain single-sex. There are also single-sex schools throughout the private sector, although their numbers are also declining.

---

In 1905 there were very few maintained mixed secondary schools in the country; by 1925 there were 300, and by 1936, 1046 (Dyhouse 1985).

In 2005, 13% of girls and 10% of boys in maintained secondary schools in England were in single-sex schools.

But in inner London, 52% of girls were in girls' schools and 27% of boys were in boys' schools (Whatford, 2005).

---

## Going co-ed

Each year some teachers face the emotive issues of their single-sex school going co-ed. In our experience the teachers' and pupils' perceptions of the implications of this mostly reflect a mixture of common sense concerns around a new kind of chaos in the school, such as behaviour management issues regarding boys' unruly behaviour, and the possibility

that the opposite sex may be a source of distraction. The majority of staff may feel they will have to change their approach to teaching in order to accommodate boys' and girls' supposedly different learning dispositions, based on views of learning styles grounded in assumptions about the differences between male and female learners. There may be little or no acknowledgement of the fact that in a single-sex school, girls or boys are already engaged in much of the behaviour that teachers feel would be typified by the opposite sex.

## Parental choice

Where they are available, single-sex schools remain a popular choice for some parents, especially for their daughters. Other parents equally resolutely support co-education, seeing it as part of the sexes learning to live together.

■ The parents of girls believe their daughters will be protected from boys' attentions, wanted or unwanted attentions in single-sex schools, and will be instilled with a hard-working academic ethos. Some also believe adolescents should be sex-segregated for religious reasons.

■ Parents are more likely to choose mixed schools for their sons, seeing girls as a civilising influence.

Where there are single-sex schools in competition with co-educational schools in a locality in the educational quasi-market, these preferences have renewed significance (Ball and Gewirtz 1997). Many co-educational schools have 60% or more boys, which raises problems for local authorities trying to balance provision and provide equal opportunities.

### Issues for all schools to consider

■ What do you consider to be the specific benefits, if any, for girls and for boys of attending single-sex schools?

■ Do staff in your schools have specific expertise in teaching girls or boys?

■ Are there opportunities for teachers to reflect upon and share this experience and knowledge with each other and with teachers in co-educational schools, especially those which are considering running some single-sex classes?

■ Are there opportunities to develop practices that encourage staff as well as students, to engage in critical reflection about negative gender stereotyping – given that some argue that gender is not an issue in single-sex schools?

## Research findings on the advantages and disadvantages of single-sex education

Historically, the segregation of the sexes is a relic of the new private schools for girls in the 19th century and state grammar schools in the 20th, following the pattern of the long established boys' public schools. This was countered by the Progressive School Movement of the early twentieth century, which produced Bedales and King Alfred School, amongst others, and the comprehensive movement of the 1950s to 1970s, both of which argued that co-education was more 'natural', would improve the relationships between the sexes at work and in the family, and would counter tendencies towards homosexuality.

Advocacy for single-sex schools re-emerged in response to feminist concerns over girls' access to teacher attention and school resources, and with how well girls achieve academically, as well as career opportunities for women teachers.

However, there is little research evidence to suggest that going to a single- or mixed-sex school makes a statistically significant difference to either boys' or girls' overall examination performance. The sector of schooling and parental background matter much more and, given the selectivity of many single-sex schools, it is not surprising they get better results at 16 and 18. However, some girls' schools do produce notably good results with girls from disadvantaged and minority ethnic backgrounds.

Whether the school attended is co-educational or single-sex doesn't seem to influence either boys' or girls' attitudes to gender equity in employment. Boys are no more or less likely to be willing to work for a woman, whichever type of school they have attended. Nor does the type of school affect either men's or women's attitudes towards the domestic division of labour. Co-educated boys are no more likely to help with the washing-up or to approve of women having jobs when they have children. Going to a co-educational school does not affect the incidence of premarital pregnancy, nor individuals' likelihood of getting married, nor the average age at which they marry. In other words, girls from single-sex schools are no more or less interested in boys than those from co-educational schools. We have no evidence whether or not single-sex schooling (or going to boarding school) affects individuals' sexual preferences in adult life (ie we don't know if co-education does discourage homosexual interests as has been asserted) (Leonard *et al*, 2006).

However, there is evidence that girls have a lower opinion of their abilities in most subjects (except English) in mixed schools; and that both sexes make more sex-stereotyped choices of subject in the presence of the opposite sex. Co-education increases educational differentiation between the sexes: it encourages more masculine choices and positioning in boys, and more feminine choices and positioning in girls. Girls from single-sex schools have been more likely to continue to study science in higher education and to earn higher wages in later life than those from mixed schools.

Thinking on co-education has shifted somewhat as a result of concerns about the underachievement of boys. Discussion concerns the relative advantages of single-sex education for boys rather than girls, linking boys' underachievement with the (supposed) feminisation of schooling and girls putting down boys in mixed classes (see the schedule Single-sex Classes in Co-educational Schools on page 144, also Martino and Frank, 2006; Martino *et al*, 2005).

### Issues to consider

Work in the UK and Australia (Francis *et al*, 2003; Lingard *et al*, 2002; Martino *et al*, 2004; Sukhnanden *et al*, 2000) has addressed issues for boys and girls within the framework of a gender-specific critical pedagogy. These encourage educationalists to:

■ stress the importance of teachers knowing about and understanding gender issues. This is essential to guide curriculum and pedagogy and especially reflective work with pupils. It urgently needs to be re-introduced into initial teacher training and continuing professional development

■ map practice within a school, in particular looking at the skills of teachers who already use strategies that challenge the social construction of gendered behaviour. This applies both to teaching boys and teaching girls, because within a single-sex girls' school, constructions of femininity often continue to limit some girls' aspirations and motivations

■ work towards a coherent whole-school approach to avoid ad hoc practices. Instead, monitor and then evaluate any supposedly gender specific teaching strategies adopted

■ provide training for all staff and governors about the social construction of gendered behaviour

■ critically reflect on curriculum materials used in single-sex schools (including library, ICT and careers resources) in order to avoid gender stereotyping

■ develop effective practices that encourage students to reflect on how notions about gender are constructed (Martino *et al*, 2004)

■ encourage open-ended and creative tasks and avoid falling into the trap of assuming that boys, in particular, need bite-size lessons. These do little to stimulate higher order thinking and critical reflection

■ help pupils and teachers to develop conflict resolution skills in order to respond to sex-based and homophobic (as well as race and class, etc) based harassment, bullying and intimidation . This is needed all the more in single-sex schools where some versions of femininity or masculinity get privileged over others (which means that there is a larger group of potential harassers since much harassment is between boys and between girls).

## References and further reading

Ball, S. and Gewirtz, D. (1997) Girls in the education market: choice, competition and complexity. *Gender and Education* 9 p207-22

Francis, B., Hutchings, M. and Read, B. (n.d.) *Science in Girls' Schools: Factors that Contribute to Girls' Engagement and Attainment.* IPSE, London Metropolitan University, for the AMGS/Girls' School Association

Francis, B., Hutchings M., Archer L. and Melling, L. (2003) Subject choice and occupational aspirations among pupils at girls' schools. *Pedagogy, Culture and Society* 11 (3)

Hey, V. *et al*, (1998) Boys' underachievement, special needs practices and questions of equity. In Epstein, D., Elwood. J., Hey, V. and Maw. J. (eds) (2004) *Failing Boys? Issues in Gender and Achievement.* Buckingham: Open University Press

Leonard, D. (2006) Single-sex schooling, in: .Skelton, C., Smulyan. L. and Francis. B (eds) *Handbook of Gender and Education.* London: Sage

Leonard, D., Sullivan, A. and Joshi H. (2006) *Single and Mixed Sex Schooling: Life-Course Consequences?* ESRC End of Project Report

Lingard, B. *et al*, (2002) *Addressing the Educational Needs of Boys.* Canberra: Department of Education, Science and Training www.dest.gov.au/NR/rdonlyres/6045BC92-B4BC-4F50-93E9-6DF

Martino W. and Frank B. (2006) The tyranny of surveillance: male teachers and the policing of masculinities in a single sex school. *Gender and Education* 18 (1)

Martino, W., Lingard, B. and Mills M. (2004) Issues in boys' education: a question of teacher threshold knowledges? *Gender and Education* 16 (4)

Martino, W., Mills, M. and Lingard, B. (2005) Interrogating single-sex classes as a strategy for addressing boys' educational and social needs. *Oxford Review of Education* 1(2)

Sukhnandan, L., Lee, B. and Kelleher, S. (2000) *An Investigation Into Gender Differences In Achievement: Phase 1 A Review Of Recent Research and LEA Information On Provision, and Phase 2 Schools and Classroom Strategies.* London: National Foundation for Educational Research

Whatford, C. (2005) *Secondary-school Places Planning in London* www.teachernet.gov.uk/wholeschool/london/las/placesplanning

Younger, M. and Warrington, M. (2002) Single sex teaching in a co-educational comprehensive school in England: an evaluation based upon students' performance and classroom interactions. *British Educational Research Journal* 28(3)

## Useful contacts

Girls School Association www.gsa.uk.com/
International Boys School Coalition www.boysschoolscoalition.org

# Single-Sex Classes in Co-Educational Schools

*Mike Younger and Molly Warrington*

■ *See also schedules: Single-Sex schools; Learning and Teaching; Assessment; English; Mathematics and Numeracy; Science; Modern Foreign Languages*

The preoccupation with raising boys' achievement in many of our secondary schools has caused a resurgence of interest in single-sex classes. In some respects, this resurgence has been ironic, since single-sex teaching was advocated in the 1970s and 1980s as an organisational strategy which had potential to raise girls' achievements and to help to achieve equality of opportunity. However, by the end of the 1980s, few single-sex classes existed in coeducational secondary schools in England. The renewed interest in single-sex teaching in secondary schools – but not, significantly, in primary schools – in the last decade or so, has been sparked almost entirely by the concern with boys' needs and with the debate about under-achieving boys.

The generalised notion of under-achieving boys is open to question. This phenomenon is encountered chiefly in specific curriculum areas such as English or modern foreign languages (MFL), and often applies more to boys from working-class backgrounds or those of Caribbean, Pakistani or Bangladeshi origin. But it is as simplistic to assume that all boys from these backgrounds under-achieve, as it is to assume that there are no under-achieving girls.

The impact of single-sex classes on outcomes, in terms of the effects on students' motivation and achievements, is open to different interpretations (Younger *et al*, 2005). Some studies have suggested that single-sex grouping of students is one factor which has appeared to contribute to the high achievement levels of both girls and boys over time,

without accompanying social disadvantages. Other studies have suggested that, when implemented within a whole school, gender inclusive context (see below), such groupings can help boys to achieve better results in English and in MFL, as can girls in mathematics and the sciences at GCSE. In some schools though, the impact on achievement has been minimal, and classroom management challenges, particularly from disengaged boys and a smaller minority of girls, have led to the abandonment of the initiative. So the key might be in the ethos and commitment the school brings to the issue.

## The whole school context

Single-sex teaching cannot work effectively in isolation. If it is to be successful in any school, it needs high profile promotion within the school community. The proactive and supportive role of senior management, monitoring but also offering public support, is absolutely vital. Where senior management has simply been accommodating or even detached, the effects have been much more limited or even counter-productive.

### *Issues to consider*

■ How committed is the school's senior management team to sustained single-sex teaching? Is there support for the teachers involved? How is this commitment conveyed to all the staff?

■ How are the outcomes to be monitored and evaluated over time? What steps can be taken accurately to ascertain the views of all participants, including students and parents or carers?

144

■ What steps are in place to ensure that students and parents or carers are fully informed of the rationale behind the school's approach, and kept up to date on progress?

■ How can middle managers support teachers who are less confident or committed to this form of organisation, so that they have access to strategies which have proved effective in other contexts, and are able to implement the teaching strategies within the set of beliefs, attitudes and expectations articulated within the ethos of the school?

■ What structures and processes exist within the school which enable students to contribute to the discussion of their own learning? How are students' voices acknowledged as valid and authentic?

■ Once single-sex classes have been introduced, what is done to create a climate in which boys and girls can perform without fear of undermining their own image or losing face with their friends of either sex?

## The case for single-sex classes: students' voices

Our research with secondary schools in different parts of the country as part of the four-year Raising Boys' Achievement Project, suggested that – under certain circumstances – boys and girls felt more comfortable when taught in boys-only or girls-only classes. The students we interviewed identified a number of advantages of such classes:

■ they had fewer distractions from learning when the other sex were not present

■ they were more willing and confident to answer questions and to participate more in the lesson; girls spoke of it 'being less embarrassing to do talks if the blokes aren't there to rubbish you'; boys talked of 'not being so nervous and afraid of messing-up in front of the girls'

■ the classroom atmosphere was more conducive to learning: less noise and display behaviour from boys, fewer disparaging comments from girls

■ they were more willing to work harder and to discuss issues without worrying about stereotypical expectations and their own image; it was easier to express feelings and opinions

■ teachers were able to teach more: girls felt they learned better because there was less need for teachers continually to discipline boys; boys felt

they received more attention and help with their learning because there were no girls present to dominate the questioning and to claim the teachers' attention.

At the same time, our research confirmed that single-sex classes were not automatically a panacea. In some schools, girls were worried about the effects of single-sex classes on their own social integration or felt that male teachers were bonding more with boys, and setting up stereotypical laddish images and expectations which made it more difficult when boys and girls came together again in other lessons. Another worry was that boys-only classes were too challenging, and caused classroom management problems. Some boys suggested that they missed the help and support girls offered them in lessons, and felt that lessons lacked stimulation and fun when no girls were present.

Whilst it is difficult to draw out generalisations which apply across all schools, it is true to say that:

■ more girls than boys favoured single-sex classes

■ in most schools, a majority of both boys and girls felt that – under certain circumstances – single-sex classes helped them to remain more motivated and to learn more effectively

■ in all schools, boys and girls did not want to be taught in single-sex classes for any more subjects than presently existed in the school; broadly, single-sex classes were offered in one or more of English, mathematics, science and MFL.

### Issues to consider

■ If there is interest in introducing single-sex classes in your school, what has been the basis for this? What does the school hope to achieve from the initiative?

■ Is this initiative driven by a concern for the motivation and achievement levels of one gender, or is it directed at particular students who might be on key borderlines at GCSE?

■ Who might lead the discussion about the introduction of single-sex classes? An innovator? A recent convert? A member of the senior management team? What is their perspective and motivation? How does this connect with your own and that of the department or faculty within which you work?

■ Where might single-sex classes be introduced? In tightly defined contexts – for example, one department, one year, particular sets in the year? Across a whole year for all subjects?

■ What opportunities can be created for pupils and parents to contribute to decision making, or making their views known on this issue? What might be the advantages and disadvantages of creating such opportunities?

### Teaching single-sex classes: an inclusive rather than a 'boy-friendly' pedagogy

Those who advocate single-sex teaching often argue that it facilitates a differentiated curriculum, with different texts, resources and exemplars, for girls' and boys' classes. They maintain it allows pedagogy to differ according to gender-biased needs and interests, so that teaching boys-only classes can be more structured, have more variety and pace, emphasise competitive rather than collaborative activities, and involve more kinaesthetic and active teaching approaches. Our research questions both these assumptions. It is significant that neither the boys nor the girls we interviewed suggested that they were taught differently in single-sex classes, despite the fact that this has been one of the main issues surrounding such classes. Little evidence has emerged to substantiate claims about gender differentiated learning styles and interests. Rather, a series of gender-neutral pre-conditions has been found which must be implemented if single-sex teaching is to sustain motivation and engagement in learning. These pre-conditions operate both at the pedagogic level, within individual classrooms, and at the whole-school level.

Extensive classroom observations and ongoing discussions with teachers identify a number of features which characterise good practice teaching in single-sex classrooms.

■ Lessons have a clear and sharp beginning, with a lesson structure which is shared with the class.

■ Lessons incorporate a variety of short-term targets, to tight and agreed time limits.

■ Teacher-pupil interactions are fast and energetic, with the teacher's input high profile, offering a variety of activities and public praise.

■ There is a constant reinforcement of high expectations, through a proactive and assertive approach, which avoids the negative or the confrontational.

■ The teacher establishes absolute base line rules which, if broken, incur known and consistent sanctions.

■ The teacher takes time and care actively to promote a team ethic with the class, to forge an identity of which the students can feel part.

■ Humour and informality are also used by the teacher, to consolidate rapport and relationships with the pupils.

This pedagogy is in fact not gender-differentiated, but is equally applicable to all-girls and all-boys classes; it relates more to the nature of effective teaching *per se*, than to anything which is specific to single-sex classes.

### Issues to consider

■ If a gender-inclusive pedagogy is at the heart of successful teaching in single-sex classes, what processes already exist in your school to support the development of interactive, collaborative teaching and learning, as outlined above?

■ Does the school recognise that some colleagues might be role models in this respect? If so, do opportunities exist for them to explore their pedagogic practices with other colleagues? Do opportunities exist for peer observation of teaching?

■ How does the school maximise its involvement in initial teacher education to develop its own pedagogy? Are specific newly qualified teachers seen as a resource in this respect?

Observations of single-sex teaching suggest that there are a number of distinct challenges associated with such classes.

■ Does the ethos in the school enable honest and constructive exchanges to take place about the challenges which staff face when teaching in single-sex contexts?

■ How might it be possible to avoid some boys becoming intimidated by the atmosphere in single-sex classes and thus reluctant to contribute?

■ What strategies might be devised, for all-girl classes, to avoid some girls assuming the role of surrogate boys, and becoming more aggressive towards other girls?

■ What safeguards are there to try to ensure that teachers avoid sexist repartee as they attempt to establish rapport and togetherness with students?

■ Do teachers encourage competition between parallel sets of boys' and girls' classes and, if this is a preferred strategy, what can be done to avoid an anti-male or anti-female ethos developing within the classes?

∎ There is more sophistication in teaching single-sex classes than might at first be apparent from these checklists. Successful teaching and learning in single-sex classes demands not only a set of pedagogic practices, but the teaching strategies need to be situated within a set of beliefs, attitudes and expectations held by teachers, and strongly supported by senior managers in the school.

## Final considerations

Single-sex classes on their own are no panacea for the problems of poor behaviour, disaffection and lack of achievement, but equally they can provide a positive and successful experience for girls and boys. Central to this is the willingness to sustain, monitor and evaluate single-sex classes as a mode of organisation over time, supported by proactive rather than passive school leadership, and to develop an accessible classroom pedagogy which opens up learning for all students. Successful teaching in single-sex classes is less concerned with developing explicit gender-specific (notably boy-friendly) pedagogies, and more concerned with teacher belief, attitude and expectation. Discussion of so-called boy-friendly teaching strategies is, in fact, simply discussion about the essence of high quality teaching, which needs to be available equally to boys and girls. All of the above also applies to single-sex

small groups, and these need to be monitored whether they have been formed by design, or by the chance that a group of pupils with a common need happens all to be of the same sex.

## References and further resources

Younger, M. and Warrington, M. with Gray, J., Rudduck, J., McLellan, R., Bearne, E., Kershner, R. and Bricheno, P. (2005) *Raising Boys' Achievement: A Study Funded by the Department for Education and Skills.* London: DfES (DfES Research Report RR63) www.dfes.gov.uk/genderand achievement

Warrington, M. and Younger, M. (2003) 'We decided to give it a twirl': single-sex teaching in English comprehensive schools. *Gender and Education* 15 (4) p339-350

JUST THE THOUGHT OF ALL THOSE BIKES PUFFS ME O~

# Working with Girls

*Debra Murphy and Emma Renold*

■ *See also schedules: 'Underachieving Boys' and 'Overachieving Girls' Revisited- Rhetoric and Reality; Working with Boys; The 14-19 Curriculum; It's My School: The Power of Pupil Voice; Study Support and Out of School Hours Learning*

### Girls on and off the policy agenda

Scanning for literature on working with girls nowadays, there seems to be a real dearth of information. This is in direct contrast to an increasing number of guidance documents dedicated to working with boys and the problems of masculinity. It is also in marked contrast to the 1970s and 1980s, when there were specialised groups for teachers and youth workers working with girls. These professionals had to struggle to establish dedicated single-sex provision for girls in and out of school – against considerable political opposition (Leonard, 2000).

It is perhaps no surprise, given the UK performance culture of testing, targets and tables, that there is such concern with the gender gap in achievement in some areas, notably literacy and language-related subjects. However, the gaps by race and social class – and the interactions of each of these with each other and with gender – remain much more significant. The differences in the achievements and educational needs between various groups of girls – even if they have more or less dropped off the agenda – are greater than the overall difference between boys and girls.

Some of the effects of the over-concern with boys' achievement include:

■ masking the continuing problems faced by girls in schools

■ justifying a greater focus and expenditure on meeting boys' needs (at the expense of girls)

■ deflecting attention from the larger achievement gaps according to race and social class (Francis and Skelton, 2005).

Defining education and educational success solely in terms of measurable outputs that can be publicised in league tables, and pitting the sexes against each other, reinforces crude gender oppositions – for example, that boys and girls as groups have different learning styles.

For instance, gender stereotypes lie behind the DfES 'Playing for Success' initiative which establishes out of school hours study support centres at football clubs and other sports' grounds to encourage 'children' to do their homework – actually targeted at boys, given the football focus.

This strategy is founded upon assumptions that oversimplify girlhood/femininity and boyhood/masculinity and overlook the diversity between girls and between boys that the feminist and pro-feminist academic literature has long highlighted. We are again having to make visible the ways in which girls' educational needs have been overlooked by the new initiatives, each of which is supposedly gender-neutral but each of which impacts differently upon girls and boys, and differently upon different groups of girls.

### Diverse girlhoods, diverse needs, diverse working practices

#### Issues to consider

Schools might start by considering how the following key areas of concern (which overlap and intersect in many different ways) impact upon, and how are they negotiated differently by girls rather than boys; and by girls according to their age, ethnicity, religion, class and sexuality:

- school exclusion and truancy (Osler and Vincent, 2003)
- bullying and violence (Alder and Worrell, 2004)
- smoking and alcohol misuse (Lloyd, 2005)
- self-harm and bodily abuse (Frost, 2001)
- low and high achievement (Skelton and Francis, 2005; Renold and Allan, 2006)
- pressures of hyper heterosexualised femininities (see Hey, 1997, Aapola *et al*, 2005) and demonisation of other femininities (eg 'laddettes', see Jackson, 2006, or 'mean girls', see Ringrose, 2006).

Much of this research emphasises the diverse range of issues affecting girls. We question the extent to which it makes sense to develop a literature on working with girls unless the sort of girl is further specified. A great deal of literature about girls' educational needs or on girls and girlhood may itself contribute to reinforcing gender stereotypes of girl learners and particular categories of girl (the mean girl, the slut, the laddette) or particular aspects of femininity (internalisation of failure, low self-esteem). Much of the research on working with underachieving working-class girls tends to focus on social problems such as teenage motherhood or presents them as being deficient in resources such as confidence and self-esteem (LB Camden, 2005).

## Working with girls in short-term intervention projects

Schools' projects such as those in inner-city secondary schools described below (Murphy, 2006) can challenge common constructions of underachieving girls. Starting from the students' perspective encourages them to think for themselves, and engage critically with their own educative and gendered experiences. However many projects intentionally and unintentionally reinforced narrow and constraining forms of femininity. A key characteristic of these projects was their non-participatory approach to working with girls, imposing their own gender agenda on working practices, interventions and strategies, rather than starting with girls' own experiences and ideas for what might work best.

### *Reinforcing gendered assumptions of girls*

It was disappointing that so many schools assumed that the solution to underachievement lay in the girls' capacity to change themselves rather than in the schools' capacity for change. One school's adoption of an emotional literacy project, aimed at raising girls' self-esteem, typified what many schools believed girls liked doing or the type of activities that they ought to be engaged in. This particular project had begun with the common (mis)conception that girls like talking about themselves. The problem with this model is that it tends to encourage introspection and assume that the root cause of most problems lie in girls' own psychological shortcomings rather than in the structure, culture or ethos of the school.

> In one school, while boys were engaged in conducting market research, visiting a local prison and burying a time capsule deep under the foundations of what was to become the site of their new school building, girls were sitting around in circles, being asked to discuss the inner contents of their handbags (presumably a metaphor for their inner thoughts and feelings).

This gender-differentiated approach to working with girls, based on homogenising girls and traditional stereotypes of femininity, is unlikely to challenge many of the inequalities already experienced by this group as it encourages introspection rather than encouraging them to engage critically with society at large, the school or the curriculum.

Where curriculum change was called for, it generally centred on the idea of off-site, work-related training for these pupils. Many off-site projects attempted to engage their girls in training pathways that further reinforced gender-specific and stereotyped choices about the future. For example, work placements tended to involve working within either hospitality, style or image industries such as hair styling or beauty. While these jobs do offer the potential for lucky or talented young people to become successful, they can equally produce low-wage sub-employment. Success in these industries often depends upon who you are, who you know and to a large extent what you look like. This example highlights once again the essentialist view of gender: here girls are constructed as preoccupied with beauty and style. Could this type of project be responsible for narrowing these girls' 'horizons for action' (Hodgkinson *et al*, 1996)?

The government's five-year strategy acknowledges that many young people are bored and frustrated.

(DfES, 2004) It does not seem to acknowledge that solutions to disadvantage must lie beyond a curriculum determined by employers and vocational training alone. Instead, we need to expand our girls' – and boys' – horizons for action in some of the ways detailed below.

### Challenging assumptions about girls

Some schools put consultation with students at the centre of their projects. Recognising girls' and women's own voices has a long history in feminist research. Some schools reported that this approach enriched their understanding of the social, cultural and emotional assets that the girls already possessed. Involving learners in thinking about the skills that they already possess and the type of learning that they enjoy can serve as a powerful tool for bringing about real change at the institutional level of the school.

### Photo-evaluation

One student voice girls' project used photo evaluation. The purpose of this was to generate discussion and exchange information about how to enhance learning in and out of the classroom. One group of girls was given disposable cameras and their photos were displayed and used as the basis for discussion. The project revealed that this group had very different concerns and experiences from those assumed by their teachers. One school using the photo evaluation technique reported that the main advantage was that it was an effective tool for opening up dialogue between the students and teachers about classroom practices that would otherwise have gone unnoticed. A theme throughout the responses was that these girls had a number of concerns over feeling included; this was reflected in their comments about how their interactions with teachers made them feel '....teachers embarrass you', as well as the school peer group culture where it was felt that cleverness marginalised you from your peers.

This tends to challenge the idea that it is mostly boys who have to negotiate peer group popularity with school success (Younger and Warrington, 2002). Another area of concern was feeling in control of learning. Pupils tended to state that they preferred learning outside the classroom environment or away from teacher surveillance. Many students commented that they felt that they were being treated as children in school whereas outside of school they had a lot of responsibility as carers, either of younger siblings or of their own parents.

### Think about girlhood differently when working with girls

Working with girls means working with a range of competing and often normative assumptions about girls, girlhood and femininity. It involves critically exploring our own assumptions about girls, girlhood and femininity. This involves recognising how other differences (such as age, ethnicity, religion, social class, locality etc) make a difference to girls' and young women's educational experiences in expected and unexpected ways.

### Issues to consider

We offer some useful starting points and related questions for critically thinking through approaches in working with girls, whether planning single-sex workshops on single issues or working in single-sex or mixed-sex environments more widely. Reflecting upon these questions and talking with girls before any strategy or programme is implemented (for example, separating girls from boys, targeting particular groups of girls for particular educational initiatives) will, we hope, encourage practices that challenge gender stereotyping.

**Critically explore your own assumptions around girls, girlhood and femininity**

- What stereotypes of femininity do you as a teacher, or practitioner working with girls, hold around girls and femininity (for example different ages, ethnicities, sexualities, class groups etc)?
- What kinds of dominant images of femininity does the school itself reflect to the children in the school?

**Learn from girls (and with girls) how they understand themselves and each other as girls within various educational contexts and settings**

- What do girls themselves think about being a girl (for example how are different kinds of femininity valued by themselves, by others)?
- What kinds of images of femininity do girls bring with them into the school context?
- How are different kinds of femininity acted out in different contexts (inside school and beyond the school gates)?

**Critically explore how dominant notions of what it means to be a girl or young woman impact upon girls' everyday lives, social interactions and aspirations and expectations**

■ What kind of dominant images of femininity (for example in the media, peer culture etc) do girls consider impact most upon their everyday lives, positively and negatively?

■ How do these dominant images of femininity influence the ways in which girls think about and plan for their futures?

**Recognise how differences (sexuality, class, gender, age) intersect and interact with each other in anticipated and unanticipated ways**

■ What differences do you think make a difference to girls' lives?

■ How are your own assumptions challenged when discussing with girls how issues of class, age, sexuality, disability or religion affect their lives and their understandings of themselves and their futures?

## Participation and voice

Finally, when planning interventions specifically for girls, or an intervention that will indirectly impact upon girls, make sure to involve girls as far as possible in the planning and design of that intervention. Reflect with girls on the anticipated positive and negative effects of such interventions upon girls and their lives.

## References

Aaopola, S., Gonick, M. and Harris, A. (2004) *Young Femininity.* Buckingham: Palgrave

Alder, A. and Worrall, C. (2004) *Girl's Violence: Myths and Realities.* New York: SUNY Press

Frost, L. (2001) *Young Women and the Body: A Feminist Sociology.* Palgrave: MacMillan

Department for Education and Skills (2004) *Five Year Strategy for Children and Learners* http://www.standards.dfes.gov.uk

Francis, B. and Skelton, C. (2005) *Reassessing Gender and Achievement: Questioning Contemporary Key Debates.* London: Routledge

Hodgkinson. P., Sparks, A. C. and Hodgkinson, H. (1996) *Triumphs and Tears: Young People, Markets and the Transition from School to Work.* London: David Fulton

Jackson, C. (2006) *Lads and Ladettes in School.* Buckingham: Open University Press

Leonard, D. (2000) Teachers, femocrats and academics: activism in London in the 1980s. In Myers, K. (ed) *Whatever Happened to Equal Opportunities in Schools? Gender Equality Initiatives in Education.* Buckingham: Open University Press

Lloyd, G. (2005) (ed) *Problem Girls: Understanding and Supporting Troubled and Troublesome Girls and Young Women.* London: Routledge

London Borough of Camden (2005) *On the Margins: a Report on Exclusion from Education and Employment.* Camden's Equalities and Social Inclusion Team

Murphy, D. (2006) *Underachievement of White Working Class Pupils in Camden Schools: A report of the PACE project.* London: Camden School Improvement Service

Osler, A. and Vincent, K. (2003) *Girls and Exclusion: Rethinking the Agenda.* London: Routledge

Renold, E. and Allan, A. (2006) Bright and Beautiful: High achieving girls, ambivalent femininities, and the feminization of success in the primary school. *Discourse* 27 (4) p457-73

Ringrose, J. (2006) A New Universal Mean Girl: Examining the Discursive Construction and Social Regulation of a New Feminine Pathology. *Feminism and Psychology* 16 (4) p405-24

Younger, M. and Warrington, M. (2002) Single-sex teaching in a co-educational comprehensive school in England: an evaluation based on students' performance and classroom interactions. *British Educational Research Journal* 28 (3)

# Working with Boys

*Trefor Lloyd*

■ *See also schedules: 'Underachieving Boys' and 'Overachieving Girls' Revisited – Rhetoric and Reality; Working with Girls; The 14-19 Curriculum; It's My School: The Power of Pupil Voice; Study Support and Out of School Hours Learning*

It has been impossible to miss the concern of the government and the media about boys' underachievement since the 1990s. Much work with boys is therefore concerned with trying to improve their current performance in school. But of course certain groups of boys and young men have always underachieved at school and, while their number may be increasing, it would be a mistake to think that this is something new.

However, changes in the workplace have had, and are still having, a disproportionate impact on young men. Many of the relatively well paid jobs that they could, in the past, have gone into without formal qualifications have disappeared: much heavy industry, many trades, and of course traditional, on-the-job apprenticeships. These have been replaced by lower paid, often service sector jobs which are often perceived as women's work.

Nevertheless, some young men still believe that they can leave school without qualifications and walk into well paid work. This just does not happen. On the other hand, five A*-Cs at GCSE can go a long way towards securing a modern apprenticeship. In working with boys, we are therefore both trying to address boys' underachievement, and also to counter a set of beliefs and attitudes (about the workplace, for example) that reinforces an anti-academic view.

## Understanding the situation

Underachievement is an issue for both young men and young women, and an understanding of gender differences helps to inform solutions for both. This is not at the basic level of 'girls do...' and 'boys do ...', but about much more careful observations of individual boys' and girls' attitudes and behaviour. So, for example, one classroom will contain within it a range of boys, such as the following:

Joe finds maths difficult, when he doesn't understand something he turns off and chats to his mates. Inevitably, his maths teacher responds to his talking and not his maths difficulty. Because this happens often, Joe feels the teacher is singling him out and starts to anticipate conflict in the classroom and the teacher starts to expect that from Joe. The teacher is surprised to hear that other teachers find Joe fine in their class.

Alex is always full of life, and bounces around the school. He wants to be in everything. He is first to get his hand up, although he doesn't always stay on point. Sometimes in class he gets so excited he just can't sit still. This is particularly the case for the science teacher, especially during experiments. Alex seems to get very frustrated when this happens and this can escalate very quickly.

These boys reflect a broad range of attitudes and behaviour, that aren't gender specific, but more common in boys. Increasingly, some girls are adopting behaviour of the type traditionally associated with boys, but statistics suggest that boys and young men continue to be excluded and underachieve in greater numbers than girls and young women.

At its crudest, strategies for dealing with boys' underachievement have offered 'stick them in front of the computer', 'try action books', or 'cool to learn' campaigns.

These fit all approaches, coming from the same school of thought as 'give me five things I can do in the classroom tomorrow', and are just too simplistic.

They inevitably miss out an initial detailed assessment of the problem, which is essential. Action books, the use of computers and other active learning styles, as well as the recognition that boys' disinterest can just be an act, can all help towards countering boys' underachievement. However, boys can be motivated to underachieve by a number of factors, and this complexity has to be reflected in the strategies we adopt.

We need first to note the broad spectrum of underachievement. At secondary level, this can range across a spectrum from those that underachieve to those that fail, or are failed, from bright boys and young men who could do better, to those who leave or are asked to leave before they are tested through GCSEs.

Some boys will leave everything until the last minute, do the absolute minimum to scrape through, work less if they are praised, and be reluctant to try in subjects they have to struggle with. For others, school is primarily a social environment and they fail, or do not engage with subjects, because there are people to see and talk to! Some boys' status goes up as a result of their apparent lack of interest and because they show no concern about getting into trouble. Other boys are only partially disengaged: some teachers find that they work and participate, while others say they are surly and either quiet or too rowdy.

For some of these groups of boys, an important contributory factor is their expectation that teachers will treat them differently in Year 9 from Year 7, and in Year 11 from Year 9. If teachers do not recognise they are getting older and treat them differently, conflict can follow.

### Issues to consider

■ Which boys in your class are underachieving, and what are the factors that contribute to this?

■ How is their attitude to the lesson expressed?

■ Are these factors that are best dealt with individually, or are there common themes that could be addressed in groups?

■ Do other teachers agree with your view and experience? Do they see pupils differently? Do they get more or less out of them? If so, why?

■ What do these boys believe their futures will hold for them?

■ How accurate do you think that view is?

### Teachers' attitudes towards boys

Interestingly, some of the lowest levels of school exclusions in the UK are in Northern Ireland (Barr *et al*, 2000; Muldoon *et al*, 2000). Such low exclusion rates are particularly interesting as research generally suggests that levels of disruptive behaviour in schools might be expected to increase as a result of such circumstances as the Troubles.

The central reason seems to lie in teachers' attitudes. Teachers in the North often recognise that the Troubles can significantly contribute towards individuals' disruptive behaviour. So they see it as important to develop their classroom management skills and their understanding of the more disruptive young people – usually boys. This is in sharp contrast to other teachers and schools which expect difficulties. They want just to teach, and see individuals as problems standing in the way of achieving this, or they group individuals and then see them as a disruptive group.

However, if, as teachers, we see classroom problems as opportunities to develop our teaching skills, rather than seeing disruptive pupils as obstacles to teaching, we can identify strategies for creating a good learning environment for all pupils. If teachers accurately identify the learning needs of their pupils, they will meet the needs of all, including underachieving boys, more accurately.

An investigation in a primary school where all the teaching staff were women suggested that attitude was more important than gender (Lloyd, 2002). While classrooms were being observed, some female teachers related well to the girls and to some of the boys, but found certain more opinionated or disruptive boys more difficult to engage. In contrast, other female teachers clearly enjoyed working with the boys (often saying they were funny, had loads of energy and got excited about things), while having more difficulties with some of the girls. The school was concerned that boys were missing out because of the gender of the teaching staff. However, it appeared to the observers – and was reported by boy pupils – that teachers' attitudes towards them were much more important than the teacher's gender.

While there is a lot of talk of the importance of male role models, boys don't always say that male teachers are that important. When asked, boys have often reported that a teacher with a positive attitude towards them is more significant than their gender. However, if it is a male teacher with a positive attitude towards them, this is still a real bonus (Lloyd, 2002).

### Issues to consider

■ Honestly review those whom you like, enjoy teaching, and engage with easily, and explore how much gender plays a part in your day-to-day teaching. While we are supposed to offer everyone the same service, we don't, of course, however professional we may be

■ When you lose control in the classroom, do you blame the pupils, or are you more self-reflective of your teaching?

■ Do you anticipate problems in the class from certain male pupils?

■ What works with the more challenging male pupils and why?

■ How could you use these methods, styles and approaches more, and would that help?

■ Is having a positive attitude towards boys and young men more important than your gender?

### Strategies to combat boys' underachievement

Secondary schooling can offer too big a challenge for an increasing number of boys. Boys at inner city primary schools often anticipate the worst and when asked what secondary school will be like, they will often say they will be beaten up every day, or that Year 10 and 11 boys will steal their dinner money. Often isolated incidents are thought to be common and a real day-to-day threat. Sometimes TV school dramas from the USA have a bigger impact on their view of secondary schools than school open evenings!

Many of those boys who will have difficulties will need to change their views of secondary school, but they often need a set of skills that too many lack. This provides an important focus for transition programmes. For example, skills that many lack include:

*working together* – most of the boys get into classroom and playground difficulties as a result of their relationships with each other (disputes, cursing, football, fighting etc)

*emotional expression* – too many of them have short fuses, and are unable to respond to emotional situations appropriately, resulting in unnecessary conflict

*negotiation skills* – most of them find negotiations difficult (whether with teachers or other pupils) and often find basic communication difficult without conflict

*learning skills* – concentration, reflection, and thinking are all areas that some boys find difficult or are inconsistent in demonstrating.

In one transition programme for Year 5 boys, these skills are introduced, practised and then boys are invited to take the 'willpower challenge', where they select 8 of 12 tasks that test their self-control, concentration and willpower. If they pass the tasks they receive a certificate, a book token and a mark. In the programme pilot, the majority emerged with

■ an increased confidence in dealing with situations with other children and teachers that they found difficult

■ an increase in self-control, willpower and concentration, which had a direct impact on their behaviour and their attainment both at primary school and later at secondary school

■ a reduction in the likelihood of exclusions in primary and later in secondary school.

Offering the boys and young men at this harder end of underachievement practical skills and strategies both to contain their behaviour and deal with situations more effectively, equips them to engage in school rather than get distracted. This type of programme engages boys on the edges of the school community and may be necessary for those boys who become disengaged and much harder to deal with within the classroom.

Many disengaged boys arrive in Year 10 having forgotten what school is for. They forget that school provides them with the means to enter the workplace and that how well they do academically will significantly affect their opportunities there. While the local careers education and guidance (CEG) provider – and schools – will usually focus on the workplace in Year 11, practical and skills-based support significantly influence underachieving young men before they take their GCSEs. This may change as the 14-19 diplomas become increasingly available.

Another style of transition programme focuses on interview and phone experience; completion of application forms; training options after school; where and how to look for jobs; and the changing workforce and workplace, including challenges to gender stereotyping and opportunities to discuss personal career options. In addition, young men themselves arrange visits to the local college, Job Centre and careers library and visits to the workplaces of their choice. As a result, young men's confidence increases and they develop skills (such as interviewing and using the telephone) and a more realistic view through engaging with the workplace. Many of the young men also realise that the workplace is a difficult environment in which to establish themselves, and, as a result, at least 50% of them become more focused on what they can get from school (as reported by young men and by teaching staff) and this is often reflected in their GCSE attainment.

## What works with boys and young men

While the two programmes described above concern different age groups of boys and young men (Year 5 and 10), they have some similar elements that indicate what might be effective with underachieving boys and young men on the edges of the school community. These can be summarised as follows:

■ the purpose and the benefits must be obvious

■ if the programme is aspirational and about their futures this will reduce problems with classroom management and disruption

■ the more practical the programme, the better the response

■ the less practical the activity, the more motivation has to be addressed

■ skills-based programmes in particular are easier for these boys to engage in

■ rehearsal of these skills and learning through doing are of particular interest

■ teachers' attitudes to the boys and young men need to be positive, and they need to be problem solvers rather than problem finders.

## Summary

Boys' underachievement is complex. This means that careful assessment of individuals is required before solutions are tried. One-stop methods do not provide effective strategies for teachers.

It is critical to understand boys' motivation, and for teachers to understand their own attitudes towards boys and young men. Often a change in teacher attitude can bring about significant changes in attainment of individuals.

Any teacher is likely to need to try a number of different approaches, styles and ways of working to get the best out of the boys in their class.

Informing underachieving boys and young men of the realities of secondary school or the workplace within a context that enables them to engage, helps them to learn the purpose of learning (something many of them have often lost sight of).

## References and further resources

For more information about programmes such as Willpower Challenge and Into Work see: Working With Men's website www.workingwithmen.org.

Barr, A., Kilpatrick, R. and Lundy, L. (2000) School exclusions: lessons from Northern Ireland. *Education and the Law* 12(3) p165-75

Lloyd. T. (2002) What Difference does a Teacher's Gender Make in the Classroom? Unpublished internal document: 'Working With Men'

Lloyd. T. (2002) *Underachieving Young Men Preparing for Work: A Report for Practitioners*. York: Joseph Rowntree Foundation

Lloyd. T. (2003) *Role Models and All That!* A 'Working With Men' discussion paper

Muldoon, O.T., Trew, K. and Kilpatrick, R. (2000) The legacy of the troubles on the young people's psychological and social life. *Youth and Society* 32 (1)

# Early Childhood Education

*Jayne Osgood*

## Introduction

Gender equality is a major concern to those working with very young children. There are many ways in which it can be addressed in early childhood education and care. Research has raised awareness and understanding of the ways in which gender operates in young children's lives (see, for example, Davies, 1989 and 1993; MacNaughton, 2000; Yelland, 1998). Practitioners and researchers have created possibilities to challenge gender discrimination. There has been a move away from biological explanations of differences in girls' and boys' behaviour to perspectives that understand gender identity as something that is largely acquired.

We learn how to understand ourselves as female or male – and while we learn this when we are very young, our understandings are constantly open to change and modification as a consequence of the social contexts in which we find ourselves. Since the 1970s, research has demonstrated how educational institutions from nurseries to universities frequently reinforce traditional gender identities. This includes acting in ways that emphasise imbalances between the genders.

## Understanding gender as socially constructed

What it means to be female or male changes with time and place, and is affected by social class, race, ethnicity, sexuality, religion and age. There are many ways of doing gender across and within cultures. For example, what it meant to be a young, white, working-class woman in Britain in the 1920s, and the expectations of how to behave and conduct oneself, are very different from those operating now. These expectations will, no doubt, differ again in the future. To understand how gender is constructed we need to look at the role that early childhood educators play in maintaining or challenging issues of gender in children's early learning experiences.

## Issues to consider

- Is the importance of gender equality made explicit in your early years setting?
- Are there strategies in place to promote gender equality in the curriculum?
- How are these strategies translated into practical pedagogical approaches, for example, the use of language?
- How are daily interactions with children informed by gender equality?
- How do you work with parents/carers to establish gender equality and challenge inequality?
- How do men and women who work in early years settings challenge or re-enforce gender stereotypes?

## Getting it right – or wrong

Contemporary feminists argue that very young children learn what society considers the correct ways of behaving as girls or boys. They argue that it is also possible to challenge thinking about gender. In short, it is not inevitable that maleness and femaleness have to be constructed in the way that they often are. However, there is often considerable resistance to doing gender differently because it can result in social isolation, teasing and sometimes violence (including bullying). For very young children, socially constructed gender boundaries are closely monitored and maintained by other children, teachers, family members and the media, especially television. Within the paradigm of child development, children who move between the categories of behavioural expectations for girls and boys may be considered to have got their gender wrong and can be therefore treated with suspicion by peers, teachers, family and society.

## Promoting sameness: denying difference

Educators are often adamant that they treat boys and girls the same, and therefore there is no need to focus on gender equality. But equal does not mean the same. The notion of sameness becomes synonymous with the characteristics of the dominant culture in contemporary Britain: white, western, heterosexual, able-bodied, Christian, and male. Some minority cultures or communities outside the dominant group may adopt its practices and perspectives, while others may react against it.

Through examining their practices and policies, early years educators are in a position to broaden children's horizons and to provide children with far greater opportunities for developing their gender identity in a broader and more inclusive way. They will need to be particularly sensitive and pragmatic about what is achievable in the context of their own early years setting while recognising that they do have opportunities to do gender differently.

### Issues to consider

- How are gender issues raised during in-service training?
- Evaluate the extent to which current policies on sexist language promote a broad or narrow definition of what it means to be a boy or girl
- Monitor, evaluate and review all policies with regard to gender equality issues
- Develop a simple set of practices which promote gender equality, for example girls and boys working and playing together, but bearing in mind any culturally specific considerations.

## Play and sexuality

Play is a critical time when gender behaviours are learnt. Equally, it is a time in which the views of adult sexuality prevail. Mock weddings, mummies and daddies, games of kiss-chase, and girl/boyfriends are all examples of play that reinforce the notion of heterosexuality as the norm. However, where transgressions occur, for example, a boy dressing in girls' or women's clothes, educators may see this as problematic, and discourage young children from such behaviours. The books, toys, cartoons and films etc used in the early childhood setting, and within the family and in wider society, can act to reinforce a limited view of acceptable gendered behaviour in young children.

A book series *Debating Play* edited by Tina Bruce has made an important contribution to encouraging early childhood educators to reflect on their practice in relation to play choices and pedagogical practices. These books examine cultural myths and taboos and so challenge readers to become committed to the promotion of play opportunities that help children to make sense of their lives. For example, Holland (2003) urges practitioners to question their reactions to the masculine field of war, weapon and superhero play in the early years. In doing so, she challenges practitioners to question their own views on appropriate, gendered forms of play. Similarly, MacNaughton (2000) confronts common myths about gender with regard to very young children that are apparent in many early childhood settings. In working directly with practitioners, the author demonstrates that the everyday teaching practices of early years educators have profound implications for young children's notions of gender identities through play. Since there is an emphasis in early childhood education on learning that occurs through play, practitioners need to reflect critically on their own attitudes to gendered play.

In addition to the growing body of literature designed to assist early years educators, there are resources available that promote gender awareness. For example, the growing use of Persona Dolls is an important trend. The dolls and their stories act as tools to explore, expose and challenge bias. Furthermore, it is claimed that they can help children to express feelings and ideas, think critically, challenge unfair treatment and develop empathy with people who are different from themselves. Through thinking critically about the assumptions behind their practice, early years educators can begin to consider alternative pedagogical approaches, designed to challenge taken-for-granted ways in which young children develop and reinforce their gender identities.

### Issues to consider

- How do staff in your early years setting view gendered play?
- Do you have resources, including books that show non-traditional families, for example single parents; same-sex parents; extended families; young mothers; children in care?

■ What is your attitude to children who do not do boy or do girl in ways that society accepts (for example the boy who likes to dress up as a fairy and play with dolls? The girls who favour being noisy and energetic, using outdoor play and behaving like tomboys)?

■ Have you thought about the way you explain the role of play to parents, for example, in exploring aspects of identity?

The issues outlined here are designed to help practitioners think about how their practices relate to how young children develop their views of what is appropriate for their gender in the early years setting. Educating educators, children and parents about the benefits of challenging gender stereotyping is crucial, and requires educators to examine their own positions in terms of gender and the impact this can have on children's choices.

## References and further resources

Alloway, M. (1995) *Foundation Stones: The Construction of Gender in Early Childhood.* Carlton: Curriculum Corporation.

Boldt, G. (1997) Sexist and heterosexist responses to gender bending. In Tobin, J. (ed) *Making a Place for Pleasure in Early Childhood Education.* New Haven: Yale

Brown, B. (1998) *Unlearning Discrimination in the Early Years.* Stoke-on-Trent: Trentham

Brown, B. (2001) *Combating Discrimination: Persona Dolls in Action.* Stoke-on-Trent: Trentham

Bruce, T. (ed) *Debating Play series.* Buckingham: Open University Press

Davies, B. (1989) *Frogs and Snails and Feminist Tales: Preschool Children and Gender.* Sydney: Allen and Unwin

Davies, B. (1993) *Shards of Glass. Children Reading and Writing Beyond Gendered Identities.* Sydney: Allen and Unwin

Holland, P. (2003) *We Don't Play With Guns Here: War, Weapon and Superhero Play in the Early Years. (Debating Play Series).* Maidenhead: Open University Press

MacNaughton, G. (2000) *Rethinking Gender in Early Childhood Education.* Sydney: Allen and Unwin

Robinson, K. (2002) Making the invisible visible: gay and lesbian issues in early childhood education. *Contemporary Issues in Early Childhood Education* 3 (3) p415-434

Robinson, K. and Jones-Diaz, C. (1999) Doing theory with early childhood educators: Understanding difference and diversity in personal and professional contexts. *Australian Journal of Early Childhood* 24 (4): p33-41

Yelland. N. (ed) (1998) *Gender in Early Childhood.* London: Routledge

Information about Persona Dolls can be found at: www. persona-doll-training.org.

# The 14-19 Curriculum

*Hazel Taylor*

■ *See also schedules: Career Support and Guidance; Inclusion of Pupils with Special Educational Needs; Assessment*

The structure and content of the 14-19 curriculum in England is changing radically over the decade from 2005 – 2015. The stakes for gender equity are high. If the changes work well, we will see sharply improved equality of access and outcome across the range of curriculum pathways. If the changes are poorly implemented, we will see increased segregation in vocational choices and a reinforcement of traditional patterns of economic differences between women and men.

## The context for change

The changes have been driven by continuing concern about the stubborn differences in educational outcomes for young people in England. This is in a global context where in most developed countries the gap between the highest and lowest achievers has narrowed. In addition, the knowledge economy requires high levels of education, and needs both men and women to be working. Unskilled jobs, many of them traditionally associated with men, continue to disappear rapidly. Work areas which traditionally required little training are now changing so quickly that continued reskilling is essential. OECD figures for 2001 show that the UK education system is a 'high excellence, low equity' performer, compared with the 'high excellence, high equity' systems of Japan, Korea and Canada.

The 14-19 curriculum has contributed to the achievement gap by continuing to value exclusive academic routes to higher education. This is often at the expense of routes which encourage more young people to stay in education beyond 16, and to move in more immediately relevant ways to higher level qualifications. The challenge is to develop a curriculum which contributes to a further rise in the numbers of students who at the 16+ examination in England gain 5 A*-C including both English and mathematics, and which increases the numbers who stay in education to 19 and beyond.

It is ironic that the National Curriculum, which did much to reduce gender difference in subject choice at 14, and to provide a more level playing field for choice at 16, is now giving way to a more differentiated set of pathways. These are intended to improve equity of outcome in terms of qualification, but may well replicate gendered inequity in choice of occupational areas, and reinforce the continuing patterns of pay difference between sectors.

The workforce is still highly gender segregated, both horizontally, on the whole with women at lower levels than men, and vertically, with considerable imbalances of numbers in the traditionally gender segregated areas. New areas for work, such as the IT industry, also have gendered patterns of recruitment. Gendered preferences are affected by other variables including ethnicity. Young people of ethnic minority heritage can be affected by double stereotyping, and occupational disadvantage due to ethnicity is greater than that due to gender. Gendered preferences of occupation contribute to skills shortages by reducing the pool of applicants, and reduce choice. The mother who would like her son to have a male role model caring for him at nursery does not usually have that option. The challenge for the implementation of the 14-19 curriculum is that, in striving to reduce overall inequity in performance, we do not increase segregation.

Another aspect of the context for the change is the 2006 Equality Act, which places a duty on public authorities to be proactive in promoting gender equality. Where employers and training organisations have a contractual duty to a public authority – the local authority or the Learning and Skills Council (LSC) – to provide elements of an educational programme, they are required to pre-empt situations where discrimination might arise, and ensure that it does not. The Act should have considerable positive impact on the delivery of the new curriculum.

## The Curriculum Model

In England, young people from 2008 have the opportunity to make choices at 14 that place them on a pathway that is vocationally linked. They continue to study the national curriculum core subjects and ICT, PE, citizenship, RE, health and careers education. They are also able to choose to study either:

■ one diploma from an ultimate choice of 14, with one other course, or

■ a minimum of one course in each of the arts, design and technology, the humanities and modern foreign languages, with an opportunity to take a course in all four areas if they wish to.

There are fourteen specialised diplomas, at three levels up to advanced level, covering the occupational sectors of the economy. Though the design of the qualifications is employer-led, they are not intended as a direct preparation for an occupation – they require young people to develop good basic skills, develop the broader skills employers want and act as a basis for further progression. Young people succeeding at Level 2 (the equivalent of five A*-C GCSEs) will be fully prepared to go on to Level 3 diploma courses, A levels or an apprenticeship. Those succeeding at Level 3 will likewise be prepared for higher education or for occupationally specific training.

Functional skills form a central part of the reformed GCSEs, the new diplomas and apprenticeships. These are the core elements of English, mathematics and ICT that provide an individual with the essential knowledge, skills and understanding that will enable them to be confident, effective and independent in life and at work.

The intention is that the great majority will opt for a diploma rather than the traditional academic route of separate subjects to GCSE. It remains to be seen whether occupationally-defined diplomas will develop parity of esteem with the still available general education route. This schedule focuses on gender equity issues in specialised diplomas.

The first five diplomas become available from 2008, increasing to fourteen by 2010. Diplomas are offered through local partnerships, making best use of specialist facilities, and students travel between their base school and other locations to access learning and training. A local prospectus gives details of the offer, and students enter a programme at a level determined by their prior achievement. The key risk moments for gender equity are:

■ during the planning and co-ordination of provision

■ during the delivery of provision in traditionally segregated areas

■ before choice takes place

■ during the choice process.

At each of these moments, thoughtful preparation can ensure that students of both sexes:

■ are aware of the opportunities in all occupational families

■ are free of the constraints of stereotyping

■ experience teaching that is inclusive of them

■ find potential barriers to participation are anticipated, and access is facilitated.

If this is achieved, then the new system could do much to break down the persistent gendered inequities in occupation and life chances, while raising attainment and well-being for all. The Equal Opportunities Commission carried out a formal investigation into occupational segregation in 2004. Its Action for Change booklets describe excellent practice in breaking down gender stereotyping and removing practical and attitudinal barriers to change (EOC, 2005). There is much good practice to be drawn on from the projects of the 1980s which encouraged girls into non-traditional areas (Myers, 2000).

## Risk moments – planning and co-ordination of provision

Provision of the full range of diplomas in every area requires major collaboration between providers and schools. Local 14-19 partnerships, convened by the local authority and the LSC, and bringing together schools, colleges, employers and other training providers, have been in development since 2006. These partnerships are central to the effective delivery of the full range of diplomas. They are responsible for ensuring that local provision is of high quality, providing specialist environments and strong links with local workplaces. They co-ordinate delivery and are responsible for ensuring transport is available between all locations for those who need it. Precise configurations of provision will always vary from area to area, as they respond to local circumstances.

The 14-19 partnership is responsible for providing a prospectus of local provision, and the local provider of careers education and guidance (CEG) works with the partnership and schools in providing information, advice and guidance on choice. Where there is a strong partnership commitment to equalities, the opportunities to address occupational segregation and discrimination are considerable. Instead of negotiating separately with a variety of training providers, each with their own perspective on these issues, schools work with a co-ordinated group of providers and employers with good communication and agreed principles about access and opportunity. Achieving this everywhere cannot be left to chance. A partnership fully committed to equalities will have in place:

■ a clear statement of principles about equality of access, experience and outcome for all students across all occupational areas, within its local curriculum policy, guiding all development

■ responsibilities for ensuring the delivery of these principles written into job descriptions of key personnel within the partnership, including the co-ordinator

■ a programme of training about equality issues for all partnership members

■ mechanisms for supporting and monitoring providers in the development and delivery of diplomas

■ contacts with industry bodies and other groups that provide information and advice about good practice in gender equality in their areas

■ a regular review forum with agreed power of follow-up where progress, retention and other concerns are reviewed and action planned. The format of this will vary from place to place. What is important is that the forum has power to influence developments in good practice

■ strong links with the local CEG provider, whose staff share the commitment to equalities and keep in touch with gender conscious developments in advice and guidance nationally

■ regular attractive publicity about successes and good practice that is widely disseminated though local press, radio, websites, and community networks.

The partnership is in a position to monitor the recruitment and retention to each diploma by gender and ethnicity, and to analyse the data by school and provider, so that it can broker good practice between schools, and between providers, and offer support where the current practice is not leading to equality. Because of targets for increasing retention of 16-year-olds in education, and further targets for course completion rates, there is pressure to guide students into areas where least effort is needed to reach these targets. This can lead to reluctance to grapple with the challenges of encouraging students to choose non-traditional areas where they may need more support to succeed. Once there is evidence of success for students locally across the range of diplomas, this issue disappears. Realistic local targets for inclusion of both sexes across all diplomas need to be set. These should become more challenging as students and parents build up confidence in making non-traditional choices, and as good practice in addressing retention issues develops.

The local prospectus is the partnership's central means of publicising its commitment to equity. It must go beyond token pictures of boys and girls in non-traditional activities, to address the questions young people, and parents and carers may have about the risks of making a non-traditional choice. It needs to:

■ emphasise the range of job opportunities in any given occupational area, and the variety of contexts for work

■ give information about measures to welcome and support the atypical gender – the girls or boys who are in a minority in any programme

■ describe how concerns about perceived discrimination will be dealt with

■ reassure about the safety of girls in any predominantly male environment

■ give information about the provision of transport.

### Issues to consider in delivering diplomas in traditionally gender segregated areas

■ How is the local 14-19 partnership demonstrating its commitment to equality of provision, access and outcome?

- How is the school represented on the partnership? Does that person have a specific responsibility for equalities?

- What monitoring processes are in place to pick up good practice and areas of imbalance in access, retention and outcome?

- How are schools and providers working together specifically to support students opting for non-traditional courses?

- What support is the local CEG provider offering in gender conscious advice and guidance?

- How does the local prospectus actively encourage non-traditional choices?

## Risk moments – delivery of provision in traditionally segregated areas

While schools can influence choice supported by a good prospectus, retention is very much a matter for the local providers, and in areas where there is little experience of removing barriers for students who find themselves in a small minority on a course, support will be needed. Providers, whether schools, colleges or other training organisations, develop their courses according to the national syllabuses provided by the awarding bodies, and have the opportunity to recognise local contexts as they do so. Providers will need to expect there to be initial unintended barriers that cause young people to feel insecure and to wish to drop out, and be ready to deal with these. Unexpected barriers may be connected with:

- feeling uncomfortable in a heavily male or female environment reflected in rest facilities and workplace conversation

- lack of confidence in using equipment and technical language that students of the other sex are already familiar with

- unthinking attitudes and low expectations conveyed by fellow students, members of the workforce or those involved in workplace training

- exemplars of new concepts and procedures that are very gender specific.

It will always be the case that good intentions and commitment at the level of those taking overall decisions may not be reflected at ground level, and that both unthinking habit and quite deep-seated prejudice may lie beneath discriminatory events. Where employers and providers are fully aware of the Gender Duty on public authorities, there will be clear procedures for ensuring it is met, but it will take time for this to become embedded. Any discrimination, whether direct or indirect, conscious or unconscious, in the delivery of diplomas will be in breach of the 2006 Equalities Act.

Providers range from schools and colleges to specialist training organisations and consortia of local employers. The range of previous experience in welcoming atypical students varies a great deal. A local employee with a skills shortage may have recognised the economic sense of widening its pool of skilled workers, while small companies coming together to get involved in the partnership may not.

One building firm with large contracts for maintenance of social housing recognised that many elderly tenants feel more secure with female contractors. It has implemented a culture change programme in the company. Its working practices are driven by an equal opportunities policy which covers recruitment, training, monitoring and disciplinary procedures. Its subcontractors are required to comply with the policy. Its female and ethnic minority staff are clearly valued, and it provides an excellent environment for workplace elements of the Construction and Built Environment diploma.

The early stages of diploma delivery are crucial in determining whether or not a young person chooses to stay in a non-traditional area. To enable atypical students to learn in an environment that is supportively challenging, providers can:

- provide trainers from the atypical sex
- mentor atypical students and trainees
- offer single-sex induction sessions
- set up a buddy system
- review the language of their occupational area and if necessary develop a new, inclusive vocabulary
- ensure staff have all undertaken diversity training
- monitor progress and intervene early where students are falling behind, taking care to identify the real cause of this
- ensure the environment is welcoming to all
- avoid creating cross-gender competitiveness which is intimidating to the minority gender
- provide opportunities for safe, open discussion of workplace experiences.

### *Issues to consider in retaining atypical students*

■ What messages does the training environment give about the place of the atypical gender?

■ How are atypical students helped to feel welcome and secure but not patronised?

■ How are the majority gender helped in recognising the benefits to them of a mixed group?

■ Who would notice if an atypical student was struggling? What would they do?

## Risk moments – pre-choice

If young people are to make informed choices at 14, their earlier education needs to have made them aware of the full range of issues around gender discrimination and employment. This needs to begin in primary schools, where many children form firm views about the gender appropriateness of certain jobs, and where they can develop prejudices about the value of some curriculum areas. These early attitudes can be highly resistant to challenge at 14, when young people are testing out their gender identity at a time of heightened awareness and confusion in mid-adolescence. Traditional attitudes and beliefs develop by default unless there are structured opportunities to discuss them, and to consider a wider view of the roles of men and women in the home and workplace. Work on raising aspirations and on the range of opportunities available to both boys and girls needs to be done with families and in communities, so that support is built for those who make more unusual choices.

It is also important from year 7 to be introducing young people to the range of work that is available in each of the occupational families – for example, that engineering covers not only mechanical and structural engineering, but also the delicate engineering processes of medical equipment design and manufacture. A great deal of self-limitation around choice is based on ignorance of what in fact is entailed in unfamiliar areas, an ignorance often shared by families and teachers.

The CEG guidelines state that by key stage 4, young people should be able to recognise stereotyping and misrepresentative images of people, careers and work, and explain why it is important to develop personal values to combat stereotyping (DfES, 2003). For these aspirations to become reality requires a school climate in which gender, as with other equalities, is consciously addressed on a day-to day

basis, and where careers guidance positively seeks to demonstrate that there is a place for either sex in any occupational area. The traditional 'gender blind' approach to careers education has been shown to be ineffective where choice has taken place later, and will be even more so at 14.

Pre-choice education about gender and work needs to include:

■ structured opportunities to discuss changes in men and women's roles across cultures and social class

■ plenty of visual material illustrating men and women in non-traditional jobs – posters, illustrations in teaching materials, and in on-line material accessed without supervision

■ visits from young adults already in non-traditional areas

■ visits to workplaces where discussion about who is doing what is part of the experience

■ a school workforce which models gender equity in all areas

■ events for parents and young people that challenge stereotypes, such as 'What's My Line?' evenings

■ family and community activities which highlight variety and stimulate discussion – for example, participation in events like 'take your daughter to work' day.

### *Issues to consider in pre-choice preparation*

■ What opportunities already exist within the primary curriculum for pre-choice work? Are they coherent? How can they be extended?

■ How does careers education in years 7 to 9 address gender equity issues? Is it gender blind or gender conscious? How might it need to develop in the light of the new 14-19 curriculum?

■ What image does the school convey of the place of men and women in different areas of the workforce? How could it be improved?

■ What community resources are there to support a wide view of men and women's roles in the home and at work? How can the school work with community organisations to challenge prejudices and stereotypes?

## Risk moments – choice at 14

Secondary schools have plenty of experience of running option choice in Year 9 that they can draw on in developing a choice process for diplomas that is gender conscious and gender fair. Some issues remain the same – ensuring that young people are both realistic and ambitious about their aspirations, and that they understand the type and amount of work required by their chosen courses. What is new is that a diploma is a complete package offering a range of subjects within one envelope, all interconnected as relevant preparation for an occupational area, and providing a variety of educational experiences on and off site, more or less directly practical and vocational. Access to the diploma is at a level determined by prior attainment, so it is stratified, and progress through the levels is dependent on progress made. Students move forward according to stage not age. From a gender equity perspective, there are possible issues about decisions about entry level but accurate key stage 3 assessment should ensure that these are made on firm evidence, not on supposition about future progress that might be based on spurious gender differences such as boys' untidiness or girls' avoidance of non-fiction.

The main challenge is that the titles of diplomas clearly indicate occupational areas and many of them immediately signal a gender connection. For example, of the first five diplomas to come on stream, one – Creative and Media – is gender neutral, while of the others, Construction and the Built Environment (CBE), Engineering, and IT have strong male connotations, and Health and Social Care has strong female ones. Within each of these areas there is a very wide range of jobs. However, unless there is a great deal of preliminary discussion, young people will interpret the titles narrowly and be influenced by gender stereotypes in their choices. The first tranche of diplomas would appear to be aimed at boys who may be disaffected by the academic curriculum and both CBE and Engineering is taught largely in off-school sites at colleges and workplaces with specialist facilities. The choice process needs to include:

- plenty of illustration of the wide range of job opportunities in every area
- opportunities to visit workplaces and teaching sites
- information about the safety of travel arrangements

- information about the welcome and safety of girls in construction and engineering environments, and the welcome of boys in health and social care environments. This includes addressing issues about the employment of young men with young children, where our society both wants male role models, and at the same time sees young men as potential abusers who may not express natural affection and concern for children through touch for fear of misinterpretation. Highly stereotyped work areas also exacerbate fears about sexuality and homophobic bullying, and these fears can affect choice
- opportunities for single-sex taster courses so that young people feel able to take a risk in the knowledge they are not irrevocably committed
- plentiful information for parents and carers
- the mobilising of role models among this group of adults.

## Issues to consider in guiding choice at 14

- How much of the current choice process needs adapting as diplomas come on stream?
- What preparation and training do all teachers need about the gender implications of the new 14-19 curriculum?
- How are the diploma providers involved in the choice process?
- Who in school champions the equalities aspects of the choice process and monitors experiences of students from this perspective?

The changes to the 14-19 curriculum offer many opportunities for young people to remain more engaged with their education and to achieve more than they imagine. The aspects that challenge gender segregation in occupational areas have the potential to transform large areas of the workforce and in doing so to bring about greater equity in representation, pay, and skills between women and men. If this is accompanied by parallel changes in distribution of labour in the home and with childcare, then the aspiration of a high equity education system will be met.

## References and further resources

Blenkinsop, S., McCrone, T., Wade, P. and Morris, M. (2005) *How do Young People make Choices at age 14 and age 16?* London: DfES Research Report 773 www.dfes.gov.uk/research/data/uploadfiles/RR773.pdf

Connexions (2006) *Connexions in Action: Challenging Gender Barriers.* Sheffield: NACP www.nacp.co.uk

DfES (2003) *Careers Education and Guidance in England: A National Framework 11-19* (DfES/0163/2003). London: DfES

Equal Opportunities Commission (2005) *Action for Change.* Manchester: EOC

Equal Opportunities Commission (2005) *Free to Choose: Tackling Gender Barriers to Better Jobs.* Manchester: EOC www.eoc.org.uk/PDF/occsegfinalrepengland.pdf

Myers, K (ed) (2000) *Whatever Happened to Equal Opportunities in Schools?* Buckingham: Open University Press

www.works4me.org is the EOC website for young people with information about breaking free of stereotypes

www.jivepartners.org.uk JIVE is a European Social Fund project which aims to create cultural change in engineering, construction and technology by addressing the barriers that prevent women from pursuing careers in these sectors

www.geriproject.org The GERI (Gender Equality and Race Inclusion) consortium help LSCs, schools, guidance professionals, training providers and employers to tackle gender and ethnic stereotyping

www.wisecampaign.org.uk WISE (Women Into Science and Engineering) promotes these sectors as career options to young women

www.womenandequalityunit.gov.uk WEU (Women and Equality Unit) provides Does Sex Make A Difference? a resource pack for those working with year 9 pupils

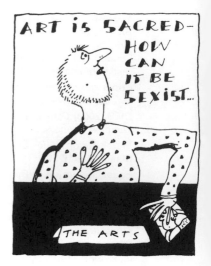

# Art and Design

*Karen Hosack*

## Introduction

Creating and learning about art can enable girls and boys to use their experiences of life to construct and develop their own view of the world and their place within it. Learning about the work of artists from different times and places helps pupils gain insight into and respect for diverse cultures, and informs their own creative practice, the outcomes of which can take many forms.

Gender issues are present in some form in all works of art, whether they are referred to in general by portraying particular attitudes of a culture towards men and women, or as an artist's personal male or female perspective on their world. It is important to emphasise that each artist's perception is unique, and the interpretation of a work of art is also a matter of debate. However, a huge amount of knowledge about a time, a place or its people, can be gleaned from careful looking and skillful questioning. From this, the particular society's attitude to women and men can be explored. For example, it was more usual in pre-1900 Western Europe for women to be the subject of art rather than be artists themselves. This reflected the aspirational values of society for women at the time. There are a few interesting exceptions to this rule, such as Artemisia Gentileschi and Vigée le Brun, who were closely related to male artists and therefore were in stronger positions to succeed in a male dominated profession. Examining the barriers for women as producers of fine art gives teachers scope to discuss social history and the politics of power and gender. Feminist art historians have given us not just a rediscovery of female artists, but have also highlighted how women's traditional roles in various societies have shaped our current artistic canon.

## Issues to consider

Ask your class – in primary or secondary school:

- does the word 'artist' suggest a man or a woman?
- how many women artists and how many male artists do you know of?
- who makes textiles? Men? Women? (Teachers: this is a rich area to explore as a global theme)
- are there any colours you think of as feminine/masculine? Why is this?
- what's the difference between art and craft? In your culture do men do one and women the other?

Gender also plays a part in how we personally respond to the visual arts. Interpretation is built on past experience, and therefore to some extent (as with reading and writing) gender, as well ethnicity, social background, religion and culture, will have an impact on children's perceptions. It is a teacher's role to recognise this and to challenge assumptions and beliefs by supporting both boys and girls in developing their questioning skills.

## Working through one picture

Evidence collected from primary schools through the Take One Picture scheme at the National Gallery, London, suggests that boys, in particular, benefit when using the visual arts as an initial stimulus for cross-subject learning. Given the opportunity to focus on just one artwork at a time, all pupils and teachers are challenged to set their own lines of enquiry using an image as a springboard. This approach allows time for pupils to interrogate the chosen image creatively. This can be done by offering different ways of recording their thoughts, for example on post-it notes, a graffiti wall or on a soundfile or film.

In a world that demands that we switch our attention between one stimulus to the next, we may expect pupils to find it difficult to focus on one work of art for a sustained period of time. The very stillness of art, however, encourages pupils to look more closely at details and to start to interpret them using their own knowledge. Both girls and boys actually feel very comfortable with this; after all, they learnt to read visual images before words. Capturing this state and rediscovering this method of learning can be both invigorating and liberating for them, while encouraging analytical, observational, communication and collaborative skills, as well as developing concentration. This strategy builds confidence in pupils and offers excellent differentiation opportunities that a whole class can enjoy.

## Making art

Pupils use their bodies to express themselves when producing artwork. They interact with their environment by manipulating materials and making responses in an immediate and real way, whether consciously or unconsciously. Some pupils will have an intuitive ability for creating art if they have a high-level of dexterity coupled with acute spatial awareness, and this interest needs to be nurtured and harnessed in a way that can support their learning across the curriculum.

### Issues to consider

■ Are there different ways in which girls and boys in your class approach creative projects?

■ Does one sex rather than the other prefer some media? (for example film, clay, or paint) How do you explain any differences?

■ Do girls and boys choose different subjects to portray? Do they prefer to use different colours? Sizes? Textures? Does this matter?

## Relevance

Pupils will be more interested in a work of art if the subject is relevant to their own lives. Hogarth's 'The Graham Children', which has been widely used by primary schools taking part in the Take One Picture scheme, is a good example of a painting that will easily engage pupils of a similar age to those depicted. Questions about the period clothes and toys will be raised in a speaking and listening session, including:

■ why the girls are wearing long, uncomfortable-looking garments?

■ why is the baby boy wearing a dress?

These can be explored by the pupils together with other aspects in or inferred in the painting, such as discovering what the objects tell us about the characters. Of course, many works of art can be presented as rich learning resources in this way, with themes such as homes, animals, families and friendship, among others, all striking a resonance with young people.

## Resources

We are now fortunate to be able to access quality images through the internet. So, although the work of, for example, Berthe Morisot is not the subject of a children's book, her paintings can be seen via the net. Text in books for adults, such as *Berthe Morisot* by Kathleen Adler and Tamar Garb, may be beyond the scope of many children, but the reproduced images can still be used in classrooms, and the ideas are stimulating and inspiring for teachers.

Consider, too, using the work of artist and illustrators of children's picture books. You can develop children's critical awareness of visual images and gender issues (through the key stages) with these. If you select carefully, especially using illustrators the children are already familiar with, such as Jane Ray, Anthony Browne and Faith Ringgold, you will find children naturally make links between different subject areas that the teacher can exploit for the purposes of expanding learning.

## Identity, beauty and relationships

These are reoccurring preoccupations for artists that make particularly good starting points for discussions linked to gender. Images can be used to explore identity and relationships from nursery to key stage 5, using known paintings and sculptures, together with children's own portraits and self-portraits.

### Issues to consider

From Early Renaissance portraits to Tracey Emin's 'My Bed', artists have used ideas about an individual's relationship with their environment and other people within works of art.

When introducing a portrait to a group of students ask them:

■ how did the artist want to portray the sitter?

- what do the objects in the work tell us about the person/people?
- can you make a comparison between images of women and men in traditional works of art and in contemporary teen magazines?
- do you think certain images can empower or disempower women/men?

With older students, ask about specific images of women – from the nude to the Madonna – to raise discussion on the relationships between artists and their models, and issues of gender and sexuality. The relationship between the male artist and his female muse can be explored by students, with discussion on how these roles are still in evidence, or not, in images produced today.

Images of beauty can be contrasted with those of domesticity. Woman as Venus, goddess of love, for example in the works of Tiepolo, Velázquez and Botticelli, can be discussed alongside images showing mother and child from a variety of sources including Mary Cassatt, Henry Moore and religious iconography of the Christ child.

### Issues to consider

- What traits are considered to be appropriate to present as female or male in art?
- How do these change as cultures change over time?

Art is a uniquely human form of communication. Producing it, seeing it, discussing it, enjoying it and even hating it, are all worthwhile creative experiences. Everyone's opinion is valid, which makes teaching and learning using art objects exciting and open to all abilities and interests.

## Resources and references

Adler, K. and Garb, T. (1987) *Berthe Morisot*. London: Phaidon

Blake, F., Schooner, D., and Steers, J. (2003) Students' gendered experiences of art portfolio assessment in Canada, The Netherlands and England. *Studies in Art Education* 44 p335-349

Bloomfield, A. (2000) *Teaching Integrated Arts in the Primary School*. London: David Fulton Publishers

Burgess, L. and Reay, D. (2005) Postmodern Feminisms: problematic paradigms in art education In: *Postmodernism and Art Education*. Hardy, T. (ed) London: Intellect Books with NSEAD

Hosack, K. (2004) *How Artists See – series*. Oxford: Heinemann (For Key Stages 1 and 2)

NACCCE Report (1999) *All Our Futures: Creativity, Culture and Education*. Sudbury: DfES

RCMG report (2004) *Inspiration, Identity, Learning: The Value of Museums*. Leicester: DCMS/DfES

Rogers, R. (2004) *State of the Art*. London: Clore Duffield Foundation

www.art-works.org.uk – Artworks (Young Artists of the Year Awards, Children's Art Day and research)

www.fwa-uk.org (Foundation for Women's Art)

www.nationalgallery.org.uk – The National Gallery, London

## Citizenship Education
### *Hilary Claire and Cathie Holden*

Child 3: We should get rid of Tony Blair and have a new prime minister.

Child 1: No, two prime ministers: a woman and a man.

Child 2: Women are more..., they don't just go straight in to wars.

Child 3: And they do think.

Child 2: They don't like wars so they wouldn't start one.

Child 3: Yeah, if they do need to have a war they would but like they don't really start them.

Child 1: I think there should be a man president and a woman president, that way it's fair.

*Gender and politics*: children aged 9.

### Introduction

Citizenship education is about equipping children with the skills and knowledge to become active, responsible citizens, able to make a difference to society. It is probably the subject with the greatest potential for addressing gender issues, as it embraces contemporary problems facing society. Yet, ironically, much as race has been marginalised, the official documentation makes little explicit reference to gender. There is no acknowledgement that citizenship education might directly address the issues and tensions associated with gender inequity in society.

For the teacher wanting to help young people understand issues of equity and justice from a gender perspective, there are opportunities but they have to be sought out. In this schedule we indicate how gender impinges on the ways in which children learn about citizenship issues, and we suggest ways to help readers find those opportunities to understand these issues.

### Background

Citizenship education entered the National Curriculum in 2002. In primary schools citizenship covers topical issues, problems and event, knowledge about rules and laws, democracy, allocation of resources and human rights as well as the skills of decision-making, debate and conflict resolution. The secondary curriculum covers, more explicitly, the criminal justice system and the law, democratic systems, cultural diversity and human rights. It aims to produce young people able to debate, discuss and participate in the processes of change. Involvement in the community is central to both (DfEE/QCA 1999).

Depending on their perception of the purposes of citizenship education, some teachers see their role as teaching the facts about political systems, while others see it as encouraging pupils to act as change agents.

### Minimalist and maximalist citizenship: where do you stand?

The Crick Report (1998), on which much of the citizenship curriculum and guidance was based, promoted the civic republican aim of an engaged, active citizen working towards a better society. But simultaneously, and confusingly, there is an assumption that citizenship education is actually about working within the status quo – for example, learning about the law, about the parliamentary system, how to vote etc. How should we understand these two extremes?

McLaughlin (1992) described citizenship as a continuum, with conservative acceptance of the status quo at one end, where pupils learn to fit in (minimalist), and at the other an engaged radical position, where pupils are encouraged to critique existing systems, challenging inequities and to work towards social justice (maximalist). So the first question that teachers concerned with gender equity in the citizenship curriculum need to ask themselves, is where they fit into this spectrum. Do they want to teach about society, accepting the status quo, or do they wish to work at the radical maximal end of the continuum, teaching about gender inequities and encouraging their pupils to question and to challenge?

## The content of the citizenship curriculum: what should we teach?

> Pupils need to be taught directly about the gendered nature of issues relevant to social life, which are typically like an iceberg beneath the water, taken for granted, but effectively sustaining inequity.

This means actively seeking out gender issues when planning each unit of work, ensuring that the content covered and the resources chosen raise issues of inequality or injustice, and challenge pupils' thinking. The curriculum content for citizenship education has been left deliberately light touch: the areas to be taught are listed but the content is largely left to the teacher, which leaves scope for such an approach.

The following suggestions indicate how key areas of the citizenship curriculum can embrace gender equity.

### Globalisation and global citizenship
Citizenship education encompasses the local, the national and the global. It follows that a curriculum which is concerned with gender equity needs to look at the situation and experience of women in different parts of the world, as well as at home. This might include, for example, the way in which the British public is implicated in exploitation of workers – usually females – producing cheap goods and services. A study of the rise of ICT and the internet might include the rise of chat rooms, which has created new forms of exploitation of young women. A more positive aspect of globalisation is to consider how women's capacities can be promoted in response to their needs. Pupils can consider the implications of the UN's concern to educate women, in order to raise the quality of life throughout a

nation, and about specific initiatives like the United Nations Development Fund for Women to fund women's projects and Fair-trade initiatives to support women to become self-sufficient.

### Economic inequalities
Learning about how the economy works is a specific area of the citizenship curriculum. Teaching this with an awareness of gender issues would include pay, jobs, conditions of work (including unpaid work in the home), poverty of women-headed single parent families (compared with two-parent families), the imbalance of gender in top jobs and the glass ceiling. *The New Feminism* (Walter, 1999) points out that economic inequalities remain the greatest source of gender inequity, despite many positive changes since the challenges to male dominance of the Women's Movement of the 1970s and 1980s. There is scope for looking at how women are affected by childcare policies, their membership and status within trade unions, and inequalities within pension provision.

### Human rights and gender
The citizenship curriculum acknowledges that learning about and expecting to promote human rights are fundamental to citizenship education. One does not have to look outside Britain to realise that human rights issues relating to gender are on our very doorstep, for example in the sex trade where young East European women are tricked into coming to Britain, and the treatment of other young women brought in as servants and then virtually enslaved. Further afield, the incidence of rape and violence against women in conflict zones has been reported (Bunch, 1995). Madeleine Arnot indicates the range of human rights issues that relate to women:

> The international human rights community, according to Bunch (1995), has begun to recognise 'gender-based violations as pervasive and insidious forms of human rights abuse'. However the mass violation of women's human rights through such gender-based violence is not generally considered an appropriate topic for citizenship education in schools. The battery of women, their physical and psychological imprisonment in the home, the violent entrapment of women in prostitution, pornography and domestic service, compulsory pregnancy, rape, female infanticide and the malnutrition of girls are human rights violations that demand urgent attention. (Arnot, 2005)

### Political knowledge and engagement

The children quoted at the opening of this schedule show that even primary pupils are interested in politics and gender, and that there are opportunities for exploring the inequities within politics from an early age. The citizenship curriculum requires that children know about how democracy works, how parliament operates, and about voting and elections. In order to understand this, there is scope for looking not only at the gender imbalance in Parliament, for example, but also why it is that women are so under-represented. Pupils can look at representation in public institutions from the local council to political parties and the work of the 300 Group to get more women into Parliament. The use of women-only short lists is always a topical, controversial issue. Other areas include the difficulties of putting women's issues on the agenda in some public forums, and the difficulties faced by women who might wish to take an active role in various groups like trade unions and local councils. Here, there are opportunities to explore just how democracy works: why is it that so few women have a voice in such institutions? Is it because of male assumptions about women's ability to act effectively? Is it because of lack of confidence, or is it because of the necessity to be at home with young children?

Compounding the issue is the fact that research shows that boys tend to know more about the political system than girls and to be more interested. Thus, bringing gender into politics may be one way of engaging girls' interest, and showing them that decisions made by politicians do affect them and that they can make their voice heard. Children can bring in newspaper articles related to current issues in the news affecting girls and women and decide what should be done about it, and which minister they should write to. There is even a website to contact MPs (Clough and Holden, 2002).

### Identity and gender

Citizenship education is concerned with identity and belonging within different communities; thus there are opportunities to address situations where women are marginalised, deprived of certain rights as citizens or treated as less than equal in public settings. In the contemporary climate, in which alienation from Western values by political Islam and Islamophobia are perhaps the most serious causes of civil breakdown, it is important to remember that some women and girls are subject to discrimination and bullying simply because of what they look like.

Under the heading of challenging racism and discrimination, pupils should be considering the experience of some minority ethnic women, particularly where they are stereotyped as not British because of clothing or religious affiliation. Although the effects of Islamophobia, which is at the basis of such treatment, affect men too, Muslim women in hijab are more visible and vulnerable than men, whose religious affiliation is less apparent.

Gender equity is never divorced from class and ethnicity. Few people nowadays take a simplistic view of gender that one size fits all. The work of the black women's movement from the 1970s and 1980s and subsequently, made it very clear that black or minority ethnic women did not have the same agenda as middle-class white women, who shared much of the privilege enjoyed by their menfolk. Writers like Diane Reay and Sue Lees have pointed out that working-class women, whether black, from ethnic minorities or white, do not share the same experiences and may suffer from very different discriminatory practices. The challenge, then, is to help pupils to understand that discrimination comes in all shapes and sizes and to appreciate the dangers of stereotyping. It is also to get pupils to consider a situation from many angles, not just gender but also race and class.

### Community

Learning about and being involved in the community is central to citizenship, and yet it is one of the areas that teachers find most difficult. This is partly because many teachers live outside the school community or inhabit very different worlds from their children, and partly because there are no packs about community: each is different with different issues. And yet research shows that children are very aware of what is going on in their community – indeed it is the backcloth to their lives. They know about the lack of safe places for women in the community, lack of things for girls to do (skate parks are mainly used by boys) and the no-go zones. Older pupils can also discuss provision for women's refuges, childcare facilities and issues around prostitution. There are also gender issues for boys, who find themselves stereotyped as troublemakers and thus rejected. There are links with PSHE here around the rise in teenage drinking and anti-social behaviour orders (ASBOs).

### Inequalities based directly on sexual mores and sexuality

This area has strong links with PSHE, as the personal and the public combine where there is discussion about sexual mores and sexuality. In PSHE, pupils might discuss current sexual mores, for example the implicit assumptions about male sexuality being less under control than that of females; violence and abuse against women and gays and lesbians; issues round sex work; rape and blame for rape. Links to citizenship education come when pupils look at how communities sanction such behaviour, the legal position, the cost to society and what can be done to bring about change. In the same way, discussions about paternal rights and responsibilities, child care and hours of work, can be discussed in terms of personal understanding, but can also be looked at through a citizenship and gender lens, with pupils able to ask who benefits, what are the costs – economic and to society – and what needs to be done to bring about change.

## Teaching citizenship: do boys and girls respond differently?

> Pupils will not respond to the content of a citizenship curriculum in identical ways, because they are themselves gendered in experience and attitudes. This means there has to be some differentiation of approach to different content and contexts.

### The effects of the pupils' own gendered attitudes

Recent research on attitudes indicates that girls are in general more tolerant of minorities and more open minded, particularly of ethnic minorities and gays, than boys (with exceptions – there is by no means a clear gender divide). Girls and boys will be the objects of patriarchal and heterosexist attitudes themselves, and this will impact on how certain important issues of social justice are dealt with by each sex. For example, girls who are aware of patriarchal attitudes may be more concerned about women's issues: abortion rights, women's roles in society, impact of attitudes to sex in spread of HIV/aids. Gay boys may be bullied more, but are potentially more aware of how discrimination against groups and stereotyping operate, through their personal experience. Boys and girls who have tried to break through gender stereotypes, or know people who have, will have different attitudes from those who have more conventional perspectives. Boys may be hostile to the introduction of some issues of gender equity, because of their own socialisation into patriarchal attitudes. This can of course mean that material is not seen as neutral when it is introduced into the citizenship curriculum, but may be viewed as threatening and loaded.

Feminist work on girls' and boys' affective responses and views on justice (for example Gilligan, 1982 and 1988; Noddings, 1988) alerts us to the possibility that pupils may respond to some of the issues in the citizenship curriculum in different ways. Girls are more likely to be concerned with relationships, to empathise with those with whom they identify, even if their experience is entirely dissimilar – for example the victims of natural disasters and people living in poverty. While the differences are less clear-cut than was originally hypothesised, and many boys do show care and concern, nevertheless teachers may find that their efforts to work on empathy and sympathy are less effective. In consequence, ways of engaging boys and girls coming with different perspectives and content need to be differentiated.

### Crime and violence in society

Citizenship education engages with issues such as the law and crime, which are themselves gendered. Boys have a higher profile than girls in some types of criminal behaviour, and the types of punishable behaviour they engage in differs – though laddish behaviour by girls is increasing. For example, teenage girls are more likely to engage in shoplifting, and teenage boys more likely to get into fights involving weapons. This may mean that different approaches to engaging boys and girls with these issues is necessary, since gender-based peer group pressure can mean some pupils may identify with antisocial behaviour and be much less amenable to citizenship-related messages. In classrooms, some polarisation of the pupils by sex/gender could result if teachers are insensitive to such socio-cultural interpretations.

## Teaching citizenship skills: are there gender issues to consider?

This second section addresses process issues in citizenship education relevant to gender equality. To start with, we need to consider in what ways girls may be disadvantaged or benefit from those interactions, and ways of working which are built into effective citizenship education.

### Skills encouraged in citizenship education

- active engagement – interactive learning styles
- debate and discussion
- reflexive and flexible attitudes to issues
- conflict resolution
- collaborative learning
- speaking in public – advocacy
- research and presentation skills.

Many girls have no difficulty with many of these skills, but all the following can disempower girls and some boys in contexts that require active participation:

- lack of confidence
- not knowing how to participate
- finding that their attempts to participate are not taken seriously or are blocked
- finding that the issues they wish to raise are marginalised
- being required to compete rather than collaborate
- feeling disengaged and that civic affairs are nothing to do with them.

Citizenship is about participation and voice, and much of this is practised and learned in schools through active approaches – debate, advocacy etc. These are not neutral – boys tend to dominate in most settings and so may deny girls full participation and opportunity to exercise their voice. Girls are often more comfortable with modes of learning involving collaboration and discussion than being individually exposed and required to speak in public. In contrast, many boys find collaboration and flexible debate more difficult, although they may enjoy public speaking, advocacy and more confrontational styles.

Approaches to conflict resolution cannot be gender blind, given that girls are more likely to be prepared to collaborate than boys. Some boys may consider some approaches to conflict resolution feminine or even effeminate. Some girls will certainly choose fighting, violence and physical strength as conflict resolution strategies, just as some boys will choose negotiation, but there may be a prior bias towards one or other solution that is gendered.

With respect to active citizenship, there is some evidence that boys may be more willing to engage in active protest, including some that is violent or illegal, whereas girls are more likely to undertake community and voluntary work seen as helpful and caring.

### Structural issues

The school and class councils may be the main places where issues affecting pupils' lives in school can be addressed in a democratic fashion. It is important that this microcosm of democracy operates democratically, so that everyone gets practice in advocacy, and learns that they can experience effective, participative, active citizenship. It is essential to monitor that different voices are represented and heard, and issues affecting all pupils – not just some – are brought to everyone's attention.

### Monitoring and evaluation to ensure positive changes

It is important to bring all the issues outlined in this chapter into the open. As part of learning about democracy and what active citizenship means in practice, children should not just discuss the gender issues mentioned above, asking how we ensure that everyone gets a chance to voice their opinion. They should also become accustomed to monitoring what is happening, evaluating their findings, and taking relevant action in a cycle of enquiry: analysis – monitoring – policy development. Self-evaluation and peer evaluation of discussions can be useful starting points (see Claire and Holden 2005 for a self-evaluation grid which has been tried and tested in school).

### Issues to consider
### A summary and checklist
#### Content issues

- Are we addressing gender inequalities in the economy and in politics directly rather than implicitly in the curriculum?
- Are we addressing gender when we look at classroom issues, the school, the community, national and international contexts?
- Are pupils encouraged to look at gender together with ethnicity/religion/disability/class when they consider discrimination and intolerance?
- Is there a gender dimension in our work on human rights?

#### Process and attitudes

- Do we recognise and help our pupils to recognise the gendered nature of interactions affecting discourses, participation and confidence?
- Do we monitor such participation and interactions, together with the pupils themselves, to make sure that good intentions are translated into action?

- Do we provide support for pupils whose voice and participation are marginalised?
- Do we consider gender issues in conflict resolution, and help pupils work towards positive, peaceful solutions?

### Structural issues within the school

- In mixed schools, are girls and boys equally represented on school or class councils? And where there is equality of representation, is there also equality of participation?
- Do gender issues get raised in the school or class councils as appropriate?

### Monitoring

- Have we audited the current situation with respect to gender content and participation?
- How does this translate into policy decisions?
- How shall we involve pupils and the wider community in this process as part of their own education in a gender-aware citizenship education?

## Resources

Arnot, M. (2005) Gender Equality and Citizenship Education, www.jsse.org/2005-2/equality_arnot.htm publishing date: 24.02.2006

Bunch, C. (1995) Transforming human rights from a feminist perspective. In Peters, J. and Wolper, A. (eds) *Women's Rights, Human Rights – International Feminist Perspectives.* New York :11-17

Claire, H. (2001) *Not Aliens: Primary School Children and the Citizenship/PSHE Curriculum.* Stoke-on-Trent: Trentham

Claire, H. and Holden, C. (2005) *Effective transition KS2 – KS3* http://www.citized.info/?strand=0andr_menu=induction

Claire, H. and Holden, C. (2007) *The Challenge of Teaching Controversial Issues.* Stoke on Trent: Trentham

Clough, A and Holden, C (2002) www.number-10.gov.uk

Crick Advisory Group (1998) *Education for citizenship and the teaching of democracy in schools.* London: QCA

DfEE – Department for Education and Employment/QCA – Qualifications and Curriculum Authority (1999) *The National Curriculum for England, Key Stages 1- 2, 3-4.* London: QCA

Gilligan, C. (1982) *In a Different Voice.* Harvard: Harvard University Press

Gilligan, C. (1988) *Mapping the Moral Domain.* Harvard: Harvard University Press

Lees, S. (1986) *Losing Out.* London: Hutchinson

McLaughlin, T. H. (1992) Citizenship, Diversity and Education: a philosophical perspective. *Journal of Moral Education* 21(3) p235-250

Noddings, N. (1988) An Ethic of Caring and its Implications for Instructional Arrangements. *American Journal of Education* 96 (2) p215-230

Osler, A. and Starkey, H. (2005) *Changing Citizenship: Democracy and Inclusion in Education.* Buckingham: Open University Press

Osler, A. (ed) (2000) *Citizenship and Democracy in Schools: Diversity, Identity, Equality.* Stoke-on-Trent: Trentham

Osler, A. and Vincent, K. (eds) (2002) *Citizenship and the Challenge of Global Education.* Stoke-on-Trent: Trentham

Reay, D. (2001) Spice girls, 'nice girls', 'girlies' and tomboys: Gender discourses, girls' cultures and femininities in the primary classroom. *Gender and Education* 13 (2) p153-166

Walter, N. (1999) *The New Feminism.* London: Virago

According to research, boys show more interest and engagement with design and technology (D&T) than girls, and a greater inclination to take up technological-related careers (Sayers, 2002). Teachers can either condone or challenge these views.

The national curriculum for England and Wales made design and technology compulsory for all five to sixteen year olds. This extended access to primary children and to all pupils post fourteen. However, post fourteen pupil choices remain in the selection of which aspect of the subject to study.

### *Curriculum and teaching – the what*
### Course choices and achievement

There is some evidence that by key stage 3 significantly fewer boys than girls reach the expected level of attainment in D&T in teachers' assessment. The examination entry patterns for pupils at the end of compulsory schooling (see Table 1) also reveal that in spite of the national curriculum, significant gender differences in course choices continue.

The entry patterns suggest that pupils have clear views of what is, and is not, appropriate for them to study, and this is not changing.

Table 2 overleaf shows that girls, across the course options, achieve significantly more passes than boys. Where there is a major imbalance between girls' and boys' entry numbers the minority group is considered to be the more highly selected, representing more able and committed pupils. It is, therefore, expected that their performance would be higher than the majority group. The figures in Table 2 indicate that this may be the case with girls, but not for those boys choosing to study textiles and food technology.

**Table1: Entry by thousands of male and female pupils in D&T GCSE subjects**

| Subject | 2002 | | 2003 | | 2004 | |
|---|---|---|---|---|---|---|
| | Male | Female | Male | Female | Male | Female |
| Electronics Products | 18 | 2 | 17.8 | 1.5 | 17.1 | 1.4 |
| Food Technology | 27 | 75 | 28.9 | 74.9 | 28.9 | 74.1 |
| Graphic Products | 61 | 47 | 59.5 | 45.9 | 57.5 | 44.4 |
| Resistant Materials | 89 | 27 | 87.8 | 24 | 85.9 | 21.3 |
| Systems Control | 13 | 1 | 13.5 | 1.1 | 12.5 | 1.1 |
| Textiles Technology | 2 | 46 | 1.6 | 48.5 | 1.7 | 50.8 |
| Other D&T | 5 | 3 | 9 | 6.7 | 11.4 | 8.1 |

*Source: www.dfes.gov.uk/rsgateway*

**Table 2: Percentage of male and females at the end of KS4 gaining a pass or higher (A*-C) by subject in 2005**

GCSE D&T

| Subject | Entries in thousands | | % achieving A*-C grades of pupils attempting the subject | |
|---|---|---|---|---|
| | Male | Female | Male | Female |
| Electronic Products | 15.9 | 1.1 | 58 | 73 |
| Food Technology | 27.2 | 66.7 | 44 | 63 |
| Graphic Products | 49.2 | 37.4 | 47 | 65 |
| Resistant Materials | 80.4 | 18.0 | 49 | 65 |
| Systems Control | 11.1 | 0.9 | 57 | 76 |
| Textile Technology | 1.6 | 46.6 | 37 | 69 |
| Other D&T | 13.3 | 8.5 | 51 | 68 |

*Source: www.dfes.gov.uk/rsgateway*

## Issues to consider
■ Are boys doing as well as girls in D&T at key stage 3 in your school? Why do you think this might be?

■ Do you monitor which boys and which girls take different courses and their reasons for this? Are there gendered patterns of entry and achievement?

## Career aspirations
Significant gender stereotyping in pupils' career choices is evident in the different vocational pathways taken by girls and boys, and the continuing reluctance of girls to take up engineering courses and technology-related careers. Roger and Duffield (2000) identified two influences underlying girls' persistent opting out of science and technology courses: pupils' view of themselves and future possibilities; and career awareness. They described the relationship between self-concept and career awareness as the 'interaction between the way pupils see themselves and the opportunities they perceive are open to them' (p374). Pupils generally lack awareness of the world of work, but for girls this is combined with a view of technology as a male occupation.

As one girl studying electronics at age fifteen commented: 'although I enjoy electronics and am fascinated by it, I am not thinking of doing it more seriously, I don't see the point' (Murphy, 2006 p235).

## Issues to consider
■ Do the pupils you teach have views about careers that are appropriate for girls and for boys?

■ Do you make reference to technological careers in your teaching and give examples that challenge pupils' thinking about future possibilities?

## D&T – a masculine domain?
How we talk about a subject determines which people are associated with it and who becomes distanced from it. Historically, as with science, males were associated with what is technical and females with what is not-technical. This emerged from the basic divide that associated femininity with nurturing, connection and the body, and masculinity with objectivity, separation, and the mind. The notion of the living female universe to be nurtured and protected emerged in Greek and early pagan philosophies. The challenge to this perspective, the right of man to have dominion over the earth, came into ascendancy in the 18th and 19th centuries as the tensions between social conventions and technological development grew. The emerging discourse surrounding technology placed aesthetics in opposition to the technical, and 'the inventor, the user, the thinker about and reactor to technology' was male (Rothschild, 1983:xix). This way of thinking about technology denied women the role of inventor even though historical, anthropological analyses of what people did challenged this.

Men could invent machines, and women and children could operate them. When there was a struggle to maintain control over access to machinery, men appropriated skilled work and women's work was restricted to the unskilled and routinised (Wajcman, 1991). Consequently, technical competence was seen as integral to masculinities and women were positioned as the technically incompetent. In schools, these practices were reflected in the separation of craft, design and technology which boys studied, often in single-sex groups, from home economics which girls studied. The notion of a common curriculum only became embedded following the introduction of the national curriculum in 1988.

### Issues to consider

■ Do you discuss with pupils their views of who is, or can be, good at D&T? Is this reflected in your feedback to pupils and whose work is valued?

■ Have you considered how you represent the ideal pupil in D&T? Are the characteristics you emphasise associated with gender?

### Teaching and learning – the how
### Teachers' expectations

Teachers have definite views about what girls and boys bring to subjects:

> You have your high technological boy...he's a very technological kiddo and he is able to work at very high level, logical, technical, mathematics etc. The girls are more artistic in their approach. They're far more quality-conscious than the boys. (Murphy, 2006, p225)

Teachers can reinforce or challenge gender stereotypes about who is, or is not, competent at design and technology. For example, a teacher faced with single-sex groups of Year 9 pupils studying joints in resistant materials, stressed for the boys their cultural heritage through references to 'man the hunter', 'man the inventor' and 'man the voyager'. When teaching the girls he made no reference to the possibility of their involvement in the subject, instead referring to their father or husbands 'doing it for them'. In the same school another male teacher drew on domestic examples for all pupils and engaged boys and girls equally.

Some girls' marginalisation in workshop settings may also arise because they have limited access to equipment, as they tend to wait until boys have used it first. The teacher who drew on domestic examples made a point of extending girls' participation by

ensuring they had access to, and felt competent with, the machinery. This same teacher assumed that in the all-boys group, boys had no problems with the workshop equipment. However, as one boy, who was anxious to drop the subject, commented: 'I am just afraid of hurting myself.' Boys like this are regarded by their peers as weak. They have to hide their anxieties, and this can often limit what they achieve, as they often have incomplete products in spite of their ambitious designs.

### Issues to consider

■ Consider your choice of examples and your use of language. Are the contributions of both males and females to the subject recognised?

■ Do you assume that all boys and all girls are equally comfortable with different aspects of D&T?

■ Do you take account of the different experiences that boys and girls will bring to subjects like textiles, food technology, resistant materials, electronics etc?

■ Do you observe who engages with equipment and how, and act on it supportively?

### What pupils pay attention to

From a young age there is a tendency for boys and girls to engage in different activities and roles even when using the same resources. Consequently, differences emerge between them in what they pay attention to, and in what they understand is purposeful activity. For example, when playing with construction kits, young boys were observed to focus on making structures that moved whereas girls were more likely to use structures as part of their social play. Similarly, when primary children were given tinkering activities like taking apart a clock mechanism, girls were observed to consider the potential of the parts to construct a robot or a flower, whereas boys were more interested in the deconstruction process and the way parts worked.

These differences in what girls and boys pay attention to influence what they focus on in D&T tasks. Girls' concern with the social context dominates their designs, and they tend to consider aesthetics and user needs. Boys are more likely to include detail about mechanisms and structures focusing on the physical aspect of needs and wants. In a study involving secondary pupils given the opportunity to generate authentic designs, it tended to be girls who placed their response in the context of the person's needs and the circumstances in which the product would be used. Thus water sensors housed in a water-drop shape were used to create a bath alarm for a grandmother (Murphy, 1999).

In assessment situations, girls are more able to deal with reflective, evaluative tasks than many boys. Boys do better on these tasks when they are practically engaged in developing solutions. They consistently outperform girls in conceptual areas like energy systems. Girls outperform boys on most aspects of communication in D&T.

These differences in learning and assessment situations reflect some of the historical constructions of feminine and masculine concerns discussed earlier.

### Issues to consider

- Do you provide opportunities for peer-review of initial plans and designs so that pupils can consider alternative perspectives?

- In your product analysis tasks, what types of products do you select? Are they equally accessible to girls and boys?

- Do you give feedback to pupils against criteria so they can develop an awareness of their strengths and weaknesses? Do you act on this feedback to support boys, for example with communication skills, and girls with conceptual understanding and its application?

### Differential learning

The differences discussed are significant as they alter the possibilities available for pupils' learning. For example in the evaluation of the Nuffield Primary Solutions, one activity was to design a bus. Most boys began with the moving parts, whereas girls focused on the interior features for the passengers and the exterior appearance. At the end, many girls' buses looked like buses, but lacked wheels or had rather inefficient wheels. Many boys' buses looked like moving cardboard boxes. In a study with 13 -14 year-old pupils, one activity was to design and make a vehicle with four wheels to carry a two-kilogram weight five metres. All the boys worked first on the structure to meet the criteria of stability, strength and movement. Appearance was a secondary consideration: 'it's the capability of the designs that's key.' The girls gave priority to presentation and appearance, so one chose to work with plastic and used vacuum formation.

### Issues to consider

- In evaluating products do you encourage pupils to make explicit what their priorities were?

- Do you monitor how pupils interpret tasks and get them to consider the impact on their learning through self-assessment?

- Do you vary learning about design and making, and sometimes use design-only tasks?

- If the emphasis is on making, do you assume that the relevance of what is being learned is understood by all pupils and in the same way?

### Ways of working

In many studies, differences in how boys and girls work have been noted. Girls state a preference for working together and boys for working alone. Some teachers discourage collaborative work in D&T as they see it as an opportunity for pupils to free wheel. Both boys and girls value collaboration. 'It works better when we're in groups, more ideas than if you work as an individual. You can see things from different perspectives.'

Girls appear more willing to consult the teacher, while for some boys this is the last resort. Girls are described as facilitators, giving lots of support to others in discussing strengths and weaknesses in designs. Girls will do this even when they are working on individual products, as they often talk out loud about their problems and potential solutions, keeping track of their own and others' designs and product issues. Their collaborative approach can be interpreted as their being less able or deficit. For example, it has been observed that when girls seek help, some teachers, instead of modelling possible solutions and offering alternatives, identify the problem and solve it without discussion, removing the girls' independence. Some boys who feel unable to ask for help, either from other boys or from the teacher, struggle and often fail to progress.

### Issues to consider

- Do you value group work and support it by providing a balance between learner independence and decision-making, and opportunities for peer interaction?

- Have you asked pupils which ways of working they prefer and why?

- In your mind's eye, which pupils seek help more than others? Is there a gender issue here?

## References and further resources

Barlex, D. (2002) *Young Foresight. Shaping Things to Come.* London: Software Production Enterprises www.youngforesight.org

Barlex, D. (2001) *Primary Solutions in Design and Technology.* London: Nuffield/DATA www.primarydandt.org.uk

Murphy, P. (1999) Supporting collaborative learning: a gender dimension. In Murphy, P. (ed) *Learners, Learning and Assessment.* London: Paul Chapman

Murphy, P. (2006) Gender and technology: gender mediation in school knowledge construction. In Dakers, J. R. *Defining Technological Literacy, Towards an Epistemological Framework.* New York: Palgrave MacMillan

Riggs, A. (1998) Gender and technology education. In Banks. F. (ed) *Teaching Technology.* Buckingham: Open University Press.

Roger, A. and Duffield, J. (2000) Factors underlying persistent gendered option choices in school science and technology in Scotland, *Gender and Education*, 12(3) 367-383.

Rothschild, J. (1983) *A Practical Guide Teaching Technology from a Feminist Perspective.* New York: Pergamon Press

Sayers, S. (2002) Is gender still on the agenda as an issue for design and technology? In Sayers, S., Morley, J. and Barnes. B. (eds) *Issues in Design and Technology Teaching.* London: RoutledgeFalmer

Spendlove, D. (2002) Boys' performance in design and technology. In Sayers, S., Morley, J. and Barnes. B. (eds) *Issues in Design and Technology Teaching.* London: RoutledgeFalmer

Wajcman, J. (1991) *Feminism Confronts Technology.* Pennsylvania: Pennsylvania State University Press

# English and Media

*Jan Shapiro*

## Introduction

It is not hard to locate endless research papers, reports and articles on aspects of gender in English and media teaching centred on the underachievement of boys (eg Arnold, 1997; Dunne and Khan, 1998; Frater, 1997; Qualifications and Curriculum Authority, 1998) – and, particularly, their status as reluctant readers and writers. This has been an educational concern since the early 1990s and there is clearly a pattern of boys underachieving in English when compared with girls at both primary and secondary levels. Nationally, girls outperform boys at all four key stages in English. Differences in English, particularly in reading and the quality of writing, emerge during key stage 1 and accumulate as pupils progress through school.

However, it is vital that this debate is situated carefully in context. There is a far greater differential within groups than between groups. Success and underachievement are evident for both girls and boys, and it can be distracting and even misleading to approach gender monitoring too crudely in our classrooms. However, schools often begin to diagnose apparent gender trends by referring to the statistics showing the relative position of males and females. This can lead to reactive teaching and the employment of pedagogy focused on raising boys' achievement through what are considered boy friendly strategies. Such strategies include delivering the lesson in short bite-sized chunks, encouraging competition and selecting readers targeted to boys with emphasis on visual literacy. These can reinforce limited learning strategies and gender stereotypes rather than extending boys as learners. Both sexes benefit from a range of learning experiences. The public debate equating boys' failure with girls' success is a huge oversimplification of the issue.

Of course it is important to reflect on any year group's progress from a gender perspective, but all teachers should bear in mind that more complex forces may be at work, and that understanding the specific context surrounding pupils may be more helpful than broad-stroke gender distinctions. While gender is one of the key factors affecting educational performance, it always functions in relation to other social variables that may be more powerful. In other words, it is necessary to take a far more holistic approach to counter underachievement in any classroom.

### Issues to consider

These questions are designed to help you reflect and review practice in relation to gender issues in the English classroom. They can form the beginning of a process of ongoing self-evaluation.

### Speaking and listening

Oral work in the English and media classroom needs to be well managed and planned. It is during these activities that gender issues specific to a particular class or school are often highlighted.

■ Do pupils work in a variety of groupings?

Is there a culture and ethos in your classroom that encourages pupils to work with each other in ways that are supportive, and that enable everyone to participate? For example, are pupils taught how to share out different roles in group discussions so that everyone has a turn at being the chairperson, reporting back and note taking? (It is all too easy for teachers to give an instruction like 'I would like you to work in groups' without being clear about what this means and ensuring that everyone is involved).

- Do girls and boys lead and report back in group discussions? Or does one gender dominate? Are pupils given the opportunity to debate? Are these debates structured, fair and balanced? Are everyone's views valued?

- Is talk valued? Do pupils have the opportunity to reflect on their own talk and discuss the ways in which groups work together? Do teachers notice any difference between the talk of girls and boys? Is this discussed as part of the lesson in a way that enables pupils to reflect on this? Has the nature of male/female talk been discussed explicitly?

- Is talk appropriately integrated with reading and writing tasks? Are there opportunities for pupils to think about and discuss the ways in which language and choice of language is value laden? Do they explore the gender assumptions that language carries? Do they discuss sexist and racist language with sensitivity and knowledge?

- What kinds of texts, be it moving image or print material, are used to stimulate discussion? Are pupils offered a range of texts, including those that explore the power of gender and racial stereotypes? Are pupils able to make reference in their talk to a range of texts?

## Reading

While it is well known that boys and girls will read different texts, pandering to this difference will only reinforce stereotypes. It is important that all pupils are exposed to a wide variety of different texts, authors and genres of writing.

- Is there discussion on the criteria for selecting texts? Are pupils introduced to texts of all kinds – stories, poems, drama, non-fiction and media texts – and are the interests of both girls and boys reflected? Do texts reflect a wide range of historical periods and cultural backgrounds? What is the balance between female and male authors?

- Do pupils in secondary schools understand and use media concepts like denotation and connotation, in order to decode texts and uncover implicit messages about gender, race and ethnicity?

- Have pupils been exposed to media texts that challenge female or male stereotypes and conventional assumptions? Discussion of the kinds of gaze assumed in films and television programmes can produce important awareness of how certain perspectives are privileged.

- Are children and young people able to analyse texts from different points of view, and do they understand that texts can be read in different ways and can have multiple meanings? Are they critical readers?

- Are pupils encouraged to talk about their reading? Does the teacher talk about her/his own reading and present a positive model of a reader? Is reading beyond the classroom given high priority?

## Writing

Pupils should be enabled to write for a range of audiences, in different formats and genres and from different points of view. Writing tasks should be balanced with opportunities for extended writing as well as shorter, more concise tasks.

- How does the department feed back to pupils about their progress as writers? Is enough done to show pupils that the writing process is valued?

- What writers are pupils exposed to? What messages are conveyed about good writing or important writing?

- What messages does the teacher give his/her class about what qualities are most valued in writing? Is this length or detail? Succinctness or elaboration? Logic or wit? Is presentation deemed more important than quality? Do teachers monitor their own responses to the writing of girls and boys? For example, is neatness expected of girls and is carelessness tolerated from boys?

- Are pupils able to exercise their choice as writers? Are they given tasks for which they are given the opportunity to express their own ideas?

- Is there a balance between giving pupils a clear structure such as a writing frame and giving them independence?

- Is writing made relevant? Does it have a function in the real world?

- Is talk used at different stages of the writing process, for example, using improvisation, role-plays and peer feedback?

## Media in the English classroom

Media literacy is a key component of the National Curriculum and pupils should be given ample opportunity to interrogate different forms of media texts. The English and media classroom can provide a space for challenging gender stereotypes and exploring identity. With the media playing such a strong role in the formation of young peoples' gender identities, it is important that they understand and engage with media representations of gender. However, this can be very challenging in some contexts, with pupils often resenting and resisting commonsense readings of their favourite media texts. In addition, they should also be given opportunities to produce their own artefacts. We need to be wary of perpetuating the idea of a gender digital divide by assuming that boys are more willing than girls to use and explore the more technical aspects of media production. Both girls and boys engage with a digital technology that is continually advancing.

## References and further resources

Arnold, R. (1997) *Raising Levels of Achievement in Boys.* Slough: NFER, EMIE

Barrs, M. and Pidgeon, S. (eds) (1993) *Reading the Difference.* London: CLPE

Dunne, J. and Khan, A. (1998) The crisis in boys' reading, *The Library Association Record*, 100(8): 408-10

The English and Media Centre www.englishandmedia.co.uk/
    A not-for-profit educational publishers and teachers' centre providing high quality teaching materials and Continuing Professional Development to teachers of English and Media in the UK and across the world

Frater, G. (1997) *Improving Boys' Literacy: A Survey of Effective Practice in Secondary Schools.* London: Basic Skills Agency

Millard, E. (1997) *Differently Literate.* London: Falmer Press

Ofsted (2003) *Boys' Achievement in Secondary Schools.* London: Ofsted

Ofsted (2003) *Yes He Can: Schools Where Boys Write Well.* London: Ofsted

Qualifications and Curriculum Authority (1998). *Can Do Better: Raising Boys' Achievement in English.* London: QCA

Younger, M. and Warrington, M. with Gray, J., Rudduck, J., McLellan, R., Bearne, E., Kershner, R. and Bricheno, P. (2005) *Raising Boys' Achievement: A Study Funded by the Department for Education and Skills.* (DfES Research Report RR63). London: DfES www.dfes.gov.uk/gender andachievement

The National Association for the Teaching of English www.nate.org.uk/
    NATE is the UK subject teacher association for all aspects of English from pre-school to university. NATE supports effective teaching and learning, keeps teachers informed about current developments and provides them with a voice at a national level

The National Literacy Trust www.literacytrust.org.uk/ index.html
    An independent charity concerned with raising literacy standards for all age groups throughout the UK

... BUT THIS IS THE IMPORTANT BIT. IT'S CALLED THE "WESTERN HEMISPHERE"

# Geography

*Margaret Caistor and Louise Lee*

Arguably, geography and its teaching have moved on from concerns over male stereotypes and eurocentricity. It is perhaps no longer necessary to check for images of female and ethnic minorities in geography textbooks as issues of discrimination are now recognised by successful publishers. Does this mean that real progress has been made in offering a geographical curriculum that offers equality of opportunity to all? The recent handbooks from the Geographical Association (Balderstone, 2206, Scoffham, 2004) include references to gender issues in a commendably wide range of chapters, but school geography too often ignores issues of gender. Some teachers are unwilling to question practice to ensure that it challenges societal stereotypes. Where stereotypical images were once a discussion tool, they are now too frequently used as objective sources and gender-biased language is not questioned.

Britain and the world today are rich and increasingly accessible environments for young geographers to learn about. Familial links give pupils an array of experiences to share in their study of geography; the use of the world wide web has transformed our perception of distant places. The subject has the power to help students make sense both of their place and role as citizens in the world and of world events. The current focus on metacognition and thinking skills enables students to ask their own questions about ethnic and gender inequality, and about the sustainable use of resources. For example, the world is shrinking for a global elite, while the development gap widens and 600 million women worldwide have no access to school education. The effects of climatic changes are not uniform around the world. We should be presenting the disparities that still do exist around the world and encouraging students to ask meaningful questions about the adult world to which they will soon belong.

## Early years (ages 3 to 5) and key stage 1 (ages 5 to 7)

In 'Knowledge and Understanding of the World', and key stage 1 geography, children learn about where they are – there is an emphasis on place and spatial awareness. This understanding of relevant concepts/vocabulary, and patterns of physical and human features are developed through exploring the local area or nearby places, or by learning about more distant places or the wider world through stories, pictures, video/DVD programmes, the internet or meeting people. Gender issues are important in the content and uses made of the resources and in the activities of the children.

There has been some research on whether there is a difference in spatial ability between boys and girls. Scoffham (2004) explores gender issues within a strong argument for developing spatial awareness, and the use of maps as a fundamental skill in nurseries and infant classes.

### Issues to consider

In planning the resources and activities to develop the geographical element in early years and infant classrooms, teachers and assistants could consider such questions as:

- are the 'people who help us' sometimes not of the stereotypical gender?
- do stories chosen to explore journeys or places have both girls and boys as key characters?
- are families varied and not always portrayed as a father, mother and two children?

- are surveys of pupils' opinions of nice and nasty areas of the school grounds analysed by gender?

- do girls have equal access to the most popular toys or artefacts in a newly focused home corner? Do boys and girl have opportunities to develop their play in the home corner in separate groups?

- do both girls and boys drive or push the most popular vehicles round the path in the outside area?

## Key stage 2 (ages 7 to 11)

Much of the research into gender differences in geography in the upper primary phase is focused on aspects of spatial ability. Taylor (1998) asked pupils to draw a map to help guests arrive at their house for a party. She found that 'boys tended to cover a greater area and were more likely to use plan views than girls. The boys also produced a wider range of map types. However, the girls drew more details and were more accurate than the boys beyond the age of eight'. Scoffham (2004) questions whether such differences are innate or the result of social and cultural upbringing. Catling (1998) refers to past research having identified gender differences in environmental knowledge and mapping competence (Matthews, 1992). However, his study of a local area with some year 5 pupils showed that in both pre-study and post-study mapping there was no difference between the girls' and boys' mapping skills, and boys were not more accurate spatially. He found that boys had more extensive knowledge than girls of the area and that this difference still existed after the study, although it was less significant than at the start. Mackintosh (1998) examines research findings that challenge assumptions that photographs are easy to understand.

- Does a published photo pack only show rural images, which could reinforce stereotypes of materialistic deprivation?

- Do these pictures challenge rather than confirm children's existing frameworks, exploiting their curiosity and flexible attitudes about other peoples and cultures?

- Do you use gender-specific questions when developing pupils' interpretation skills from concrete and descriptive, through speculative and reasoning, to evaluative and problem solving?

The key stage 2 curriculum continues and develops knowledge and understanding of the immediate locality, nearby places, distant places and the wider world. Questions about age groups, gender groups, ethnicity and social class, inform and enhance an enquiry-based study of a locality. For example:

- who lives there? What do they do?

- who is affected by the changes in the locality?

- are leisure facilities (for example parks) considered in relation to the age, gender and ethnicity of users?

Enquiry into physical topics usually includes questioning the impact of the physical pattern or process on people, and what people do to affect the pattern or process. Do you, as a teacher or assistant:

- use gender-neutral terms such as 'people' whenever possible?

- allow separate groups of girls and boys sometimes to determine some of the questions that are used to structure the enquiry, rather than always assuming that they have similar interests?

- ensure that a range of views is explored in decision-making exercises?

Enquiry in human topics raises other questions:

- are you careful to be specific about whether women or men are undertaking work? Do you differentiate between paid and unpaid work?

- do you refer to the 'built' rather than the 'man-made' environment?

- are women and people of ethnic minority backgrounds ever shown in positions of authority?

- do visitors to the school who contribute to geography (such as local planners), include both women and men?

Environmental geography and, in particular, work on sustainability is an important element of the curriculum in key stage 2.

- Do both girls and boys take an active role in organising and taking part in practical tasks such as recycling or redeveloping the school grounds, both for the present and sustainably for the future?

## Key stage 3 (ages 11 to 14) and upper secondary (ages 14 to 19)

Recent work on gender in the secondary phase has focused not on the subject as such, but on the fact that girls attain significantly better than boys in geography examinations at GCSE and A level. Butt *et al* (2006) explore the ways in which the performance and attainment of some students in geography may be linked to their gender and list some useful suggestions based on four implications for practice.

■ How do we ensure that internal assessment opportunities are varied in nature to allow both genders an opportunity to show themselves at their best?

■ How can we ensure that longer assessments are broken down into smaller elements to ensure full understanding?

■ Is it important to vary the formats for assessment and feedback for students?

■ Is it important to be conscious of gender differences in the level of classroom interaction? (p384-349)

The Geographical Futures programme developed by QCA (2005) suggests five key concepts – big ideas – and seven distinctive experiences, skills and attitudes. These are used as a framework in the table below with questions, many from Connolly (1992), added. These concepts and skills can equally well be applied to the 14 to 19 geography curriculum of academic, applied and vocational courses.

---

Geographical imagination – a sense of place, identity and an ability to negotiate in and about place:

■ When pupils record their perception of the environment on a survey sheet, do you ask them if they think that pedestrian areas are safe, both by day and night?

■ Do you avoid middle-class eurocentric assumptions about homes and families?

■ Does fear limit access to leisure? For example, are pubs inviting to lone women? Do young men feel comfortable in all areas of the town centre?

■ What public and private community facilities exist? Are they equally accessible to all residents regardless of gender, race, class and disability?

■ Are large, central services complexes (like out-of-town shopping centres) accessible to the people who need to use the shops or services?

■ Do inhabitants perceive buildings and housing estates as safe by day and night?

Spatial awareness – the importance of where things are and how they relate to other phenomena, and why it matters:

■ Do you study leisure facilities in relation to age, gender and ethnicity of users?

■ Do you sometimes use resources which depict females involved in active leisure pursuits and males in passive pursuits?

■ Do you explore ways in which boys and girls spend their leisure time? What might any differences tell us?

■ Is the local provision of open space adequate for young children and girls, for example is there adequate provision of open space within 120 metres of home?

■ How is choice of leisure governed by access to time and money?

■ Is work in the home shared equally between males and females? How does this affect the pattern of leisure provision and access to leisure facilities in an area?

Interdependence – the interconnections and interrelationships operating in a complex, diverse, interconnected world – explaining and coping with the dynamics of change:

■ Do you sometimes present alternatives to the classic workplace, for example working at home, working in a cooperative?

■ Do you differentiate between paid and unpaid work?

■ Do you spend a suitable amount of time (given their economic importance) on tertiary in comparison with primary and secondary occupations?

■ Do you recognise the importance of the contribution of women and children to farming, especially in Africa?

■ Do you explore the way men may become relatively more important in agriculture when development projects are introduced?

■ Do you ask female pupils to 'imagine you work on an oil rig' when the stimulus material depicts a man?

Scale and scale linkages – how all scales from the personal and local to the global are linked and the importance of recognising this in the way we conduct our lives:

■ Are the case studies used to illustrate global links attractive/interesting to both girls and boys?

■ Are there opportunities for girls and boys to develop personal examples of ways in which individual action may have global repercussions?

Interactions – the way in which geographers draw across the physical and human worlds to understand environmental change, sustainable development, social and cultural exchange, and to clarify the big picture for human society.

■ Do you show male and female experts and male and female recipients involved in development schemes? Do you ensure that not all the experts are white and the recipients black?

■ Do you show local women participating in organising and running self-help schemes?

■ When relevant, do you question westernised assumptions about family size, and the value of children to the family?

■ Do you present positive images of and discuss reasons for poverty?

■ Do you explore different opinions about controversial global issues, for example the notion of human rights as a Western idea?

The distinctive experiences, skills and attitudes

Valuing and building on students' own experiences of their lives, their communities and the wider world:

■ Do you take account of the fact that there are gender specific aspects of students' own experiences? Do you recognise that the starting point may be different and routes through an enquiry may differ? (Roberts, 2006)

Promoting an active and critical approach to enquiring about the world around them, and so developing thinking skills, problem-solving approaches and the ability to recognise, clarify and confirm their own attitudes and values:

■ Do you find that girls prefer to work in groups? What are the implications for classroom practice?

Contributing to political literacy by providing opportunities to explore the values dimension of issues concerning society and environment:

■ Do you find that girls feel they are more likely to be listened to and effect change in single-issue groups than in politics?

Emphasising fieldwork and outdoor learning, providing a distinctive opportunity to investigate and explore in the real world. Practical, social and behavioural skills developed:

■ Do both girls and boys take a leading role in organising practical work?

■ Is your classroom free of verbal abuse and physical intimidation?

Developing graphic skills and visual literacy through geography's distinctive use of maps, diagrams, computer images, multimedia, geographical information systems:

■ Are you aware of whether you are assessing the maps drawn by students for the information shown or for neatness?

■ Do girls and boys have equal opportunity to develop their skills on computers?

Promoting social awareness, environmental responsibility and understanding of cultural diversity through real-world issues at different scales, so assisting students in identifying personal routes for action – a unique contribution to global citizenship:

■ Are there some opportunities for choice between real-world issues?

■ Are all pupils encouraged to consider the position of people of other ethnic backgrounds and/or gender?

Developing young people's social and emotional development, for example through group work, fieldwork, individual enquiry and addressing real and significant questions and issues:

■ Do you structure the gender composition of groups? If boys or girls are in a small minority (in an A level group for example), do you make their position easier?

■ Do you take account of the fact that girls and boys may have different interests when studying real issues?

## References and further resources

Butt, G. with Bradley-Smith, P. and Wood, P. (2006) Gender Issues in Geography in Balderstone, D. (ed) *Secondary Geography Handbook*. Sheffield: Geographical Association pp384 -393

Catling, S. (1998) Children as Mapmakers, In Scoffham, S. (ed) *Primary Sources, Research findings in primary geography*. Sheffield: Geographical Association pp10-11

Connolly, J. (1992) Geography: Equal Opportunities and the National Curriculum. In Myers, K. (ed) *Genderwatch! After the ERA*. Cambridge: Cambridge University Press

Mackintosh, M. (1998) Learning from Photographs. In Scoffham, S. (ed) *Primary Sources, Research Findings in Primary Geography*. Sheffield: Geographical Association,

Matthews, H. (1992) *Making Sense of Place*. Hemel Hempstead: Harvester Wheatsheaf

QCA. *Futures: Meeting the Challenge* – www.qca.org.uk/futures The website, in December 2006, groups the concepts and skills differently. The format of the list used is from Rawling (2006)

Rawling, E (2006) Changing the subject – What's it got to do with me? In Balderstone, D (ed) *Secondary Geography Handbook*. Sheffield: Geographical Association

Roberts, M. (2006) Geographical Enquiry. In Balderstone, D. (ed) *Secondary Geography Handbook*. Sheffield: Geographical Association

Scoffham, S. (2004) Young Geographers In Scoffham, S. (ed) *Primary Geography Handbook*. Sheffield: Geographical Association

Taylor, S. (1998) Progression and Gender Differences in Mapwork. In Scoffham, S. (ed) *Primary Sources, Research Findings in Primary Geography*. Sheffield: Geographical Association

According to this, there's about 3½ women in the whole of British History.

Would that be with or without Boadicea?

..with

# History

*Kate Moorse and Hilary Claire*

History can play a major role in the development of young people's identities and the ways in which they perceive and understand the world. By providing young people with the knowledge and skills to comprehend the forces that have shaped their world, they can be equipped to reflect and consider how attitudes and experiences have, or might need to, change. Thus through history, one can explicitly address 'isms' like sexism, racism, and classism, since interpretation and making statements about your own and the sources' perspective is built into the methodology of history.

In content terms, gender appears within the 'knowledge and understanding' or 'breadth of study' sections of the history curriculum and follows through into GCSE and AS/A level examinations via the subject and assessment criteria. However, the national curriculum and subject specifications constitute only the core entitlement for young people, and schools are at liberty – even encouraged – to enhance and tailor the curriculum to suit their pupils and the priorities of their community.

This schedule highlights opportunities for gender related work at each key stage, then presents issues to consider when teaching history to any age group, under the themes of curriculum organisation, content, historical enquiry, pedagogy, and resources

## The early years (3 to 7)
The focus for very young children in history is to develop the language and concepts relating to the past and time passing, and to lay the foundations for future learning within the humanities. Investigations and discussions involving questioning and critical thinking establish an active mode of learning. In

engaging with the past, children become familiar with the concept of evidence through encountering a range of source types, especially artefacts, photos, film and other visual material, stories and picture books and oral testimony. In thinking about how the past is different from or similar to the present, young children will encounter issues of gender amongst others. Developing a culture of probing such matters will set up expectations that they warrant attention, as well as establishing a basis for tackling increasingly complex ideas in the later key stages.

The breadth of study for key stage1 (in England 5 to 7 years) facilitates a gender-inclusive approach through the requirements to teach about the child's family and community in the local and wider world, significant events and the lives of significant people. As part of work for Women's History Month (March), but also in their general schemes of work, they might focus on grandmothers, sisters and aunts, and not just significant females much further afield.

Choices for 'significant people' can focus on women's and men's efforts to challenge stereotypes, restrictive conventions and injustice. For example, children can learn about Harriet Tubman, Rosa Parks, Sojourner Truth, Marie Curie, Indira Gandhi, Rosa Luxembourg, Amy Johnson, Bessie Coleman, the Pankhurst women and many others who challenged the attitudes of their day about what women could do. When children learn about a significant event, for example Remembrance Day, they can consider the role of women as well as men, and members of the Commonwealth countries in the two world wars.

## The upper primary years (7 to 11)
In England, the key stage 2 curriculum is expressed as a series of study units. Under *knowledge and*

*understanding*, pupils should be taught 'about characteristic features of the periods and societies studied, including the ideas, beliefs, attitudes and experiences of men, women and children in the past and about the social, cultural, religious and ethnic diversity of the societies studied in Britain and the wider world'. This is reinforced within the descriptions of the local, world and most of the British study units. It follows that boys and girls should continue to gain experience of men's and women's lives, and to understand that history is about *all* people. It is vital in primary school to consider gender, class and ethnicity in choice of content and approach, since these are the years in which children's attitudes and views are formed.

*Excellence and Enjoyment* (2003) encourages primary schools to take greater ownership of the curriculum and to become increasingly innovative and creative; teachers are encouraged to devise and teach their own schemes of work and, where the QCA scheme of work is used as a basis, teachers may wish to customise the units exemplified. These might have a specific focus on the lives of girls and women in the past. For example, in Unit 11a, in addition to learning about the gendered conventions about work, education and home life in the Victorian period, children can learn about feminists in the Victorian period who challenged these conventions.

### The secondary curriculum (11 to 19)

The 11 to 14 curriculum (key stage 3) will be organised around key concepts and key processes, with a set of criteria determining the selection of content. Whilst 'diversity' has the most explicit mention of gender ('understanding the diverse experiences and the range of ideas, beliefs and attitudes of men, women and children in past societies, and how these have shaped the world'), chronology, change and continuity, causation, significance and interpretations, all give rise to both a gender dimension and opportunities to dig deep into the social and gendered construction of the historical record. There is synergy between key stage 3, GCSE and A level, and gender informs the curriculum at each stage.

As with all subject areas, it is also important to consider the learning environment and children's preferred learning styles and groupings. This will be particularly pertinent if gender is explicitly addressed in the history content, as some children may feel silenced, patronised or derogated for

unconventional views. A complete swap of gender roles can be a useful way to deal with lack of empathy for unfamiliar experience, and single-sex groups considering certain issues can also allow franker expression of opinions.

### *Issues to consider*
### Curriculum organisation

■ What is the level of understanding and knowledge about gender and history within the department/school, particularly of women's history/histories and its relationship to ethnicity and social class? What training or staff development can be provided to raise levels of awareness?

■ To what extent does the development of historical understanding appear to differ according to gender? How often do you, as a team of teachers, discuss your perceptions – and act on them?

■ How do you conceive or think about your history scheme of work? Do you have a rationale for the key stage? – for the year? – for the term?

■ How do you select the content and contexts to study? Have you considered what has the greatest potential for addressing gender issues?

■ Is gender explicit within the curriculum plans? In terms of content and historical method? How is it expressed?

■ What is the balance in terms of scale: local, regional, national, international? – bearing in mind that retrieving lost histories and sources through local and regional contexts often provides rich opportunities for exploring gender issues

■ Do you use the opportunity provided by Women's History Week or Month (March) to show-case work on gender undertaken throughout the year? Has the school thought about how such opportunities might be used?

### Content

■ When women's history is planned for, have you considered whether it should be taught through the lives of famous women or the experiences of groups of women? What role might each of these play? What should the balance be?

■ What opportunities are there to study women's history or the history of specific groups, for example, minority ethnic communities in British history studies?

■ Do you make good use of oral, family, local and social history in which women and minority groups can be more easily recovered from the past and/or more fairly represented in the present or recent past?

■ What opportunities are there to study aspects of mainstream topics, mainly or exclusively through sources relating to women or from a female perspective?

■ Is there a balance in terms of topic choice and emphasis in terms of the matters which may be of interest to either sex within a teaching group or relate to the experiences of other specific groupings within the class?

■ Do you monitor, as a matter of course, girls' and boys' responses to the content you and they select? Do pupils participate in collaborative reflection over what they study?

■ To what extent does your choice of content lend itself to a positive approach and counter stereo-typing? Is there a sufficiently varied and complex range of sources which will allow a genuine and thorough enquiry and resist a simplistic and schematic treatment?

## Historical enquiry

■ What range of sources do our pupils encounter? How do pupils work with sources? Are there opportunities to work both in a sustained way and with substantial or detailed sources which allow questions and reflections on gender issues to follow?

■ When pupils are engaged in historical enquiry, and especially when engaging with historical sources, are they noticing the presence – or absence – of females? Are they asking about what is missing or biased? Are they encouraged to identify further questions that they wish to ask or would like answers to?

■ Are pupils evaluating the sources they use, or have presented to them, especially where they are selected by others – the publishers, authors or you?

■ Do you actively seek out sources which reflect the lives and experiences of women from other cultures?

■ Have you considered what questions might be asked of those sources?

■ Will they differ from those you might ask of British or European sources? If so, how? Why?

■ What implications could this have for your usual practice?

■ How has the historical record been constructed? How were those decisions made?

■ How is historical significance understood? How do pupils come to appreciate how this affects women and minority groups, and how they are represented in history?

■ How has the writing of history changed over the years and at different periods? What factors have contributed to the change?

■ Do you raise questions about distortion, omission or emphasis?

## Pedagogy

■ In setting about historical enquiries, do pupils work in a variety of groups? Do they sometimes work in single-sex groups? When in a mixed group, do they take on a variety of roles?

■ In work which the pupils initiate themselves, how do you make sure that women are not ignored?

■ Do you find ways of helping each sex to develop those skills and abilities which research shows are generally impeded? For example:

　□ for girls – opportunities for extended oral work to develop conceptual frameworks through discussion?

　□ for boys – opportunities to empathise with people of different time and place, especially women or girls? In developing the ability to empathise, girls have historically been expected frequently to identify with male, and white, historical figures. How often does either sex empathise with the opposite sex? What about a figure from another cultural context?

## Resources

■ In primary and lower secondary phases, topics will often be introduced through storybooks and/or historical fiction. Does the library/classroom collection carry a range of such books with girls or women as central characters?

■ Do stories, books, posters and other sources selected to explore and display the past and people living in the past show girls and boys and men and women in both conventional and non-conventional contexts, and activities?

■ What is the balance of representation of both males and females in the sources you provide? Where representation is conventional for the time, do you discuss how things have changed over time or, if not, how they might change? Do you ensure that over time, visitors who give oral testimony provide a balance of males and females and ethnicities?

■ Do you include historical photos and other pictorial material showing people and events from other places in the world? How do you introduce these to the children? How might you use the opportunities they provide?

■ Do girls and boys both experience wearing – or are they encouraged to imagine wearing – the clothes from another time and reflect on similarities or differences especially where gender is concerned, for example thinking about riding an early bicycle clothed as a man, as a woman?

■ When working with artefacts, for example when studying the Victorians or the 20th century do you use the opportunity to explore gendered roles and to compare these with pupils' experiences today?

■ Do you try to give pupils sources which contain alternative or non-conventional role models, especially in photos and other visual sources?

■ Do you make use of alternative sources such as literature, art, theatre, film?

■ Do you ask pupils to look at the language of sources – both primary and secondary, and then to place it in its historical/social context?

■ How do new and different questions of sources challenge the orthodoxy of history?

■ Do you, with pupils, regularly assess books, websites and other sources for sexism, racism or bias more generally?

■ Do you have a range of primary and secondary sources to present alongside a textbook to demonstrate errors in fact and/omission? And to select from, to supplement existing material?

■ What strategies do you have for using books and other resources which present negative or biased images?

■ Are you and the librarian/library postholder aware of available resource lists/websites and regularly check for new publications, websites, developments, teaching materials?

■ Do you allocate preparation time specifically for seeking out resources and source material which may be found in less usual places or from alternative sources?

## In a boys' school

■ Is women's history seen as part of mainstream history and perceived as important as it might be in a mixed or all girls' school?

■ Has a policy decision been taken by the school or department as a whole, or is women's history seen as the female staff members' concern?

## References and further resources

Bellamy, L. and Moorse, K. (1996) *The Changing Role of Women.* London: John Murray

Bourdillon, H. (ed) (1994) *Teaching History.* London: Routledge and Open University

Claire, H. (1996) *Reclaiming Our Pasts: Equality and Diversity in the Primary History Curriculum.* Stoke-on-Trent: Trentham

Cooper, H. (2002) (2nd ed) *History in the Early Years.* London: RoutledgeFalmer

Early Modern History www.earlymodernweb.org.uk/emr/index.php/category/themes/gender/

Women's History: research guide www.womenshistory.about.com

# Information and Communication Technology (ICT)

*Pippa Totraku and Avril Loveless*

## The story of gender and ICT

There are relatively small differences between girls' and boys' performance in ICT at GCSE. Of the 14% of boys and 12% of girls who took ICT in 2006, 65% of the girls and 57% of the boys got grade C or above. A similar pattern is found in GNVQ at 16. However, by 18, the gender gap in numbers taking the subject has widened, and by the time young people reach the workplace, men are in the majority. Getting more women into ICT is an important challenge. It is not only an equal employment or opportunity issue. It is also an issue of how the world in which we live is designed, and for whom it is designed. It is important to ensure that women are involved throughout the processes and practices of shaping technological innovation (Wajcman, 2000).

Social scientists recognise that technological innovation is itself shaped by the social circumstances within which it takes place. Women's participation in the ICT industry is influenced by a number of factors. They are often alienated from joining the profession by the male culture of the working environment and of computers, where systems and artefacts are shaped in a masculine image. There are negative stereotypes about computer workers and a shortage of female role models. Unfortunately there is also a lack of accurate information about ICT careers. The issues are not about girls' or boys' ability in ICT, but about how choices are made, and what schools might do to lead to different patterns of engagement with the technology.

## How is the framework for ICT set out in the National Curriculum?

Teachers need an understanding of how ICT is set out in the National Curriculum in England and the knowledge, resources and resolve to address gender equity within the subject (Sanders, 2005a). The requirements of teachers are clearly identified in the National Curriculum for Information and Communication Technology, which:

> prepares pupils to participate in a rapidly changing world in which work and other activities are increasingly transformed by access to varied and developing technology. Pupils use ICT tools to find, explore, analyse, exchange and present information responsibly, creatively and with discrimination. They learn how to employ ICT to enable rapid access to ideas and experiences from a wide range of people, communities and cultures. Increased capability in the use of ICT promotes initiative and independent learning, with pupils being able to make informed judgments about when and where to use ICT to best effect, and to consider its implications for home and work both now and in the future. (DfEE, 1999:96)

The framework for the knowledge, skills, and understanding that children must develop are identified by the following distinctive, but not mutually exclusive, strands:

- finding things out
- developing ideas and making things happen
- exchanging and sharing information
- reviewing, modifying and evaluating work as it progresses.

These strands reflect how people normally work with ICT in the wider world and reflect a capability with

ICT. An ICT capable person is skilful in applying ICT both technically and cognitively to access, develop, create and communicate information appropriately.

### ICT in schools

Early in the 1980s, it was noted that it was nearly always the boys who took advantage of the opportunity to use computers. During the early 1990s teachers reported that girls were using computers more, but only in order to develop their secretarial skills. By the late 1990s girls were enthusiastic about computer multimedia and the internet, as they encompassed the traditional female interests of art and socialising. It was still mostly boys who enrolled in programming courses. At the end of the 1990s it was generally accepted that there was a computer gender gap and that this mattered.

While the primary curriculum can enable positive experiences for both girls and boys, the secondary ICT curriculum is not fully engaging young women and does little to encourage positive attitudes towards technology. The strategies we can use to address stereotypes within the subject of ICT can be grouped into two broad themes: attitudes and access.

### The attitudes to ICT of boys and girls

In general, boys and girls show equal ability in using computers but there is a definite gender difference in their attitudes. Relatively small at younger ages, the differences increase as they become older, because of the socialisation processes: the longer children are in school, the greater the gender difference becomes. Various researchers have noted the attitudes described in the box below:

### The stereotypes underpinning these attitudes

Assumptions about gender roles continue to limit girls' aspirations and achievements in computing. Children pick up and adopt notions of male and female roles and activities at an early age, and in some circumstances, some boys and some girls will behave in stereotypical ways when encountering ICT. Boys can act disruptively when engaged with computers and girls can take a passive role. However, not all young girls will be powerless and not all young boys will be powerful. Parents often reinforce gender stereotypes to computing by giving less encouragement and computer-related help to girls than to boys. Similarly, girls are less interested in computers if they think that their parents believe them to be more suitable for boys. In computer magazines, advertisements, the internet and movies, the media presents a computer culture in which enthusiasts are often portrayed as male social isolates or geeks. Children are highly susceptible to the influence of gender role models and many of these stereotypes are not models to which girls aspire.

### How can we counter these attitudes?

Although teachers and adults need to be explicit with pupils about gender bias, merely modelling

### Girls
- have a less positive attitude than boys towards computing
- believe it will be useless to them in their work or home life
- have an interest in computers related to its use as a tool to accomplish specific tasks in particular contexts
- regard technology as a means to an end
- prefer activities that involve online collaboration, connectedness and interaction
- have negative attitudes which diminish with age as their sense of computers' value and usefulness increases
- become less confident in their computer skills the more experienced with computers they become

### Boys
- think about computers differently to girls
- have alternative motivations for using them
- see technology as having intrinsic value
- are attracted to computers by a sense of enjoyment, mastery and accomplishment
- show a preference for action-oriented software
- by as young as 4, consider computers to be more important to them than to girls
- recognise links to possible future careers
- gain a sense of active enjoyment and fascination from using computers
- feel more positive about computers

exemplary behaviour is seldom enough to counteract the pupils' sexist notions. If teachers seem anxious and uneasy with technology or appear incapable, there is a chance that they will pass these attitudes or behaviours on to the pupils in their class. Sanders (2005a) suggests several steps a school might take, including in-service training, to raise the awareness of adults and teachers to gender equity issues. She recommends staff development that emphasises no personal blame for universally learned gender stereotypes as likely to work to improve teachers' gender-related behaviour.

## How do boys and girls access ICT?

Teachers enable pupils to have access to the ICT curriculum through the physical organisation of resources and the pedagogical organisation of group work. Each school will design different models of access to ICT: ICT suites, local area networks, mini-suites in classrooms and portables. The key issue is how pupils are able to work at the computer in ways that are sensitive to the interests of both sexes.

### What do we need to consider when choosing resources?

It is important to have a critically informed approach to selecting resources such as software, and awareness of the role marketing might play in the construction of gender stereotypes. The themes of football, motor racing, skateboarding or other predominately male orientated interests typically appear in many educational software programs. Software which features sports, war, or competition is less likely to encourage girls to participate. It is not the computer or software that is at the root of the sex bias, but the expectations and stereotypes of the software designers. Computer games advertised for children predominantly target a male audience. This is significant, since the first experience most young children have of using computers is of playing games. Boys tend to start doing this at a younger age and for long periods of time, and persist with gaming as they get older; girls tend not to follow these patterns. The games industry is beginning to address the issue of gender bias. Computer consoles and games are becoming as popular with girls as with boys, and have titles which appeal to both sexes. Games for girls represent an important growth area in the market, so there is a push to promote software that appeals to feminine interests, such as the Barbie Fashion Designer game. However, this is still a case of ICT being used to perpetuate gender stereotypes.

### What do we need to consider when organising group work?

Boys and girls may work differently in different groupings and this has implications for the organisation of access to the ICT curriculum. Group work plays an important role in pupils' social, linguistic and cognitive development. There are social advantages to collaborative work, but there are also underlying gender issues. Through working together at the computer, children learn to deal with each other, cope in social situations, sort out conflicts and make friends. However, boys can often dominate in groups and prefer to work individually, whereas girls tend to be more collaborative in their interactions with each other and with the computer task. Group composition can also change the quality of talk in the group and the extent to which individuals are genuinely involved in discussions and decision-making. Students who work collaboratively tend to have better language and communication skills than those who consistently work individually. Computers can provide a focal point for debate and reference, and can support the development of ideas and higher order thinking (Wegerif and Dawes, 2004).

### Do we need to challenge the current curriculum?

Curriculum improvement will need to reflect two principles: counteracting the perpetuation of gender stereotypes, and making pupils' experiences relevant to real world concerns. A curriculum that bases change on commonly accepted gender differences can perpetuate stereotypes. It is important to have a flexible curriculum to accommodate people's diverse paths to technology. If we adopt different curricular approaches and teaching methods to appeal to diverse learning styles, we might also address gender differences. Some schools have created taster courses to attract more girls and extracurricular intervention projects for girls only, which focus on wider experiences than current course work. An emphasis on problem-solving as opposed to basic skills and programming might also be more appealing to girls. A curriculum in which computing and technology in general are seen as tools for solving humanity's problems and enriching humanity's experiences should also promote gender equity: it will be relevant to real-world concerns, embedded in human and social contexts, and make real life connections. Many teachers are using this approach both in the discrete ICT curriculum and the use of ICT in other subjects. But there is still room for development in understanding and practice.

### Issues to consider
### What questions do schools need to ask to ensure gender equity in ICT?
### Access

■ Are measures in place to ensure equal access for boys and girls? What steps are being taken to increase their comfort and confidence in using computers?

■ What types of extra curricular ICT courses are offered? Do any specifically address either girls' or boys' interests? (for example, 'Computer Clubs for Girls' www.cc4g.net)

■ Do you monitor uptake of optional or extra curricular ICT courses by gender?

■ What steps do you take if you find either girls or boys are under-represented?

### Software and activities

■ Is computer software monitored for gender bias and for whether it promotes stereotypes?

### Role models

■ Are there enough trained women teachers to motivate and mentor girls' use of computers in the classroom?

■ Are images presented of computer workers which are gender-neutral or gender-inclusive?

### Training and teachers

■ Are teachers aware of gender equity issues in regard to ICT?

■ Do teachers make a conscious effort to treat girls and boys equally when using technology?

■ How are pupils grouped or organised for work with technology?

■ What types of activities are pupils asked to do with technology (for example problem solving)?

■ Is planning checked to ensure that there are opportunities for hands-on activities that look at the benefits of ICT to the human race?

### Some useful websites
This is where you will find help to address the issues discussed.

www.josanders.com

Jo Sanders has published over 50 books and articles on gender equity and given three international lecture tours. Resources available on the site include: books to order or download, web links for more information and guidance on how to ensure equity in the IT classroom. The website includes materials for planning audits and strategies for gender inclusion.

www.cc4g.net/partners.aspx

'Computer Clubs for Girls' (CC4G) is funded by the DfES and supported by Naace, Becta, and The Specialist Schools and Academies Trust. The project aims to:

■ combat the negative misconceptions about the nature of IT jobs formed during – or before – early teenage years

■ use motivational opportunities within CC4G to bring professional and technical skills to girls

■ develop skills that are embedded within fun educational activities based on girls' interests – music, celebrity, media and fashion, to name a few

■ provide an opportunity that is recognised by industry as developing skills that will be valued by employers, recognised by teachers as making a direct contribution to the capability of pupils, and enhancing delivery of the school curricula

www.teem.org.uk

The TEEM site offers an easy-to-use software directory for teachers and adults to find relevant titles quickly. Evaluations of all titles listed can also be read. There is a section on helping teachers to get the best from their hardware and advice on buying new equipment.

### References
Cook, D. and Finlayson, H. (1999) *Interactive Children, Communicative Teaching*. Buckingham: Open University Press.

DfEE (1999) *The National Curriculum*. London: DfEE and QCA

Faulkner, W. (2003) *Teaching the Teachers: a Gender Blind Approach to IT Training*. Available at http://www.rcss.ed.ac.uk/sigis/ Accessed 25nd August 2006

Huyer, S. (2003) *Gender, ICT and Education*. Available at http://www.wigsat.org/engenderedICT.pdf

McFarlane, A. (ed) (1997) *Information Technology and Authentic Learning: Realising the Potential of Computers in the Primary Classroom*. London: Routledge

O'Hara, M. (2004) *ICT in the Early Years*. London: Continuum

Sanders, J. (2005a) *Crossing Cultures, Changing Lives: Integrating Research on Girls' Choices of IT careers*. Available at www.josanders.com/pdf/Oxford.pdf Accessed 27th August 2006

Sanders, J. (2005b) *Gender and Technology: A Research Review*. Available at www.josanders.com/resources Accessed 27th August 2006

Schofield, J. (1995) *Computers and Classroom Culture*. Cambridge: Cambridge University Press

Wajcman, J. (2000) 'Reflections on gender and technology studies': in what state is the art? *Social Studies of Science*, 30(3) p 447-464

Wegerif, R. and Dawes, L. (2004) *Thinking and Learning with ICT: Raising Achievement in Primary Schools*. London: RoutledgeFalmer

# Mathematics and Numeracy

*Tamara Bibby, Pat Drake, Heather Mendick and Hilary Povey*

## Introduction

Since 1994, the gender gap in maths at all stages to GCSE has become negligible, with girls pulling slightly ahead of boys. Maths is boys' most popular A level, while for girls it is the sixth most popular (2006 figures), but girls get slightly more of the top grades than boys. In international comparisons, England is one of the minority of countries where there is no statistical gender difference in overall school maths scores (PISA, 2000).

Girls no longer under-perform in maths in the way they once did, but when it becomes voluntary their active participation remains low. This is despite our knowing that most university students need to continue with maths in some form as part of their studies, and that mathematical proficiency is part of most vocational skills. People who have maths skills have better life chances than those who do not.

Internationally, girls report much less interest in and enjoyment of mathematics, lower self-related beliefs and much higher levels of helplessness and stress in mathematics classes in spite of the small differences in performance between the sexes. That is why it is so important to scrutinise what happens in maths classrooms and to be aware of the mathematical experience of every young person. For a subject believed to be more calmly rational and logical than others, maths can summon up the most powerful emotions, in teachers as well as pupils. This schedule is concerned with the social and psychological elements of learning in maths, because it is these which currently act as barriers to engagement with maths beyond school.

Pupils can often talk fluently about their experiences of learning in practical subjects and subjects they can relax in. However, such conversations tend not to happen about maths. It is useful to consider *why* we so seldom have those discussions in maths and whether we could. What might happen? The activities presented in the following sections are designed to help you, and your classes, to think about the intended and unintended effects that words and actions can have. Hopefully they will enable you to make maths lessons more enjoyable and engaging for everyone – including yourself.

### Issues to consider

*The activities here are intended to be accessible to pupils of all ages and teachers in all phases – please feel free to adapt them to suit the needs of particular groups. Many can be used as mathematical activities.*

### What is maths?

It's the language of nature, or about structure and pattern, or something you either can or cannot do.... There are so many stories about what maths is and these stories often have different implications for girls and boys, for learners from different social class backgrounds, or from different ethnic groups. They contain important clues about beliefs and anxieties that affect learning.

*What do you and your learners think maths is? Ask a class to draw spider diagrams mapping all their ideas and associations about maths, and analyse them*

- What surprises you? Why? What does not surprise you? Why?
- What are the similarities and differences between girls' views and boys'?
- What are the differences between the views of learners from different ethnic groups?

- Do the spider diagrams relate maths to any other school subjects or any out-of-school activities?
- Are any of these gendered – ie associated mainly with masculinity or femininity – or mainly with boys or girls from particular ethnic or social class backgrounds?

How can you use the findings to connect maths to pupils' positive beliefs about it, and to explore their negative ones?

## What are mathematicians like?

Maths is often seen as distant from human activity. This can make many learners, particularly girls and women, find it difficult to relate to. What would an audit of maths resources reveal about the gender, ethnicity, background of any mathematicians actually named? What possibilities are there for learners to relate to them?

*Ask your students to imagine a mathematician. Get them to write a description or draw a picture. Use some of the questions below as prompts. Discuss with the class their descriptions and pictures.*

- What sort of people have they imagined? Are their mathematicians alive or dead? Old or young? Male or female? What is their ethnic background? What part of the world do they come from?
- What were their mathematicians like when they were at school?
- Do their mathematicians have children? What sort of houses do they live in? What jobs do they do? Would you and would they like to meet them?
- Are there patterns in the responses from the class? How do they account for what they have produced?
- How can you open up the idea of being a mathematician to a wider variety of people?

(See the suggested reading section for material about real mathematicians and ideas on how to use mathematicians' stories in the classroom.)

## How is maths taught?

How we teach maths can have enormous effects on the *hidden curriculum* as experienced by learners in our classrooms. The arrangement of space, the teaching methods used, how you assess and give feedback, the interactions between you and the learners and between the learners themselves, the expectations you have, will all give out strong messages to the girls and boys you teach. The next two activities address the way teachers' actions can directly improve pupils' feelings about themselves as learners of maths.

*Audit the range of learning activities you use, and observe which pupils respond well and which respond badly to each type of activity.*

- What patterns do you notice in your teaching?
- Are there patterns in the ways learners responded? Are the patterns gender related? Are some types of activity better suited to high attainers than others?
- How do learners from different ethnic and social class backgrounds respond?
- Does the way your space is organised suit some of these ways of working better than others?

Adjusting the balance of activities can increase enjoyments levels and feelings of mastery, with powerful long term effects for pupils.

*Audit your feedback to learners. For each person in the class, note the types of comments you make and the amount of feedback you give each individual, whether it is concerned with the maths or with how the maths is presented, if you use praise or criticism or both. Ask a colleague to observe your interaction in lessons.*

- Are there patterns in who receives the most feedback?
- Is your feedback different for girls and boys?
- How do your expectations of the learners colour your comments?
- Which comments take you longest to produce?
- Are some comments better than others in helping learners to progress? Are there patterns in this?
- Are there particular girls and boys who seem to have been invisible?
- Do some types of learners seem to seek to hide from or to escape your attention?

Assessment for learning that values the learner while giving clear guidance for improvement is particularly important in maths, because of the negative beliefs so many maths learners have. Small adjustments in assessment styles can make a big difference.

## Who are the teachers of maths?

What and how pupils learn are bound up, not just with the activities we deliberately present to them, but also with the relationships in the class; relationships between adults and individuals and groups, as well as relationships amongst the pupils. The messages associated with how we communicate – consciously and unconsciously – through our words, actions, tone of voice, demeanour and so forth, are all studied with great attention by those we teach. In other words, when we think we are teaching maths, we will also be teaching about appropriate things to do and say in maths lessons and appropriate ways of relating to maths as a subject. Primary and non-specialist maths teachers in particular can transmit their own anxieties about the subject without realising.

## Who are the learners of maths?

In any maths class, the learners are significantly different from each other. Each brings into the classroom different hopes and fears, different attitudes, values and expectations – and a very different sense of self. How the pupils are grouped, in sets or streams or all attainment classes, has a significant effect on this – and the experience of setting often affects boys and girls differently. In trying to meet each learner's needs, you will want to consider what they think about themselves in the maths class and what they think is the point of it all.

*What do your learners think of themselves in maths lessons? The questionnaire below will reveal attitudes and confidence levels*

* I prefer to work on my own
* You have to be brainy to do well in maths
* I enjoy working with friends
* I usually understand a new idea in maths quickly
* If I do well in maths it's usually because I work hard
* Boys generally do not like it if girls beat them at maths
* Knowing maths will help me get a job
* I always feel nervous when I look at a maths problem
* I'm lucky when I do well on a maths test

* I do not see the point of the maths we do
* My last maths teacher thought I was useless
* If I do well in maths it's because I have a good teacher
* If I do well in maths some people make fun of me
* I cannot understand how anyone can like maths
* My last maths teacher enjoyed teaching me
* If I do well in maths it's usually because the work is easy

■ Are there patterns in the responses? Are any of these patterns gendered?

■ Do any of them relate to levels of attainment? If your pupils are grouped by attainment, how does this appear to affect their response?

■ Did the responses of any individuals surprise you? If so, which of your assumptions about the individual were challenged?

■ What could you do to challenge any negative beliefs revealed?

## Why learn maths?

Many pupils find it difficult to see the point of learning maths. A survey of their reasons for doing it or not would give more material to use in efforts to improve their engagement. Many young people have little appreciation of the importance of maths in occupational areas they see as social – for example, the travel industry, or many parts of health and social care. Widening understanding about its applications can help increase motivation. Addressing learners' self belief, motivation and interest in maths does much to increase their chances of staying engaged with it beyond 16.

## Authors' note

Although this schedule is called 'Mathematics and Numeracy', we have reservations about the term numeracy. We think perhaps that the re-labelling of primary school mathematical activity by the UK government as numeracy is problematic from gender and class perspectives and we wonder how long it will be before we have mathematics for the middle-class boys and numeracy (or even functional mathematics) for the rest.

## References and further resources

Alic, M. (1986) *Hypatia's Heritage: a History of Women in Science from Antiquity to the Late Nineteenth Century.* London: The Women's Press

Bibby, T. (1997) *Developing Mental Maths with 9-11 Year Olds.* Leamington: Scholastic

Boaler, J. (1997) *Experiencing School Mathematics: Teaching Styles, Sex and Setting.* Buckingham: Open University Press (Revised and expanded edition (2002) Mahwah, NJ: Lawrence Erlbaum Assoc.

Burton, L. (ed) (1986) *Girls into Maths Can Go.* London: Cassell

Burton, L. (ed) (1990) *Gender and Mathematics: An International Perspective.* London: Cassell

Burton, L.(2004) *Mathematicians as Enquirers: Learning about Learning Mathematics.* Dordrecht: Kluwer Academic Publishers

Buxton, L. (1981) *Do You Panic About Maths? Coping With Maths Anxiety.* London: Heinemann

Greenwald, S. (2006) *Incorporating the Mathematical Achievements of Women and Minority Mathematicians into Classrooms.* Available from: http://www.mathsci.appstate.edu/~sjg/history/womenrecenthistory2.pdf

Harris, M. (1997) *Common Threads: Women, Mathematics and Work.* Stoke-on-Trent: Trentham

Kaiser, G. and Rogers, P. (eds) (1995) *Equity in Mathematics Education: Influences of Feminism and Culture.* London: Falmer

Mendick, H. (2006) *Masculinities in Mathematics.* Maidenhead: Open University Press

Paechter, C. (2001) Gender, reason and emotion in secondary mathematics classrooms. In Gates, P. (ed) *Issues in Mathematics Teaching.* London: RoutledgeFalmer

Perl, T. (1993) *Women and Numbers: Lives of Women Mathematicians Plus Discovery Activities.* San Carlos, California: World Wide Publishing

PISA (Programme for International Student Assessment) (2000) reported by OECD (2001). Paris: OECD

Povey, H. (1998) That spark from heaven or 'of the earth': girls and boys learning mathematics. In Clark, A. and Millard, E. (eds) *Gender in the Secondary Curriculum: Balancing the books.* London: Routledge

Tobias, S. (1978) *Overcoming Math Anxiety.* New York: W. W. Norton and Company

Walkerdine, V. (1998) (2nd ed) *Counting Girls Out.* London: Falmer

# Modern Foreign Languages

*Vee Harris*

## Introduction: looking at the research

Powell (1986) revealed that girls' attainment level and motivation in modern foreign languages (MFL) was significantly greater than boys'. This is true also in other countries (Carr and Pauwels, 2005). The Nuffield Languages Inquiry (2000) notes that boys achieve far less well than girls. The gender gap is greater in languages than in most other subjects. The table below (Ofsted, 2004) indicates the discrepancy in 2003:

|  | Boys | Girls |
|---|---|---|
| Number of pupils entered for MFL GCSE | 128,962 | 140,305 |
| Average points score French | 3.8 | 4.6 |
| Average points score German | 4.2 | 4.7 |
| Average points score Spanish | 3.9 | 4.7 |

The situation has been exacerbated now that pupils in England are again allowed to opt out of MFL post-14. Powell's study, conducted at a time when MFL was an option, found that while 62% of the pupils choosing to continue were girls, only 38% were boys. Davies (2004) notes that even before the statutory implementation in England of the 2003 Education Act, 6% of girls had given up French at the end of key stage 3, compared to 26% of boys. Studies of teenage boys in Australia (Carr and Pauwels, 2005) and in Canada (Kissau, 2006) reveal a similar level of disenchantment. Both studies conclude that societal perceptions of what is appropriate for males lie at the root of the differences.

It seems probable, furthermore, that the pupils most likely to opt out of languages are from the more socially disadvantaged schools. The majority of schools planning to abandon compulsory language lessons are in inner-city areas, raising fears that learning a foreign language will become an elitist activity, confined to middle class schools (Chitty, 2002). The proportion of maintained schools with languages as a compulsory element had dropped from one third in 2004 to one quarter in 2005, with schools in the lowest quintile of educational achievement least likely to offer languages (7%), while schools in the highest quintile were most likely to do so (63%) (CILT, 2005). It is not yet clear whether the advent of MFL in primary schools will redress or further aggravate the problem.

The situation is not unique to Britain. The issue of the macho culture in languages is revisited at the end of this schedule.

## Keeping a sense of proportion

Some boys continue to make excellent progress, particularly later in their educational career, and we should be wary of stereotyping all boys as failing in this area. We need to avoid devoting all our attention to making the subject more appealing to boys and in the process marginalising the girls, especially if this means encouraging masculinities that are socially damaging. Perceptions that girls' behaviour in the MFL classroom is generally less disruptive than their male peers can mask that they have mentally switched off. The generally tidier presentation of their work can hide very real difficulties they are having in coming to grips with a new language. Finally, an underpinning principle of good equal opportunities practice in MFL, as in other subjects, is that it meets the needs of both boys and girls, favouring neither.

## Whole-school or departmental strategies – what's your policy?

### Choice of languages

It is worth reviewing the choice of languages on offer. Some language colleges are responding to the vocational dimension of language learning and the new markets, by offering Arabic and Mandarin Chinese. Community languages offer another opportunity for real contexts for language learning, particularly in schools with high numbers of bilingual pupils. Williams *et al* (2002) indicate that boys are more motivated to learn German than French, regarding French as 'the language of love and stuff' – such stereotypical notions surrounding languages are unhelpful and need to be challenged.

### Single-sex classes

Barton (2002a) found that the evidence for single-sex classes is inconclusive. On the one hand, all-boy classes can result in a deterioration of discipline. On the other, it can lead to raised achievement for both boys and girls. She notes that it is the teacher's engagement with their pupils that determines the effectiveness of such classes. It is important however to ensure that girls are not used to civilise boys' behaviour.

### Setting

Clark (1998) examines the impact of setting within modern languages and offers different options for tackling the all too familiar problem of the preponderance of girls in top sets, while bottom sets are full of demotivated boys.

### Vocational courses

Pupils find vocational courses, such as the Certificate of Business Language Competence, more relevant and motivating than the usual GCSE diet (CILT, 2005). Boys and girls often find it difficult to relate MFL to their future careers, and this may, in particular, be the case for pupils from less privileged backgrounds. Inviting speakers from local businesses to make the vocational links explicit can be particularly effective. (Visit www.nepbn.org for details of English companies who will sponsor schools through a range of activities. Further information is available at www.languageswork.org.uk.)

### Teaching methods

Two particular areas of pedagogy are helpful in relation to gender and MFL. The first returns us to the principles of meaningful activities and a real audience inherent in Communicative Language Teaching. The second relates to perhaps the other side of the coin: initiatives to develop the more conscious, analytic and reflective side of language learning.

## How can we make the content of the MFL curriculum more meaningful for girls and boys?

Many pupils find MFL tourist-type topics boring. Although the growth of content and integrated learning (CLIL) is a promising development (see Grenfell, 2002), even regular classroom activities can become more meaningful on an immediate level with a slightly different slant. GCSE topics such as 'Personal Information' and 'House and Home', assumed to be of less interest to boys, need to be handled with particular care to avoid both sexes becoming trapped within gender roles.

■ Pupils can ask and answer questions about age, hobbies etc in the style of a particular type of film, or in line with the personality of two well-known characters drawn from soap operas, celebrities, or in the context of a particular situation (doctor and patient, police officer and lost child etc). Other pupils then have to guess from the performance what was written on their class-mates' cue cards.

■ Adams (1998) provides a range of interesting alternatives to writing the inevitable letter to an imaginary pen pal. For example, whilst using similar vocabulary and structures, describing a ghost house may have more appeal.

■ 'Who does what in the home?' can be used both as a context for learning the vocabulary of household tasks and for challenging gender stereotypes (see Harris 1992 for further suggestions). As always, we need to be alert to the images in our teaching materials.

■ Cultural awareness is often marginalised or trivialised in textbooks, reduced to a few photos of public buildings or regional landscapes, for example. Although girls express a greater desire than boys to identify with speakers of a foreign language (Williams *et al*, 2002), Barton (2002b) found that underachieving boys are also curious about cultural background information. Whilst it would be foolish to ignore opportunities like the World Cup, we should be aware of the danger of reinforcing stereotypes. Jones (1995) offers a wealth of alternative ways in which cultural awareness can be developed, and Brown and

Brown (1996) show how discovering about other life styles, for example in the francophone countries of Africa, may make language classes more interesting. Project work using the new technologies to give on line access to such real contexts can allow pupils to research and present House and Homes or Daily Routines in a way that both increases motivation and fosters independence.

■ Self-confidence in oral work is an issue for both boys and girls. Some girls' over-anxiety about grammatical accuracy can inhibit them from participating. Younger boys are often risk-takers, but as they approach adolescence, they may become less and less willing to make fools of themselves in public. Spontaneity can be built up gradually through short bursts of pair work and exploiting everyday classroom routines. This provides pupils with the confidence and skills needed to engage in more extended and real world problem-solving tasks, such as allocating families to homes in a new block of flats according to their size, daily routines, disabilities etc (Harris *et al*, 2001).

## How can we make MFL activities more thought provoking?

No child relishes the thought of spending hours just listening, repeating and being called upon to answer questions to which the answer is already known. (Powell, 1986:62)

Boys' comments appear to reflect a general concern about the lack of independence and of opportunities for thinking things out:

Maths, physics and that focus on you having to work things out for yourselves... in French, there's nothing you have to work out, the only thing you have to work out is to put words together to make a phrase. (Harris, 2002)

A number of initiatives such as the key stage 3 framework for modern foreign languages (2003) invite us to pay greater attention to developing pupils' ability to analyse, reason and reflect on their learning.

■ In boys' opinion, a good MFL lesson is one in which the teacher shares with the pupils the reason for the activities s/he organises (Jones and Jones, 2001). This is not simply a matter of stating the lesson objectives, but of explaining how choral repetition or pair work is going to contribute to reaching them.

■ Assessment for learning emphasises sharing assessment criteria with pupils, and Barnes and Hunt (2003) offer practical examples of pupil-friendly level descriptors and constructive target setting on pupils' work. Clearly stated assessment criteria and meaningful outcomes help boys to take oral work seriously and not view it as an opportunity to muck about

■ The peer and self-review encouraged by assessment for learning is part and parcel of understanding, and then applying the criteria. Pupils are also likely to pay greater attention to their work if there is a real audience

■ A focus on thinking skills can render even mundane topics more interesting. Encouraging pupils to categorise vocabulary according to likes/dislikes or to 'find the odd word out' can make it more challenging. In the latter case, it can also increase grammatical awareness, as 'reasons' can include gender, tense, or accents. (See Lin and Mackay (2004) for imaginative photocopiable materials to develop categorising, sequencing, and creative thinking skills. Jackson *et al* (2004) also focus on thinking skills, concentrating on useful starters)

■ Macaro and Erler's work (2005) suggests that pupils may struggle with the relationship between the written and the spoken form, particularly in French. The pronunciation of words ending in 'eau' or 'ent' for example may be confusing. Encouraging pupils to deduce the new spelling rules may be important in addressing many boys' perception that MFL is a hard subject.

Understanding how to go about their learning may be particularly important for low attainers. Studies (Macaro, 2001; Grenfell and Harris, 1999), suggest that they have a narrower range of learning strategies and use them less frequently than their more successful peers. Macaro (2001) and Harris and Snow (1999) outline how the strategies involved in each of the skill areas can be taught. Turner (1995) suggests that we tend to test listening skills rather than teach them and suggests ways of explicitly teaching the strategies involved.

Teaching pupils these strategies gives them greater control over their own learning and might challenge under-achieving boys' notion that their lack of success is due to fixed causes, since they all too readily attribute it either to the task – 'it's boring, a waste of time' – or inherent factors – 'I'm no good at

French'. Second, it makes it more possible for all pupils to work independently.

It is not enough to offer pupils greater independence in their learning; they need the tools or strategies that will enable them to understand how to go about it. Even though boys report enjoying group work, the socialisation process is likely to have developed their competitive rather than collaborative skills. Barton (2002b) reports that one boy stated 'If we're in groups everyone just tends to just cheat' and she notes that girls appeared more confident that they were able to work effectively in groups. A number of recent studies suggest that we should capitalise on boys' enjoyment of competitive games. Whilst this might prove effective in the short term, if the macho culture is to be challenged and boys enabled to work collaboratively, then we need to devote more time to making explicit exactly what is involved here. Pupils can be encouraged to draw up their own ground rules for working in groups, and teachers can recognise and validate pupils' collaborative skills (Harris, 1992).

## Conclusion

As in other subject areas, there is a risk that the under-achievement of boys in MFL dominates the debate. This schedule makes suggestions that characterise quality teaching and, as such, are just as suitable and desirable for girls as for boys (Younger *et al*, 2005:15). A combination of maximising familiar communicative principles, coupled with exploiting new opportunities for reflection and analysis, may enable all pupils to enjoy and achieve in MFL, and allow them to extend their horizons.

### *Issues to consider*

■ Is there a MFL gender gap in your school? Are particular groups underachieving, for example according to their gender, race, class, attainment level? Is this also reflected in the number of those choosing to opt out of MFL post 14?

■ How feasible would it be to change the languages taught or offer vocational courses?

■ How could the content of the curriculum be made more relevant to all pupils? Which tasks could be extended to have a more meaningful perspective?

■ Do the images in your textbooks and other resources reflect the lives and experiences of your pupils?

■ To what extent is cultural awareness, assessment for learning and explicit learning strategy instruction, embedded in the scheme of work?

■ Choose one particular class. How can a more collaborative ethos be established?

■ How are languages viewed within the school as a whole? How could their status be enhanced?

## Acknowledgements
I am very grateful to the students on the Goldsmiths' PGCE Modern Languages course for their willingness to reflect on and share with me the results of their discussions with the boys they interviewed.

## References and further rtesources
Adams, J. (1998) *On Course for GCSE Coursework.* London: CILT

Barnes, A. and Hunt, M. (2003) *Effective Assessment in MFL.* London: CILT

Barton, A. (2002a) Teaching Modern Foreign Languages to single sex classes. *Language Learning Journal* 25: 8-14

Barton, A. (2002b) Learning Style: the Gender Effect, in: Swarbrick, A., *Aspects of Teaching Modern Foreign Languages.* London: Routledge

Brown, K. and Brown, M. (1996) *New Contexts for Modern Language Learning; Cross-curricular Approaches.* London: CILT

Carr, J. and Pauwels, A. (2005) *Boys and Foreign Language Learning: Real Boys Don't Do Languages.* Palgrave Macmillan

Chitty, C. (2002) The inclusive curriculum: an education for the benefit of all young people? *Forum* 44, 3. 99-102

Clark, A. (1998) *Gender on the Agenda: Factors Motivating Boys and Girls in MFLs.* London: CILT

CILT (2005) *Languages in Key Stage 4. Language Trends 2005.* London: CILT

Davies, B. (2004) The gender gap in Modern Languages: a comparison of attitude and performance in Year 7 and Year 10, *Language Learning Journal* 29: 53-58

Department for Education and Skills (2003) *Key Stage 3 National Strategy. Framework for teaching modern foreign languages: Years 7, 8 and 9.* London: HMSO

Grenfell, M. (2002) *Modern Languages across the Curriculum.* London: RoutledgeFalmer

Grenfell, M. and Harris, V. (1993) 'How do Pupils Learn? (Part 1)', *Language Learning Journal*, 8, 22-25

Grenfell, M. and Harris, V. (1994) 'How do Pupils Learn? (Part 2)', *Language Learning Journal*, 9, 7-11

Grenfell, M. and Harris, V. (1999) *Modern Languages and Learning Strategies In Theory and in Practice.* London: Routledge

Harris, V. (2002) Treading a tightrope: supporting boys to achieve in Modern Foreign Languages, in Swarbrick, A. (ed) *Teaching Modern Foreign Languages in Secondary Schools.* London: Routledge

Harris, V. (1992) *Fair Enough? Equal Opportunities and Modern Languages.* London: CILT

Harris, V., Burch, J., Darcy, J. and Jones, B. (2001) *Something to Say? Promoting Spontaneous Classroom Talk.* London: CILT.

Jackson, J., Richards, K., Redford-Hernandez, H. and Bains, B. (2004) *Modern Foreign Languages Starters: Developing thinking skills.* Stevenage: Badger Publishing

Jones, B. (1995) *Exploring Otherness: An Approach to Cultural Awareness.* London: CILT

Jones, B. and Jones G. (2001) *Boys' Performance in Modern Foreign Languages: Listening to Learners*. London: CILT

Kissau, Scott (2006) Gender differences in motivation to learn French. *Canadian Modern Language Review,* 62,3:401-22

Lin, M. and Mackay, C. (2004) *Thinking through Modern Foreign Languages*. London: CILT

Macaro, E. (2001) *Strategies in Foreign and Second Language Classrooms: Learning to learn*. London: Cassell

Macaro, E. and Erler, L. (2005) Raising achievement of young beginner learners of French through strategy instruction. Unpublished paper

Mitchell, R. (2003) Rethinking the concept of progression in the National Curriculum for Modern Foreign Languages: a research perspective. *Language Learning Journal*, 27: 15-23

Nuffield Languages Inquiry (2000) *Languages: The Next Generation*. London: The Nuffield Foundation

Ofsted (2004) *Modern Foreign Languages at a Glance 2002/03*. London: HMSO

Powell, B. (1986) *Boys, Girls and Languages in School*. London: CILT

Turner, K. (1995) *Listening in a Foreign Language. A Skill We Take for Granted?* London: CILT

Williams, M., Burden, R., Lanvers, U. (2002) 'French is the language of love and stuff': student perceptions of issues related to motivation in learning a foreign language. *British Educational Research Journal* 28 (4): 503-528

Younger, M. and Warrington, M. with Gray, J., Rudduck, J., McLellan, R., Bearne, E., Kershner, R. and Bricheno, P. (2005), *Raising Boys' Achievement: A Study Funded by the Department for Education and Skills*, (DfES Research Report RR63). DfES Publications (also published on the DfES Gender and Achievement website, www.dfes.gov.uk/genderandachievement

# Performing Arts: An Introduction
## *Veronica Jobbins*

The performing arts of dance, drama and music have much in common, not least in their ability to deal with equal opportunities issues both directly and indirectly.

However, the national curriculum in England has made a distinction between the arts in terms of their place on the curriculum. Thus, drama has been subsumed under English, and dance included with PE, while music has its own place as a foundation subject. The situation varies between schools, and there is often a hierarchy of arts provision in the way in which some subjects are offered only to certain groups of pupils. In secondary schools, for instance, dance and drama may be available to the younger pupils, but not within the examination option scheme. In primary schools, dance may be taught in mixed groups, but when pupils go into their secondary school, only girls may have dance included in the PE curriculum. Thus progression through the key stages can be problematic in the performing arts. This is contrary to the notion of a broad and balanced curriculum which is fundamental to the National Curriculum. Ideally, schools should provide opportunities in all the arts to all their pupils. Some consider that teaching one or two art forms is sufficient, failing to appreciate that each art form makes a special and unique contribution to the education of the child, and that one cannot be substituted for another.

It is also important to draw a distinction between opportunity and genuine access. For example, are the girls in a music class actively encouraged to take a turn on the drum kit or to use music technology? Do the boys in a mixed school feel confident about attending an after-school dance club? When it comes to choosing examination courses, are the teachers who advise pupils aware of equality issues and able to challenge the prejudice that may influence the pupils' choices? Equally, are the performing arts examination syllabuses offered accessible to all pupils? In recent years there have been interesting developments in GCSE syllabuses for dance, drama and music which take account of a multi-cultural perspective, but some A/AS Levels are still eurocentric in their perceptions of culture.

Tokenism, be it in a racial or a gender context, is still a central issue for the performing arts. Where a school is looking for an easy way of fulfilling its equal opportunities policy, the performing arts can provide an obvious means, for example, bringing in an Indian dance teacher or an African drummer to work with pupils. Great care is needed if the accusation of tokenism is to be avoided. With appropriate planning, such experiences can make a vital contribution to the way a school addresses diversity, but only if they are set in context and are part of an ongoing programme that gives equal respect and value to all arts irrespective of their cultural origin.

There are still inequalities to be addressed in the access for young people from more disadvantaged backgrounds with regard to opportunities in dance, drama or music. For example, more affluent families are able and willing to pay for specialist tuition in dance or instrumental lessons. However, more schemes concerning all the performing arts are being established through schools, local authorities or nationally, to enable all children, whatever their background, to have access to high quality specialist provision from primary age through to secondary.

Schools can have a vital role in identifying and supporting pupils who are talented in any of the performing arts. Many specialist schools have well-developed policies and strategies that provide excellent opportunities for talented pupils to improve and develop their skills, and thus progress in their chosen art form. However, all schools can give effective support, particularly if they link with outside community and youth arts organisations, such as youth dance or theatre groups or orchestras.

Regrettably, senior staff and careers advisers do not always recognise the career opportunities that are open to young people in the performing arts and may well give advice based on stereotypical perceptions. In secondary schools, subject teachers can help to combat this by seeking ways to inform the careers staff in their school, by offering individual help and, on all occasions, by challenging stereotypical notions of career possibilities. Government policies to widen participation in higher education have significantly increased the number of people going to university. The performing arts have benefited from this trend, but there is still work to do to ensure that all young people, whatever their background, are given sound advice as to appropriate courses and, where necessary, support with audition and interview preparation.

Where disability is concerned, policies of integration have enabled many pupils to take part in dance, drama or music lessons. Some teachers have been helped by extra staffing and resources to provide special opportunities for disabled pupils. However, teachers frequently struggle to find ways of challenging all their pupils irrespective of ability or disability. This can be hard in practical subjects when the nature of the disability is physical. Often, it is necessary to look at the appreciative and creative aspects of the art form rather than the technical skills, to enable those pupils to gain enjoyment and satisfaction from their arts experience.

There is no reason why the disabled should not dance, play musical instruments or act. Recent advances in technology have opened up enormous potential for the disabled to participate alongside more physically able pupils. An example in music would be the case of a GCSE music student suffering from cerebral palsy who was able to use midi equipment to play synthesiser sounds on an electric drum kit.

Finally, it is important to be clear about the difference between arts education and therapy. Pupils with special needs have an equal right to participate in the performing arts as a part of their arts entitlement.

# Dance

*Veronica Jobbins*

The provision for dance in schools across England is patchy and variable. The time available for dance, the content of the dance curriculum and the specialist skills, knowledge and understanding of the teacher varies between schools and local authorities. For the purposes of the national curriculum, dance is placed within physical education (PE) providing an artistic and cultural dimension to the PE curriculum. Dance is named as one of six activities essential to a balanced physical education programme and is compulsory in key stages 1 and 2, and optional in key stages 3 and 4. While dance is placed within PE in the national curriculum in secondary schools, it may be located within PE departments or taught within the creative or performing arts. With the development of specialist performing arts and sports colleges, dance has become increasingly popular at key stage 3 and at examination level. GCSE dance is one of the fastest growing GCSE subjects, and the demand for post-16 dance courses such as AS or A Level dance has increased rapidly in recent years.

However, there are still considerable problems to overcome before dance is available for all young people in our schools, irrespective of age, gender, race, ability or disability.

One of the major difficulties is that dance in western society, and certainly in Great Britain, with the exception of some traditional forms, such as highland and Morris dancing, has been seen as a largely female activity. There has been considerable prejudice in our society against boys dancing, which has only partly been dispelled by recent popular forms such as street dance. This has been reflected in the amount and way in which dance is offered in schools, especially secondary schools. Where dance takes place in primary schools, it is mostly taught in mixed groups, but not all mixed schools offer dance to male pupils, and it is rare for boys-only schools to have dance on the curriculum.

In recent years the situation has been changing, with a growing awareness that boys should have equal entitlement and access to dance as girls, and thus new initiatives have aimed at encouraging more boys to dance, both in and out of schools. The problems in so doing are numerous and deep rooted, but improved understanding of appropriate lesson content and teaching strategies have significantly increased boys' participation in dance. Sadly, there are still few male dance teachers to challenge the misconception that dance is not for boys and to provide much needed role models, and homophobic stereotypes remain.

In our eagerness to provide adequate dance provision for male pupils in our schools, it is important not to forget the female pupils. Equally, there are important issues concerning cultural diversity and anti-racist teaching to be addressed. Dance, with its unique combination of the physical, artistic and intellectual, can play an important part in challenging stereo-typical roles and behaviour, and giving all young people an understanding of, and respect for, cultural values and traditions other than their own.

Unfortunately, many teachers feel that their own knowledge is too limited to make even a start at introducing a range of dance styles to their pupils. For instance, it would certainly take most teachers considerable additional training to be able to teach African or Asian dance styles adequately. However, this is not the only way of giving their pupils some experience of dance forms other than western, and promoting a truly equal opportunities policy regarding dance.

Increasingly schools are working with professional dance artists and companies through projects such as Creative Partnerships. Inviting dancers and choreographers from dance forms other than western, as well as contemporary dance and ballet, to work for short periods of time with particular classes, or to perform to the whole school, can provide a refreshing new perspective to pupils' understanding of the arts. Fortunately, dance video and DVD resources are now freely available to enable teachers to show that dance is much wider than contemporary dance or ballet.

It is interesting to remember that dance is not seen as a separate and discrete art form in all cultures. The links with music and drama in particular, are very strong in African and Asian cultures, so much so that in some cultures the same word is used for music and dance. Cooperation and collaboration between performing arts teachers can offer a richness of experience that is vital to good equal opportunities practice.

### Issues to consider

The following questions are intended to help dance teachers in primary, special and secondary schools to examine their own teaching and the dance curriculum, in terms of equity.

### Policy

- In your school, is dance offered equally to all male and female pupils/all the male pupils/or all the female pupils? How is it presented to boys?

- If offered, are male pupils taking up dance options? If not, what are their reasons?

- If dance is taught by a female teacher, do you invite male dancers, teachers or choreographers to your school to work with the male and/or female pupils?

- Do you invite dancers, teachers and choreographers from traditions other than western to teach in the school?

- If dance performances take place during assemblies, lesson time or after school, are the dancers, be they pupils or visiting professionals, mainly male, female, or in groups of equal representation? Are a number of different cultural groups and dance styles represented?

- Are attempts being made to combat prejudice among pupils, staff (teaching and non-teaching), governors and parents?

- Do your dance clubs, option groups and examination groups consist mainly of female or male pupils, or children from a particular ethnic group?

- In a mixed school do you think it is ever appropriate to work with single-sex groups for dance?

### Lesson content and organisation

- In a mixed school, is the content of your dance lessons geared to the interests of male pupils, female pupils or both sexes?

- Should there be differences in the material used in dance lessons for mixed classes, for single-sex girls' classes and for single-sex boys' classes?

- Do you present traditional gender models in your teaching? For example, stereotypical roles such as in Oklahoma: cowboys are macho, violent, knee slapping: cowgirls are dainty, flirtatious; or stereotypical sexual behaviour as in disco style dances: girls are desirable, available objects, boys are aggressive, dominant exploiters?

- If you teach mixed dance classes, does mixed partner work or small group work happen naturally? If not, do you encourage it?

- If you teach mixed classes, do you monitor the way you use praise, reprimands, questions and support? Do you expect the same level of achievement from both female and male pupils?

- Does teaching mixed classes with an unequal ratio of male and female pupils affect your teaching methods? The lesson content? The achievement of the female/male pupils?

- If you teach single-sex dance classes, do you find yourself restricted to a narrow range of movement? For example, for male pupils, strong, fast movement; for female pupils, light, flowing movement?

- Do you ever use dance as a medium to explore gender roles and behaviour with your pupils? Or to look at issues such as racism or positively to contribute to the school's anti-racist education?

- How frequently is music from cultures other than western used as an accompaniment or starting point for a dance lesson?

- How frequently are poems, books, stories etc from black authors or black cultures used in dance lessons and schemes of work?

## Language

■ Are stereotypes implied in your choice of descriptive language – for example: 'don't move like an old woman'?

## Resources

■ Do you identify and comment on the stereotypes frequently found in dance books, photos, magazines, etc, when talking to your pupils? For example, men lifting women, women showing soft and flowing movement, predominance of white ballet dancers.

■ Do you attempt to combat stereotypical visual images by searching out photos and other artefacts that portray men and women in a variety of dance contexts? For example, women lifting men, black ballet dancers?

■ Are there a variety of dance images always on display in the dance studio, gym, hall or corridor?

■ Does your DVD/video collection include a range of dance material that can provide examples of women and men dancing in non-stereotypical ways, and dance from different cultures?

■ Does your CD collection include a variety of popular, classical and world music?

■ Does the school library have a good collection of dance books and magazines that present positive images of male and female dancers, and a range of dance styles? For example, Indian dance, African dance, jazz dance and books showing men dancing?

## Clothing

■ In mixed dance lessons, should boys and girls be allowed the same choice of clothing?

■ Does the clothing that you allow pupils to wear for dance highlight sexual stereotypes or make it embarrassing for pupils to perform certain movements, such as sitting with legs wide open on the floor or making large energetic jumps?

■ Are the school regulations sensitive to the needs of children from religious groups who have particular concerns about clothing, for example, Jewish and Muslim pupils?

## References and further resources

Bland, A. and Percival, J. (1984) *Men Dancing.* London: Macmillan

Dance Matters (2004). NDTA 40, Summer Dance Network www.dancenetwork.org.uk

DFES Music and Dance Scheme www.dfes.gov.uk/mds

Jobbins, V. (2005) Entitled to Dance: Boys in Schools. *Animated* Winter p10 – 11

National Dance Teachers Association www.ndta.org.uk

# Drama

*Jan Shapiro*

## Introduction

The status of drama in schools is an ongoing concern for practitioners. There are those who argue that the subject should be taught as a discrete art form, and are convinced that being regarded as anything less, fundamentally compromises the integrity of the subject. There are others who believe that a statutory framework for drama would give it the status it deserves. There are also those who feel that drama benefits from being considered as a learning tool, and resist the potential limiting of the subject were it to be ascribed aims, objective and assessment criteria as other discrete statutory subjects. This ongoing dialogue has become a backdrop to drama teaching in both secondary and primary contexts.

Many more girls than boys choose to do drama as an option at GCSE level and at higher education institutions, and the subject is too often seen as an easy option at secondary school level. Drama programmes are rigorous and demanding, and the lessons, with their emphasis on group work, discussion and creativity, are often the ones which most challenge pupils and their teachers.

Despite the disproportionate take-up of drama by girls at schools, females remain under-represented in the theatre industry in most aspects of theatre making, with the exception of traditional female roles like the wardrobe mistress and make-up artist. While there are far more parts written for females by females today, males still have a better chance of a successful career in the performance aspects of theatre, although in such a competitive industry it is a difficult and complex career for anyone.

## Issues to consider
### Curriculum provision

It is important to consider the drama offer in your school and interrogate the nature of the drama experience for your pupils, as your approach to drama teaching will inform the outcomes, especially when dealing with equality and equity issues.

- What is drama used for in your school? Is learning through drama more valued than learning in drama?

- What is seen as more important? Is it the process or the product? Is the emphasis always on performance? Are pupils taught the value of the drama experience without having to show an end result? Do they see the advantages of the subject as teaching understanding, sympathy and empathy?

- Are pupils given the tools to 'read' live theatre, and do you think they will be become discriminating audiences in the future? Do pupils respond to both the dramatic narrative and as an audience? In other words, are they able to articulate their experience as observers and what they may bring to an interpretation of a piece?

- Are pupils given the opportunity to improvise and make their own drama as well as interpreting the drama of others?

### Drama for younger pupils – in England, key stages 1-3

- Where does drama happen? Is drama seen as an extra-curricular activity or is it given status within your school curriculum? If takes place outside school hours, who participates? Is there a representative gender mix? Is drama seen as being for girls rather than boys? Are sessions timetabled against other activities? Does this affect the uptake?

■ What opportunities exist for teachers to talk with colleagues, including the headteacher, about the purpose and the potential of drama? Do you have discussions about the democratising nature of drama and the way in which it enables an equal voice if used effectively? Drama is about working collaboratively, and boys and girls, who may normally find it difficult to engage with each other in different contexts, often find it enlightening to work together in a drama classroom where working as a team is crucial to success.

■ Are there ways in which you can make the spaces welcoming and encouraging for both girls and boys?

■ How do you communicate what kinds of behaviour are appropriate – for example, not showing off, not being aggressive?

■ How do you ensure that activities appeal to girls and boys?

■ How do you and your colleagues work together to capitalise on the opportunities, including exploring gender issues, presented by drama?

### For older pupils – in England, key stage 4

■ What do the statistics tell you about the choice of drama by girls and boys?

■ Do you know what pupils think of the subject? Are there any differences here between girls and boys and/or different ethnic groups?

■ Is drama offered against other subjects with a particular gender profile? Is it presented to attract pupils from both sexes?

■ What do you know about pupils' aspirations to study drama post 16? What encouragement and information can you give, including in the areas of back-stage work, lighting and sound design or writing? Is gender an issue? Would you be more or less likely to encourage a girl or boy to enter the world of stage lighting? Production? Costume? Make-up?

### Aims and assessment

■ Do your aims express values and attitudes that counter and challenge sexist, racist and homophobic behaviour?

■ How does your scheme of work relate to pupils' experience at each phase of learning? How do

you plan for continuity and progression of anti-sexist and anti-racist drama?

■ In defining drama, how do you make sure that the values, experiences and interests of women have their place in the art form?

■ How do you make sure that the sexist and racist notions of beauty are not perpetuated? Is the pretty blonde girl always given the lead role? Does the big, handsome boy always get the male lead?

### Lesson content

When drama is used to support the whole curriculum, examine the content for gender-bias, whether this is in a novel that pupils are studying in English or a scenario in a history lesson. This is a great opportunity for dialogue with other colleagues who may be equally concerned about bias.

■ Do you seek the help of others, such as colleagues in your school including the librarian, and the school library service, to find suitable material, and to establish a gender balance? Do you have access to the work of female playwrights?

■ How do you make sure that both girls and boys value themselves and their experiences as positive and not negative? Are sexist views challenged?

■ Do you give pupils the skills to consider some traditional female roles, and the reasons behind these roles? Do you give pupils the chance to discuss sex-roles within their drama roles?

■ Are the social and political contexts of texts explored? What opportunities existed for women in those contexts?

■ Do you give girls the chance to play male characters, and boys the chance to play females? Do they feel safe in doing this? Do your pupils know why males used to play women, for example in Shakespeare plays? Do they explore how cross-gender casting is used in contemporary theatre?

### Group work: the talented few – or drama for all?

Group work is essential in good drama practice.

■ Do you focus on the talented child while relegating the others to support roles? Are boys favoured here?

■ How are those who work supportively, and give opportunity to others, rewarded?

- What role models do the pupils draw on in their own work? What do you do to widen the range, challenging gender bias?

- Are pupils given the opportunity to direct each other? Is this role equally shared out? Are girls at ease with directing boys and vice versa?

### *Activity*

The hierarchy of the playground may well be replicated in the drama classroom, and this may prevent girls, in particular, from literally taking centre stage.

- Observe the actions of the children in mixed groups, focusing on gender. Watch one girl through the stages of group work and analyse her learning.

- Consider who demands your attention – boys or girls?

- How do you challenge unacceptable behaviour including bullying and offensive language? How often is that behaviour linked to sexist, racist, homophobic attitudes? How are children with different abilities/disabilities given opportunities within the group?

- How do you influence the gender dynamics of your group? Work with a colleague to observe your lessons, paying particular attention to the equality issues and gender dynamics.

### Teachers

We are all role models for children. Our professional behaviour carries messages often more powerful than the taught curriculum.

Ask yourself:

- how do my teaching strategies foster and encourage equal opportunities?

- do children see me challenging inequalities, in the curriculum content I select, in the ways I use materials, practice my craft, and in the opportunities I create for all my pupils?

- when planning the school productions do I keep equal opportunity issues in mind?

- what opportunities do I make for pupils to see women and men in professional theatre, and experience Theatre in Education – for example, seeking out a group that works on or presents sexual harassment, sexist bullying in the playground, the difficulties and complexities of relationships, or challenges gender stereotypes?

Drama has much to offer the whole curriculum. All teachers should be given training to enable them to utilise a full range of drama strategies, conventions and approaches, and have the confidence to use these flexibly and creatively in their lessons. It is also an aesthetic art form, and pupils should be given the opportunity to see it as such. Moreover, it offers the whole school community a space for debate and reflection, and is a mechanism for bringing people together. It is a subject that should be respected and celebrated.

*Based on the schedule in Genderwatch! After the ERA 1992 by Pauline Mason*

### References and further resources

Baldwin, P. (1997) *Stimulating Drama*. London: National Drama

Bennathan, J. (2000) *Developing Drama Skills 11-14.* London: Heinemann

Dickinson, R. and Neelands, J. (2006) *Improving your Primary School through Drama.* London: Fulton Publishers.

*Drama Research: the Research Journal of National Drama*

Fleming, M. (2003) *Starting Drama Teaching*. Second Edition. London: Fulton Publishers

Goode, T. and Neelands, J. (2003) *Structuring Drama Work: A Handbook of Available Forms in Theatre and Drama.* Cambridge: Cambridge University Press.

*The Journal of National Drama* www.dramamagazine.co.uk/

Kempe, A. (2000) *Progression in Secondary Drama*. London: Heinemann

# Music

*Brigitte Charles and Lucy Green*

In most schools, girls tend to be more enthusiastic and involved in musical activities than boys, particularly when it comes to singing in the choir and playing in the orchestra or band. Yet once women have grown up, their musical roles are much less obvious than men's. In some areas of music, such as playing the drums in a rock band or conducting an orchestra, women are still in a small minority.

Music books and most standard histories of music rarely mention women except as the wives, mistresses, sisters or mothers of famous male musicians. Overall, women's involvement in music has not generally been seen as a valid or interesting aspect of musical studies. Even the possibility that girls and women might have different musical roles from those of boys and men, was for many years overlooked as being of no importance.

During the 1980s and 1990s a number of musicologists and music educationalists turned their attention to this area. It is now known that women have been involved as performers and composers in all periods of history in western classical, folk, jazz and popular musics, from antiquity to the present day. In some musics though, including much traditional African drumming and gamelan, women and girls are banned from playing certain instruments, or sometimes from any musical activities at all apart from singing.

It is significant that girls and boys in schools tend to choose different instruments, musical styles and musical activities from each other. Although there are always exceptions to the general rule, attitudes and assumptions about gender and music are established by the time children are six years old, and are maintained through the teenage years.

Children and teachers often have unexamined expectations that girls and boys not only are, but ought to be, involved in different musical activities, for different reasons and with different results.

## Issues to consider
### Lyrics

Male and female stereotypes are prominent in nursery rhymes and children's songbooks, and these play a major role in children's first experiences of music in school. Much popular music, for example some hip-hop, contains words that are explicitly violent against women. Most operas portray women as fickle, mad or valued only for marriage.

- Do you ask the children to discuss gender stereotypes in nursery rhymes and children's song lyrics?
- Have you ever discussed the portrayal of women and men in the lyrics of popular music or opera?

### Books and other resources

Books, including textbooks, and other learning resources still tend to under-represent women and portray them in limited musical roles.

- Are women portrayed in non-stereotypical roles in your resources?
- Do you examine how women musicians are portrayed in books? Do you examine the books with your children to raise their awareness?
- Have you asked children to examine their own perceptions of gender and how this affects their attitudes to musical practices? Listening to a range of musical styles, and guessing the sex of the composer and reasons for the guess could be a fruitful starting point.

■ Do your wall displays and posters celebrate the achievement of women in music?

## Singing

Many boys have a negative attitude towards singing because it is associated with femininity. They often regard it as a girl thing and not a macho activity. As a result school choirs and singing groups in schools are very often girl heavy.

■ Are there positive role models in the form of male singing teachers, visiting male singers to the school and displays showing male singers?

## Instrumental choice

Musical instruments are perceived as gendered by pupils of all ages, and boys and girls tend to play instruments that are considered appropriate to their gender.

■ How many girls in your school play feminine instruments such as the violin and flute, compared to boys?

■ How many girls play drums and electric guitar in your school, compared to boys?

■ If there is an obvious imbalance, have you discussed this with the pupils?

## Music technology

Music software design in almost all cases is monopolised by men, and this may mean that the approach, layout or design of the programmes used for music do not instantly appeal to girls. In the classroom, girls tend to use the computer less than boys. Even in classrooms where technology usage appears to be equal, girls often lack confidence, compared to boys. Pupils and teachers often expect girls to be less competent in their use of technology.

■ How do you ensure that girls are positively encouraged to use ICT as a compositional tool?

■ What expectations do you have of girls and ICT?

## Pupils' involvement in musical styles

There is an assumption that classical music is for girls. Many boys avoid joining the choir and orchestra in some schools for this reason. Alternatively, popular music is associated with boys, and they tend to dominate the rock bands as well as computers.

■ Do you have boys in the orchestra; girls in the jazz/rock band?

■ If not, how are you addressing this with pupils to promote and encourage an equal representation of gender?

## The music in the curriculum: composition and improvisation

Many teachers are unfamiliar with the many female composers across all fields of music. When choosing music for children to listen to and/or perform, teachers seldom seek out music that has been composed by women. Many recordings of music by women are readily available.

■ Do you play music and mention that a woman composed it?

■ Are the children exposed to a range of different musical styles that are composed by women?

■ Do you include women improvisers in your curriculum?

## The music in the curriculum: performance

Many recordings and videos of music used in the curriculum contain males and females playing stereotypical instruments, or under-represent women performers. Whilst a few orchestras and many pop and jazz bands are still dominated by male instrumentalists, there are ample opportunities to select music performed by women.

■ Do you have pictures of orchestras containing only, or mainly, men on your classroom wall?

■ Do you play pupils recordings of music that are performed by women?

■ If so, do you tell the pupils women are playing it?

■ Do you play pupils recordings of women playing stereotypically masculine instruments such as drums, bass guitars and trombones?

## World music

When teachers present music from around the world, they often treat it as gender-neutral. An alternative approach might be, for example, to discuss the fact that girls and women are not always allowed to play some or all of the instruments in some styles, including music from Bali, and many parts of Africa and the Middle East.

■ Do you present music such as gamelan or African drumming as if it were a gender-neutral area?

■ Have you discussed this issue with pupils?

## Small-group work

Boys and girls tend to work in single-sex groups when given a classroom performance or composition task.

■ As a teacher, do you expect boys and girls to work differently in groups?

■ To what extent do children conform to a gendered way of working, for example, girls working cooperatively and boys working individually?

## Role models

Bruce and Kemp (1993) showed that primary children tend to choose instruments that they saw being played by role models of their own sex, regardless of whether the instrument was seen as a masculine or a feminine one beforehand. Media images of instruments as gendered are pervasive and it is very difficult for teachers to change pupils' perceptions by the use of role models. However, that is no reason for not trying!

■ Have you ever attempted to provide live role models that challenge stereotypes in musical activities?

## Teacher expectation of pupils' musical products

Many primary teachers tend to expect music composed and performed by boys to be forceful, loud, erratic and funky. Contrastingly, music that is thought to have been composed by girls is placed within the context of classical music. Girls' music is often judged as quiet, restrained, pretty, melodic and unadventurous.

■ Do you have expectations, perhaps unconsciously, that boys and girls will produce different kinds of music when they compose or improvise?

■ Do you expect girls and boys to treat instruments in different ways, for example, boys to play the drums loudly, and girls to play softly?

■ Have you ever noticed such tendencies, either in yourself or in your pupils?

## Teacher expectation of pupils' musical behaviour

Many teachers have an expectation that boys will not co-operate in groups, whereas girls will work well together. Many teachers also assume that boys create music spontaneously rather than persevering and planning out ideas. However, this may not be the case.

■ Do you assume that boys create music spontaneously whereas girls discuss and plan their musical ideas as a group?

■ Do you expect girls, but not boys, to record their musical ideas using traditional or graphic notation?

■ Do boys appear more confident and do girls appear tentative whilst creating music?

■ How can you challenge rather than reinforce stereotypical behaviour?

## References and further resources

Bayton, M. (1998) *Frock Rock: Women Performing Popular Music.* Oxford: Oxford University Press

Brewer, H. (1995) Sexism and stereotyping in the text of children's song-books. *Primary Music Today* (April) p20-22

Bruce, R. and Kemp, A. (1993) Sex-stereotyping in children's preference for musical instruments. *British Journal of Music Education* 10 (3) p213-17

Charles, B. (2004) Boys and girls' constructions of gender through musical composition in the primary school. *British Journal of Music Education* 21 (3) p265-277

Comber, C., Hargreaves, D. J. and Colley, A. (1993) Girls, boys and technology in music education. *British Journal of Music Education* 10 (2) p123-34

Green, L. (1997) *Music, Gender, Education.* Cambridge: Cambridge University Press

Harrison A. C. and O'Neill, S. (2002) Children's gender-typed preferences for musical instruments: an intervention study. *Psychology of Music* 28 p81-97

Morgan, L., Hargreaves, D. J. and Joiner, R. W. (1997) How do children make music? Composition in small groups. *Early Childhood Connections* Winter 1997/8 p15-21

Women's Revolutions Per Minute(WRPM) w.w.w.wrpm.net/about.asp

Women in Music w.w.w.womeninmusic.org.uk

Worldwide Internet Resources: Women Composers and Women's Music

w.w.w.music.indiana-edu/music_ resources/women.html

# Personal, Social and Health Education

*Janice Slough*

Personal, social and health education (PSHE) in schools is both a discrete element within the curriculum and a dimension of the whole curriculum. The former may take the form of a series of lessons on, for example, a topic within health education, or may be a carefully planned programme over a number of years. The latter is concerned with the whole-school ethos, the quality of interactions between adults, adults and pupils, and pupils with their peers. These patterns of behaviour which are modelled may be as influential as taught lessons – or more so – and are the responsibility of all adults in the school. Gender issues are implicit in all relationships between people and are important in different ways for both girls and boys.

Under pressures to attain targets, and given the fact that in the English national curriculum PSHE is not statutory, it is often a poor relation when the timetable is planned, teachers are assigned, and resources allocated. Both boys and girls benefit in schools where PSHE is given priority within the whole-school ethos and as a discrete subject.

## What is PSHE?

There are three main elements in the teaching of PSHE:

■ the acquisition of knowledge in order to make informed choices

■ the development of life skills to understand oneself and build positive relationships

■ the exploration of attitudes and values to understand others' points of view.

In England, these strands can be identified in the statement (QCA, 2000) that children and young people need the self-awareness, positive self-esteem and confidence to:

■ stay as healthy as possible

■ keep themselves and others safe

■ have worthwhile and fulfilling relationships

■ respect the differences between people

■ develop independence and responsibility

■ play an active role as members of a democratic society

■ make the most of their own and others' abilities.

Our gender identity is an intrinsic part of how we see ourselves, how we develop self-esteem and self-confidence, and how we relate to others. Recognition of the importance of gender identity is essential in well-developed PSHE provision.

## Why is PSHE particularly important in addressing gender equality?

It is generally accepted that children tend to behave in accordance with their sex-role stereotypes from an early age. Stereotypes are limiting for both sexes and are subtly different for boys and girls depending on their social class, ethnicity and culture, as well as their gender. However, whatever the other variables, the dominant patterns are related to sex roles. Sex-role stereotyping most significantly affects:

■ the home – domestic roles and responsibilities

■ sexual behaviour and child care

■ the workplace – types of work, hours and levels of seniority

■ health- self-care, patterns of physical and mental illness

■ emotional development

■ violence and offending behaviour.

In all these areas there are traditional patterns of male dominance and female compliance, expressed culturally in differing ways. The legacy of this continues to influence young people's gender development, although the world around them increasingly requires different patterns of behaviour, linked to moral commitments to equity in rights and responsibilities, and socio-economic ones based on the changing needs of the economy.

Gender has considerable influence on how we see ourselves, our social interactions and lifestyles. The disparity between girls and boys in reaching their potential appears to have three main causes:

■ inborn differences between the sexes
■ acquired characteristics and self-perception, and social and economic influences
■ influence of the school and teachers' attitudes.

A good PSHE curriculum particularly supports girls to address conditioning and repression, and to examine the pressures on young women and their function in society, and can enable boys to examine different models of masculinity. As the provision in school is so important, girls and boys need to be given the opportunity to experience personal, social and health education of high quality.

### Issues to consider

■ Is gender equality a guiding principle of the PSHE curriculum?
■ How is the classroom climate for respectful discussion established for PSHE and maintained across all year groups?
■ What use is made of single-sex and mixed groups in developing a broad and inclusive view of gender roles?

### The PSHE taught curriculum

In England the framework for personal, social and health education has three elements:

■ about myself
■ developing relationships
■ being part of the community – locally, nationally and in the world.

> When I was asked 'What do I want out of life?' I didn't know what to say. No one had ever asked me anything like that before. (15 year old girl after a PSHE lesson)

Girls and boys need to be able to understand themselves emotionally, physically, psychologically and spiritually. They need to know what is happening to their bodies as they grow; be challenged about concepts of body image; and understand that they have the right to privacy and respect from others.

They need to be able to identify and express their feelings, especially those that are strong or perceived as negative. They need to know to whom or where they can go for help. Developing good family, friend and sexual relationships are important aspects of growing up for girls and boys. Exploring attitudes and values around relationships; understanding personal needs, strengths and weaknesses and developing skills to maintain good relationships, are all part of the quality PSHE programme.

### Self-esteem in school and society

There is overwhelming evidence that pupils who believe in themselves, and who have mature social skills, can express their emotions assertively. Those who are happy at school learn more effectively. It could be argued that girls will be able to contribute to PSHE more because they are deemed more empathetic, more sensitive in relationships and are able to articulate their feelings (Goleman,1996). However, research has shown that they also tend to have lower self-esteem and confidence. Girls and young women need more help to value themselves and to act assertively (Balding, 1998; Patterson and Burns, 1990). Girls have often been brought up not to show negative feelings such as anger as it is not deemed ladylike, and PSHE can help them to identify and express negative feelings. Herman (1994) showed that, when girls are faced with difficulties and conflicts, they will often become passive and frozen. This may explain why some women stay in negative relationships, continuing to be abused. They can suffer from a learned helplessness, attributing success to luck and therefore succumbing to a downward spiral of underachievement. Girls need help in developing the skills that help them stand up for themselves and address their needs and their rights.

Boys too can be disadvantaged by their upbringing. They are often brought up to be boisterous and exuberant, but are not encouraged to show sensitivity or empathy. Boys' health is an area for concern too. The suicide rate is much higher for young men than for young women. Boys may also need more encouragement to eat healthily and to see the importance of a healthy life style. Boys need to develop a greater sense of responsibility for their sexual behaviour. They need help in becoming more aware of and open about their emotions, and able to express them in safe ways. Peer group pressures about a masculinity which does not value educational achievement also need to be examined openly.

In general, girls and boys are seen to gain self-esteem from different sources. Girls are more likely to gain self-esteem from who they are, what they look like and how other people view them. They are influenced by the media and can become very conscious of their body shape and appearance. Anorexia and eating disorders are far more common amongst girls and young women than boys and young men. In contrast, boys tend to gain self-esteem from what they do and achieve, such as sporting success. They are also more likely than girls to blame others for any lack of success. Teaching and learning in PSHE needs to consider these views and differences, and to challenge and support girls and boys to reach their full potential personally, socially and academically.

### Issues to consider

- Are gender differences (and exceptions to the general patterns) in self-esteem taken into account in the taught PSHE sessions?
- Does your PSHE curriculum cover the development of personal and social skills, such as being assertive?
- Do girls and boys have the opportunity to think positively about themselves – what they look like, who they are and what they are able to do?
- Does your curriculum encourage girls and boys to think about their aspirations, needs and behaviour?
- Are girls speaking confidently and assertively in the classroom?
- Are boys offered safe opportunities to talk about the pressures of stereotypes of masculinity?

## Sex and Relationship Education

Good sex and relationship education is about more than plumbing although it is important for both girls and boys to know and understand what is happening to their bodies. They need to know, for example, that menstruation is a normal and healthy process, and that everyone's body is unique. Sex and relationship education for girls and boys should cover forming relationships; loving and caring; taking responsibility; dealing with strong emotions; knowing what each person wants out of life and relationships; and being assertive about keeping safe.

Girls and boys pick up misinformation and feel the pressure to do what everyone else is doing, whether this is slimming or having sex. Young people also need to understand that good sex starts in the mind and involves how they feel about themselves, their

body and their sexuality. It is about communicating wants and needs assertively, and not just allowing themselves to be pressured into doing anything that they do not want to do, nor forcing themselves on someone else.

### Issues to consider

- Does your course help girls and boys to feel good about their sexuality, however that may be expressed?
- Do you look at current issues and focus on issues of sexism or good role modelling for women and men?
- Are you a good non-sexist role model in the classroom?

## Drug and alcohol education

Goleman (1996) suggests that the root causes for dependency on drugs or alcohol are often emotional. People who depend on alcohol or drugs often use them to soothe feelings of anger, anxiety or depression. Girls who lack self-esteem may find that they become addicted to smoking or may use cigarettes to keep themselves thin. If they do not have the confidence to present themselves as they are, they may use cigarettes, alcohol or drugs as a support. Boys' abuse of alcohol can be seen as a normal part of what young men do, and therefore ignored as the health issue that it is. The social norms around drugs need to be addressed in the classroom, exploring such things as the existence of the ladette culture, and gendered attitudes to alcohol abuse.

Drug education is more than knowledge of drugs. Girls and boys should be encouraged to explore why people use and abuse substances and how, as young adults, they can learn to cope and to enjoy life without depending on them.

### Issues to consider

- Do girls know that they are particularly vulnerable to alcohol, and do you help them look at issues around drinking?
- Do you help girls and boys to look at body image and examine how the media can manipulate women, in particular, into being discontented with how they look?
- Do you help boys to understand and control their attraction to excitement and danger?
- Do you include content on healthy lifestyles? Are girls and boys encouraged to eat healthily and have fun exercising?

Girls and boys need to experience PSHE that enables both genders to communicate openly and honestly. In heterosexual relationships, women need men who: know and understand themselves and others; who can express their feelings in an assertive, non-violent way; and who have the skills to build positive relationships of trust and respect. Men need women who: are able to express their feelings and needs assertively; and who can resist falling back into stereotyped patterns of dependency and compliance. In same-sex relationships, the same good communication is needed.

## The whole school approach

All adults in the school, both within the classroom and outside it, are involved in developing the whole school ethos which demonstrates respect, allows opportunities for pupils to practise taking responsibility and make decisions, and to develop positive self-esteem and confidence to enable them to make the most of their abilities. Both girls and boys need to develop confidence in expressing their feelings in an assertive, non-violent way both within single-sex and mixed groups. Adults in the school interacting with each other and with the pupils can act as positive role-models in helping girls realise that they can be confident and assertive, and boys that they can be sensitive and caring.

### Issues to consider

■ Is there gender analysis of incidents of bullying (an example of lack of respect) in the school?

■ Are both girls and boys able to take responsibility and not always for the stereotypical female or male tasks?

■ Do both girls and boys explore ways of expressing their feelings in assertive, non-violent ways?

■ Do the adults in the school show that they can be assertive without being aggressive?

■ Are the adults non-judgemental, and do they have common expectations of the behaviour and aspirations of boys and girls?

■ Are women seen in managerial and leadership positions?

■ Do the adults show appreciation and give praise to all pupils regardless of their gender?

■ Do adults label the act and not the pupil, and expect the same behaviour from girls and boys?

## The whole school approach – values and expectations

While attitudes and values can be explored in the classroom, they also tend to rub off from older children and adults. It is therefore very important that there is a shared understanding within the school and the classroom of what is acceptable and unacceptable in how people behave and what they say.

■ Do you have an equal opportunities policy?

■ Is there regular staff training on aspects of equal opportunities?

■ Are there negotiated, agreed class ground rules for acceptable behaviour?

■ Do you challenge sexual stereotypes and ensure that there are positive and non-traditional images of girls and boys, and women and men around school and in any handouts or text books?

■ Do adults expect the best of every child irrespective of their gender?

■ Do you avoid segregation of pupils by sex, for example in lining-up and registers?

■ Do you challenge sexist attitudes: 'That's not very ladylike'; 'Girls should be neat and tidy'; 'I need a strong boy to help me move the furniture'?

■ Does the school celebrate differences whether they are about gender, sexuality, ethnicity, religion, special needs or disability?

■ Does the school treat every person as an individual whatever sex they are?

■ Do you encourage girls and boys to experiment with activities that are not traditionally associated with their sex?

Personal, social and health education is an exciting aspect of education. We have a great responsibility to help young women and young men reach their full potential and live self-determined lives. All young people need to understand themselves and others. They need to be able to express their feelings in an assertive, non-violent way and to have the skills to build positive relationships of trust and respect.

### References
Balding, J. (1998) *Young People in 1997*. Exeter: University of Exeter Health Education Unit

Claire, H. (2001) *Not Aliens: Primary School Children and the Citizenship/PSHE Curriculum*. Stoke-on-Trent: Trentham

Gordon, J and Grant, G. (1997) *How We Feel: An Insight Into the Emotional World of Teenagers*. London: Jessica Kingsley

Goleman, D. (1996) *Emotional Intelligence*. London: Bloomsbury

Herman, J. (1994) *Trauma and Recovery*. London: Pandora

# Physical Education and School Sport

*Anne Flintoff and Sheila Scraton*

Gender equality in physical education (PE) has been a concern for teachers, sports coaches and researchers for some time. There is now an extensive body of research seeking to understand how gender operates within PE, and teachers have been involved in numerous initiatives aimed at challenging inequities. Yet PE remains one of the most gendered subject areas on the school curriculum, particularly in secondary education. There are still significant issues to address. For example, the PE curriculum is often differentiated by gender; boys significantly outnumber girls in choosing examination PE; and girls, particularly those from ethnic minority backgrounds, are under-represented in extra-curricular sports clubs.

Government legislation and policy in the UK have recognised the important contribution of PE to pupils' wider education and schooling, not least for its role in the promotion of healthy lifestyles and the reduction of child obesity. For example, the national PE and School Club Links strategy focuses on schools and other agencies working together in partnership to raise standards and levels of participation in PE and school sport (PESS). In addition, London's hosting of the Olympic Games in 2012 means that interest in, and commitment to, PE and youth sport has never been greater. The national strategy and its associated initiatives provide important opportunities for pupils to be physically active – in and out of school. The challenge for teachers will be to ensure that these opportunities are not just high quality and open to all, but that they meet the varying needs of all pupils.

Sound advice for teachers on challenging stereotypical attitudes and practices limiting the opportunities for girls and boys to develop a wide range of physical abilities and skills accompanied the introduction of the national curriculum in England (DES, 1991). It highlighted, for example, the fact that providing access is not the same as providing opportunity and that mixed-sex groupings might not be the best way to ensure a positive learning environment for all pupils. It also noted the complex ways in which different boys and girls respond to PE. There remains a tendency to talk about girls' or boys' experiences of PE as if they were homogeneous, separate groups, but ethnicity, religion, sexuality, social class, disability and ability, as well as geographical location, all contribute to boys and girls doing gender differently.

However, acknowledgement of this diversity brings with it difficult questions about what this means for gender equitable practice. Some important recent initiatives have focused on making PE more girl-friendly (see for example, Nike/Youth Sport Trust, 2000), but there is also a need to challenge the assumptions that the PE we offer boys is automatically boy-friendly. Many boys dislike the often highly competitive and physical nature of their sport-dominated PE lessons, and seek refuge in alternative leisure activities, such as music or literature (Bramham, 2003).

Teachers are asked to question whether their practice is providing high quality PESS experiences, and if it 'enables all young people, whatever their circumstances or ability, to take part in and enjoy PE and sport' (DfES/DPMS, 2005). This will entail careful consideration of the range of experiences on offer in PESS, so that pupils can move beyond limited, stereotypical notions of masculine and feminine movement vocabularies. Pupils themselves can also be engaged in questioning the social construction of gender through PE and sport, particularly within examination PE sessions.

The following questions will help you assess whether you have high quality, gender equitable, PESS.

### *Issues to consider*
### Curriculum content

■ How does the curriculum, across and within phases, ensure girls and boys get a balanced and coherent experience of the six National Curriculum categories of physical activities?

■ How does your sports partnership ensure equity of experience for boys and girls through the primary/secondary phases?

■ Do you teach different games to boys and girls? Can you challenge the unhelpful stereotype of girls' and boys' games through exploring the common features of a category of games, for example, striking and fielding, in cricket and rounders?

■ Do you offer different categories of activities to boys and girls at particular ages? Some schools begin to teach single-sex PE at key stage 2, and offer a narrower, games-based curriculum to boys, keeping a wider, more balanced curriculum for girls of the same age.

■ Does your curriculum link to opportunities to continue activities in extra curricular or community clubs and settings? There may be fewer opportunities for girls than boys to continue with games out of school, particularly for primary aged girls. Do you signpost opportunities? How does your school partnership take this into account when planning activities?

■ Do all pupils experience different aspects of health-related PE – for example, strength training as well as activities focused more on holistic health, such as yoga or relaxation; healthy lifestyles and eating; as well as fitness testing?

■ How does the PE curriculum contribute to the whole-school approach to health and well-being?

■ Are boys able to experience dance and gymnastic activities as well as games? Many schools include dance and gymnastics activities for boys at primary level, but not as they progress through secondary school. Do men and women teachers deliver particular aspects of the curriculum? What messages does this give to the pupils?

■ What is the take-up of GCSE, A level and other certification courses in PE by girls and boys? Nationally, more boys than girls appear to opt for examinations in PE. What can you do to make the subject more attractive to girls? Which staff deliver particular aspects of the syllabus, for example, do all the male staff deliver the hard sciences such as biomechanics, or physiology? And what messages does this give to pupils?

■ What resources are used for examination PE (and PE classes more generally)? Do they offer positive role models from each sex? Do you involve students in critical analysis of gender equity in PE and sport? Do you introduce organisations and policy initiatives designed to improve gender equity in sport and physical activity, such as the Women's Sports Foundation (www.wsf.org.uk)?

■ If you work in a single-sex school, do you avoid making curriculum choices based on gendered assumptions about the most suitable activities, for example, excluding dance for boys?

### Extra-curricular opportunities

■ Are participation statistics regularly collected, and importantly, used to inform future strategies to widen the numbers and range of pupils taking part?

■ Does your school sport partnership provide particular clubs or activities aimed at interesting previously under-represented groups, such as Asian girls, disabled pupils or particular age groups? National evaluations of the school sport partnership programme show that schools presently offer fewer opportunities for children at key stages 1 and 4 than at key stages 2 and 3.

■ Do you offer both competitive and non-competitive activities, as well as opportunities for informal physical activity for girls and boys?

■ Do pupils have a say in which activities are made available, for example, through a pupil council?

■ Are sessions provided at different times of the day to provide for a wide range of pupils' home circumstances?

■ Does your partnership ensure that all coaches and other professionals working in extra-curricular clubs provide positive and appropriate learning environments for all pupils?

221

## Teaching methods

■ Do you include opportunities for pupils to get involved in different roles beyond the performer, for example, coach, referee, choreographer? Can you find ways to help each sex take on roles where they are underrepresented, for example, leadership roles for girls.

■ Do you find out when religious festivals such as Ramadan fall during the year and allow alternative activities for Muslim pupils who may be tired and hungry?

■ Do you monitor how boys and girls work together in your lessons? Do you encourage interaction and cooperation between boys and girls, for example by using grouping strategies that actively promote this?

■ Do you offer opportunities for skill-based learning that is differentiated on the basis of ability, rather than gender? How do these include pupils with special educational needs or disabilities?

■ Do you monitor the use and distribution of equipment and space, to ensure that girls have the same access as boys?

■ Do you use teaching models, such as Sport Education, that encourage pupils to learn leadership and teamwork skills, as well as physical ones?

■ Do you monitor the gender balance of pupils you ask to demonstrate or answer a question?

■ Do boys and girls experience different teaching styles, including problem solving, reciprocal or student-led learning? Ofsted (2005) noted that boys are less likely than girls to experience problem solving and other, less structured, teaching styles, particularly at secondary school age.

■ Do you offer the same physical challenge to girls as to boys?

■ Do you take up in-service training opportunities to increase your knowledge and understanding of gender, and other equity issues in PE? The Nike Girls in Sport programme (Nike/Youth Sport Trust, 2000) is one example.

■ Are teaching assistants and other professionals involved in in-service training?

■ Are there opportunities for single-sex classes where appropriate? Mixed-sex teaching in PE is not always the answer to providing a positive experience for all pupils. There may be times when single-sex-classes would provide better learning experiences – if one sex is new to an activity, or when teaching swimming to Muslim girls, for example.

■ Do men and women teachers use different behaviour management strategies? For example, some men teachers use intimidatory physical activities as punishments for boys' poor behaviour, such as press-ups, or laps around the field. What messages does this send pupils about appropriate masculine behaviour?

## Language

■ Do you avoid sexist stereotypes like 'You're throwing like a girl'?

■ Do you avoid terms such as 'batsman', 'man to man' and use less gendered language, such as 'batter' or 'one-on-one' in a positive and non-tokenistic way?

■ Do you always challenge inappropriate language, for example sexist, homophobic, able-ist and racist put-downs between pupils?

■ Do you draw on women's sporting achievements as well as men's in your teaching?

## PE clothing and changing rooms

■ Do you allow boys and girls choice in what they wear for PE? Is there a range of items such as shorts, skirts, leggings and tracksuit bottoms from which pupils can choose? The Nike Girls into Sport programme (Nike/Youth Sport Trust, 2000) and other research shows that PE kit remains a major issue for girls in their enjoyment of PE, and they particularly dislike being forced to wear short skirts. Why not involve the pupils themselves in helping to promote a new kit for all?

■ Secondary school PE changing rooms are notoriously cold and unwelcoming. What can you do to make them more attractive? Do you use wall space to help brighten them, as well as helping with learning, by, for example displaying learning objectives for a block of work; key words or concepts, and positive images of role models?

■ Can you provide privacy for pupils when they are changing and/or showering? This may be particularly difficult in some primary schools without specialist PE facilities, but the issues remain equally pertinent

## Department/subject policy, organisation and ethos

The organisation of a department, its rules and its overall ethos, including imagery and symbols, can all contribute to a gender equitable PE.

■ If your PE department is organised so that boys' PE is separate from girls' PE, what messages does this convey to pupils?

■ Who teaches PE at primary level? Is there an assumption that men teachers will feel happier and be willing to teach more PE than women teachers? How are coaches/teaching assistants used in the delivery of curriculum PE? Do they replace class teachers and, if so, what message does this give about the status of PE, in relation to other subject areas?

■ Do your notice boards advertise important sporting events/achievements for girls as well as boys?

■ Are girls' achievements noted and praised in the same way as boys'?

■ Are facilities and equipment used equitably between boys and girls?

■ Do other teachers help with girls' extra curricular clubs as well as with the boys'?

## References and further resources

Bedward, J. and Williams, A. (2000). Girls' experiences of physical education – voting with their feet? In Williams, A. (ed) *Primary Physical Education: Research into practice.* London: Falmer

Bramham, P. (2003). Boys, masculinity and PE. Sport, *Education and Society* 8 p57-71

Cockburn, C. (2001) Year 9 Girls and physical education: a survey of pupil perception. *The Bulletin of Physical Education* 37 p5-24

Department for Education and Skills, Department for Culture, Media and Sport (2005) *Do you have High Quality Physical Education and Sport?.* Annesley: DfES

Department of Education and Science (1991). *Physical Education for Ages 5 -16 years: Proposals to the secretary of state of education and science.* London: HMSO

Flintoff, A. and Scraton, S. (2001) Stepping into active leisure? Young women's perceptions of active lifestyles and their experiences of school physical education. *Sport Education and Society* 6 p5-22

Flintoff, A. and Scraton, S. (2005) Gender and PE. In Hardman, K. and Green, K. (eds) *An Essential Reader in Physical Education.* London: Routledge

Green, K. and Scraton, S. (1998) Gender, coeducation and secondary physical education: a brief review. In Green, K and Hardman, K (eds) *Physical Education: A Reader.* Aachen: Meyer and Meyer

Harris, J. and Penney, D. (2002) Gender, health and physical education. In Penney, D. (ed) *Gender and Physical Education: Contemporary Issues and Future Directions.* London: Routledge

Kay, T. (2005) The voice of the family: influences on Muslim girls' responses to sport. In Flintoff, A., Long, J. and Hylton, K. (eds) *Youth Sport and Active Leisure: Theory, Policy and Practice.* Brighton: Leisure Studies Association

Nike/Youth Sport Trust (2000) *Girls into Sport: Towards Girl-friendly Physical Education.* Loughborough: Institute of Youth Sport

Penney, D. (2002) *Gender and Physical Education: Contemporary Issues and Future Directions.* London: Routledge

Scraton, S. (1992) *Shaping Up to Womanhood: Gender and Girls' Physical Education.* Buckingham: Open University Press

Scraton, S. and Flintoff, A. (2006) Girls and PE. In Kirk, D., O'Sullivan, M. and MacDonald, D. (eds) *Handbook of Research on Physical Education.* London: Sage

# Religious Education

*Joveriah Idrees and Anna Sallnow*

All religions have evolved over time and have been influenced by the cultures and traditions of which they have formed a part. In many of those cultures men did have prominent roles. However women have always been there with their own distinctive place and contribution.

There is also huge diversity within religions, and women's role in these will often differ radically.

## Issues to consider
## What are the issues for the classroom?

Questions form an integral part in RE teaching, and these can begin to explore what it means to be religiously educated and how gender issues contribute.

- What role do women play in particular religions?
- Has it changed over time?
- Are there differences within the religion and what impact does this have?
- What issues and tensions can this raise?
- How are they resolved?
- Where does the evidence for the different interpretations of women's roles come from?
- Is it based on religious texts, tradition or culture?
- What does it mean to be a woman in a particular religion?
- What is it is like to see the world through the eyes of another?
- Are there similarities between faiths on these issues?
- What do the religions teach about equality between men and women?

## Activity

Ask the pupils to add other questions to the list above for a class discussion.

In order for these discussions to take place we need to ensure that in the classroom there is:

- respect for the opinions and ideas of others
- the ability to listen even if the opinions are ones that the children and young people disagree with
- acknowledgment that there are a number of views and all will be held with firm commitment and passion. Religion is something very close to the heart!
- an agreement to be open-minded and to question the prejudices that lurk within us all.

## Teaching and learning styles

Utilising a variety of teaching styles to match different learning styles plays an important role in promoting equality and accessible learning for all pupils. Learning style is defined here as an 'individual's characteristic ways of processing information, feeling, and behaving in learning situations' (Smith, 1982:24).

RE has great potential in this area:

- visual (artwork, written material, artefacts, diagrams, maps)
- kinaesthetic (ICT, creative arts, drama, role-play, games, debates)
- auditory (story, discussions, explanation).

Activities should use all three styles on a regular basis and can be good starters or plenary activities.

## RE and the Curriculum

In all religions there are examples of women who have made a real impact.

### Key Women

As Dinah Hanlon wrote in the 1992 edition of *Genderwatch*, women have played important roles as:

- judges, for example, Deborah (Judaism)
- leaders, for example, Rani of Jhansi (Sikhism)
- prophetesses, for example, Nehanda of Zimbabwe (African religion)
- mystics, for example, Rabia'al Adawiyyah (Sufism/Islam)
- shamans and visionaries (in primal religions)
- saints, for example, St Theresa of Avila (Christianity)
- martyrs for their faith, for example, Bahai women in Iran (Bahai)
- devotees and followers of religious leaders, for example, Bebe Pani (Sikhism)
- courageous and inspirational figures, for example, Sojourner Truth and Mary Seacole (Christianity)
- early believers, for example, women were among the first converts in Islam and Christianity.

### Issues to consider

As a suggested classroom activity or whole-school display, ask pupils to find out what other examples they can add to the list from all the beliefs and religions represented in the school community.

Are there individuals in the local community who could be added to this list? Could they be invited into school to address the children?

### Media

- What are the images of women and religion that are shown in the media?
- Are they accurate?
- Do they need to be challenged?
- Do they emphasise the exotic and unusual rather than the similarities in human experience?
- What images would you use?

### Displays

- Do displays represent men and women, girls and boys, in a variety of roles and from a number of cultures?

- Do they challenge children and young people to think about issues of equality?
- Are the children and young people and their faith backgrounds featured?

### Visitors in schools

- Are visitors from a range of beliefs and faiths included in the curriculum?
- Are women from different faiths invited in to talk about their day-to-day experiences and patterns of life?
- Are there local examples of women as religious leaders?
- Are there examples of men or boys taking on caring roles such as whispering Adhan in a baby's ear or preparing food in the Langar in Sikhism?

### Resources

- Do pupils have the resources to help them develop critical skills, so that they are able to challenge materials for accuracy?
- Do they present a real portrait of the world: one that includes women and people from all backgrounds and ages?
- As well as books and posters, consider:
  - [ ] AVA materials
  - [ ] artefacts
  - [ ] your displays
  - [ ] internet resources
- Many schools have access to invaluable resources to support learning. These are the pupils, parents, the school community and the wider community, including religious and cultural institutions.

### Places of worship

- Have there been visits to local places of worship? Do you have books, videos and posters showing many places of worship?

### Finally

The voices of the young people and those of the faith communities are important. Let the religions speak for themselves rather than have outsiders interpret what is unfamiliar. And remember that what may seem restrictive in one culture may be the opposite in another. Power has many aspects and, for many cultures, women's roles are central to religion.

*Any errors are ours but thanks and acknowledgements to David Hampshire, County Adviser in Cornwall, and for the original article by Dinah Hanlon.*

## References and further resources

The subject of gender in teaching RE has been studied in many countries. The following website deals with Australian research:

www.detya.gov.au/schools/boyseducation/

The following site gives links to a variety of sites (some of them Australian):

www.simonmidgley.co.uk/achieving/gender.htm

Ansari, S. and Martin, V. (2001) *Women, Religion and Culture in Iran.* London: Routledge

Astley, J and Francis, L. J. (1994) *Critical Perspectives on Christian Education.* Leominster: Gracewing

Griffith, R.M. and Savage, B.D. (2006) (eds) *Women and Religion in the African Diaspora: Knowledge, Power, and Performance.* Baltimore: John Hopkins

Hanlon, D. (1992) Religious Education in *Genderwatch: After the ERA.* Cambridge: Cambridge University Press

Morgan, P. and Lawton, C. (eds) (2007) *Ethical Issues In Six Religious Traditions.* Edinburgh: Edinburgh University Press

*RE Today* (Journal) www.retoday.org.uk

Sawyer, D. F. (1996) *Women and Religion in the First Christian Centuries.* London: Routledge

Wilkinson, P. and Charming, D.(2004) *The Encyclopaedia of Religion.* London: Dorling Kindersley

# Science

*Patricia Murphy*

The national curriculum, introduced in 1988, ensured girls' inclusion in science up to 16. However, the general decline in pupils' interest in science raised concerns about whether pupils were leaving school adequately prepared for the rapid pace of technological and scientific change. In spite of the national curriculum, there has been little impact on girls' recruitment to science courses post 16, and girls' entry to physics A-level continues to decline.

## The historical perspective

To understand what lies behind these trends it is important to remember the gendered history of science education. Even the academic curriculum that a minority of girls experienced in the 19th century relied on domestic examples. The curriculum for males to enable them to take up their roles in the public domain included the physical sciences, while aspects of the biological sciences were neglected. Polarisation between the biological and physical sciences continued and the content of girls' lessons remained different to boys'. Gender differences in access at secondary level remained until the introduction of the national curriculum in

1988. This historical heritage is important if gender is understood not as fixed and innate but as a historical, social construction.

## Who chooses to do what science?

One teacher described the ideal physics pupil as having a 'logical, analytical, mathematical brain' (Benson in Murphy and Whitelegg, 2006). You can imagine which pupils might feel included in that classroom, though this view of masculinity may not be one that all boys identify with or that all girls reject.

Far fewer girls than boys are entered for physics at 16 in England, Wales, Scotland and Eire, in contrast to biology. In 2005, physics was the sixth most popular A level for boys. For girls, physics was the nineteenth most popular. In 2005, only 14% of girls who were awarded an A* or A in GCSE Double Award science or physics, sat A-level physics. As Table 1 shows, there is a decline in entry for the physical sciences in contrast to biology, particularly for physics and particularly for girls.

**Table 1**

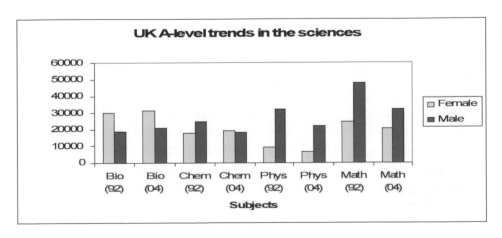

227

## Issues to consider

■ You might ask pupils what language is typical of the ways in which science is talked about. Is there a difference in girls' and boys' responses to this?

■ If you offer the separate sciences, who gets entered for these subjects? Are girls and boys equally represented across the three sciences?

■ How many girls and boys go on to study which A-level sciences?

## Perceptions of relevance and gender identity

Browne and Ross (1991) observed that very young children identify and engage with 'gender-appropriate' activities. Girls chose creative activities including drawing, or talking to an adult. Boys chose constructional activities.

Of school age pupils responding to science questions, boys noticed structures and mechanism, and avoided questions with feminine content such as flowers, textiles, or babies. Girls noticed aesthetic factors such as colour and textures and avoided tasks with what they considered masculine connotations such as cars or building sites. This occurred even though pupils knew the science required to answer the task. It is not the task itself, but what the task is about and whether pupils feel competent in these situations that affects their response (Murphy and Elwood, 1998). These differences connect back to the roles and activities that girls and boys have learned.

## Relevance and interest

As pupils progress through compulsory schooling, their interest in science declines. They feel science becomes more abstract, irrelevant and not connecting with their interests and experiences. Girls' view of their competence in science also declines (see Reid and Skryabina, 2002). By the end of key stage 4, more boys than girls report that they enjoy science. Few girls name physics as their favourite subject compared to boys, and girls continue to prefer biology to chemistry, and chemistry to physics, mirroring the pattern of entry in Table 1 on page 227.

In primary schools, boys show interest in physical science and girls in biological and environmental sciences. Pupils, especially girls, are interested in science that applies to their lives. By the end of secondary school, pupils report that biology is relevant to them, eg their bodies, and their concerns with health and disease. However, they see little purpose in learning the theoretical content of physics and chemistry. Boys can make links between physics and its relevance to everyday life through specific experiences, whereas girls cannot. This suggests that out-of-school experiences matter, connecting boys with physics, and girls with biology. Boys' distance from biology appears less dramatic than girls' from physics, because boys share with girls an interest in their bodies and their health.

## Issues to consider

■ To find out if interest in science declines, ask pupils to rate on a simple scale how much they enjoyed different topics, and how interesting they found them. You could use their different responses to find out more:

*Lots of people rated X as very interesting. Can you tell me what makes that topic interesting in your view?*

By listening to each other, pupils may start to see topics in a different light.

## Relevance and purpose

Krogh and Thomsen (2005) explored pupils' purposes in learning physics. Pupils who studied physics for future careers – predominantly boys – referred to science and technology and content concerned with society. Pupils who studied physics in order to know more for its own sake – mainly boys – preferred content concerned with calculations and fundamental principles. Pupils who studied physics in order to help people – predominantly girls – showed a greater preference for content related to human aspects.

## Issues to consider

■ Do you explore with your pupils what they see as the purpose for learning science? They could rate their responses to the following statements:

*I like science because I get to discuss issues that are important to me*

*I like science because it helps me understand the world and myself*

*I like science because it is important for the job I want to do*

■ Are pupils well-informed about science-related careers? Is there a difference between girls' and boys' awareness of careers?

Invite the class to discuss the following issue:

*Far more girls than boys said that science was not relevant to their future careers. Why do you think they feel like this?*

- Explore your pupils' initial understanding of a science topic – not the abstract scientific knowledge, but their views about what it relates to in the real world.
- Start lessons not only with the scientific criteria to be learned, but also the purpose of learning them.

## Relevance and difficulty

At key stages 4 and 5, prior achievement and career aspirations influence pupils' decisions to continue science. Many pupils consider science A-levels to be especially difficult, and their teachers think this is a main reason why they do not choose it. Boys are more likely than girls to consider studying science irrespective of their achievements. More girls than boys report a decline in feeling competent in science as they go through secondary school. One key stage 4 girl who gave up science commented:

> I'm not enjoying science at all at the moment ... You don't enjoy things when you can't understand a thing they are saying. Like if you keep not being able to do things, you just end up not bothering. (Sharp, 2004:196)

She got B grades in physics and chemistry and an A grade in biology in her examinations. However, she felt that she was failing. Girls need to be encouraged not to discount their prior achievement.

### Issues to consider

- Have you asked your pupils to rate how well they feel they are doing in science and how well they consider you think they are doing?
- You could use the traffic lights self-assessment technique to find out pupils' views of their understanding of science topics.

### Curriculum and teaching – the what and the how of science
### Context and content in the curriculum

Some parts of the science curriculum will be more familiar to boys and others to girls. The content of the physics curriculum at both primary and secondary level, and the contexts in which this content occurs, is likely to be more familiar to boys. Girls prefer to understand science in social contexts, whereas teachers and boys focus on the abstract. Curriculum changes that increase girls' self-concept have no detrimental effect on boys' overall achievement, and in some cases they have improved all pupils' performance. The changes that are beneficial include:

- using social situations to organise the science content to be studied
- using a social situation and the problems within it to provide the purposes for pupils' learning of science
- making values implicit in science matters for discussion and critique between pupils and their teachers.

The first two changes are part of the 2006 changes to the key stage 4 science curriculum in England.

### Issues to consider

- Think of some typical content and situations that you tend to use. Are they school-based or everyday? Who might have experience of them outside school?
- Do you ever discuss with pupils how they see the content of the tasks you set and whether they can imagine situations which connect with them?
- If you use contextualise learning activities, to what extent do you treat them as important?
- Have you asked pupils whether they consider context important in relation to their perception of the nature and purpose of the learning activity?

### Teacher expectations and support

There is evidence that in science, teachers tend to have lower expectations of girls than boys. and this is particularly the case in physics, where girls are seen as less able than boys to manage mechanics, electric circuits and electromagnetism and to lack the mathematical ability necessary to study physics. The feedback pupils receive can also differ, with girls more likely than boys to receive feedback on the quality of their work rather than their behaviour. Boys tend to receive more feedback than girls, both positive and negative. Negative feedback is usually about their behaviour.

The more supportive their science teacher, the more likely pupils are to have a positive attitude to science. Pupils, both girls and boys, report that science teachers are less supportive than teachers of other subjects. The size of science classes is a factor in this.

## Issues to consider

■ Who, in your minds' eye, are the high fliers in your subject? Is gender an issue here? Why do you think that might be?

■ Do you have any views of areas of your subject that boys find more difficult than girls and vice versa? What evidence do you have for this? Do your colleagues share these views?

## Teaching strategies

Both policy and teachers themselves advocate a fast-paced and well-structured lesson to support boys' learning. Many girls struggle in classrooms where the pace is fast. Girls value having the time to discuss and revisit scientific ideas with their teachers. Natasha, a pupil who achieved A grades in the three science subjects, explained her experience of science teaching:

> She goes, well if you don't understand it you should not be in this group [the higher group]... she didn't try to explain it. [She] doesn't seem to care really...It's just science that there's a problem in ...that does annoy me ...because science is my favourite subject. (Sharp, 2004, p176)

## Issues to consider

■ How do you organise the pace of your lessons? Do you allow time for reflection?

■ Have you tried selecting pupils to answer rather than asking for hands up? Do you allow wait time so pupils realise that a thoughtful response is valued, not necessarily the quickest response?

■ In your mind's eye, which pupils:
  – take your time up because of their behaviour?
  – seek most help?
  – do you rely on to give the right answer?
  – do you tend to challenge so they take their thinking further?

■ Do either girls or boys predominate in these groups?

Girls particularly value collaborative group work, which allows opportunities to discuss and share ideas. To achieve this, roles need to be carefully managed and tasks selected that require joint discussion and decision-making.

■ Have you asked pupils in what ways they like to work and their reasons for this?

■ Do you allow pupils to choose their groups or do you select them? Which grouping arrangements do you find work best?

Other teaching strategies which increase the motivation and achievement of pupils, particularly girls, include investigative group work, problem-solving and project-based activities, and group and whole class discussions. In the evaluation of the science course *21st Century Science*, pupils welcomed the opportunities for discussion, and girls in particular, who had thought science lacked relevance and interest, dramatically changed their views after implementation (Murphy *et al*, 2006).

■ Have you asked pupils about the activities you use and their enjoyment of and interest in them?

## Assessment procedures

Gender differences in response to assessment methods are discussed in the assessment schedule in this volume. Girls tend to gain higher marks on the continuous assessment aspect of science examinations and with coursework than boys. Some boys don't understand the significance of assessment procedures like coursework and mock exams, and find difficulty organising themselves to meet schedules. Girls do better on questions that allow a short free-response compared with multiple-choice response questions. Boys do equally well on both. This has been reported for primary and secondary pupils. There is evidence, too, that girls' performance relative to boys is lower on questions that involve graphical and figural data requiring the same form of response. This is often used in physics questions in the Standard Assessment Tasks (SATs) and in GCSE examinations.

## Issues to consider

■ Do you analyse science performance outcomes if there are gender differences in achievement by science subject?

■ Do you find that girls do better than boys in science coursework in your school? Why do you think this is? Have you discussed this with pupils?

■ Do you go through past papers to find out which questions pupils found difficult and their reasons for this? Which ones do they avoid?

## References and further resources

Browne, N. and Ross C. (1991) Girls' stuff, boys' stuff: Young children talking and playing. In Browne, N. (ed) *Science And Technology In The Early Years*. Buckingham: Open University Press

Krogh, L. B. and Thomsen, P. (2005) Studying students' attitudes towards science from a cultural perspective but with a quantitative methodology: Border crossing into the physics classroom. *International Journal of Science Education*. 27 (3) p281-302

Murphy, P. and Elwood J. (1998) Gendered experiences, choices and achievement – exploring the links. *International Journal of Inclusive Education*. 2 (2) p95-118

Murphy, P. and Whitelegg, E. (2006) *Girls in the Physics Classroom: A Review of the Research on the Participation of Girls in Physics*. London: Institute of Physics

Murphy, P., Lunn, S. and Jones, H. (2006) The impact of authentic learning on students' engagement with physics. *The Curriculum Journal* 17 (3) p229-46

Murphy, P., Ponchaud, B. and Whitelegg, E. (2006) *Girls in the Physics Classroom: A Teachers' Guide for Action*. London: Institute of Physics

Osborne, J. and Collins, S. (2001) Pupils' views of the role and value of the science curriculum, a focus group study. *International Journal of Science Education* 23 (5) p441-467

Sear, J. and Sorensen, P. (2000) *Issues in Science Teaching*. London: Routledge

Sharp, G. (2004) A Longitudinal Study Investigating Pupil Attitudes Towards Their Science Learning Experiences From A Gender Perspective. Unpublished Ph.D. Milton Keynes: The Open University

Warrington, M. and Younger, M. (2000) The other side of the gender gap. *Gender and Education* 12 (4) p493-508

# Bibliography

*Sue Adler*

Individual schedules have their own references and resources, including websites and useful organisations.

This bibliography does not duplicate all those sources but includes more general books. It is not intended to be comprehensive but it supports the central concerns of this book.

Aaopola, S., Gonick, M. and Harris, A. (2004) *Young Femininity*. Basingstoke: Palgrave

Adler, S., Laney, J. and Packer, M. (1993) *Managing Women: Feminism and Power in Educational Management*. Milton Keynes: Open University Press

Alder, A. and Worrall, C. (2004) *Girl's Violence: Myths and Realities*. New York: State University of New York Press

Arnot, M. (2002) *Reproducing Gender? Critical Essays on Educational Theory and Feminist Politics*. London: RoutledgeFalmer

Arnot, M. and Mac an Ghaill, M. (eds) (2006) *The RoutledgeFalmer Reader in Gender and Education*. London: Routledge

Arnot, M., Gray, J., James, M., Ruddock, J. with Duveen, G. (1998) *Recent Research on Gender and Educational Performance*. London: Office for Standards in Education

Ashley, M. and Lee, J. (2003) *Women Teaching Boys: Caring and Working in the Primary School*. Stoke-on-Trent: Trentham

Barrs, M. and Pidgeon, S. (eds) (1993) *Reading the Difference: Gender and Reading in the Primary School*. London: Centre for Language in Primary Education (CLPE)

Barrs, M. and Pidgeon, S. (eds) (1998) *Boys and Reading*. London: Centre for Language in Primary Education (CLPE)

Barrs, M. and Pidgeon, S. (eds) (2002) *Boys and Writing*. London: Centre for Language in Primary Education (CLPE)

Bhavnani, R. (2006) *Moving on Up? Ahead of the Game: The Changing Aspirations of Young Ethnic Minority Women*. Manchester: Equal Opportunities Commission

Bleach, K. (1998) *Raising Boys' Achievement in Schools*. Stoke-on-Trent: Trentham

Brown, B. (2001) *Combating Discrimination: Persona Dolls in Action*. Stoke-on-Trent: Trentham

Cameron, C., Moss, P. and Owen, C. (1999) *Men in the Nursery: Gender and Caring Work*. London: Paul Chapman

Cameron, D. (2006) *On Language and Sexual Politics*. London: Routledge

Claessen, M. (2006) *Gender and Class Differences in GCSE Results*. Cambridge: Cambridge Assessment Internal Report

Clauss-Ehlers, C. (2006) *Diversity Training for Classroom Teaching: A Manual for Students and Educators*. New York: Springer-Verlag

Claire, H. (ed) (2005) *Gender in Education 3-19: A Fresh Approach*. London: Association of Teachers and Lecturers

Cole, M. (ed) (2006) *Education, Equality and Human Rights: Issues of Gender, Race, Sexuality, Special Needs and Social Class*. London: Routledge

Coleman, M. (2002) *Women as Headteachers: Striking the Balance*. Stoke-on Trent: Trentham

Connolly, P. (1998) *Racism, Gender Identities and Young Children*. London: Routledge.

Cortina, R. and Roman, S.S. (eds) (2006) *Women and Teaching: Global Perspectives on the Feminization of a Profession*. Basingstoke: Palgrave Macmillan

Crozier, G. and Reay, D. (eds) (*2004*) *Activating Participation: Parents and Teachers Working Towards Partnership*. Stoke-on-Trent: Trentham

Cruddas, L. and Haddock, L. (2003) *Girls' Voices: Supporting Girls' Learning and Emotional Development.* Stoke-on-Trent: Trentham

Davies, B. (1993) *Shards of Glass. Children Reading and Writing Beyond Gendered Identities.* Sydney: Allen and Unwin

Dennison, C. and Coleman, J. (2000) *Young People and Gender: A Review of Research.* London: Women's Unit and Cabinet Office.

Drake, P. and Owen, P. (1998) *Gender and Management Issues in Education: An International Perspective.* Stoke-on-Trent: Trentham

Drudy, S., Martin, M., Woods, M. and O'Flynn, J. (2005) *Men and the Classroom: Male Teachers in Today's Primary Schools.* London: Routledge

Epstein, D. (1994) *Challenging Lesbian and Gay Inequalities in Education.* Milton Keynes: Open University Press

Epstein, D., Elwood, J., Hey, V. and Maw, J. (2004) *Failing Boys: Issues in Gender and Achievement.* Buckingham: Open University Press

Equal Opportunities Commission (2006) *What is the Gender Equality Duty?* Manchester: Equal Opportunities Commission website http://www.eoc.org.uk/Default.aspx?page=17686

Francis, B. and Skelton, C. (2005). *Reassessing Gender and Achievement: Questioning Contemporary Key Debates.* London: Routledge.

Francis, B. (2000) *Boys, Girls and Achievement: Addressing the Classroom Issues.* London: RoutledgeFalmer

Frost, L. (2001) *Young Women and the Body: A Feminist Sociology.* Basingstoke: Palgrave MacMillan.

Gaine, C. and George, R. (1999) *Gender, Race and Class in Schooling: An Introduction for Teachers.* London: Falmer Press

Gaskell, J. (1992) *Gender Matters from School to Work.* Milton Keynes: Open University Press

Gillborn, D. and Mirza, H. (2000) *Educational Inequality: Mapping Race, Class and Gender.* HMI 232. London: Ofsted

Gillborn, D. and Youdell, D. (2000) *Rationing Education: Policy, Practice, Reform and Equity.* Buckingham: Open University Press

Gilligan, C. (1982) *In a Different Voice.* Harvard: Harvard University Press

Gilligan, C. (1988) *Mapping the Moral Domain.* Harvard: Harvard University Press

Hey, V. (1997) *The Company She Keeps: Ethnography of Girls' Friendships.* Buckingham: Open University Press.

Jackson, C. (2006) *Lads and Ladettes in School, Gender and a Fear of Failure.* Buckingham: Open University Press

Lees, S. (1986) *Losing Out.* London: Hutchinson

Lees, S. (1993) *Sugar and Spice: Sexuality and Adolescent Girls.* London: Penguin

Lloyd, G. (ed) (2005) *Problem Girls: Understanding and Supporting Troubled and Troublesome Girls and Young Women.* London: Routledge

Mac an Ghaill, M. (1994) *The Making of Men: Masculinities, Sexualities and Schooling.* Milton Keynes: Open University Press

Mahony, P. (1985) *Schools for the Boys: Coeducation Reassessed.* London: Hutchinson

Martino, W. and Meyenn, B. (2001) *What about the Boys? Issues of Masculinity in Schools.* Milton Keynes: Open University Press

Millard, E. (1997) *Differently Literate: Boys, Girls and the Schooling of Literacy.* London: Falmer Press

Mirza, H. (1992) *Young, Female and Black.* London: Routledge

Myers, K. (ed) (2004) *Teachers Behaving Badly: Dilemmas for School Managers.* London: RoutledgeFalmer

Myers, K. (ed) (2000) *Whatever Happened To Equal Opportunities in Schools? Gender Equality Initiatives in Education.* Milton Keynes: Open University Press

Neall, L. (2002) *Bringing the Best Out In Boys: Communication Strategies for Teachers.* Stroud: Hawthorn Press

Noble, C. (2003) *How To Raise Boys' Achievement.* London: David Fulton

Osler, A. (ed) (2000) *Citizenship and Democracy in Schools: Diversity, Identity, Equality.* Stoke-on-Trent: Trentham

Osler, A. and Starkey, H. (2005) *Changing Citizenship: Democracy and Inclusion in Education.* Buckingham: Open University Press

Osler, A. and Vincent, K. (2003) *Girls and Exclusion: Rethinking the Agenda.* London: Routledge

Ozga, J. (1993) *Women in Educational Management.* Buckingham: Open University Press

Reay, D. (1998) *Mothers' Involvement in Their Children's Primary Schooling.* London: Routledge

Reed, L. R. (2006) *Creating Gender-fair Schools and Classrooms: Engendering Social Justice for 5-13 Year Olds.* London: Paul Chapman

Rowan, L., Knobel, M., Bigum, C. and Lankshear, C. (Central Queensland University) (2002) *Boys, Literacies and Schooling: The Dangerous Territories of Gender-*

*based Literacy Reform.* Buckingham: Open University Press

Rudduck, J. (1994) *Developing a Gender Policy in Secondary Schools.* Milton Keynes: Open University Press

Sewell, T. (1997) *Black Masculinities and Schooling: How Black Boys Survive Modern Schooling.* Stoke-on-Trent: Trentham, 1997

Shain, F. (2003) *The Schooling and Identity of Asian Girls.* Stoke-on-Trent: Trentham

Siraj-Blatchford, I. (1993) *Race, Gender and the Education of Teachers.* Milton Keynes: Open University Press

Skelton, C. (2001) *Schooling the Boys.* Buckingham: Open University Press

Skelton, C. and Frances, B. (2005) *Feminist Critique of Education.* London: Taylor Francis

Skelton, C., Francis, B. and Smulyan, L. (eds) (2006) *The Sage Handbook of Gender and Education Handbook.* London: Sage

Walkerdine, V. (1990) *Schoolgirl Fictions.* London: Verso

Walter, N. (1999) *The New Feminism.* London: Virago

Weiner, G. (1994) *Feminisms in Education: An Introduction.* Buckingham: Open University Press

Younger, M. and Warrington, M., with McLellan, R. (2005) *Raising Boys' Achievement in Secondary Schools: Issues, Dilemmas and Opportunities.* Buckingham: Open University Press

Younger, M. and Warrington, M. with Gray, J., Rudduck, J., McLellan, R., Bearne, E., Kershner, R. and Bricheno, P. (2005), *Raising Boys' Achievement: A Study Funded by the Department for Education and Skills,* DfES Research Report RR63. London: DfES Publications

# Index

14-19 provision 97-8, 111, 154, 159-65

academies 30
admissions criteria 26-7
anti-racism 207-8, 211
art and design 29, 166-8
assemblies 16, 36, 73-6
assessment/attainment 1-4, 51, 65-6,
    118-123, 164, 175, 178, 185, 188,
    197, 202-3, 210-11, 229-30
autistic spectrum disorder (ASD) 100

behaviour 27, 65-70, 108, 131, 133, 152,
    211, 222
behavioural, emotional and social
    difficulties (BESD) 65-6, 100
bilingualism see English as an
    Additional Language
books/textbooks 64, 73, 76, 80, 125,
    138-9, 157, 167, 183, 188, 190-1,
    203, 208-9, 213, 225
    see also learning materials/
    resources
breaktimes 67, 77-81, 109
British Educational Communications
    Technology Agency (BECTA) 56
budgets 27, 29-31
Building Schools for the Future (BSF)
    32
buildings 16, 31, 32-7
bullying 13-4, 19-20, 27, 65-70, 79, 89-
    91, 143, 156, 219
    see also harassment

care; childcare 13, 21, 25, 51, 62, 70
careers 5-6, 94-5, 206, 210, 228
    and children's choices 5, 15, 93-7,
    17
    and teachers' progression 25
    education 15, 94, 154, 161-3, 206
carers see parents
Children Act 2004 12
Children's centres 13
Children's Trusts 12
citizenship 169-74
classroom assistants see learning
    assistants
clothing, dress 27, 82-4, 222
    religious 171, 209
Commission for Equality and Human
    Rights 10, 24

communities 12, 14, 16, 59, 71, 83, 86,
    91, 139, 17
    school 16-18, 57, 67, 73, 82, 87,
    104
Construction and Built Environment
    diploma 162
continuing professional development
    (CPD) 21, 46-9, 52-3, 57-8
coursework 3-4
crime/anti-social behaviour 171-2
critical friends 45, 87
cultural diversity 10, 189, 205, 207-8,
    220
    see also ethnicity
culture
    school and classroom 13, 23, 40,
    51, 67, 120-1, 130-133

dance 31, 205-9
design and technology 175-7
Department for Education and
    Employment (DfEE) 169, 192
Department for Education and Skills
    (DfES) 7, 12-15, 33, 39, 50, 52, 55,
    67, 82, 84, 94, 104, 108, 134, 150,
    220
digital divide see ICT
disabilities, children with 16, 33, 43, 63,
    101, 206, 219-21
Disability Discrimination Act 2005 82,
    101
Disability Equality Duty 101
displays 16, 76, 139, 214, 225
drama 205-6, 210-212
drug and alcohol education 218

early years 156-8, 183, 188
eating disorders 90, 100, 218
Education Act 1944 74
Education Act 1988 74
emotional
    difficulties 69
    intelligence 48, 51
    literacy 149
Employment Act 2000 9
Employment Equality (Age)
    Regulations 2006 10
Employment Rights Act 1999 9
employment/jobs 5-6, 8-11, 22, 25, 31,
    59-61, 93-7, 142, 152, 159, 184,
    186, 192
    see also workforce

English 3, 30, 40, 144, 160, 180-2, 205
English as an Additional Language
    (EAL) 38, 104-6, 108-9
Equal Opportunities Commission 11,
    22, 24, 27, 93, 160
Equal Pay Act 1970 8-9
Equality Act 2006 8, 10, 24, 160, 162
Ethnic Minority Achievement (EMA)
    105, 108
ethnicity 12-13, 33, 46-7, 66-7, 79, 84,
    100, 105, 111-3, 159, 189,
    and achievement 6, 28-30, 38-40,
    43-4, 108
    and employment; staff 20-2, 24-6,
    31, 46-7, 49-50; 53, 60
    and parents 62-3, 106
European Union legislation 8, 10-11
Every Child Matters 2003 12-15, 29-30,
    44, 52, 59, 101
Excellence for All Children 101
exclusions 12, 27, 65, 100, 107-8, 127
extended schools 13-14., 33

faith 74, 82, 224-6
    see also religion
families 62-3, 67, 71, 156-7, 184
    see also parents
femininity 148-51, 176, 197, 214
feminisms/feminists 124, 131, 142, 148,
    150, 156, 166, 170, 172, 189
Fixed Term Employees (Prevention of
    Less Favourable Treatment)
    Regulations 2002 10
flexible working patterns, flexi-time 9,
    21, 22
friendship 3, 65-8, 115

games 56-7, 77, 79-80, 84, 194, 203,
    220-1
Gender Equality Duty (GED) 2007 8,
    10, 22, 24, 27, 42, 49, 60, 162
General Teaching Council 20, 25, 46,
    47, 48
Geographical Futures Programme 185
geography 49, 183-7
gifted and talented programme 98-9,
    134
globalisation 170
governors 24-28, 29, 31, 44, 53, 59, 82
groupwork 70-1, 180-1, 194, 203, 215,
    230
    see also single-sex groups

harassment 13, 20, 22, 27, 68, 79, 143
    sexual 9, 13, 18, 20, 60, 130, 140, 143, 224
    see also bullying; homophobia/ homophobic abuse; racist attitudes/behaviour
Health and Safety at Work Act 1974 9
Health Education Authority 91
healthy schools programme 134
homophobia/homophobic abuse 14, 27, 66, 89-91, 131-2, 143, 164, 207, 211-2, 222
human rights 169-70, 173, 186
Human Rights Act 82

identities 73, 82, 95, 101, 167, 171, 185, 188
    gender 2, 52, 89-92, 117, 120, 156-7, 163, 171, 182, 216
    sexual 89-92, 157, 219

Information and Communication Technology (ICT) 33, 55-58, 160, 170, 182, 192-195, 214
Islamophobia 171

leaders/leadership 16, 19-23, 42, 51-2, 104-5, 135
    and pupils 85-8
league tables 38, 62, 148
learned helplessness 114, 217
learning materials/resources 26, 57, 64, 76, 190-1, 194, 208-9, 213-4, 219, 225
    see also books/textbooks
learning mentors 18, 31, 59, 69-70, 105, 126-9
    see also mentoring
legislation 8-15
lesbian, gay, bisexual, transgender (LGBT) 20, 22, 63, 89-92, 136, 172
    see also homophobia/ homophobic abuse; sexuality
libraries 134, 138-140, 209, 211
literacy 40, 123-5
lunchtimes 67-8, 77-81, 109

management 16, 25, 29, 43-4, 144-5
    see also leaders/leadership
masculinity 130-1, 143, 148, 176, 197, 217-8, 227
maternity leave 9, 21, 22
mathematics 2, 4-5, 105, 120, 144, 152, 160, 196-9
media 1-2, 56, 193, 215, 225 see also English and Media 180-2
mentoring 88, 109, 126-9, 134
    see also learning mentors
modern foreign languages (MFL) 29, 144, 200-3
music 205-6, 213-5

National Agreement for Workforce Reform 48
National College for School Leaders (NCSL) 48
national curriculum 1988 4-5, 159-160, 175, 177, 181, 188, 192, 205, 207, 227
National Qualifications Framework 48
Nike Girls in Sport programme 222

Office for Standards in Education (Ofsted) 1, 24, 46, 48, 50, 95, 101, 107-8, 113, 200, 222
option/subject choices 5-6, 15, 23, 26, 30, 39, 164, 175, 210
Organisation for Economic Co-operation and Development (OECD) 1-2, 93, 159
out of hours learning 134-7

parents 44, 59, 62-4, 79, 80, 82, 83, 91, 95, 101, 106, 144, 158
    see also families
partnerships 30, 57, 61-2, 64, 86, 160, 208
    civil 89
part-time staff 10, 21, 52-3
pastoral care 69-71
paternity leave 9, 21
pay 5, 25, 50, 93
    see also performance management
peer
    groups 1, 71, 86, 114-5, 150
    support 128-9
performance
    data 38-41
    management 25-6, 50-4 , 60
persona dolls 157
personal, social and health education (PSHE) 71, 90, 171-2, 216-9
personalisation 55, 111
personalised learning 13
physical education (PE) 84 205, 207, 220-3
play 157-8
playgrounds 77-81, 130
policies 16, 18, 26-7, 68, 77, 208
poverty 6, 100, 172
prenatal development 1
private finance initiative (PFI) 30, 31
Programme for International Student Assessment (PISA) 1-2, 196
progressive school movement 142
pupil
    mobility 29, 33, 107-110
    voice 36, 44, 85-8, 102, 116, 131, 145, 150-1, 171, 173, 226

Qualifications and Curriculum Authority (QCA) 169, 185, 189, 216

Race Relations Act 1976 82
Race Relations (Amendment) Act 2000 82
racist attitudes/behaviour 18, 20, 27-8, 66-8, 81, 96, 100, 104-6, 131, 211
Raising Boys' Achievement Project 145
reading choices 125, 138-9, 181
recruitment 9, 22, 31, 60
religion 17, 33-4, 66, 73-5, 82, 84, 91, 141, 222, 224-6
    and clothing 171, 209
religious education (RE) 224-6
role models 54, 56-7, 60, 95, 146, 153, 159, 192, 195, 207, 212, 214-5, 221

safety in school 32-4, 67-8, 90
school
    climate 16-18
    councils 13, 44, 77, 79, 84, 87, 174
    ethos 16-17, 56, 57, 73, 106, 146
    self-evaluation 42-5, 52, 180

school evaluation forms (SEF) 86
school improvement plans (SIP) 27
science 4-5, 30, 40, 105, 144, 227-31
self-harm 66, 90, 100
Sex Discrimination Act 1975 8-9, 24, 82
sex education 26, 90, 218
sexuality 89-92, 101-2, 157, 172, 219-20
single-sex
    groups 95, 105, 112, 144-7, 208, 215, 217, 221-2
    schools 4-5, 26, 29, 39, 87, 112, 141-3, 148
social class 13, 24, 39, 43, 100, 111-2, 115, 144, 148-9, 156, 184, 189, 216, 220
    and parents 62
social, emotional and behavioural difficulties (SEBD) 65-6, 100
spatial awareness 183-5
special education needs (SEN) 100-103
Special Educational Needs and Disability Act 2001 101
sport 27, 30-1, 79, 80, 134, 148, 194, 220-3
staff/staffing 24-6, 31, 44, 48-9, 51, 59-61, 63, 68, 77-8, 101-2, 136
study support 134-7
succession planning 20-21
suicide 66, 90, 217
supplementary school 62-3

Take One Picture scheme 166-7
Teacher Development Agency (TDA) 46, 48
teaching assistants 31, 38, 40, 49-50, 59, 69-70, 88, 101, 105, 222
teamwork 52, 211
teenage pregnancy 13, 149
toilet facilities 29, 31, 77-8
tokenism 205
trade unions 9, 11
transition
    primary to secondary 88, 154-5
tribunals 10, 11

uniform 27, 82-4
United Nations 170
    Declaration of Rights of the Child 12

Women and Work Commission 94
Women's History Month 188-9
Women's Sports Foundation 221
work placements 57, 149
workforce 10, 31, 48, 59-61, 155, 159, 163
    see also employment/jobs
work-life balance 21, 51